# *The* Ultimate
# CHICKEN
# Cookbook

# The Ultimate CHICKEN Cookbook

## OVER 400 TASTY AND NUTRITIOUS RECIPES FOR EVERY OCCASION

EDITOR SIMONA HILL

southwater

This edition is published by Southwater, an imprint of Anness Publishing Ltd, Blaby Road, Wigston, Leicestershire LE18 4SE
Email: info@anness.com
Web: www.southwaterbooks.com; www.annesspublishing.com

If you like the images in this book and would like to investigate using them for publishing, promotions or advertising,
please visit our website www.practicalpictures.com for more information.

ETHICAL TRADING POLICY
Because of our ongoing ecological investment programme, you, as our customer, can have the pleasure and reassurance of knowing
that a tree is being cultivated on your behalf to naturally replace the materials used to make the book you are holding.
For further information about this scheme, go to www.annesspublishing.com/trees

Publisher: Joanna Lorenz
Managing Editor: Helen Sudell
Editor: Simona Hill
Designer: Nigel Partridge
Illustrator: Anna Koska and Lucinda Ganderton
Editorial Reader: Penelope Goodare

Previously published as *The Every Day Chicken Cookbook*

PUBLISHER'S NOTE
Although the advice and information in this book are believed to be accurate and true at the time of going to press, neither the authors nor the
publisher can accept any legal responsibility or liability for any errors or omissions that may have been made nor for any inaccuracies nor for any
loss, harm or injury that comes about from following instructions or advice in this book.

NOTES
· For all recipes, quantities are given in both metric and imperial measures and, where appropriate,
measures are also given in standard cups and spoons. Follow one set, but not a mixture
because they are not interchangeable.

Standard spoon and cup measures are level. 1 tsp = 5ml, 1 tbsp = 15ml, 1 cup = 250ml/8fl oz

Australian standard tablespoons are 20ml. Australian readers should use 3 tsp in place of
1 tbsp for measuring small quantities of gelatine, flour, salt etc.

Medium (US large) eggs are used unless otherwise stated

# Contents

# INTRODUCTION

Chicken is possibly the most versatile cooking ingredient of all, and it is used all around the world. It is nourishing, low in fat and, if you buy good-quality produce, it is full of flavour too. Included here are recipes using chicken as well as poussin, guinea fowl and turkey, to provide you with a wide choice of poultry dishes using a range of cooking techniques. Because the book has an international flavour, the recipes use a selection of ingredients, herbs and spices from different countries. Some of the more unusual ingredients will need to be bought at specialist food stores, but most are readily available in supermarkets.

The book opens with a comprehensive introduction to choosing, buying and storing chicken, turkey and other poultry, along with guides to preparation and serving methods and cooking times. This collection of recipes has been gathered from around the globe so that you can enjoy chicken at its best.

# Chicken and Other Small Poultry

Perhaps because they are small and easy to keep chickens have been domesticated for thousands of years. The chickens we eat today are descended from jungle fowl that were first domesticated in India more than 4,000 years ago.

The idea of hens pecking about a farmyard conjures up an idyllic image, but in reality chickens and other poultry were just as often kept in domestic backyards or small gardens. Originally, chickens were farmed for their eggs and killed for their meat only when they were past their laying best. Many birds were undernourished and forced to scavenge in every unhygienic nook and cranny. So the chicken or cockerel that made it to the average table was likely to be a sad culinary offering, with little meat and the necessity for hours of boiling, rendering minimal flavour to all but the stock.

It wasn't until the last 150 years that attitudes towards chicken rearing changed. Chickens were bred for pleasure and the number of breeds increased. Chicken became an expensive luxury food and a roast bird was an occasional treat. Modern, intensive farming methods over the last few decades have brought chicken to many more

*Above: The conditions in which a chicken is reared will affect the quality of the meat.*

tables, not only as an occasional treat, but also as an everyday food. However, intensive-rearing methods often meant that quantity superseded quality as birds were fattened quickly, and flavour and texture diminished. As the conditions in which many hens are reared have been exposed and the resulting hygiene and health problems realized, so public outcry has forced a reversal towards

traditional methods of free-range farming, and organic poultry has become more widely available.

Farmers have developed different breeds for a specific purpose, whether it is high egg yields or improved meat quality, and their breeding methods are geared to meet market demands.

Where farming methods are strictly regulated, organic poultry often offers better quality, more flavourful meat. As a rule, the better the conditions under which poultry are reared, the better the end product. Whether the end concern is the welfare of the poultry or the quality of the meat, the means to both are the same: if you want quality chicken, buy those that have been well reared.

**Nutrition**

Chicken and other small poultry are rich in high-quality protein, providing all the essential amino acids required by the body for growth. The meat provides B-group vitamins, especially niacin. It also provides iron (more in the leg meat than the breast meat) as well as the minerals copper and selenium. The white meat is low in fat (the fat is found in and under the skin) and contains a lower pro-portion of saturated fat than meat.

*Left: Corn-fed chickens are easy to pick out because of their yellow skin but identifying a free-range (middle top) or organic (right) chicken is not so easy. A reputable supplier is the key to obtaining good quality meat.*

*Right: For a roaster, look for a plump breast and creamy skin.*

## Buying

Poultry can be bought fresh, chilled or frozen. When choosing, look for birds with a clear, soft skin (there should be no blemishes or bruises). A soft, thin skin shows that the bird is young; the tougher the skin, the older the bird. A fresh chicken should have a plump breast and the skin should be creamy in colour. The top of the breastbone should be pliable.

A bird's weight is taken after plucking and drawing and may include the giblets (neck, gizzard, heart and liver) packaged separately. The bigger the bird, the better its value because the proportion of meat to bone will be higher.

As well as whole birds, chicken is available in a choice of cuts such as quarters, legs, wings, thighs, breast fillets and drumsticks. Portions may be on the bone or boneless, with or without skin. Sliced, diced and minced (ground) chicken breast is also available. Stir-fry strips, marinated cuts and stuffed portions are all sold fresh or frozen.

## Storing

Always keep poultry chilled, as bacteria thrive in warmth. Select poultry towards the end of a shopping session and avoid leaving it in a warm car before going home. Unpack and chill it promptly. Store poultry in the refrigerator until you are ready to cook it.

Place poultry loose in a deep dish and cover it closely. Check pre-packed poultry to make sure that the packs are sealed before placing them in the refrigerator. Store in the coldest part of the refrigerator; the lowest part is best, where the chicken cannot accidentally drip on to other foods. Use loose poultry within about two days of purchase.

Raw, fresh poultry can be frozen whole or in portions. If they are included, remove the giblets from a whole bird before freezing. Wrap chicken portions tightly in clear film (plastic wrap) or freezer film. Pack the portions in a freezer bag and seal. Once out of the freezer, the best way to thaw poultry is in the refrigerator. Place in a suitable container, cover closely and leave overnight. Always thaw poultry completely before cooking. Never put a frozen chicken in hot water, as this will toughen the flesh and is dangerous, as it allows bacteria to multiply.

## Handling

Poultry is particularly susceptible to bacterial growth. This can cause food poisoning if the poultry is eaten without being thoroughly cooked, or if it is allowed to contaminate other foods. Contamination occurs when the chicken meat touches other foods, if liquid from the meat drips on to other foods.

Before preparing raw poultry, assemble all the utensils and dishes you will need. Weigh out all the other ingredients you are using, then unpack and cut, coat or prepare the poultry.

When making a meal that includes dishes that are to be served uncooked such as salads or desserts, or ready-cooked foods, such as cooked fish or meat, it is a good idea to prepare these foods first before handling the raw poultry to avoid cross-contamination.

Thoroughly wash utensils, surfaces and hands after handling and cooking all types of poultry. Use a cutting board that can be washed at a high temperature, and always keep a cutting board just for the preparation of raw poultry. Remember to wash utensils used to lift or stir part-cooked poultry before using them with cooked poultry.

---

### Cook Well, Eat Well

It is very important to cook poultry properly to ensure that any bacteria are destroyed. To check if poultry is cooked, pierce the thickest area of the meat with a thin metal skewer or sharp knife. If there is any sign of pink in the flesh or if the juices are not clear, then the chicken or poultry is not properly cooked and it must be returned to the heat or the oven for further cooking.

# *Types of Small Poultry*

There is now a great variety of poultry available in shops and supermarkets. A recipe will usually make it clear what type of bird you need to choose.

**Poussin**

This is the French name for a young chicken, four to six weeks old and weighing 350–675g/12oz–1½lb. They are bred for flavour and tenderness. Each bird provides enough meat for an individual portion. Poussins, which are also sometimes called spring chickens, have a tender, delicate flavour. They can be roasted, when they benefit from a moist stuffing, and they can also be spatchcocked and grilled (broiled), pan-fried or barbecued.

**Double poussin**

A variation on the poussin, these are larger, older birds that weigh about 900g/2lb. Double poussins usually have enough meat for two people. Like poussins, the meat is tender and has a delicate flavour.

**Rock Cornish hen**

This small North American cross-breed was developed from White Rock and Cornish chickens and is sometimes called a Rock Cornish game hen. These small birds are four to six weeks old and can weigh up to 1.2kg/2½lb. The flesh is white and flavourful, though the ratio of bone to meat is high.

**Roasting chicken**

Sometimes called a roaster, this is a young cockerel or hen about 12 weeks old. Roasting chickens usually weigh about 1.3kg/3lb, but may be as big as 3kg/7lb. Older birds (up to 20 weeks old) are up to

*Above: Poussin.*

*Below: Double poussin.*

4.5kg/10lb in weight and are available from specialist butchers.

**Stewing or boiling chicken**

Also known as a boiling hen or fowl, a chicken for stewing requires long, slow simmering as the flesh is tough, but its flavour is excellent. As a guide to age, the older the chicken, the harder and more rigid the breastbone. Boiling fowl (stewing chicken) are

not readily available these days as demand is low, so they have to be sourced from a specialist butcher. They are used for pies, fricassées, ballottines and galantines and, most often of all, in soups, stews and casseroles.

**Capon**

This is a young cockerel that has been castrated and then fattened on a special diet to make it plump and flavourful. The practice is prohibited in many countries, including Britain. Capons are large birds and can weigh 2.75–4.5kg/6–10lb. In the past they were often cooked for celebration meals at Christmas and Thanksgiving in

*Below: Cockerels are not often eaten, although castrated birds, or capons, are available in some countries.*

*Right: A stewing or boiling chicken.*

*Above: A capon.*

centuries, but originally came from the coast of Guinea in West Africa. They are tender with slightly dry flesh that resembles pheasant. The flesh is not distinctly game-like in flavour, but it leans more in that direction

than towards chicken. Guinea fowl are generally cooked as for chicken or pheasant, but at a high temperature – for example the birds should be barded and roasted in an oven preheated to 230°C/450°F/Gas 8 for 25–30 minutes. The birds can also be braised or casseroled.

place of turkey. They have a fairly large proportion of white meat to dark.

**Guinea fowl**
These are domestic fowl, which have been raised in Europe for

*Right: An oven-ready guinea fowl.*

## CUTS OF CHICKEN
A wide range of different portions is available, on and off the bone. Choose the cut to suit your taste and the recipe.

**Quarters** include either the leg or the wing joint, the latter having a large portion of breast meat. The leg joint includes the thigh and also the drumstick.

*Above: Chicken portions include the leg quarter (top middle), drumsticks (left) and thighs (right).*

**Other portions** include **thighs**, which are small, neat joints, **drumsticks**, which take a long time to cook, and **wings**, which have very little meat. **Breast portions** are sold on the bone and breast fillets are sold off the bone, both are available skinned or unskinned; these portions include only the white meat. **Supremes** include the wing bone.

*Below: Chicken breast fillet (top) and a chicken supreme, which includes part of the wing bone.*

*Right: Wing.*

**Part-boned breasts** still have the short piece of bone leading into the wing and the fine strip of breastbone.
**Liver** is often used in pâtés, risottos, soups and terrines.

*Above: The whole leg is useful for casseroles and poaching. Left: Liver.*

# Preparing Chicken and Other Small Poultry

These techniques are suitable for chicken as well as other poultry, such as guinea fowl and poussin, and game birds such as pheasant.

### Jointing a bird

Many recipes specify particular joints of poultry or game. Although you can buy them ready-prepared, if you have the right equipment it is fairly straight-forward to joint a bird to suit the recipe. Use a large, sharp knife and poultry shears for cutting through meat and bone. The following gives four small portions from each side of the bird, eight in total – two wings, two breasts, two drumsticks and two thighs.

**1** Put the bird breast side up on a chopping board. Remove the leg by cutting through the skin and then through the thigh joint. Repeat with the leg on the other side.

**2** Following the line of the breast-bone and using poultry shears, cut the breast in half.

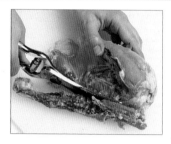

**3** Turn the bird over and cut out the backbone, leaving the wings.

**4** Cut each breast in half, leaving a portion attached to the wing.

**5** Cut through the knee joint.

**6** Cut off the wing tip.

### Preparing a bird for roasting

Little preparation is needed to roast a bird, but the following techniques will produce better results.

### Removing the wishbone

Breast meat is carved more easily if this arched neck bone is removed.

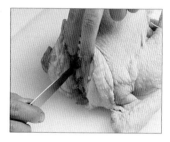

**1** Using a sharp knife pull back the skin from the neck cavity and carefully cut around the wishbone.

**2** Scrape off the meat from the wishbone, then cut it away at the base and pull it out.

---

#### Make a Lucky Wish

It is traditional for two people to pull the wishbone until it snaps. Each person is allowed to use their little finger to hold the end of one side of the bone. The person who ends up with the larger arched top of the bone is entitled to make a wish.

**Trussing with skewers**

This is a quick method for a larger bird that has a greater quantity of meat so it keeps its shape better.

**1** Push one metal skewer through both sections of the wing, into the skin of the neck and straight out through the wing on the other side.

**2** Push the second skewer through the thighs and the tail cavity.

**Trussing with string**

Tying a bird with string keeps it neat and helps it to cook evenly.

**1** Season the bird and tuck the wing tips and neck flap underneath.

**2** Tie string around the legs and under the flap of skin.

**3** Bring it towards the neck end.

**4** Turn the bird over and wrap the string around the wings.

**5** Pull tightly and tie neatly.

**Spatchcocking a bird**

This is a method of splitting and flattening a whole bird so that it can be grilled (broiled) or roasted.

**1** Tuck the wings under the bird. Remove the wishbone. Split the bird along each side of the backbone. Remove the backbone.

**2** Place the bird on a chopping board breast side uppermost. Press down firmly with the heel of one hand on the middle of the breast to flatten the bird against the board.

**3** Push a metal skewer through the wings and breast. Push a second skewer through the thighs.

## Tunnel boning a bird

This is a method of part-boning a bird from the breast to the joints. The skin is left in one piece and the bird is ready to stuff. This is easy with a larger bird, but can be fiddly and difficult with small birds.

**1** Pull back the skin around the neck, then cut out the wishbone.

**2** Feel inside the cavity for the wing joint, then use a sharp knife to cut the breastbone from the meat and skin from one side of the bird.

**3** Pull out the curved bone. Cut the meat from the bone until you reach the wing joint.

**4** Cut through the wing joint using the tip of the knife. Repeat on the other side of the bird. Pull the meat back from the carcass and cut away the flesh, keeping the knife close to the bone. Sever the leg joints when you reach them, leaving the bones attached to the leg meat.

**5** Cut and ease the skin away from the breastbone, then turn the bird so that the skin is on the outside. The finished bird retains the joints, but the central part of the body is completely boneless.

## Stuffing

Chickens and other poultry can be stuffed before roasting. This improves the flavour as well as making the meat moist. Stuffings

---

### Stuffing Tips

Do not stuff the body cavity of a large bird because this could inhibit heat penetration, and harmful bacteria may not be destroyed. For smaller birds, use stuffing that is cool or at room temperature, not hot or chilled. Pack the stuffing loosely in the neck end of the bird and cook any leftovers separately – stuffing balls can be cooked around the edges of the roast poultry. Stuff poultry just before cooking.

---

are usually based on breadcrumbs with flavourings such as onions and herbs added. Rice, meat and nuts can also be used. Stuffing swells during cooking so pack the bird loosely to allow for this.

## Basic Herb Stuffing

This simple stuffing will keep your chicken moist and flavoursome.

1 small onion, finely chopped
15g/½oz/1 tbsp butter
115g/4oz/2 cups fresh breadcrumbs
15ml/1 tbsp chopped fresh parsley
5ml/1 tsp mixed dried herbs
1 egg, beaten
salt and ground black pepper

**1** Cook the onion gently in the butter until tender. Transfer to a bowl and allow to cool.

**2** Add the remaining ingredients and then mix thoroughly. Season well with salt and pepper.

## Preparing breast fillets

If you prepare fillets from a whole chicken the rest of the carcass can be jointed and used to make stock.

**1** Joint the bird into portions, but keep the breasts whole.

**2** Use your fingers to pull the skin and thin membrane from the breast. Slice the meat off the rib bone and any remaining breastbone.

**3** Cut the thin, white central tendons from the breast.

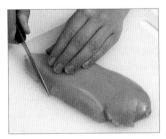

**4** Trim away any pieces of fat and untidy edges from the breast.

**Preparing escalopes**
A chicken breast yields two escalopes. A turkey breast can be sliced into several escalopes, depending on the size of the breast.

**1** Place the skinless breast fillet flat on a chopping board and, using a large, sharp knife, carefully slice the breast in half horizontally. To cut a thin, even slice, hold your hand flat on top of the chicken breast as you cut, to prevent it from moving.

**2** Arrange the chicken between sheets of baking parchment and beat out gently until thin and flat, using a meat mallet or rolling pin.

**Cutting strips for stir-frying**
Use a flattened escalope for stir-fry strips (see above).

Cut the escalope into fine strips. When cut across the grain in this way, the meat cooks quickly.

**Skinning and boning thighs**
When boned, chicken thighs yield a neat nugget of well-flavoured meat.

**1** Use a knife to loosen the skin, then pull it away from the meat.

**2** Cut the flesh lengthways along the main thigh bone, then cut the bone out, trimming the meat close to the bone. Continue cutting out the bones, leaving the meat open and flat.

**Making kebabs**
The thigh meat is ideal for kebabs. Skin and bone the thigh (as above).

**1** Cut the meat across the grain into four pieces, using a sharp knife.

**2** Thread the meat on to skewers. Add pieces of vegetable (try mushrooms, small onions, red and green (bell) pepper); they will cook in the same time as the chicken.

# Cooking Chicken and Other Small Poultry

Young, tender birds can be poached, roasted, grilled (broiled), barbecued, griddled or fried in a shallow pan or, once coated in breadcrumbs or batter, in deep oil. If you do have an older bird it should be cooked by long, gentle and moist methods such as braising and stewing.

### Roasting

Small poultry, such as chickens, poussins and guinea fowl, are easy to roast and require the minimum of attention. For a larger bird that requires longer cooking the breast should be covered loosely with foil. Remove the foil for the final 15 minutes' cooking time to complete the browning.

**1** Rub the breast and the top of the bird generously with butter. Season with salt and pepper, and add herbs or other flavourings if required.

**2** Place the bird breast side down in the roasting pan for the first 30 minutes of the cooking time.

**3** Turn and baste the bird, then cook for the calculated time, basting the bird every 15 minutes.

**4** When the bird is cooked (see Careful Cooking), remove from the oven and cover the bird tightly with foil. Leave to rest in a warm place for 10–15 minutes before carving and serving.

---

#### Roasting Times

Preheat the oven to 200°C/400°F/Gas 6, or 230°C/450°F/Gas 8 for guinea fowl. Calculate cooking times using the weight of the bird (including stuffing).
**Chicken:** allow 20 minutes per 450g/1lb, plus 20 minutes.
**Poussin:** allow 50–60 minutes total roasting time.
**Guinea fowl:** allow 15 minutes per 450g/1lb, plus 15 minutes.
**Rock Cornish hen:** allow 40 minutes per 450g/1lb, plus 20 minutes.

---

### Grilling (broiling)

This is a quick-cooking method for smaller birds and portions. For even, thorough cooking, split a whole bird in half or spatchcock it. Rub flavouring ingredients into the bird 1–2 hours in advance to allow the flavours to infuse (steep).

**1** Preheat the grill (broiler). Brush the meat with oil and season well.

**2** Place skin side up on a rack in a grill (broiling) pan and cook below the heat source so the meat cooks through before it over-browns.

**3** Allow about 40 minutes cooking for poussin, turning frequently.

**Griddling boneless breast fillets**

This is a healthy way of cooking, allowing fat to drain away between the ridges of the pan and preventing the meat from being greasy.

1 Brush the breast fillets with a little vegetable oil.

2 Preheat the griddle until almost smoking, then lay the fillets on it – don't overload the pan, or the meat will steam rather than brown.

3 Cook until the meat is well browned underneath, and firm and white inside. Turn the fillets over. Cook until well browned and the meat is white throughout.

**Cooking on a barbecue**

Ensure that the barbecue is properly heated and fuelled with enough charcoal to burn hot and long enough to cook the poultry thoroughly. Position the barbecue rack away from the hot coals so that the meat has plenty of time to cook before the skin is overcooked.

1 Cut slashes into thick portions. This will ensure that they cook through. Make two or three cuts across larger drumsticks or poultry quarters. There is no need to slash small drumsticks or breast meat.

2 Marinating poultry before cooking adds flavour and keeps it moist during cooking. Mix together olive oil, chopped garlic, chopped fresh herbs and chopped fresh red or green chillies in a deep, non-metal container.

3 Add the poultry to the marinade and turn the pieces to coat them. Cover and chill for at least 30 minutes or for up to 24 hours.

4 To cook, place the portions on the barbecue rack, brush with marinade and cook over the hot coals. Turn the pieces frequently to ensure that they cook evenly, brushing with more of the marinade to keep the meat moist.

---

**Careful Cooking**

**Checking cooking progress:** Pierce the thickest area of meat with the point of a small, sharp knife. Check the juices – if there is any sign of pink the meat is not cooked. Then check the meat at the base of the cut, when cooked it will be firm and look white, if it is pink and soft, the bird is not cooked. Use this test on portions and whole birds. On a whole bird, the area behind the thigh takes longest to cook.

**Barbecues:** Chicken tastes excellent when cooked on a barbecue, but it does require attention to ensure that it is cooked through. One solution is to poach the portions gently in just enough stock to cover until they are only just cooked – this will take about 20–30 minutes. Leave to cool in the stock, then transfer to the marinade and chill overnight. Slash the meat and cook until thoroughly reheated and well browned.

### Pan-frying

Escalopes (thin slices) and boneless breasts cook quickly, so they are ideal for pan-frying over a high heat. Breast meat on the bone takes longer and must be evenly cooked through. Denser thigh and leg meat on the bone require careful cooking and turning. With larger pieces, reduce the heat to low once the chicken is browned. Cook it very slowly so that it does not over-brown, and always ensure that it is cooked through.

**1** Heat a little olive oil in a large, non-stick frying pan.

**2** Add the pieces to the hot oil in the frying pan and cook until they are lightly browned underneath.

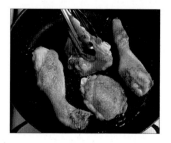

**3** Turn the joints and cook until they are lightly browned on the second side. Reduce the heat and continue cooking gently until the meat is cooked. Boneless thighs take 15–20 minutes. Drumsticks take at least 30 minutes.

### Stir-frying

Fine strips of poultry cook quickly and are tender. Try diced or thinly sliced pieces.

**1** Cut pieces of breast crossways into thin, even-size strips.

**2** Heat the empty wok or a large, heavy frying pan until hot before adding a little oil to the pan. Heat the oil until it is very hot.

**3** Add the meat (in batches, if necessary – take care as the oil will spit) and stir-fry on a high heat until brown, about 3–5 minutes. Cooking times depend on amounts of meat, oil and the type of pan.

### Casseroling

This moist cooking method allows the herbs, spices and aromatics to infuse (steep) the light meat. Whole birds, joints and pieces of meat can be casseroled.

**1** Brown the poultry all over. Remove from the pan, then soften chopped onion, carrot, and celery in the fat remaining in the pan.

**2** Replace the poultry, add the wine, stock, canned tomatoes or water. Season, then bring it to simmering point. Cover, then simmer on the hob (stove top) or cook in the oven at 180°C/350°F/Gas 4.

---

#### Casserole Cooking Times

**Whole bird:** allow 20 minutes per 450g/1lb, plus 20 minutes.
**Large portions:** 45–60 minutes.
**Breast fillets:** about 30 minutes.
**Chunks or diced poultry:** 20–40 minutes, depending on size.

**Poaching whole poultry**

This is a gentle method that brings out the delicate flavour of a bird. Serve the cooked bird hot with a light cream sauce, or allow to cool in its cooking liquid. The bird can then be jointed, or the meat can be carved from the bones. Poached chicken is tender and juicy, and ideal for using in salads or cold dishes. To cook a whole bird you will need a large pan or flameproof casserole, flavourings and plenty of cooking liquid.

**1** Truss the bird neatly and tightly with string and then place it in a large pan, or flameproof casserole.

**2** Pour in enough liquid to come just to the top of the bird. Heat gently until the liquid is just starting to simmer. Using a large spoon, carefully skim off any scum that rises to the surface of the liquid during the first few minutes of cooking, before adding any flavouring ingredients, spices or herbs.

**3** Add the chosen flavourings to the pan or casserole. A selection of the following work well: sliced onions, carrot sticks, a bouquet garni, a strip of pared lemon rind, six black peppercorns and a sprinkle of salt.

**4** Bring the liquid back to simmering point, reduce the heat if necessary and then cover the pan. Cook for 1½ hours or until tender.

**5** Use a large slotted spoon to lift the bird from the pan. Transfer it to a large dish and use poultry shears and a sharp knife to cut it into serving portions or use as required.

---

**Flavourings for Poached Small Poultry**

Water is the essential base and makes a good stock. Dry white wine or cider may be used – about half and half with water. Dry sherry or vermouth can be added in small quantities to intensify the flavour. Carrots and onions are another essential; leeks, fennel, and turnips can also be added. Use herbs such as tarragon or thyme with bay leaves and parsley. Add them to the cooking liquid, or freshly chopped, to a plain cream sauce for serving with the poached poultry.

---

**Chicken Stock**

Good stock gives a fuller flavour to soups and casseroles than stock (bouillon) cubes. (Turkey can be used instead of chicken.)

*Makes about 2.4 litres/4 pints/10 cups*

1.2–1.3kg/2½–3lb chicken wings, backs
   and necks
2 onions, unpeeled and quartered
4 litres/7 pints/17 cups cold water
2 carrots, coarsely chopped
2 celery stalks, coarsely chopped
a small handful of fresh parsley
a few fresh thyme sprigs or 5ml/
   1 tsp dried thyme
2 bay leaves
10 black peppercorns, lightly crushed

**1** Put the chicken and onions in a pan and cook at a medium heat. Stir occasionally until browned.

**2** Add the water and stir in the sediment on the base. Bring to the boil and skim. Add the other ingredients. Partially cover the pan and gently simmer for 3 hours.

**3** Strain the stock into a bowl and allow to cool, then chill. When cold, remove any fat from the surface. Store in the refrigerator and use within a few days or freeze.

---

**Stock Tips**

• Stock can be made from the carcasses of any roasted poultry cooked with vegetables and flavourings. Freeze carcasses in plastic bags until you have three or four, then make the stock.
• No salt is added to stock because as it reduces, the flavour becomes concentrated and the saltiness increases.

# *Turkey*

The turkey is the largest game bird in North America. Turkeys were first domesticated by the Aztecs in Mexico. When the Spanish conquered the Aztecs they brought some of the domesticated birds back to Europe.

For the Pilgrim Fathers who landed at Massachusetts in 1620, wild turkeys were an invaluable source of food. The Pilgrims survived the winter with the help of the native population, who shared their stores of berries, nuts and maize to supplement the settlers' diet of wild turkey. In November 1621, on the first anniversary of their arrival in North America, the Pilgrims entertained the Native Americans with a feast. The feast is said to have lasted three days and turkey was established in the United States as the traditional bird for Thanksgiving celebrations.

Well before turkey became popular in Europe, large birds such as the bustard and peacock were served, as well as the goose and smaller fowl. Unlike the unfamiliar vegetables that were brought from the Americas to Europe and treated with suspicion and caution, Europeans recognized the benefits of cooking and eating such large birds, so turkey soon became part of affluent feasts. In England, the birds were raised in Norfolk and Suffolk, then herded on foot into London. Gradually the turkey took over from the goose as a popular Christmas treat.

Inevitably, turkey's popularity led to the bird being farmed more intensively. Turkeys were first reared for their meat on a large scale in the late 1940s, and modern intensive breeding and rearing have created birds with an even larger proportion of breast meat.

*Above: The turkeys that are farmed today are descended from game birds native to North America.*

### Nutrition

Turkey meat is lean and a source of high-quality protein. It provides B-group vitamins, particularly niacin, and is a good source of iron, zinc, phosphorous, potassium and magnesium.

### Buying

Turkeys are available fresh, chilled or frozen. When buying a whole bird, look for soft evenly coloured skin and plump, well-rounded breast and legs. Avoid birds that are bruised, with blemishes or torn skin. Although there are likely to be small cavities left from plucking (particularly on dark-feathered birds), there should not be any patches of feathers. The bird should smell fresh.

Turkeys vary enormously in weight, from about 2.75kg/6lb to over 11.25kg/25lb. A hen turkey matures much more quickly than a male turkey (known as a stag or tom). Turkeys can grow up to vast sizes, such as 18kg/40lb, but the average weights available are 4.5–6.3kg/10–14lb.

### Storing

Place the turkey in a large, deep dish and cover it completely with clear film (plastic wrap). Keep it in the coolest part of the refrigerator, making sure that it (or any drip from the bird) does not come into contact with other foods.

### Handling

When you have been preparing raw turkey you should always wash your hands thoroughly before handling other foods to avoid cross-contamination.

*Left: Bronze turkeys like this have a wonderful flavour.*

*Right: The majority of turkeys are white-feathered birds, like this Norfolk turkey.*

## TYPES OF TURKEY

Intensive farming methods mean that turkeys are specially bred so that they will have plenty of meat. Both free-range and organic birds are available. However, free-range labels alone are not a guarantee of good quality. For the best tasting turkey, seek out a source of organic birds from a reputable farm.

### Bronze birds

These are dark-feathered birds and the skin may be spotted with dark stubble remaining after plucking. Norfolk Bronze is a popular breed and Norfolk Black is a very plump-breasted bird. American Bronze is another traditional breed. Cambridge turkeys are traditional in Britain and they have been crossed with American Bronze to breed the Cambridge Bronze.

### White birds

In North America the White Holland is a popular breed. The majority of British turkeys are white, and traditional breeds include the Norfolk turkey. However, the superior-flavoured bronze and dark-feathered birds are becoming more popular.

## CUTS OF TURKEY

As well as whole birds, there are a variety of prepared cuts of turkey available.

### Part-boned breast

This is a large roasting joint consisting of the whole breast, meat and bone, with skin on. Usually taken from large birds, these can weigh as much as a small turkey and provide a large number of portions.

### Boneless breast

This is usually taken from one side of the breast, and neatly rolled or shaped with the skin around the outside. Take care to distinguish between a boneless breast and a joint of "re-formed" meat, made up of scraps and off-cuts moulded into a joint.

### Turkey drumstick

The leg of the bird is usually enough to provide a meal for four people. Turkey drumsticks have plenty of sinew running through the brown meat. They are better browned, then braised, until the meat is tender, when they make full-flavoured casseroles.

### Diced turkey

Used mainly for pies and casseroles, this is often darker meat from the thigh or leg.

### Stir-fry turkey

These thin strips of white breast meat cook very quickly.

### Minced (ground) turkey

This is good for pies, meat sauces and burgers.

*Left: A Norfolk Black, which has a very plump breast and a full flavour.*

# *Preparing Turkey for Roasting*

Turkeys are generally sold cleaned and ready for stuffing or cooking. Methods of preparing small poultry also apply to turkey, for example, trussing and tunnel boning are both relevant. The same rules also apply to hygiene when handling turkey. In addition, there are a few points to check before stuffing or roasting a large bird.

### Preparation checks
Use tweezers to remove any feathers remaining on the skin. Then use a long lighted match to singe off any tiny feathers or hairs, allowing the smoke to burn away before drawing the flame across the surface of the skin. Birds with dark plumage have dark "stubble", which may look unpleasant, but these small pits from which the feathers have been removed will melt away during the roasting process.

It is also a good idea to check inside the neck end of the bird for any lumps of excess fat and pull or cut them away.

### Preparing the stuffings
Stuffing can be made in advance, but the turkey should not be stuffed until just before it is placed in the oven. It is important to remember to weigh the stuffing and add this to the weight of the bird to calculate the cooking time. Truss the bird, then cook for the calculated time; never shorten the cooking time because the meat appears cooked – time must always be allowed for cooking the stuffing.

Stuffings and fillings are highly flavoured mixtures of ingredients. They are added to plain foods to introduce complex flavours. Minced (ground) meat, such as veal, pork or sausage meat (bulk sausage), is a traditional main ingredient. Mixtures are also often based on breadcrumbs or rice. Alternatively, the stuffing may not be bound into a mixture that can be sliced or spooned out easily, but consist of loose combinations of chopped fruits or vegetables.

### Cooking stuffing separately
Stuffing can be cooked separately to the turkey because not everyone likes the flavouring. Also bear in mind that stuffing will increase the overall cooking time. So for a very large bird, cooking the stuffing in a separate tray can help time-wise and it reduces anxiety about the bird being cooked through.

Also any leftover stuffing can be rolled into small balls about the size of walnuts. Place these in a separate baking tin (pan) or add them to the roasting pan, for the final 15 minutes' cooking time, and then serve with the carved meat.

### Flavouring variations
A popular method is to place aromatics such as onions or citrus fruits in the body cavity and to add the stuffing under the skin covering the breast. All these aromatics can be added to the body cavities so the flavours suffuse the meat as it cooks: a large onion cut in half and each half studded with four to six cloves. An orange and a lemon cut into quarters with three bay leaves, four sage sprigs and three thyme sprigs. A cinnamon stick or a blade of mace for a festive hint.

If you prefer to add stuffing to the breast you can loosen the skin over the breast meat and insert stuffing underneath it. It is a good idea to add stuffing here, even when stuffing the cavity, as this protects the delicate breast meat during long cooking.

## STUFFING RECIPES AND METHODS
There are a number of traditional recipes that will add moistness and flavour to the cooked meat. All of the recipes can be adapted to suit different tastes and occasions.

### Sausage Meat and Chestnut Stuffing
This is a favourite for stuffing turkey. You can buy sausage meat (bulk sausage) with a high proportion of meat, to make the best stuffing. Use fresh chestnuts in season, or look for ready-prepared, vacuum-packed chestnuts.

**1** Peel 900g/2lb fresh chestnuts, by slitting the peel and pulling it off. Remove the brown skin inside the shell. Cook the chestnuts in boiling water for 10–15 minutes. Drain, then crumble into a large bowl.

**2** Melt 25g/1oz/2 tbsp butter in a pan and add two finely chopped onions. Cook for 10 minutes, until the onions are soft.

**3** Add the onions to the chestnuts and mix. Return the pan to the heat and add 450g/1lb pork sausage meat. Cook over a medium-low heat, stirring until the sausage meat is crumbly and well browned.

**4** Add to the chestnut mixture with 115g/4oz/2 cups fresh white bread-crumbs. Season, add chopped fresh herbs. Beat an egg and add it to the stuffing to bind the ingredients.

---

### Variations for Sausage Meat and Chestnut Stuffing

This stuffing is often left plain, especially when combined with sage and onion stuffing, but complementary herbs can be added. Try the following simple combinations:
**Parsley and thyme:** add 15ml/1 tbsp chopped fresh thyme and 45ml/3 tbsp chopped fresh parsley.
**Tarragon and parsley:** add 30ml/2 tbsp chopped fresh tarragon and 30ml/2 tbsp chopped fresh parsley.
**Marjoram and orange:** add 15ml/1 tbsp dried marjoram and the grated rind of 1 orange.
**Sage and parsley:** add 45ml/3 tbsp chopped fresh sage and 45ml/3 tbsp chopped fresh parsley.

---

### Sage and Onion Stuffing

This is a classic stuffing, which is suitable for all types of poultry.

**1** Melt 25g/1oz butter in a pan. Add four finely chopped onions and cook for 10–15 minutes, or until soft. Set aside to cool.

**2** Add the onions to 115g/4oz/ 2 cups fresh white breadcrumbs and 60ml/4 tbsp chopped fresh sage. Season, then add one beaten egg and about 120ml/4fl oz/½ cup stock to bind the stuffing.

### Stuffing the body cavity

This stuffing can be prepared in advance and chilled separately from the bird.

**1** Rinse the body cavity under cold running water, then drain it well. (Wash the sink afterwards.) Then dry the turkey, inside and out, with kitchen paper.

**2** Insert the stuffing, packing it lightly, using your hands.

### Stuffing the neck end

It is traditional to stuff the neck end with sage and onion stuffing. Remove the wishbone to make carving the breast easier.

**1** Fold back the flap of skin at the neck end and then use a small, sharp knife to cut out the wishbone, working right round the bone and cutting the meat as close to the bone as possible. Cut the bone free at the base on both sides.

**2** Press the stuffing inside the shallow neck cavity.

**3** Turn the bird over on to its breast and pull the neck skin over the stuffing.

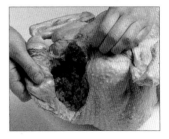

**4** Truss the bird to keep the flaps of skin at the neck and body cavities in place. If necessary, use a metal skewer to secure the skin while trussing the bird with string. Weigh the bird and the stuffing, and use both weights to calculate the cooking time.

# Cooking and Serving Turkey

Turkey and chicken are fairly similar in taste and consistency so turkey can be cooked by several methods used for chicken. Turkeys have a slightly stronger flavour so it is usually just a question of preference. However, when choosing bear in mind that thighs and leg meat can be a little tough because they contain more sinew.

## Roasting

Turkeys are easy to roast, but require a little more attention than smaller birds. Check that the oven shelves are in the correct position before heating the oven.

1 Put the prepared, stuffed bird on a rack in a large roasting pan.

2 Smear the breast with butter. Season well and place in the oven.

### Thawing Frozen Turkey

Turkey must be thawed completely before cooking. Place it on a rack in a dish, so that the liquid that drips from the bird as it thaws runs into the dish. Cover with clear film (plastic wrap). Place in the refrigerator.
**For a 4.5kg/10lb bird:** allow 2–3 days in the refrigerator.
**For a 6.8kg/15lb bird:** allow 3–4 days in the refrigerator.

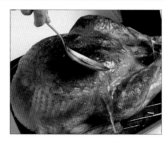

3 Baste frequently during cooking. When the breast has browned, cover the bird with foil and continue cooking and basting.

4 To check if the meat is cooked, insert a metal skewer into the thickest part of the thigh. If the juices run clear it is cooked. If they run pink it is not ready. Return it to the oven and check again after 20 minutes. Remove the foil for the final 20 minutes of cooking to finish browning the skin and give it a crisp texture.

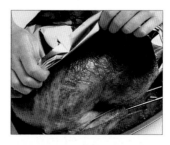

5 Remove it from the oven and cover with foil. Leave it to rest for 15 minutes before carving.

### Roasting Times for Turkey

Preheat the oven to 180°C/350°F/Gas 4. Calculate the cooking time, according to the weight of the bird (including the stuffing weight). It is difficult to estimate the exact cooking time when roasting large birds, as the shape and proportion of breast meat and the quantity and position of stuffing all influence the finished result.
**For birds up to 4.5kg/10lb:** allow 20 minutes per 450g/1lb plus an extra 20 minutes.
**For birds over 4.5kg/10lb:** allow 18 minutes per 450g/1lb, plus an extra 20 minutes.
**For birds over 6.8kg/15lb:** allow 15 minutes per 450g/1lb, plus an extra 20 minutes.

## Carving turkey

A sharp carving knife is essential.

1 Remove the trussing string. Hold the bird with a carving fork. Cut off the legs, then cut these in half, or carve the meat from the bones.

2 Make a horizontal cut across the breast just above the wing. Carve slices off the breast, then repeat on the other side. Arrange the slices on a warmed serving platter. Add the leg joints or meat to the platter.

## Stir-frying turkey

Fillets of turkey breast are best for stir-frying, as thigh and leg meat can be slightly tough. Combine turkey with Asian ingredients, or stir-fry strips of meat with onions, mushrooms and a dash of sherry for a lightly sauced dish.

**1** Cut the breast meat across the grain into thin, even strips.

**2** Heat a little oil in a wok or large, heavy frying pan. Sunflower, corn or groundnut (peanut) oils are useful for stir-frying as they can be heated to a high temperature without smoking. Olive oil gives a good flavour, but it burns easily.

**3** Stir-fry the turkey until golden brown. Cook the turkey in batches if necessary and remove the strips from the pan, continue until all the pieces are browned. Stir-fry the vegetables in the same pan, then return the turkey to the pan to finish cooking for a few minutes before serving.

## Pan-frying turkey

This is a useful method for cooking fillets of turkey breast or fine escalopes. It is also the first stage for braising or casseroling poultry. Small, neat portions of turkey thigh are ideal for casseroles.

**1** Heat a little olive oil in a frying pan. Add the turkey pieces and cook, turning occasionally, for about 15 minutes, or until the meat is golden on all sides.

**2** Once the turkey has turned golden brown, season it well and reduce the heat, then cover the pan and continue cooking gently for 15–20 minutes, or until the meat is cooked through and succulent. Serve immediately.

## Stewing and braising

Prepared diced turkey or portions cut from the thigh are a good choice of turkey cuts for stewing or braising. Drumsticks can also be cooked by this method, rendering them succulent and flavoursome.

**1** Brown the pieces of turkey as for pan-frying. Instead of using a frying pan, a flameproof casserole can be used for browning and simmering or oven cooking.

**2** When the pieces are browned, use a slotted spoon to remove them from the pan and set them aside.

**3** Cook thickly sliced vegetables in the fat remaining in the casserole. As a simple base, try one onion and two carrots. Add other ingredients to taste such as one sliced fennel bulb, two sliced celery sticks, two sliced garlic cloves, a bay leaf and parsley, sage or thyme.

**4** Replace the turkey and pour in enough stock just to cover them. Bring to simmering point, then reduce the heat and cover the pan. Simmer on the hob (stovetop) for about 1 hour or place in the oven at 180°C/350°F/Gas 4 for 1–1½ hours.

---

### Wines to Serve with Turkey

You can drink some of the same wines with turkey as you enjoy with chicken. However, turkey does have a stronger flavour and it can take a fuller, fruitier wine. Try a bright fruity red from the Côtes du Rhône or a lightly oaked white Burgundy.

# THE RECIPES

A range of recipes suitable for all occasions: light soups for lunches, quick meals for midweek suppers, salads for summer evenings, and feasts for special dinners as well as roasts, pastries and pies, pasta, rice and grain dishes, simple one-pot dishes, barbecues, tasty stir-fries and spicy meals.

# SOUPS &
# APPETIZERS

A good chicken stock is often used as a base for many tasty soups, but in this chapter chicken plays a star role. There are hearty chicken soups for lunch or supper and light soups that are perfect for a first course.

This selection of first courses and appetizers uses imaginative ingredients and methods of cooking and preparation. With unusual examples from all around the world, you are sure to find something that is just right for any occasion.

# Cream of Chicken Soup

*A rich and flavoursome creamy chicken soup makes a fabulous lunch served with crispy bread. It is essential to use a really strong, home-made chicken stock for this recipe to give the soup a full flavour.*

### INGREDIENTS

*Serves 6*

50g/2oz/$^1$/4 cup butter
2 onions, chopped
2 medium potatoes, chopped
1 large carrot, diced
1 celery stick, diced
750ml/1$^1$/4 pints/3 cups chicken stock
25g/1oz/$^1$/4 cup plain (all-purpose) flour
150ml/$^1$/4 pint/$^2$/3 cup milk
175g/6oz cooked chicken
300ml/$^1$/2 pint/1$^1$/4 cups single
   (light) cream
salt and ground black pepper
parsley leaves, to garnish

1 Melt the butter in a large pan and cook the onions, potatoes, carrot and celery gently for 5 minutes. Do not allow the vegetables to brown.

2 Add the stock and simmer gently for 30 minutes. Season with salt and pepper to taste. Purée the soup in a food processor or blender until smooth and then return to the pan. Blend the flour with the milk and stir into the soup. Cook over a low heat, stirring, until the soup thickens.

3 Meanwhile, chop the chicken finely. Add to the soup and heat through for 5 minutes. Add 75ml/ 2$^1$/2 fl oz/$^1$/3 cup of the cream and simmer for 5 minutes more.

4 Serve in individual bowls topped with a swirl of the remaining cream and garnished with ground black pepper and parsley leaves.

# Corn and Chicken Soup

*This popular classic Chinese soup is a delicious warming dish and is very easy to make.*

*Serves 4–6*

1 chicken breast fillet (about 115g/4oz), skinned and cubed

10ml/2 tsp light soy sauce

15ml/1 tbsp Chinese rice wine

5ml/1 tsp cornflour (cornstarch)

60ml/4 tbsp cold water

5ml/1 tsp sesame oil

30ml/2 tbsp groundnut (peanut) oil

5ml/1 tsp grated fresh root ginger

1 litre/1³/4 pints/4 cups chicken stock

425g/15oz can creamed corn

225g/8oz can corn kernels

2 eggs, beaten

2–3 spring onions (scallions), green parts only, cut into tiny rounds

salt and ground black pepper

1 Mince (grind) the chicken in a food processor, taking care not to over-process it. Transfer the chicken to a bowl and stir in the soy sauce, rice wine, cornflour, water, sesame oil and seasoning. Cover and leave for about 15 minutes to absorb the flavours.

2 Heat a wok over a medium heat. Add the groundnut oil and swirl it around. Add the ginger and stir-fry for a few seconds. Then add the stock, creamed corn and corn kernels. Bring to just below boiling point.

3 Spoon about 90ml/6 tbsp of the hot liquid into the chicken mixture until it forms a smooth paste, and stir. Return to the wok. Slowly bring the liquid to the boil, stirring constantly, then simmer for 2–3 minutes, or until cooked.

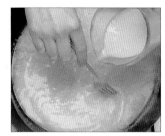

4 Pour the beaten eggs into the soup in a slow, steady stream, using a fork or chopsticks to stir the top of the soup in a figure-of-eight pattern. The egg should set in lacy shreds. Serve immediately with the spring onions sprinkled over.

# Chicken, Leek and Celery Soup

*This makes a substantial main course soup when served with fresh crusty bread. You will need nothing more than a salad and cheese or just fresh fruit to follow.*

### INGREDIENTS

*Serves 4–6*

1 chicken, about 1.3kg/3lb
1 small head of celery, trimmed
1 onion, coarsely chopped
1 fresh bay leaf
a few fresh parsley stalks
a few fresh tarragon sprigs
2.5 litres/4 pints/10 cups cold water
3 large leeks
65g/2$^1$/2 oz/5 tbsp butter
2 potatoes, cut into chunks
150ml/$^1$/4 pint/$^2$/3 cup dry white wine
30–45ml/2–3 tbsp single (light)
   cream (optional)
salt and ground black pepper
90g/3$^1$/2 oz pancetta, grilled (broiled)
   until crisp, to garnish

1 Cut the breasts off the chicken and set aside. Chop the rest of the chicken carcass into 8–10 pieces and place in a large pan.

2 Chop four or five of the outer sticks of the celery and add them to the pan with the onion. Tie the bay leaf, parsley and tarragon together and add to the pan. Pour in the cold water to cover the ingredients and bring to the boil. Reduce the heat and cover, then simmer for 1$^1$/2 hours.

3 Remove the chicken, and then cut off and reserve the meat. Strain the stock, then return it to the pan and boil rapidly until it has reduced to about 1.5 litres/2$^1$/2 pints/6$^1$/4 cups.

4 Meanwhile, set about 150g/5oz of the leeks aside. Slice the remaining leeks and the remaining celery, reserving any celery leaves. Chop the celery leaves and set aside to garnish the soup.

5 Melt half the butter in a large, heavy pan. Add the sliced leeks and celery, cover and cook over a low heat for about 10 minutes, or until softened but not browned. Add the potatoes, wine and 1.2 litres/2 pints/5 cups of the stock.

6 Season with salt and pepper, bring to the boil, then reduce the heat. Part-cover the pan and simmer the soup for 15–20 minutes, or until the potatoes are cooked.

7 Meanwhile, skin the reserved chicken breasts and cut the flesh into small pieces. Melt the remaining butter in a frying pan, add the chicken and fry for 5–7 minutes, or until cooked.

8 Thickly slice the remaining leeks, add to the pan and cook, stirring occasionally, for a further 3–4 minutes, or until just cooked.

9 Process the soup with the cooked chicken from the stock in a blender or food processor. Taste and adjust the seasoning, add more stock if the soup is very thick.

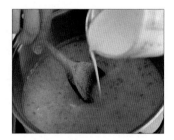

10 Stir in the cream, if using, and the chicken and leek mixture. Reheat the soup and ladle into warmed bowls. Crumble the pancetta over the soup and sprinkle with the chopped celery leaves.

# Chicken, Avocado and Chickpea Soup

*Chilli gives the chicken, chickpeas and creamy avocado a delicious kick. Enjoy this substantial soup for lunch or dinner on its own.*

### INGREDIENTS

*Serves 6*

1.5 litres/2$^1$/$_2$ pints/6$^1$/$_4$ cups chicken stock

$^1$/$_2$ chipotle chilli, seeded

2 chicken breast fillets, skinned

1 medium avocado

4 spring onions (scallions), finely sliced

400g/14oz can chickpeas, drained

salt and ground black pepper

1 Pour the stock into a pan and add the chilli. Bring to the boil, add the chicken, lower the heat and simmer for 10 minutes.

2 Remove the pan from the heat and lift out the whole chicken breasts with a slotted spoon. Leave to cool a little.

3 Using two forks, shred the chicken into small pieces. Set the shredded chicken aside.

4 Pour the chicken stock into a blender or food processor. Process the mixture until smooth, then return to the pan.

5 Cut the avocado in half, remove the skin and stone (pit), then slice the flesh into 2cm/$^3$/$_4$in pieces. Add it to the stock, with the spring onions and chickpeas. Return the shredded chicken to the pan, with salt and ground black pepper to taste, and heat gently.

6 When the soup is heated through, spoon into warmed bowls and serve.

# Chicken and Leek Soup with Prunes

*This recipe is based on the traditional Scottish soup, Cock-a-leekie. The unusual combination of prunes and leeks is surprisingly delicious.*

## INGREDIENTS

Serves 6

1 chicken, about 2kg/4$^{1}/_{2}$ lb
900g/2lb leeks
1 fresh bay leaf
a few fresh parsley stalks and thyme sprigs
1 large carrot, thickly sliced
2.5 litres/4 pints/10 cups chicken stock
115g/4oz/generous $^{1}/_{2}$ cup pearl barley
400g/14oz/$^{1}/_{2}$ cup ready-to-eat prunes
salt and ground black pepper
chopped fresh parsley, to garnish

1 Cut the breasts off the chicken and set aside. Place the remaining chicken carcass in a large pan. Cut half the leeks into 5cm/2in lengths and add to the pan. Tie the bay leaf, parsley and thyme together and add to the pan with the carrot and stock. Bring to the boil, then reduce the heat and cover. Simmer for 1 hour. Skim off any scum when the water first boils and during simmering.

2 Add the chicken breasts and cook for another 30 minutes. Leave until cool, then strain the stock. Reserve the chicken breasts and meat from the carcass. Discard the skin, bones, vegetables and herbs. Skim the fat from the stock, then return the stock to the pan.

3 Meanwhile, rinse the pearl barley thoroughly in a sieve under cold running water, then cook it in a large pan of boiling water for about 10 minutes. Drain, rinse well and drain thoroughly.

4 Add the pearl barley to the stock. Bring to the boil, then lower the heat and cook gently for 15–20 minutes. Season the soup.

5 Add the prunes. Slice the remaining leeks and add them to the pan. Bring the ingredients to the boil, then simmer very gently for 10 minutes, or until the leeks are just cooked.

6 Slice all the chicken meat and add to the soup. Reheat, then ladle the soup into deep plates and sprinkle with chopped parsley.

# Mulligatawny Soup

2 Add the onion, carrot and turnip to the pan and cook, stirring occasionally, until lightly coloured. Stir in the curry powder, cloves and peppercorns, and cook for 1–2 minutes. Add the lentils.

3 Pour in the stock and bring to the boil. Add the sultanas and chicken and any juices from the plate. Cover and simmer gently for about 1¹/₄ hours.

4 Remove the chicken from the pan and discard the skin and bones. Chop the flesh, return to the soup and reheat. Check and adjust the seasoning before serving the soup piping hot.

*A good chicken stock makes the base for this popular spicy soup. It was adapted from a Tamil recipe –* milakutanni *(pepper water) – during the British Raj in India.*

INGREDIENTS

*Serves 4*

50g/2oz/¹/₄ cup butter or 60ml/4 tbsp oil
2 large chicken joints, about
    350g/12oz each
1 onion, chopped
1 carrot, chopped
1 small turnip, chopped
about 15ml/1 tbsp curry powder, to taste
4 cloves
6 black peppercorns, lightly crushed
50g/2oz/¹/₄ cup red lentils
900ml/1¹/₂ pints/3³/₄ cups chicken stock
40g/1¹/₂ oz/¹/₄ cup sultanas
    (golden raisins)
salt and ground black pepper

1 Melt the butter or heat the oil in a large pan and brown the chicken over a brisk heat. Transfer the chicken to a plate.

COOK'S TIP

Red split lentils will give the best colour for this dish, although green or brown lentils could be used if you prefer.

# Chicken and Lentil Soup

*A chunky soup that will make a
good lunchtime dish.*

*Serves 4*

25g/1oz/2 tbsp butter or margarine

1 large carrot, chopped

1 onion, chopped

1 leek, white part only, chopped

1 celery stick, chopped

115g/4oz/1$^1$/$_2$ cups mushrooms, chopped

45ml/3 tbsp dry white wine

1 litre/1$^3$/$_4$ pints/4 cups chicken stock

10ml/2 tsp dried thyme

1 bay leaf

115g/4oz/$^1$/$_2$ cup brown or green lentils

225g/8oz/2 cups diced cooked chicken

salt and ground black pepper

1 Melt the butter or margarine in a large pan. Add the carrot, onion, leek, celery and mushrooms. Cook for 3–5 minutes, or until softened.

2 Stir in the wine and chicken stock. Bring to the boil and skim off any foam that rises to the surface. Add the thyme and bay leaf. Reduce the heat, cover, and simmer for 30 minutes.

3 Add the lentils and continue cooking, covered, for another 30–40 minutes, or until they are just tender, stirring the soup from time to time.

4 Stir in the diced chicken and season to taste with salt and pepper. Cook until just heated through. Ladle the soup into bowls and serve hot.

# Greek Chicken and Egg Soup

*Avgolemono soup is a great favourite in Greece and is a fine example of how a few ingredients, if carefully chosen and cooked, can make a marvellous-tasting dish. It is essential to use a well-flavoured stock.*

## INGREDIENTS

*Serves 4*

900ml/1¹/₂ pints/3³/₄ cups chicken stock

50g/2oz/generous ¹/₃ cup long grain rice, soaked and drained

3 egg yolks

30–60ml/2–4 tbsp lemon juice

30ml/2 tbsp finely chopped fresh parsley

salt and ground black pepper

lemon slices and parsley sprigs, to garnish

1 Pour the stock into a pan, bring to simmering point, then add the drained rice. Half-cover and cook for about 12 minutes, or until the rice is just tender. Season with salt and pepper.

2 Whisk the egg yolks in a bowl, then add about 30ml/2 tbsp of the lemon juice to the eggs, whisking constantly until the mixture is smooth and bubbly. Add a ladleful of stock with the rice and whisk again.

3 Remove the stock and rice from the heat and slowly add the egg mixture, whisking constantly. The soup will turn a lemon colour and will thicken slightly.

4 Taste and add more lemon juice if necessary. Stir in the parsley. Serve immediately, without reheating, garnished with lemon slices and parsley sprigs.

# Pasta Soup with Chicken Livers

*This is a mouthwatering soup that can be served as either a first or main course. Even those who do not normally like chicken livers may well change their minds when they taste this delicious soup.*

## INGREDIENTS

*Serves 4–6*

115g/4oz chicken livers, thawed if frozen

15ml/1 tbsp olive oil

knob (pat) of butter

4 garlic cloves, crushed

3 sprigs each of fresh parsley, marjoram
    and sage, chopped

leaves from 1 fresh thyme sprig, chopped

5–6 fresh basil leaves, chopped

15–30ml/1–2 tbsp dry white wine

2 × 300g/11oz cans condensed
    chicken consommé

225g/8oz/2 cups fresh shelled or
    frozen peas

50g/2oz/$^1/_2$ cup dried pasta shapes, such
    as farfalle

2–3 spring onions (scallions), sliced

salt and ground black pepper

1 Cut the livers into small pieces. Heat the oil and butter in a frying pan, add the garlic and herbs, with salt and pepper to taste, and fry gently for a few minutes. Add the livers, increase the heat to high and stir-fry for a few minutes, or until they change colour and become dry. Pour the wine over the livers. Cook until it evaporates, then remove the livers from the heat and taste for seasoning.

2 Tip both cans of condensed chicken consommé into a large pan and add water to the condensed soup as directed on the labels. Add an extra can of water, then stir in a little salt and pepper to taste, and bring to the boil.

3 Add the peas to the pan and simmer for about 5 minutes, then add the pasta and bring the soup back to the boil, stirring. Allow to simmer, stirring frequently, until the pasta is only just *al dente*: about 8 minutes or according to the instructions on the packet.

4 Add the fried chicken livers and spring onions and heat through for 2–3 minutes. Taste for seasoning. Serve hot, in warmed bowls.

# Chicken Soup with Dumplings

*This traditional soup is served with matzo dumplings. It is a hearty and comforting meal, ideal for those recovering from illness, and is traditionally often known as the Jewish antibiotic.*

### INGREDIENTS

*Serves 6–8*

1 chicken, about 1–1.5kg/2¼–3¼ lb, cut into portions

2–3 onions

3–4 litres/5–7 pints/12–17 cups water

3–5 carrots, thickly sliced

3–5 celery sticks, thickly sliced

1 small parsnip, cut in half

30–45ml/2–3 tbsp roughly chopped fresh parsley

30–45ml/2–3 tbsp chopped fresh dill

1–2 pinches ground turmeric

2 chicken stock (bouillon) cubes

2 garlic cloves, finely chopped (optional)

salt and ground black pepper

*For the dumplings*

175g/6oz/¾ cup medium matzo meal

2 eggs, lightly beaten

45ml/3 tbsp vegetable oil or rendered chicken fat

1 garlic clove, finely chopped (optional)

30ml/2 tbsp chopped fresh parsley, plus extra to garnish

½ onion, finely grated

1–2 pinches of chicken stock cube or powder (optional)

about 90ml/6 tbsp water

1 Put the chicken pieces in a very large pan. Keeping them whole, cut a large cross in the stem end of each onion and add to the pan with the water, carrots, celery, parsnip, parsley, half the fresh dill, the turmeric, and salt and ground black pepper.

2 Cover the pan and bring to the boil, then immediately lower the heat to a simmer. Skim and discard the scum that surfaces. (Scum will continue to form but it is only the first scum that rises that will detract from the clarity and flavour of the soup.)

3 Add the crumbled stock cubes and simmer for 2–3 hours. Skim off the fat. Alternatively, chill the soup and remove the layer of solid fat that forms.

4 To make the dumplings, in a large bowl combine the matzo meal with the eggs, oil or fat, chopped garlic, if using, parsley, onion, salt and pepper. Add only a little chicken stock cube or powder, if using, as these are salty. Add the water and mix together until the mixture is of the consistency of a thick, soft paste.

5 Cover the matzo batter and chill for 30 minutes, during which time the mixture will become firm.

6 Bring a pan of water to the boil and have a bowl of water next to the stove. Dip two tablespoons into the water, then take a spoonful of the matzo batter. With wet hands, roll it into a ball, then slip it into the boiling water and reduce the heat so that the water simmers. Continue with the remaining matzo batter, working relatively quickly, then cover the pan and cook for 15–20 minutes.

7 Remove the dumplings from the pan with a slotted spoon and transfer to a plate for about 20 minutes to firm up.

8 To serve, reheat the soup, adding the remaining dill and the garlic, if using. Put two to three dumplings in each bowl, pour over the soup and garnish with parsley.

# Pumpkin, Rice and Chicken Soup

*This is a warm, comforting soup, mildly spiced with cardamom. It makes an ideal autumnal lunch or supper when pumpkins are readily available.*

### INGREDIENTS

*Serves 4*

1 wedge of pumpkin, about 450g/1lb
15ml/1 tbsp sunflower oil
25g/1oz/2 tbsp butter
6 green cardamom pods
2 leeks, chopped
115g/4oz/generous ¹/2 cup basmati
   rice, soaked
350ml/12fl oz/1¹/2 cups milk
salt and ground black pepper
strips of pared orange rind, to garnish
Granary or wholemeal (whole-wheat)
   bread, to serve

*For the stock*

2 chicken quarters
1 onion, quartered
2 carrots, chopped
1 celery stalk, chopped
6–8 peppercorns
900ml/1¹/2 pints/3³/4 cups water

1 First make the chicken stock. Place the chicken quarters, onion, carrots, celery and peppercorns in a large pan. Pour in the water and slowly bring to the boil. Skim the surface if necessary, then lower the heat, cover and simmer gently for 1 hour.

2 Strain the chicken stock into a clean, large bowl, discarding the vegetables. Skin and bone the chicken pieces and cut the flesh into strips.

3 Skin the pumpkin and remove all the seeds and pith, so that you have about 350g/12oz flesh. Cut the flesh into 2.5cm/1in cubes.

4 Heat the oil and butter in a pan and fry the cardamom pods for 2–3 minutes, or until slightly swollen. Add the leeks and pumpkin. Cook, stirring, for 3–4 minutes over a medium heat, then lower the heat, cover and sweat for 5 minutes more, or until the pumpkin is quite soft, stirring once or twice.

5 Measure out 600ml/1 pint/2¹/2 cups of the stock and add to the pumpkin mixture. Bring to the boil, then lower the heat, cover and simmer gently for 10–15 minutes, or until the pumpkin is soft.

6 Pour the remaining stock into a measuring jug (cup) and make up with water to 300ml/¹/2 pint/1¹/4 cups. Drain the rice and put it into a pan. Pour in the stock, bring to the boil, then simmer for about 10 minutes, or until the rice is tender. Add seasoning to taste.

7 Remove the cardamom pods, then process the soup in a blender or food processor until smooth. Pour back into a clean pan and stir in the milk, chicken and rice (with any stock that has not been absorbed). Heat until simmering. Garnish with the strips of pared orange rind and freshly ground black pepper, and serve with Granary or wholemeal bread.

# Rich Minestrone

*Served with crusty Italian bread,
this delicious soup makes a
filling meal.*

### INGREDIENTS

*Serves 4–6*

15ml/1 tbsp olive oil

2 chicken thighs

3 rindless streaky (fatty) bacon rashers
   (strips), chopped

1 onion, finely chopped

a few fresh basil leaves, shredded

a few fresh rosemary leaves, finely chopped

15ml/1 tbsp chopped fresh flat leaf parsley

2 potatoes, cut into 1cm/$^1$/$_2$in cubes

1 large carrot, cut into 1cm/$^1$/$_2$in cubes

2 small courgettes (zucchini), cut into
   1cm/$^1$/$_2$in cubes

1–2 celery sticks, cut into 1cm/$^1$/$_2$in cubes

1 litre/1$^3$/$_4$ pints/4 cups chicken stock

200g/7oz/1$^3$/$_4$ cups fresh shelled or
   frozen peas

90g/3$^1$/$_2$ oz stellette or other dried tiny
   soup pasta

salt and ground black pepper

coarsely shaved Parmesan cheese, to serve

fresh basil leaves, to garnish

1 Heat the oil in a large pan, add the chicken and fry for about 5 minutes on each side. Remove with a slotted spoon and set aside.

2 Lower the heat, add the bacon, onion and herbs to the pan and stir. Cook gently for 5 minutes. Add the potatoes, carrot, courgettes and celery, and cook for 5–7 minutes.

---

COOK'S TIP

~

For extra flavour, add any
Parmesan rind to the soup.

---

3 Return the chicken thighs to the pan, add the stock and bring to the boil. Cover and cook over a low heat for 35–40 minutes, stirring the soup occasionally.

4 Remove the chicken thighs with a slotted spoon and place them on a board. Stir the peas and pasta into the soup and bring back to the boil. Simmer, stirring frequently until the pasta is *al dente*: 7–8 minutes or according to the instructions on the packet.

5 Meanwhile, remove and discard the chicken skin, then remove the meat from the bones and cut it into 1cm/$^1$/$_2$in pieces. Return the meat to the soup and heat through. Taste for seasoning and ladle into warmed bowls. Scatter over Parmesan shavings, garnish with one or two basil leaves and serve.

# Italian Minestrone

Use a leftover carcass from a roast chicken to make this tasty Italian soup. The sprinkling of salty ricotta salata at the finish is typical of Puglian cooking.

## INGREDIENTS

Serves 4

1 roast chicken carcass
1 onion, quartered lengthways
1 carrot, roughly chopped
1 celery stick, roughly chopped
a few black peppercorns
1 small handful mixed fresh herbs, such as parsley and thyme
1 chicken stock (bouillon) cube
about 1.5 litres/2$^1$/$_2$ pints/6$^1$/$_4$ cups water
50g/2oz tubetti, or other soup pasta
salt and ground black pepper
50g/2oz ricotta salata, coarsely grated or crumbled (see Cook's Tips), and 30ml/2 tbsp fresh mint leaves, to serve

1 Break the carcass into pieces and place in a large pan. Add the onion, carrot, celery, peppercorns and herbs, then crumble in the stock cube and add a good pinch of salt. Cover the chicken generously with cold water and bring to the boil over a high heat.

2 Lower the heat, half cover the pan and simmer gently for about 1 hour. Remove the pan from the heat and leave to cool, then strain the liquid through a colander or sieve into a clean large pan.

3 Remove any meat from the carcass, cut it into bitesize pieces and set aside. Discard the carcass and flavouring ingredients.

4 Bring the stock in the pan to the boil, and add the pasta. Simmer, stirring frequently, until only just *al dente*: 7–8 minutes, or according to the instructions on the packet.

5 Add the pieces of chicken and heat through for a few minutes, by which time the pasta will be ready. Taste for seasoning. Serve hot in warmed bowls, sprinkled with the ricotta salata and mint.

## COOK'S TIPS

• Ricotta salata is a salted and dried version of ricotta cheese. It has a firmer texture, and can be diced, crumbled and even grated. It is available from some delicatessens, good cheese stores and large supermarkets. If you can't locate it, use feta cheese.
• Use other small, hollow pasta shapes for this soup, if you like.

# Christmas Tortellini

*These tortellini are served on the day after Christmas in Emilia-Romagna, Italy. Traditionally they were made with minced leftover capon from Christmas Day, but nowadays chicken or turkey is often used.*

*Serves 6–8*

200g/7oz/1³/4 cups plain (all-purpose) flour, plus extra for dusting

2 large (US extra large) eggs, beaten

15ml/1 tbsp oil

2 litres/3¹/2 pints/9 cups beef stock made with stock cubes or diluted canned consommé

salt and ground black pepper

freshly grated Parmesan cheese, to serve

*For the filling*

25g/1oz/2 tbsp butter

250g/9oz minced (ground) chicken or turkey

5ml/1 tsp chopped fresh rosemary

5ml/1 tsp chopped fresh sage

freshly grated nutmeg

250ml/8fl oz/1 cup chicken stock

60ml/4 tbsp freshly grated Parmesan cheese

90g/3¹/2 oz mortadella sausage, very finely chopped

1 small egg

1 To make the filling, melt the butter in a medium skillet, then add the minced chicken or turkey and chopped herbs.

2 Add a little nutmeg and salt and pepper to taste. Cook gently for 5–6 minutes, stirring frequently and breaking up any lumps in the meat with a wooden spoon.

3 Add the stock and mix well, then simmer gently, uncovered, for 15–20 minutes, or until the meat is cooked and quite dry.

4 Transfer the meat to a bowl with a slotted spoon and leave to cool. Add the grated Parmesan, mortadella and egg to the meat and stir well to mix.

5 Sift the flour and a pinch of salt on to a clean work surface and make a well in the centre with your fist. Pour the eggs and oil into the well. Gradually mix in the eggs with your fingers. Knead the pasta until smooth, then wrap and allow to rest for at least 30 minutes.

6 Using a pasta machine, roll out one-quarter of the pasta into two 45cm/18in lengths. With a 5cm/2in fluted ravioli or biscuit (cookie) cutter, cut out 8–10 discs from one of the pasta strips.

7 Using a teaspoon, put a little mound of filling in the centre of each disc, then brush a little water around the edge of the pasta filling. Fold the disc in half over the filling so that the edges do not quite meet. Press to seal.

8 Wrap each tortellini shape around your index finger and pinch the bottom corners together to seal.

9 Put the tortellini in a single layer on floured dish towels, dust lightly with flour and leave to dry while repeating the process with the remaining dough to make 64–80 tortellini altogether. If you have any stuffing left, re-roll the pasta trimmings and make more tortellini.

10 Bring the beef stock to the boil in a large pan. Drop in the tortellini, then bring back to the boil and boil for 4–5 minutes. Taste the stock and season with salt and pepper if necessary.

11 Pour the tortellini and stock into a warmed, large soup tureen, sprinkle with a little grated Parmesan cheese and serve immediately. Hand around more Parmesan separately.

# Chicken Stellette Soup

2 Add the spring onions and mushrooms to the stock.

3 Slice the chicken thinly, then set aside.

*Tiny pasta stars – stellette – look attractive in soup, and add taste and texture. This low-fat soup with mushrooms, chicken and wine is full of flavour.*

### INGREDIENTS

*Serves 4–6*

900ml/1$^1$/2 pints/3$^3$/4 cups chicken stock
1 bay leaf
4 spring onions (scallions), sliced
225g/8oz/3 cups button (white) mushrooms, sliced
115g/4oz chicken breast fillet, cooked and skinned
50g/2oz soup pasta (stellette)
150ml/$^1$/4 pint/$^2$/3 cup dry white wine
15ml/1 tbsp chopped fresh parsley
salt and ground black pepper

1 Put the stock and bay leaf into a pan and bring to the boil.

4 Add the pasta to the pan, cover and simmer for 7–8 minutes. Just before serving, add the chicken, wine and parsley, and heat through for 2–3 minutes.

# Chicken Vermicelli Soup with Egg Shreds

*This light soup can be put together in a matter of moments and is full of flavour.*

INGREDIENTS

*Serves 4–6*

3 large (US extra large) eggs

30ml/2 tbsp chopped fresh coriander
   (cilantro) or parsley

1.5 litres/2$^1$/2 pints/6$^1$/4 cups good chicken
   stock or canned consommé

115g/4oz/1 cup dried vermicelli or angel
   hair pasta

115g/4oz cooked chicken breast, sliced

salt and ground black pepper

3 Roll up each pancake and slice thinly into shreds. Set aside.

4 Bring the stock or consommé to the boil and add the pasta, breaking it into short lengths. Cook for 3–5 minutes, or until the pasta is almost tender, then add the chicken, salt and pepper. Heat through for 2–3 minutes, then stir in the egg shreds. Serve immediately.

1 First make the egg shreds. Whisk the eggs together in a small bowl and stir in the chopped coriander or parsley.

2 Heat a small, non-stick frying pan and pour in 30–45ml/ 2–3 tbsp egg, swirling to cover the base evenly. Cook until set. Transfer to a chopping board. Repeat until all the mixture is used up.

# Thai Chicken Soup with Ginger and Lime

*A fragrant blend of lemon grass,*
*ginger and lime, with a hint of chilli.*

INGREDIENTS

*Serves 4*

5ml/1 tsp oil

1–2 fresh red chillies, seeded and chopped

2 garlic cloves, crushed

1 large leek, thinly sliced

600ml/1 pint/2$^1$/$_2$ cups chicken stock

400ml/14 fl oz/1$^2$/$_3$ cups coconut milk

450g/1lb skinless chicken, cut into pieces

30ml/2 tbsp Thai fish sauce

1 lemon grass stalk, split

2.5cm/1in piece fresh root ginger, peeled
and finely chopped

5ml/1 tsp sugar

75g/3oz/$^3$/$_4$ cup frozen peas, thawed

45ml/3 tbsp coriander (cilantro), chopped

1 Heat the oil in a large pan and cook the chillies and garlic for about 2 minutes. Add the leek and cook for a further 2 minutes.

2 Stir in the stock and coconut milk and bring to the boil.

3 Add the chicken, with the fish sauce, lemon grass, ginger and sugar.

4 Simmer, covered, for 15 minutes, or until the chicken is tender, stirring occasionally. Add the peas and cook for a further 3 minutes. Remove the lemon grass and stir in the coriander just before serving.

# Thai Chicken Soup

*Piquant Thai flavourings blended
with coconut give this soup a
terrific taste.*

## INGREDIENTS

*Serves 4*

15ml/1 tbsp vegetable oil

1 garlic clove, finely chopped

2 chicken breast fillets, about 175g/6oz
    each, skinned and chopped

2.5ml/$^{1}/_{2}$ tsp ground turmeric

1.5ml/$^{1}/_{4}$ tsp hot chilli powder

75g/3oz creamed coconut (coconut cream)

900ml/1$^{1}/_{2}$ pints/3$^{3}/_{4}$ cups hot
    chicken stock

30ml/2 tbsp lemon or lime juice

30ml/2 tbsp crunchy peanut butter

50g/2oz/1 cup thread egg noodles, broken
    into small pieces

15ml/1 tbsp spring onions (scallions),
    finely chopped

15ml/1 tbsp coriander (cilantro)

salt and ground black black pepper

30ml/2 tbsp desiccated (dry unsweetened
    shredded) coconut and $^{1}/_{2}$ fresh red
    chilli, seeded and finely chopped,
    to garnish

1 Heat the oil in a pan and fry the
garlic for 1 minute. Add the
chicken and spices and stir-fry for
3–4 minutes.

2 Crumble the creamed coconut
into the hot chicken stock and
stir until dissolved. If using
coconut cream, stir this into the
stock. Pour on to the chicken and
add the lemon juice, peanut butter
and egg noodles.

3 Cover the pan and simmer for
about 15 minutes.

4 Add the spring onions and
fresh coriander, then season
well and cook for a further
5 minutes. Meanwhile, place the
desiccated coconut and chilli in a
small frying pan and heat for
2–3 minutes, stirring frequently.

5 Ladle the soup into bowls,
sprinkle with the coconut and
chilli, and serve.

# Pot-cooked Chicken and Udon in Miso Soup

*Udon is a white wheat noodle, cooked here with a rich miso soup topped with eggs. Chicken is the main ingredient in this authentic Japanese dish.*

*Serves 4*

200g/7oz chicken breast fillet, skinned

10ml/2 tsp sake

2 abura-age (see Cook's Tip)

900ml/1$^1$/$_2$ pints/3$^3$/$_4$ water mixed with 7.5ml/1$^1$/$_2$ tsp dashi-no-moto (dashi stock granules) (see Cook's Tip)

6 large fresh shiitake mushrooms, stalks removed, quartered

4 spring onions (scallions), trimmed and chopped into 3mm/$^1$/$_8$ in lengths

30ml/2 tbsp mirin

about 90g/3$^1$/$_2$oz aka miso or hatcho miso

300g/11oz dried udon noodles

4 eggs

1 Cut the chicken into bitesize pieces. Sprinkle with sake and leave to marinate for 15 minutes.

2 Put the abura-age in a sieve and rinse with hot water from the kettle to wash off the oil. Drain and cut each into four squares.

## COOK'S TIP

Abura-age are pouches made from tofu that have been deep-fried. Dashi-no-moto are freeze-dried granules for making dashi stock – traditionally used in Japanese cooking. All the ingredients for this recipe are available from Japanese supermarkets.

3 Heat the water and dashi-no-moto in a large pan. When it has come to the boil, add the chicken pieces, shiitake mushrooms and abura-age and cook for 5 minutes. Remove the pan from the heat and add the spring onions.

4 Put the mirin and miso paste into a small bowl. Scoop 30ml/2 tbsp soup from the pan and mix this in well.

5 To cook the udon, boil at least 2 litres/3$^1$/$_2$ pints/9 cups water in a large pan. The water should not come higher than two-thirds the depth of the pan. Cook the udon for 6 minutes and drain.

6 Put the udon in a large, flameproof clay pot or casserole. Mix the miso paste into the soup and check the taste. Add more miso if required. Ladle in enough soup to cover the udon, and arrange the rest of the soup ingredients on top of the udon.

7 Put the soup on a medium heat and break the eggs on top. When the soup bubbles, wait for 1 minute, then cover and remove from the heat. Leave to stand for 2 minutes before serving in individual bowls.

# Chicken Steamboat

*This chicken dish is named after the utensil in which it is cooked – like a fondue pot, with a funnel and a moat. Electric steamboats or traditional fondue pots can be used instead.*

### INGREDIENTS

*Serves 8*

8 Chinese dried mushrooms, soaked for
    30 minutes in warm water to cover
1.5 litres/2$^1$/2 pints/6$^1$/4 cups chicken stock
10ml/2 tsp rice wine or medium-
    dry sherry
10ml/2 tsp sesame oil
225g/8oz each lean pork and rump steak,
    thinly sliced
1 chicken breast, skinned and thickly sliced
2 chicken livers, trimmed and sliced
225g/8oz/2 cups raw prawns
    (shrimp), peeled
450g/1lb white fish fillets, skinned
    and cubed
200g/7oz fish balls (from Asian stores)
115g/4oz fried tofu, each piece halved
leafy green vegetables, such as lettuce,
    Chinese leaves, spinach leaves and
    watercress, cut into 15cm/6in lengths
225g/8oz Chinese rice vermicelli
8 eggs
$^1$/2 bunch spring onions
    (scallions), chopped
salt and ground white pepper
selection of sauces, including soy sauce
    with sesame seeds; soy sauce with
    crushed ginger; chilli sauce; plum sauce
    and hot mustard, to serve

1 Drain the mushrooms, reserving the soaking liquid. Cut off and discard the stems; slice the caps.

2 Pour the stock into a large pan, with the rice wine or sherry, sesame oil and reserved mushroom liquid. Bring the mixture to the boil, then season with salt and white pepper. Reduce the heat and simmer gently.

3 Put the meat, fish, tofu, green vegetables and mushrooms in bowls on the table. Soak the vermicelli in hot water for 5 minutes, drain and place in eight soup bowls. Crack an egg for each diner into a small bowl. Put the sauces in bowls beside each diner.

4 Add the spring onions to the stock, and bring to the boil. Pour the liquid into a lighted steamboat at the table. Each guest lowers a few chosen morsels into the boiling stock, using chopsticks or fondue forks. After a minute or two, they are removed and eaten with the sauces.

5 When all the ingredients have been cooked, the stock will be concentrated and enriched. Add boiling water if necessary. Pour the hot soup into the soup bowls containing the soaked noodles and slide a whole egg into each, stirring until it cooks and forms threads.

# Celebration Soup

*This chicken brunch soup is traditionally served at new year in Japan. The ingredients can be bought from a Japanese supermarket.*

Serves 4

4 dried shiitake mushrooms

300g/11oz chicken thighs, bones removed and reserved

300g/11oz salmon fillet, skin on, scaled

30ml/2 tbsp sake

50g/2oz satoimo or Jerusalem artichokes

50g/2oz daikon, peeled

50g/2oz carrots, peeled

4 spring onions (scallions), white part only, trimmed

4 mitsuba sprigs, root part removed

1 yuzu or lime

4 large raw tiger prawns (shrimp), peeled, but with tails left on

30ml/2 tbsp shoyu

8 canned gingko nuts (optional)

8 mochi slices

salt

1 First, make the soup stock. Soak the dried shiitake overnight in 1 litre/1³/₄ pints/4 cups cold water. Remove the shiitake and pour the water into a pan. Bring to the boil, add the chicken bones, then reduce the heat to medium. Skim frequently to remove the scum. After 20 minutes, reduce the heat to low. Simmer for 30 minutes, or until the liquid has reduced by a third. Strain the stock into another pan.

2 Chop the chicken and salmon into small cubes. Par-boil them both in boiling water with 15ml/ 1 tbsp sake for 1 minute. Drain and wash off the scum.

3 Scrub the satoimo or arti-chokes, and peel thickly. Put in a pan and add water to cover. Add a pinch of salt and bring to the boil. Reduce the heat to medium, cook for 15 minutes and drain. Rinse the satoimo (to remove the sticky juice) under running water. Wipe gently with kitchen paper. Cut the satoimo or artichokes, daikon and carrots into 1cm/½ in cubes.

4 Remove and discard the stalks from the shiitake, and slice the caps thinly. Chop the spring onions into 2.5cm/1in lengths.

5 Put the mitsuba sprigs into a sieve and pour hot water over them. Divide the leaf and stalk parts. Take a stalk and fold it into two, then tie it in the middle to make a bow. Make four bows.

6 Cut the yuzu or lime into four 3mm/¹/₈ in thick round slices. Hollow out the inside to make rings of peel.

7 Add the remaining sake to the soup stock and bring to the boil. Add the daikon, carrot and shiitake, then reduce the heat to medium and cook for 15 minutes.

8 Put the prawns, satoimo or artichokes, spring onions, chicken and salmon into the pan. Wait for 5 minutes, then add the shoyu. Reduce the heat to low and add the gingko nuts, if using.

9 Cut the mochi in half cross-ways. Toast under a medium preheated grill (broiler). Turn every minute, or until both sides are golden and the pieces have started to swell like a balloon; this will take about 5 minutes.

10 Quickly place the toasted mochi in individual soup bowls and pour the hot soup over the top. Arrange a mitsuba leaf in the centre of each bowl, put a yuzu or lime ring on top, and lay a mitsuba bow across. Serve at once.

# Ginger, Chicken and Coconut Soup

*This aromatic soup is intensely flavoured with galangal, lemon grass and kaffir lime leaves.*

### INGREDIENTS

*Serves 4–6*

4 lemon grass stalks, roots trimmed

2 × 400ml/14fl oz cans coconut milk

475ml/16fl oz/2 cups chicken stock

2.5cm/1in piece galangal, peeled and thinly sliced

10 black peppercorns, crushed

10 kaffir lime leaves, torn

300g/11oz chicken breast fillet, skinned and cut into thin strips

115g/4oz/1 cup mushrooms, halved

50g/2oz baby corn on the cob, quartered

60ml/4 tbsp lime juice

45ml/3 tbsp Thai fish sauce

chopped chillies, spring onions (scallions) and coriander (cilantro), to garnish

1 Cut off the lower 5cm/2in from each lemon grass stalk and chop the end finely. Bruise the remaining pieces of stalk. Bring the coconut milk and chicken stock to the boil in a large pan. Add the lemon grass, the galangal, peppercorns and half the lime leaves, lower the heat and simmer gently for 10 minutes. Strain the liquid into a clean pan.

2 Return the soup to the heat, then add the chicken, mushrooms and corn. Simmer for 5–7 minutes, or until the chicken is cooked.

3 Stir in the lime juice and Thai fish sauce, then add the remaining lime leaves. Serve hot, garnished with chillies, spring onions and coriander.

# Mini Chicken Spring Rolls

*Light filo pastry encloses a chicken
and vegetable filling for these dainty
rolls. For a spicier version, sprinkle
with a little cayenne pepper.*

### INGREDIENTS

*Makes 20*

1 green chilli
120ml/4fl oz/$^1$/$_2$ cup vegetable oil
1 small onion, finely chopped
1 clove garlic, crushed
75g/3oz cooked chicken breast fillet, skinned
1 small carrot, cut into fine matchsticks
1 spring onion (scallion), finely sliced
1 small red (bell) pepper, seeded and
   cut into fine matchsticks
25g/1oz/$^1$/$_4$ cup beansprouts
15ml/1 tbsp sesame oil
4 large sheets filo pastry, thawed if frozen
1 egg white, lightly beaten
fresh chives, to garnish (optional)
45ml/3 tbsp light soy sauce, to serve

1 Carefully remove the seeds
from the chilli and chop finely,
wearing rubber gloves to protect
your hands, if necessary.

2 Heat a wok or large frying pan,
then add 30ml/2 tbsp of the
vegetable oil. When hot, add the
onion, garlic and chilli. Stir-fry for
1 minute.

3 Slice the chicken thinly, then
add to the wok and fry over a
high heat, stirring and tossing
constantly until browned.

4 Add the carrot, spring onion
and red pepper and stir-fry for
2 minutes. Add the beansprouts,
stir in the sesame oil, remove from
the heat and leave to cool.

> COOK'S TIP
> ∼
> Always keep filo pastry sheets
> covered with a damp, clean cloth
> until needed, to prevent them
> drying out.

5 Cut each sheet of filo into
five short strips. Place a small
amount of filling at one end of
each strip, then fold in the long
sides and roll up the pastry. Seal
and glaze the parcels with the egg
white, then chill, uncovered, for
15 minutes before frying.

6 Wipe out the wok with kitchen
paper, heat it, and add the
remaining vegetable oil. When the
oil is hot, fry the rolls in batches
until crisp and golden brown.
Drain on kitchen paper. Garnish
with chives, if using, and serve with
light soy sauce for dipping.

# Spicy Chicken Canapés

*These tiny little cocktail sandwiches have a spicy filling, and are finished with different toppings. Use square bread so that you can cut out more rounds and have less wastage.*

*Makes 18*

75g/3oz/³/4 cup finely chopped
   cooked chicken

2 spring onions (scallions), finely chopped

30ml/2 tbsp chopped red (bell) pepper

90ml/6 tbsp curry mayonnaise

6 slices white bread

15ml/1 tbsp paprika

15ml/1 tbsp chopped fresh parsley

30ml/2 tbsp chopped salted peanuts

1 In a bowl mix the chicken with the spring onions, pepper and half the curry mayonnaise.

2 Spread the mixture over three of the bread slices and sandwich with the remaining bread, pressing well together. Spread the remaining curry mayonnaise over the top and cut into 4cm/1¹/2 in circles using a plain cutter.

3 Dip into paprika, chopped parsley or chopped nuts and arrange on a plate.

# Chicken Cigars

*Serve these small crispy rolls warm as canapés with a drink before a meal, or as a first course with a crisp, colourful salad.*

INGREDIENTS

*Serves 4*

275g/10oz packet of filo pastry, thawed
   if frozen
45ml/3 tbsp olive oil
fresh parsley, to garnish

*For the filling*

350g/12oz/3 cups minced (ground)
   raw chicken
1 egg, beaten
2.5ml/$^1$/$_2$ tsp ground cinnamon
2.5ml/$^1$/$_2$ tsp ground ginger
30ml/2 tbsp raisins
15ml/1 tbsp olive oil
1 small onion, finely chopped
salt and ground black pepper

1 To make the filling, mix the chicken, egg, cinnamon, ginger and raisins together in a bowl. Season to taste. Heat the oil in a large frying pan and cook the onion until tender. Leave to cool. Add the mixed filling ingredients.

2 Preheat the oven to 180°C/ 350°F/Gas 4. Once the filo pastry packet has been opened, keep the pastry covered at all times with a damp dishtowel. Work fast, as the pastry dries out very quickly when exposed to the air. Unravel the pastry and cut into 25 x 10cm/ 10 x 4in strips.

3 Take a strip, brush with a little oil and place a spoonful of filling 1cm/$^1$/$_2$in from the end.

4 Fold the sides inwards and roll into a cigar shape. Place on a greased baking sheet and brush with oil. Bake for about 20–25 minutes, or until golden brown and crisp. Garnish with fresh parsley.

# Chicken Goujons

*Serve these crisp goujons and the herby dip as a first course for eight people or as a filling main course for four. Delicious served with new baby potatoes and a green salad.*

## INGREDIENTS

*Serves 8*

4 chicken breast fillets, skinned
175g/6oz/3 cups fresh breadcrumbs
5ml/1 tsp ground coriander
10ml/2 tsp ground paprika
2.5ml/$^1$/$_2$ tsp ground cumin
45ml/3 tbsp plain (all-purpose) flour
2 eggs, beaten
oil, for deep-frying
salt and ground black pepper
lemon slices, to garnish
sprigs of fresh coriander (cilantro),
    to garnish

*For the dip*
300ml/$^1$/$_2$ pint/1$^1$/$_4$ cups Greek
    (US strained plain) yogurt
30ml/2 tbsp lemon juice
60ml/4 tbsp chopped fresh coriander
60ml/4 tbsp chopped fresh parsley

3 Mix the breadcrumbs with the spices and seasoning. Toss the chicken into the flour, keeping the pieces separate.

4 Dip the goujons into the egg, then coat in the breadcrumbs.

5 Thoroughly mix all the ingredients for the dip together and season to taste. Cover and chill until required.

6 Heat the oil in a heavy pan. It is ready for deep-frying when a piece of bread tossed into the oil sizzles on the surface. Fry the goujons in batches until golden and crisp. Drain on kitchen paper and keep warm in the oven until all the chicken has been fried. Garnish with lemon slices and sprigs of fresh coriander and serve with the yogurt dip.

1 Divide the chicken breast fillets into two natural fillets. Place them between two sheets of clear film (plastic wrap) and using a rolling pin, flatten each one to a thickness of 1cm/$^1$/$_2$ in.

2 Cut the chicken into diagonal 2.5cm/1in strips.

# Chinese Chicken Wings

*Choose these tasty chicken wings as a
first course for an informal meal as
they are best eaten with the fingers.
Make sure you provide finger bowls
and plenty of paper napkins.*

### INGREDIENTS

*Serves 4*

12 chicken wings

3 garlic cloves, crushed

4cm/1¹/2 in piece fresh root ginger, peeled
and grated

juice of 1 large lemon

45ml/3 tbsp soy sauce

45ml/3 tbsp clear honey

2.5ml/¹/2 tsp chilli powder

150ml/¹/4 pint/²/3 cup chicken stock

salt and ground black pepper

lemon wedges, to garnish

1 Remove the wing tips and use
to make the stock. Cut the
wings into two pieces.

2 Mix the remaining ingredients
together, apart from the stock,
and pour over the chicken. Cover
with clear film (plastic wrap) and
marinate overnight.

3 Preheat the oven to 220°C/
425°F/Gas 7. Remove the wings
from the marinade and arrange
in a single layer in a roasting pan.
Bake for 20–25 minutes, basting at
least twice with the marinade
during cooking.

4 Place the wings on a serving
plate. Add the stock to the
marinade in the roasting pan, and
bring to the boil. Cook to a syrupy
consistency and spoon a little over
the wings. Serve garnished with
lemon wedges.

# Sesame Seed Chicken Bites

*Stir-fry these crunchy bites in a wok, then serve them warm with the spicy sauce. A glass of chilled dry white wine is the perfect accompaniment.*

### INGREDIENTS

*Makes 20*

175g/6oz chicken breast fillets, skinned
2 garlic cloves, crushed
2.5cm/1in piece fresh root ginger, peeled and grated
1 egg white
5ml/1 tsp cornflour (cornstarch)
25g/1oz/$^1/_4$ cup shelled pistachio nuts, roughly chopped
60ml/4 tbsp sesame seeds
30ml/2 tbsp grapeseed oil
salt and ground black pepper

*For the sauce*
45ml/3 tbsp hoisin sauce
15ml/1 tbsp sweet chilli sauce

*For the garnish*
fresh root ginger, peeled and finely shredded
pistachio nuts, roughly chopped
fresh dill sprigs

1 Place the chicken, garlic, grated ginger, egg white and cornflour in a food processor or blender and process them to a smooth paste.

2 Add the pistachio nuts and season with salt and pepper.

3 Roll into 20 balls and coat with sesame seeds. Heat a wok and add the oil. When the oil is hot, stir-fry the chicken bites in batches, turning regularly until golden. Drain on kitchen paper.

4 Make the sauce by mixing together the hoisin and chilli sauces in a bowl. Garnish the bites with shredded ginger, pistachio nuts and dill. Serve hot, with a dish of sauce for dipping.

# Little Chicken Turnovers

*These savoury Russian turnovers are often served with soup or as a snack.*

## INGREDIENTS

*Makes 35*
225g/8oz/2 cups strong white bread flour
2.5ml/$\frac{1}{2}$ tsp salt
2.5ml/$\frac{1}{2}$ tsp caster (superfine) sugar
5ml/1 tsp easy-blend (rapid-rise)
    dried yeast
25g/1oz/2 tbsp butter, softened
1 egg, beaten, plus extra for brushing
90ml/6 tbsp warm milk

*For the filling*
1 small onion, finely chopped
175g/6oz/1$\frac{1}{2}$ cups minced
    (ground) chicken
15ml/1 tbsp sunflower oil
75ml/5 tbsp chicken stock
30ml/2 tbsp chopped fresh parsley
pinch of freshly grated nutmeg
salt and ground black pepper

1 Sift the flour, salt and sugar into a bowl. Stir in the dried yeast, then make a well in the centre.

2 Add the butter, egg and milk and mix to a soft dough. Turn on to a lightly floured surface and knead for 10 minutes, or until smooth and elastic.

3 Put the dough in a clean bowl, cover with clear film (plastic wrap) and leave in a warm place to rise for 1 hour, or until the dough has doubled in size.

4 Meanwhile, fry the onion and chicken in the oil for 10 minutes. Add the stock and simmer for 5 minutes. Stir in the parsley, nutmeg and salt and pepper. Leave to cool.

5 Preheat the oven to 220°C/425°F/Gas 7. Knead the dough, then roll out until 3mm/$\frac{1}{8}$in thick. Cut out 7.5cm/3in rounds.

6 Brush the edges with beaten egg. Put a little filling in the middle, then press the edges together. Leave to rise on oiled baking sheets, covered with oiled clear film, for 15 minutes.

7 Brush with a little more egg. Bake for 5 minutes, then for 10 minutes at 190°C/375°F/Gas 5, until well risen.

# Nutty Chicken Balls

*Serve these tasty bites as a first course with the lemon sauce, or make them into smaller balls and serve on cocktail sticks as canapés.*

### INGREDIENTS

Serves 4

350g/12oz chicken breast fillet, skinned

50g/2oz/¹/₂ cup pistachio nuts, finely chopped

15ml/1 tbsp lemon juice

2 eggs, beaten

plain (all-purpose) flour, for shaping

75g/3oz/³/₄ cup blanched chopped almonds

75g/3oz/generous 1 cup dried breadcrumbs

salt and ground black pepper

*For the lemon sauce*

150ml/¹/₄ pint/²/₃ cup chicken stock

225g/8oz/1 cup cream cheese

15ml/1 tbsp lemon juice

15ml/1 tbsp chopped fresh parsley

15ml/1 tbsp chopped fresh chives

1 Skin and mince (grind) or chop the chicken finely. Mix with salt and freshly ground black pepper, pistachio nuts, lemon juice and 1 beaten egg.

2 Shape into 16 small balls with floured hands (use a spoon as a guide, so that all the balls are roughly the same size). Roll the balls in the remaining beaten egg and coat firstly with the almonds and then the dried breadcrumbs, pressing them on firmly. Chill until ready to cook.

3 Preheat the oven to 190°C/375°F/Gas 5. Place the balls on a greased baking sheet and bake for about 15 minutes, or until golden brown and crisp.

4 To make the lemon sauce, gently heat the chicken stock and cream cheese together in a pan, whisking until smooth. Add the lemon juice, herbs and seasoning. Serve with the chicken balls.

# Chicken Roulades

*These tender chicken rolls enclosing a filling of pine nuts and spinach make a light lunch dish for two or a first course for four. They can be sliced and served cold with a salad.*

### INGREDIENTS

*Makes 4*

4 chicken thighs, boned and skinned

115g/4oz chopped fresh or frozen spinach

15g/$^1$/2oz/1 tbsp butter

25g/1oz/$^1$/4 cup pine nuts

pinch of grated nutmeg

25g/1oz/$^1$/2 cup fresh white breadcrumbs

4 rashers (strips) rindless streaky
   (fatty) bacon

30ml/2 tbsp olive oil

150ml/$^1$/4 pint/$^2$/3 cup white wine or
   chicken stock

10ml/2 tsp cornflour (cornstarch)

30ml/2 tbsp single (light) cream

15ml/1 tbsp chopped fresh chives

salt and ground black pepper

1 Preheat the oven to 180°C/ 350°F/Gas 4. Place the chicken thighs between clear film (plastic wrap) and flatten with a rolling pin.

2 Put the spinach and butter into a pan. Heat gently until the spinach has defrosted, if frozen, then increase the heat and cook rapidly, stirring occasionally until all the moisture has evaporated. Add the pine nuts, seasoning, nutmeg and fresh breadcrumbs.

3 Divide the filling among the chicken pieces and roll up neatly. Wrap a rasher of bacon around each piece and tie securely with fine string.

4 Heat the oil in a large frying pan and brown the rolls all over. Lift out using a slotted spoon to drain off the oil and place in a shallow ovenproof dish.

5 Pour over the wine or stock. Cover, and bake for 15–20 minutes, or until tender. Transfer the chicken to a serving plate and remove the string. Strain the cooking liquid into a pan.

6 Blend the cornflour with a little cold water and add to the juices in the pan, along with the cream. Bring to the boil, stirring until thick. Adjust the seasoning and add the chives. Pour the sauce around the chicken and serve.

# Drunken Chicken

*As the chicken is marinated for several days, it is important to use a very fresh bird from a reputable supplier. Serve cold as part of an appetizer, or cut into neat pieces and serve as a snack with cocktails.*

## INGREDIENTS

*Serves 4–6*

1 chicken, about 1.3kg/3lb

1cm/$^1$/$_2$ in piece of fresh root ginger, peeled and thinly sliced

2 spring onions (scallions), trimmed

1.75 litres/3 pints/7$^1$/$_2$ cups water to cover

15ml/1 tbsp salt

300ml/$^1$/$_2$ pint/1$^1$/$_4$ cups dry sherry

15–30ml/1–2 tbsp brandy (optional)

spring onions, shredded, and fresh herbs, to garnish

3 Remove the skin from the chicken, and joint it neatly. Divide each leg into a drumstick and thigh. Make two more portions from the wings and some of the breast. Finally, cut away the remainder of the breast pieces (still on the bone) and divide each breast into two even-size portions.

5 Lift off any fat from the stock. Mix the sherry and brandy, if using, in a jug, add the stock and pour over the chicken. Cover again and leave in the refrigerator to marinate for 2 or 3 days, turning occasionally.

6 When ready to serve, cut the chicken through the bone into chunky pieces and arrange on a serving platter garnished with spring onion shreds and herbs.

1 Rinse and dry the chicken inside and out. Place the ginger and spring onions in the body cavity. Put the chicken in a large pan or flameproof casserole and just cover with water. Bring to the boil, skim and cook for 15 minutes.

2 Turn off the heat, cover the pan or casserole tightly and leave the chicken in the cooking liquid for 3–4 hours, by which time it will be cooked. Drain well. Pour 300ml/$^1$/$_2$ pint/1$^1$/$_4$ cups of the stock into a measuring jug (cup). Freeze the remaining stock for future use.

4 Arrange the chicken portions in a shallow dish. Rub salt into the chicken and cover with clear film (plastic wrap). Leave in a cool place for several hours or overnight in the refrigerator.

## VARIATION
~

To serve as a cocktail snack, take the meat off the bones, cut it into bitesize pieces, then spear each piece on a cocktail stick (toothpick).

# Grilled Skewered Chicken

*This dish is actually a Japanese snack as an accompaniment for drinks. The grilled skewered chicken is dipped in yakitori sauce and eaten as finger food.*

*Serves 4*

8 chicken thighs with skin, boned
8 large, thick spring onions
   (scallions), trimmed
shichimi togarashi, sansho or lemon
   wedges, to serve (see Cook's Tip)

*For the sauce*
60ml/4 tbsp sake
75ml/5 tbsp shoyu
15ml/1 tbsp mirin
15ml/1 tbsp caster (superfine) sugar

1 First, make the yakitori sauce. Mix all the ingredients together in a small pan. Bring to the boil, then reduce the heat and simmer for 10 minutes, or until the sauce has thickened.

2 Cut the chicken into 2.5cm/1in cubes. Cut the spring onions into 2.5cm/1in long sticks.

3 To grill (broil), preheat the grill (broiler) to high. Oil the wire rack and spread out the chicken cubes on it. Grill both sides of the chicken until the juices drip, then dip the pieces in the sauce and put back on the rack. Grill for 30 seconds on each side, repeating the dipping process twice more.

4 Set aside and keep warm. Gently grill the spring onions until soft and slightly brown outside. Do not dip. Thread about four pieces of chicken and three spring onion pieces on to each of eight bamboo skewers.

5 Arrange the skewers on a platter and serve sprinkled with shichimi togarashi or sansho, or accompanied by lemon wedges.

COOK'S TIP
Shichimi togarashi is a blend of flavourings and sansho is a spice. They are both used as condiments and are available from Japanese supermarkets.

# Grilled Chicken on Bamboo Skewers

These tasty chicken balls, known as tsukune, *are a favourite family dish in Japan, as it is easy for children to eat them directly from the skewer. You can make the balls in advance up to the end of step 2, and they also freeze well.*

## INGREDIENTS

Serves 4

300g/11oz skinless chicken, minced (ground)

2 eggs

2.5ml/$^1$/$_2$ tsp salt

10ml/2 tsp plain (all-purpose) flour

10ml/2 tsp cornflour (cornstarch)

90ml/6 tbsp dried breadcrumbs

2.5cm/1in piece fresh root ginger, grated

shichimi togarashi or sansho (optional), to serve

*For the sauce*

60ml/4 tbsp sake

75ml/5 tbsp shoyu

15ml/1 tbsp mirin

15ml/1 tbsp caster (superfine) sugar

2.5ml/$^1$/$_2$ tsp cornflour (cornstarch) blended with 5ml/1 tsp water

1 Soak eight bamboo skewers in water for 30 minutes.

2 Put all the ingredients for the chicken balls, except the ginger, in a food processor and blend well. Wet your hands and scoop about a tablespoonful of the mixture into your palm. Shape it into a small ball. Make another 30–32 balls.

3 Squeeze the juice from the grated ginger into a small mixing bowl. Discard the pulp.

4 Add the ginger juice to a pan of boiling water. Add the chicken balls, and boil for about 7 minutes, or until the colour of the meat changes and the balls float to the surface. Scoop out and drain on a plate covered with kitchen paper.

5 In a small pan, mix all the ingredients for the yakitori sauce, except for the cornflour paste. Bring to the boil, then reduce the heat and simmer for about 10 minutes, or until the sauce has slightly reduced. Add the cornflour paste and stir until the sauce is thick. Transfer to a small bowl.

6 Thread three to four balls on to each skewer. Cook under a medium grill (broiler) or on a barbecue, keeping the skewer handles away from the fire. Turn them frequently for a few minutes, or until the balls start to brown. Brush with sauce and return to the heat. Repeat the process twice. Serve, sprinkled with shichimi togarashi or sansho, if you like.

# Chicken, Juniper and Peppercorn Terrine

*This is an ideal dish for entertaining, as it can be made several days in advance.*

### INGREDIENTS

*Serves 10–12*

225g/8oz chicken livers, trimmed
450g/1lb minced (ground) chicken
450g/1lb minced (ground) pork
225g/8oz cubetti pancetta
50g/2oz/$^1$/$_2$ cup shelled pistachio nuts,
  roughly chopped
5ml/1 tsp salt
2.5ml/$^1$/$_2$ tsp ground mace
2 garlic cloves, crushed
5ml/1 tsp drained green peppercorns
  in brine
5ml/1 tsp juniper berries
120ml/4 fl oz/$^1$/$_2$ cup dry white wine
30ml/2 tbsp gin
finely grated rind of 1 orange
8 large vacuum-packed vine leaves in
  brine, rinsed and drained
oil, for greasing
spiced kumquats, red pepper chutney or
  chilli jelly, to serve

1 Chop the livers finely. Put them in a bowl with the pork, minced chicken, pancetta, pistachio nuts, salt, mace and garlic. Mix well.

2 Crush the peppercorns and juniper berries. Add to the mix. Stir in the wine, gin and orange rind. Cover and chill overnight.

3 Preheat the oven to 160°C/325°F/Gas 3.

4 Oil a 1.2 litre/2 pint/5 cup loaf tin (pan). Line the tin with the leaves, so that the ends hang over the sides. Pack the mix into the tin and fold the leaves over to enclose the filling. Brush lightly with oil.

5 Cover the terrine with its lid or with foil. Place it in a roasting pan and pour in boiling water to come halfway up the sides of the terrine. Bake for 1$^3$/$_4$ hours, checking the level of the water occasionally, so that the roasting pan does not dry out.

6 Leave the terrine to cool, then pour off the surface juices. Cover with clear film (plastic wrap), then foil and place weights on top. Chill overnight. Serve at room temperature with a pickle or chutney.

# Chicken and Pistachio Pâté

*This simplified version of a classic French dish can be made using a whole boned bird, or chicken pieces. Serve it as a first course for a large gathering or for an elegant picnic or a cold buffet accompanied by a herb mayonnaise.*

### INGREDIENTS

*Serves 20 as a first course, 10–12 as a main course*

900g/2lb boneless chicken meat

1 chicken breast fillet, about 175g/6oz, skinned

25g/1oz/$^1$/$_2$ cup fresh white breadcrumbs

120ml/4fl oz/$^1$/$_2$ cup whipping cream

1 egg white

4 spring onions (scallions), finely chopped

1 garlic clove, finely chopped

75g/3oz cooked ham, cut into 1cm/$^1$/$_2$ in cubes

50g/2oz/$^1$/$_2$ cup shelled pistachio nuts

45ml/3 tbsp chopped fresh tarragon

pinch of freshly grated nutmeg

4ml/$^3$/$_4$ tsp salt

7.5ml/1$^1$/$_2$ tsp pepper

green salad, to serve

1 Trim all the fat, tendons and connective tissue from the chicken meat and cut into 5cm/2in cubes. Put in a food processor fitted with the metal blade and pulse to chop the meat to a smooth purée, in two or three batches (depending on capacity). Or alternatively pass the meat through the medium or fine blade of a mincer. Remove any white stringy pieces.

2 Preheat the oven to 180°C/ 350°F/Gas 4. Cut the chicken breast fillet into 1cm/$^1$/$_2$ in cubes.

3 In a large bowl, soak the breadcrumbs in the cream. Add the puréed chicken, egg white, spring onions, garlic, ham, pistachio nuts, tarragon, nutmeg and seasoning. Using a wooden spoon, mix until well combined.

4 On a piece of foil about 45cm/ 18in long, brush oil on a 30cm/ 12in square in the centre. Spoon the chicken on to the foil to form a log about 30 x 9cm/12 x 3$^1$/$_2$ in. Bring together the long sides of the foil and fold over securely. Twist the ends and tie with string.

5 Transfer to a baking dish and bake for 1$^1$/$_2$ hours. Leave to cool in the dish and chill until cold. Serve sliced with a green salad.

---

COOK'S TIP

You could use turkey meat in place of some or all of the chicken.

---

# Chicken, Bacon and Walnut Terrine

*Walnuts, warm spices and Madeira give this chicken terrine a wonderful flavour.*

INGREDIENTS

*Serves 8–10*

2 chicken breast fillets, skinned
1 large garlic clove, crushed
$1/2$ slice bread
1 egg
350g/12oz bacon chops (the fattier the better), minced (ground)
225g/8oz chicken livers, finely chopped
25g/1oz/$1/4$ cup chopped walnuts, toasted
30ml/2 tbsp sweet sherry or Madeira
2.5ml/$1/2$ tsp ground allspice
2.5ml/$1/2$ tsp cayenne pepper
pinch each of ground nutmeg and cloves
8 long rashers (strips) streaky (fatty) bacon, rind removed
salt and ground black pepper
chicory leaves and chives, to garnish

1 Cut the chicken breast fillets into thin strips and season.

2 Mash the garlic, bread and egg together. Work in the chopped bacon (using your hands is really the best way) and then the finely chopped livers. Stir in the chopped walnuts, sherry or Madeira, spices and seasoning to taste.

3 Preheat the oven to 200°C/ 400°F/Gas 6. Stretch the bacon rashers with a palette knife or metal spatula and use to line a 675g/1$1/2$ lb loaf tin (pan), then pack in half of the meat mixture.

4 Lay the chicken strips on the top and spread the rest of the mixture over. Cover the loaf tin with lightly greased foil, seal well and press down very firmly.

5 Place the terrine in a roasting tin half-full of hot water and bake for 1–1$1/2$ hours, or until firm to the touch. Remove from the oven, place weights on the top and leave to cool completely. Drain off any excess fat or liquid while the terrine is warm.

6 When really cold, turn out the terrine, cut into thick slices and serve at once, garnished with a few chicory leaves and chives.

# Chicken Liver and Marsala Pâté

2 Transfer the livers to a blender or food processor, using a slotted spoon, and add the Marsala and chopped sage.

3 Melt 150g/5oz/10 tbsp of the remaining butter in the frying pan, stirring to loosen any sediment, then pour into the blender or processor and blend until smooth. Season well.

*This is a really quick and simple pâté to make, yet it has a delicious and quite sophisticated flavour. It contains Marsala, a soft and pungent fortified wine from Sicily. If it is unavailable, use brandy or a medium-dry sherry.*

### INGREDIENTS

Serves 4

350g/12oz chicken livers,
    defrosted if frozen
225g/8oz/1 cup butter, softened
2 garlic cloves, crushed
15ml/1 tbsp Marsala
5ml/1 tsp chopped fresh sage
salt and ground black pepper
8 sage leaves, to garnish
thin, crisp toast, to serve

1 Rinse the chicken livers and dry with kitchen paper. Melt 25g/1oz/2 tbsp of the butter in a frying pan, and fry the chicken livers with the garlic over a medium heat for about 5 minutes, or until they are firm but still pink in the middle.

4 Spoon the pâté into four individual pots and smooth the surface. Melt the remaining butter in a separate pan and pour over the pâtés. Garnish with sage leaves and chill until set. Serve with triangles of toast.

# Chicken and Pork Terrine

*This delicately flavoured Ukrainian pâté can be served with salad as a first course or with warm, crusty bread for a light lunch.*

INGREDIENTS

*Serves 6–8*

225g/8oz rindless, streaky (fatty) bacon
375g/13oz chicken breast fillet, skinned
15ml/1 tbsp lemon juice
225g/8oz/1 cup lean minced
    (ground) pork
$^1\!/_2$ small onion, finely chopped
2 eggs, beaten
30ml/2 tbsp chopped fresh parsley
5ml/1 tsp salt
5ml/1 tsp green peppercorns, crushed
fresh green salad, radishes and lemon
    wedges, to serve

1 Preheat the oven to 160°C/
325°F/Gas 3. Put the bacon on a board and stretch it using the back of a knife so that it can be arranged in overlapping slices over the base and sides of a 900g/2lb loaf tin (pan).

2 Cut 115g/4oz of the chicken into 10cm/4in strips. Sprinkle with lemon juice. Put the rest of the chicken in a food processor or blender with the pork and the onion. Process until fairly smooth.

3 Add the eggs, parsley, salt and peppercorns to the meat mixture and process again briefly. Spoon half the mixture into the loaf tin and then level the surface.

4 Arrange the chicken strips on top, then spoon in the remaining meat mixture and smooth the top. Tap the tin sharply to knock out any pockets of air.

5 Cover with a piece of oiled foil and put in a roasting pan. Pour in enough hot water to come halfway up the sides of the loaf tin. Bake for about 45–50 minutes.

6 Allow to cool in the tin before turning out and chilling. Serve sliced, with a green salad, radishes and wedges of lemon.

# Chicken Liver Pâté with Garlic

*This smooth, garlicky pâté is
wickedly indulgent and absolutely
delicious. It is ideal as a first course,
with toast and pickled gherkins.*

### INGREDIENTS

*Serves 6–8*

225g/8oz/1 cup unsalted (sweet) butter

400g/14oz chicken livers, chopped

45–60ml/3–4 tbsp Madeira

3 large shallots, chopped

2 large garlic cloves, finely chopped

5ml/1 tsp finely chopped fresh thyme

pinch of ground allspice

30ml/2 tbsp double (heavy)
    cream (optional)

salt and ground black pepper

small fresh bay leaves or fresh thyme
    sprigs, to garnish

1 Melt 75g/3oz/6 tbsp butter in a
small pan over a low heat, then
allow it to bubble gently until it is
clear. Pour off the clarified butter
into a bowl.

2 Melt 40g/1½ oz/3 tbsp butter
in a frying pan and fry the
chicken livers for 4–5 minutes, or
until browned.

---

COOK'S TIP

~

The flavour of the pâté deepens
and matures on chilling, so it is
best if you make it a day before it
is required.

---

3 Add the Madeira and set it
alight, then scrape the contents
of the pan into a food processor
or blender.

4 Melt 25g/1oz/2 tbsp butter in a
pan and cook the shallots for
5 minutes. Add the herbs and allspice and cook for 2–3 minutes.
Add to the livers with the butter
and cream, if using, then process.

5 Add about 7.5ml/1½ tsp each of
salt and pepper and more
Madeira to taste. Scrape the pâté
into a serving dish and place a few
bay leaves or thyme sprigs on top.

6 Melt the clarified butter, if
necessary, then pour it over
the pâté. Cool and chill in the
refrigerator for at least 4 hours
or overnight.

# Chicken Liver Mousse

*This mousse makes an elegant yet surprisingly easy first course. The onion marmalade is a delicious accompaniment, along with a salad of chicory or other bitter leaves.*

*Serves 6–8*

175g/6oz/³/4 cup butter, diced
1 small onion, finely chopped
1 garlic clove, finely chopped
450g/1lb chicken livers
2.5ml/¹/2 tsp dried thyme
30–45ml/2–3 tbsp brandy
salt and ground black pepper
green salad, to serve

*For the onion marmalade*
25g/1oz/2 tbsp butter
450g/1lb red onions, thinly sliced
1 garlic clove, finely chopped
2.5ml/¹/2 tsp dried thyme
30–45ml/2–3 tbsp raspberry or red
    wine vinegar
15–30ml/1–2 tbsp clear honey
40g/1¹/2 oz/¹/4 cup sultanas
    (golden raisins)

1 Trim the chicken livers, removing any filaments or fat.

2 In a heavy frying pan, melt 25g/1oz/2 tbsp of the butter over a medium heat. Add the onion and cook for 5–7 minutes, or until soft and golden, then add the garlic and cook for 1 minute more.

---

COOK'S TIP

The mousse will keep for 3–4 days. If made ahead, cover and chill until ready to use. The onion marmalade can be made up to 2 days ahead and gently reheated over a low heat or in the microwave until just warm.

---

3 Increase the heat and add the livers, thyme and seasoning. Cook for 3–5 minutes, stirring frequently; the livers should remain pink inside. Add the brandy and cook for a further minute.

4 Transfer the livers to a food processor fitted with the metal blade. Pour in the cooking juices and process for 1 minute, or until smooth, scraping down the sides once. With the machine running, add the remaining butter, until it is incorporated.

5 Press the mousse mixture through a fine sieve with a wooden spoon or rubber spatula.

6 Line a 475ml/16fl oz/2 cup loaf tin (pan) with clear film (plastic wrap), smoothing out as many wrinkles as possible. Pour the mousse mixture into the lined tin. Cool, then cover and chill until firm.

7 To make the onion marmalade, heat the butter in a heavy frying pan over a medium-low heat, add the onions and cook for 20 minutes, or until softened, stirring frequently. Stir in the garlic, thyme, vinegar, honey and sultanas and cook, covered, for 10–15 minutes, or until the onions are completely soft and jam-like, stirring occasionally. Spoon into a bowl and cool to room temperature.

8 To serve, dip the loaf tin into hot water for 5 seconds, wipe dry and invert on to a board. Lift off the tin, peel off the clear film and smooth the surface with a knife. Serve sliced with a little of the onion marmalade and a green salad.

# SALADS &
# BARBECUES

Whatever the time of year, crisp, fresh salads are always a popular choice.
In this chapter warm salads feature. They combine cooked chicken with crisp
raw vegetables or salad leaves. All kinds of cold salads are included too
– perfect for hot summer days.
Summer is also the time for outdoor eating, and as well as fresh salads,
everyone enjoys a barbecue. There are plenty of mouthwatering chicken recipes
here, with a variety of exciting marinades and accompaniments,
to enable you to create the perfect outdoor meal.

# Classic Chicken Salad with Green Beans

*A piquant dressing makes this salad of chicken, young spinach and green beans simply delicious.*

INGREDIENTS

*Serves 8*

1 chicken, about 1.8kg/4lb
300ml/$^1$/$_2$ pint/1$^1$/$_4$ cups white wine
   and water, mixed
24 x 5mm/$^1$/$_4$ in slices French bread
1 garlic clove, peeled
225g/8oz green beans, cut into
   5cm/2in lengths
115g/4oz fresh young spinach leaves,
   torn into small pieces
2 sticks celery, thinly sliced
2 sun-dried tomatoes, chopped
2 spring onions (scallions), thinly sliced
fresh chives and parsley, to garnish

*For the vinaigrette*
30ml/2 tbsp red wine vinegar
90ml/6 tbsp olive oil
15ml/1 tbsp wholegrain mustard
15ml/1 tbsp clear honey
30ml/2 tbsp chopped mixed fresh herbs
10ml/2 tsp finely chopped capers
salt and ground black pepper

1 Preheat the oven to 190°C/
375°F/Gas 5. Put the chicken,
wine and water into a casserole.
Roast for 1$^1$/$_2$ hours, until tender.
Leave to cool in the liquid. Remove
the skin and bones and cut the
flesh into small pieces.

2 Put all the ingredients for the
vinaigrette into a screw-topped
jar and shake vigorously. Adjust the
seasoning to taste.

3 Toast the French bread until
golden brown to make croûtes.
Rub with garlic.

4 Cook the green beans in
boiling water until just tender.
Drain and rinse under cold water.

5 Arrange the spinach on serving
plates with the celery, green
beans, sun-dried tomatoes,
chicken and spring onions. Spoon
over the dressing, add the toasted
croûtes and garnish with chives
and parsley.

# Dijon Chicken Salad

*Here is an attractive dish to serve for lunch with herb and garlic bread.*

INGREDIENTS

*Serves 4*

4 chicken breast fillets, skinned
mixed salad leaves, such as frisée and
    oak leaf lettuce or radicchio, to serve

*For the marinade*
30ml/2 tbsp Dijon mustard
3 garlic cloves, crushed
15ml/1 tbsp grated onion
60ml/4 tbsp white wine

*For the mustard dressing*
30ml/2 tbsp tarragon wine vinegar
5ml/1 tsp Dijon mustard
5ml/1 tsp clear honey
90ml/6 tbsp olive oil
salt and ground black pepper

1 Mix all the marinade ingredients together in a shallow dish that is large enough to hold the chicken in a single layer.

2 Turn the chicken over in the marinade to coat it completely. Cover with clear film (plastic wrap) and then chill in the refrigerator overnight.

3 Preheat the oven to 190°C/ 375°F/Gas 5. Transfer the chicken and the marinade into an ovenproof dish, cover with foil and bake for about 35 minutes or until tender. Leave to cool.

4 Put all the mustard dressing ingredients into a screw-topped jar, shake vigorously to emulsify, and adjust the seasoning. (The dressing can be made several days in advance and stored in the refrigerator.)

5 Slice the chicken thinly, fan out the slices and arrange on a serving dish with the salad leaves.

6 Spoon over some of the mustard dressing, and serve.

# Swiss Cheese, Chicken and Tongue Salad

*The rich sweet flavours of this salad marry well with the peppery watercress or rocket. A minted lemon dressing freshens the overall taste. Serve with new potatoes.*

## INGREDIENTS

*Serves 4*

2 chicken breast fillets, skinned
$^1/_2$ chicken stock (bouillon) cube
225g/8oz sliced ox tongue or ham,
   5mm/$^1/_2$ in thick
225g/8oz Gruyère cheese
1 lollo rosso lettuce
1 round (butterhead) or Batavian
   endive lettuce
1 bunch watercress or rocket (arugula)
2 green-skinned apples, cored and sliced
3 sticks celery, sliced
60ml/4 tbsp sesame seeds, toasted
salt, ground black pepper and nutmeg

*For the dressing*
75ml/5 tbsp groundnut (peanut) or
   sunflower oil
5ml/1 tsp sesame oil
45ml/3 tbsp lemon juice
10ml/2 tsp chopped fresh mint
3 drops Tabasco sauce

1 Place the chicken breasts in a shallow pan, cover with 300ml/ $^1/_2$ pint/1$^1/_4$ cups water, add $^1/_2$ stock cube and bring to the boil. Put the lid on the pan and simmer for 15 minutes. Drain, reserving the stock for another occasion, then cool the chicken under cold running water.

2 To make the dressing, measure the two oils, lemon juice, mint and Tabasco sauce into a screw-top jar and shake. Cut the chicken, tongue and Gruyère cheese into fine strips. Moisten with a little dressing and set aside.

3 Arrange the salad leaves, apple and celery on four large plates. Pile the chicken, tongue and cheese in the centre, scatter with toasted sesame seeds, season with salt, pepper and freshly grated nutmeg and serve, with the dressing.

# Chicken and Avocado Mayonnaise

*Creamy avocados complement chicken in this tasty first course. Serve with crisp nacho or tortilla chips for dipping.*

*Serves 4*

30ml/2 tbsp mayonnaise

15ml/1 tbsp fromage frais or ricotta cheese

2 garlic cloves, crushed

115g/4oz/scant 1 cup chopped
   cooked chicken

1 large ripe, but firm, avocado,
   peeled and stoned (pitted)

30ml/2 tbsp lemon juice

salt and ground black pepper

nacho chips or tortilla chips, to serve

2 Chop the avocado and toss immediately in lemon juice.

3 Mix the avocado gently into the chicken mixture. Check the seasoning and chill until required.

4 Serve in small serving dishes with the nacho or tortilla chips as scoops, if liked.

1 Mix together the mayonnaise, fromage frais, garlic, and seasoning to taste, in a small bowl. Stir in the chopped chicken.

COOK'S TIP

This mixture makes a great, chunky filling for sandwiches, baps or pitta bread. It can also be served as a main course salad, heaped on to a base of mixed salad leaves.

# Chicken and Fruit Salad

*Refreshing cantaloupe melon makes this salad ideal for a warm summer's day. The chickens may be cooked the day before.*

INGREDIENTS

*Serves 8*

4 tarragon or rosemary sprigs
2 chickens, about 1.8kg/4lb each
65g/2$^1$/2 oz/5 tbsp softened butter
150ml/$^1$/4 pint/$^2$/3 cup chicken stock
150ml/$^1$/4 pint/$^2$/3 cup white wine
115g/4oz/1 cup walnut pieces
1 small cantaloupe melon
lettuce leaves
450g/1lb seedless grapes or pitted cherries
salt and ground black pepper

*For the dressing*
30ml/2 tbsp tarragon vinegar
120ml/4 fl oz/$^1$/2 cup light olive oil
30ml/2 tbsp chopped mixed fresh herbs,
    such as parsley, mint and tarragon

1 Preheat the oven to 200°C/ 400°F/Gas 6. Put the herb sprigs inside the chickens and season. Tie the chickens with string. Spread the chickens with 50g/2oz/4 tbsp of the softened butter, place in a roasting pan and pour in the stock. Cover loosely with foil and roast for about 1$^1$/2 hours, basting twice, until browned and the juices run clear. Remove the chickens from the roasting pan.

2 Add the wine to the roasting pan. Bring to the boil and cook until syrupy. Strain and leave to cool. Heat the remaining butter in a frying pan and gently fry the walnuts until browned. Drain and cool. Scoop the melon into balls or cut into cubes. Joint the chickens.

3 To make the dressing, whisk the vinegar and oil together with a little salt and freshly ground black pepper. Remove all the fat from the chicken juices and add these to the dressing with the herbs.

4 Arrange the chicken pieces on a bed of lettuce, scatter over the grapes or pitted cherries, melon balls or cubes and spoon over the herb dressing. Sprinkle with toasted walnuts.

# Citrus Chicken Salad

*Oranges and limes give a zest to this salad that makes a delicious change from rich food. It is a good choice for a post-Christmas buffet, when cooked turkey can be used instead of chicken.*

## INGREDIENTS

*Serves 6*

120ml/4fl oz/$^1$/$_2$ cup extra virgin olive oil

6 chicken breast fillets, skinned

4 oranges

5ml/1 tsp Dijon mustard

15ml/3 tsp clear honey

300g/11oz/2$^3$/$_4$ cups finely shredded white cabbage

300g/11oz carrots, peeled and finely sliced

2 spring onions (scallions), finely sliced

2 celery sticks, cut into matchstick strips

30ml/2 tbsp chopped fresh tarragon

2 limes

salt and ground black pepper

1 Heat 30ml/2 tbsp of the oil in a large, heavy frying pan. Add the chicken breasts to the pan and cook for 15–20 minutes, or until the chicken is cooked through and golden brown. (If your pan is too small, cook the chicken in two or three batches.) Remove the chicken from the pan and leave to cool.

2 Cut a thin slice of peel and pith from each end of two of the oranges. Place a cut-side down on a plate and cut off the peel and pith. Cut out each segment leaving the membrane behind. Set aside.

3 Grate the rind and squeeze the juice from one of the remaining oranges and place in a bowl. Stir in the mustard, 5ml/1 tsp of honey, 60ml/4 tbsp of the oil and seasoning. Mix in the cabbage, carrots, spring onions and celery.

## VARIATION

For a creamy result, mayonnaise, crème fraîche or sour cream can be used to dress the chicken.

4 Meanwhile, squeeze the juice from the remaining orange and mix it with the remaining honey and oil, and the tarragon. Peel and segment the limes, as for the oranges, and lightly mix the segments into the dressing with the reserved orange segments and seasoning to taste.

5 Slice the cooked chicken breasts and stir into the dressing. Spoon the vegetable salad on to plates and add the chicken mixture, then serve at once.

# Chicken and Broccoli Salad

*Gorgonzola makes a tangy dressing that goes well with both chicken and broccoli. Serve for a lunch or supper dish, with crusty Italian bread.*

### INGREDIENTS

*Serves 4*

175g/6oz broccoli florets, divided into small sprigs

225g/8oz/2 cups farfalle

2 large chicken breast fillets, cooked and skinned

*For the dressing*

90g/3$^{1}$/$_{2}$ oz Gorgonzola cheese

15ml/1 tbsp white wine vinegar

60ml/4 tbsp extra virgin olive oil

2.5–5ml/$^{1}$/$_{2}$–1 tsp finely chopped fresh sage, plus extra sage sprigs to garnish

salt and ground black pepper

1 Cook the broccoli florets in a large pan of salted boiling water for 3 minutes. Remove with a slotted spoon and rinse under cold running water, then spread out on kitchen paper to drain and dry.

2 Add the pasta to the broccoli cooking water, then bring back to the boil and cook according to the packet instructions. When cooked, drain the pasta into a colander, rinse under cold running water until cold, then leave to drain and dry, shaking the colander occasionally.

3 Cut the chicken into bitesize pieces.

4 To make the dressing, put the cheese in a large bowl and mash with a fork, then whisk in the wine vinegar followed by the oil and sage, and season with salt and pepper to taste.

5 Add the pasta, chicken and broccoli. Toss well, then season to taste. Serve, garnished with sage.

# Chicken and Pasta Salad

*This is a delicious way to use up leftover cooked chicken.*

*Serves 4*

225g/8oz/2 cups tri-coloured pasta twists

30ml/2 tbsp pesto

15ml/1 tbsp olive oil

1 beefsteak tomato

12 pitted black olives

225g/8oz/1¹/₂ cups cooked green beans

350g/12oz/3 cups cubed cooked chicken

salt and ground black pepper

fresh basil, to garnish

1 Cook the pasta in plenty of salted boiling water until *al dente* (about 12 minutes or as directed on the packet).

2 Drain the pasta and rinse in plenty of cold running water. Put into a bowl and stir in the pesto and olive oil.

3 Plunge the tomato in boiling water for about 30 seconds, then refresh in cold water. Peel away the skin.

4 Cut the tomato into small cubes and add to the pasta with the olives, seasoning and green beans cut into 4cm/1¹/₂ in lengths. Add the cubed chicken. Toss gently together and transfer to a serving platter. Garnish with fresh basil.

# Chicken and Mango Salad with Orange Rice

*The combination of sweet and savoury has always been popular. In this recipe, ripe mango and curried chicken mayonnaise top delicious citrus rice.*

Serves 4

15ml/1 tbsp sunflower oil
1 onion, chopped
1 garlic clove, crushed
30ml/2 tbsp red curry paste
10ml/2 tsp apricot jam
30ml/2 tbsp chicken stock
about 450g/1lb cooked chicken, cut into
    small pieces
150ml/$^1$/4 pint/$^2$/3 cup natural
    (plain) yogurt
60–75ml/4–5 tbsp mayonnaise
1 large mango, cut into 1cm/$^1$/2 in dice
fresh flat leaf parsley sprigs, to garnish
poppadums, to serve

*For the rice*
175g/6oz/scant 1 cup white long grain rice
225g/8oz/1$^1$/2 cups grated carrots
1 large orange, cut into segments
40g/1$^1$/2 oz/$^1$/3 cup roasted flaked
    (sliced) almonds

*For the dressing*
45ml/3 tbsp olive oil
60ml/4 tbsp sunflower oil
45ml/3 tbsp lemon juice
1 garlic clove, crushed
15ml/1 tbsp chopped mixed fresh herbs
    (tarragon, parsley, chives)
salt and ground black pepper

1 Heat the oil in a frying pan and fry the onion and garlic for 3–4 minutes, or until soft.

2 Stir in the curry paste, cook for about 1 minute, then lower the heat and stir in the apricot jam and stock. Mix well, add the chopped chicken and stir until the chicken is thoroughly coated in the paste. Spoon the mixture into a large bowl and leave to cool.

3 Meanwhile, boil the rice in plenty of lightly salted water until just tender. Drain, rinse under cold water and drain again. When cool, stir into the grated carrots and add the orange segments and flaked almonds.

4 Make the dressing by whisking all the ingredients together in a bowl.

5 When the chicken mixture is cool, stir in the yogurt and mayonnaise, then add the mango, stirring it in carefully so as not to break the flesh. Chill for about 30 minutes.

6 To serve, pour the dressing into the rice salad and mix well. Spoon on to a platter and mound the cold curried chicken on top. Garnish with flat leaf parsley and serve with poppadums.

COOK'S TIP

A simple way of dicing a mango is to take two thick slices from either side of the large flat stone (pit) without peeling the fruit. Make criss-cross cuts in the flesh on each slice and then turn inside out. The cubes of flesh will stand proud of the skin and can be easily cut off.

# Orange Chicken Salad

*A colourful and very delicately flavoured rice salad.*

*Serves 4*

3 large seedless oranges

175g/6oz/scant 1 cup long grain rice

475ml/16fl oz/2 cups water

175ml/6fl oz/³/4 cup vinaigrette dressing, made with red wine vinegar and a mixture of olive and vegetable oils

10ml/2 tsp Dijon mustard

2.5ml/¹/2 tsp caster (superfine) sugar

450g/1lb/3¹/4 cups diced cooked chicken

45ml/3 tbsp chopped chives

75g/3oz/³/4 cup roasted cashew nuts

salt and ground black pepper

cucumber slices, to garnish

1 Thinly peel 1 orange, taking only the coloured part of the rind and leaving the white pith.

2 Combine the orange rind, rice and water in a pan. Add a pinch of salt. Bring to the boil, then cover and steam over very low heat for 15–18 minutes, or until the rice is tender and all the water has been absorbed.

3 To segment the oranges, using a sharp knife, cut a thin slice of peel from each end of the remaining oranges. Place cut side down on a plate and cut off the peel and pith in strips. Remove any remaining pith. Cut out each segment leaving the membrane behind.

4 Add the orange juice to the vinaigrette dressing. Add the mustard and sugar and whisk to combine well. Taste and add more salt and pepper if needed.

5 When the rice is cooked, remove it from the heat and cool slightly, uncovered. Discard the orange rind.

6 Turn the rice into a bowl and add half of the dressing. Toss well and cool completely.

7 Add the chicken, chives, cashew nuts and orange segments to the rice with the remaining dressing. Toss gently. Serve at room temperature, garnished with cucumber slices.

# Vinaigrette Dressing

*A good vinaigrette can do more than dress a salad. It can also be used to baste meat, poultry, seafood or vegetables during cooking, and it can be used as a flavouring and tenderizing marinade. The basic mixture of oil, vinegar and seasoning lends itself to many variations.*

*Vinaigrette dressing will keep in the refrigerator, in a tightly sealed container, for several weeks. Add flavourings, especially fresh herbs, just before using.*

*Makes just over 175ml/6 fl oz/³/4 cup*

45ml/3 tbsp wine vinegar

75ml/5 tbsp vegetable oil

75ml/5 tbsp extra virgin olive oil

salt and ground pepper

1 Put the vinegar, salt and pepper in a bowl and whisk to dissolve the salt.

2 Gradually add the oil, stirring with the whisk. Taste and adjust seasoning as necessary.

# Maryland Chicken Salad

*Barbecue-cooked chicken, corn, bacon and banana combine here in a sensational main-course salad. It's perfect served with baked potatoes, topped with butter.*

### INGREDIENTS

*Serves 4*

4 chicken breast fillets, skinned
oil, for brushing
225g/8oz rindless unsmoked bacon
4 corn on the cob
45ml/3 tbsp melted butter
4 ripe bananas, peeled and halved
4 firm tomatoes, halved
1 escarole or round (butterhead) lettuce
1 bunch watercress or rocket (arugula)
salt and ground black pepper

*For the dressing*
75ml/5 tbsp groundnut oil
15ml/1 tbsp white wine vinegar
10ml/2 tsp maple syrup
10ml/2 tsp mild mustard

1 Prepare a barbecue. Season the chicken breasts, brush with oil and cook for 15 minutes, turning once. Cook the bacon for 8–10 minutes, or until crisp.

2 Boil the corn cobs for 20 minutes in a large pan of salted water, then brush with butter and brown over the barbecue. Brush the bananas and tomatoes with butter too, if you like, and cook over the barbecue for 6–8 minutes.

3 To make the dressing, combine the oil, vinegar, maple syrup and mustard with seasoning and 15ml/1 tbsp water in a screw-top jar and shake well.

4 Toss the salad leaves in the dressing.

5 Distribute the salad leaves among four large plates. Slice the chicken and arrange over the leaves with the bacon, banana, corn and tomatoes.

# Grilled Chicken Salad with Lavender

*Lavender may seem like an odd salad ingredient, but its delightful scent has a natural affinity with sweet garlic, orange and other wild herbs. Golden polenta makes this salad both filling and delicious.*

## INGREDIENTS

*Serves 4*

4 chicken breast fillets, skinned
900ml/1½ pints/3¾ cups light
   chicken stock
175g/6oz/1½ cups fine polenta
50g/2oz/¼ cup butter
450g/1lb young spinach
175g/6oz lamb's lettuce
8 fresh lavender sprigs
8 small tomatoes, halved
salt and ground black pepper

*For the marinade*

6 fresh lavender flowers
10ml/2 tsp finely grated orange rind
2 garlic cloves, crushed
10ml/2 tsp clear honey
30ml/2 tbsp olive oil
10ml/2 tsp chopped fresh thyme
10ml/2 tsp chopped fresh marjoram

1 To make the marinade, strip the lavender flowers from the stems and combine with the orange rind, garlic, honey and salt to taste. Add the olive oil and herbs. Slash the chicken deeply, spread the mixture over the chicken and leave to marinate in a cool place for at least 20 minutes.

2 To cook the polenta, bring the chicken stock to the boil in a heavy pan. Add the polenta in a steady stream, stirring all the time until thick; this will take 2–3 minutes. Turn the cooked polenta out on to a 2.5cm/1in deep buttered tray and allow to cool.

3 Heat the grill (broiler) to medium. Grill (broil) the chicken for about 15 minutes, turning once.

4 Cut the polenta into 2.5cm/1in cubes with a wet knife. Heat the butter in a large frying pan and fry the polenta until golden.

5 Divide the salad leaves among four large plates. Slice each chicken breast and lay the slices over the salad. Place the polenta among the salad and decorate it with sprigs of lavender and tomatoes. Season to taste with salt and ground black pepper and serve.

# Warm Chicken Salad with Rice

*Succulent cooked chicken pieces are combined with vegetables in a light chilli dressing.*

Serves 6

50g/2oz mixed salad leaves

50g/2oz baby spinach leaves

50g/2oz watercress or rocket (arugula)

30ml/2 tbsp chilli sauce

30ml/2 tbsp dry sherry

15ml/1 tbsp light soy sauce

15ml/1 tbsp tomato ketchup

10ml/2 tsp olive oil

8 shallots, finely chopped

1 garlic clove, crushed

350g/12oz chicken breast fillet, skinned
   and cut into thin strips

1 red (bell) pepper, seeded and sliced

175g/6oz mangetouts (snow peas)

400g/14oz can baby corn, drained
   and halved

275g/10oz can brown rice

salt and ground black pepper

parsley sprig, to garnish

1 Arrange the mixed salad leaves, tearing up any large ones, and the spinach leaves on a serving dish. Add the watercress or rocket and toss to mix.

2 In a small bowl, mix together the chilli sauce, sherry, soy sauce and tomato ketchup and set aside.

3 Heat the oil in a large, non-stick frying pan or wok. Add the shallots and garlic and stir-fry over a medium heat for 1 minute.

4 Add the chicken and stir-fry for 3–4 minutes.

5 Add the pepper, mangetouts, corn and rice and stir-fry for 2–3 minutes.

6 Pour in the chilli sauce mixture and stir-fry for 2–3 minutes, or until hot and bubbling. Season to taste. Spoon the chicken mixture over the salad leaves, toss together to mix and serve immediately, garnished with fresh parsley.

# Warm Chicken Liver and Grapefruit Salad

*There are times when warm salads are just right. Serve this delicious combination as either a first course or a light meal, with hunks of bread to dip into the dressing.*

## INGREDIENTS

*Serves 4*

115g/4oz each fresh young spinach leaves, rocket (arugula) and lollo rosso lettuce
2 pink grapefruit
90ml/6 tbsp sunflower oil
10ml/2 tsp sesame oil
10ml/2 tsp soy sauce
225g/8oz chicken livers, chopped
salt and ground black pepper

3 To make the dressing, mix together 60ml/4 tbsp of the sunflower oil with the sesame oil, soy sauce, seasoning and grapefruit juice to taste.

4 Heat the rest of the sunflower oil in a small pan and cook the liver, stirring gently, until firm and lightly browned.

5 Tip the chicken livers and dressing over the salad and serve immediately.

---

### COOK'S TIP

Chicken or turkey livers are ideal for this recipe, and there's no need to leave them to defrost completely before cooking.

---

1 Tear up all the salad leaves. Mix together in a large salad bowl.

2 Using a sharp knife, cut the peel and pith from each end of the grapefruit. Place cut side down on a plate and cut off all the peel and pith in strips. Cut out each segment leaving the membrane behind. Reserve the juice. Add the segments to the leaves.

# Chicken Liver, Bacon and Tomato Salad

*This salad is especially welcome during the autumn months when the evenings are growing shorter and cooler. Try this rich salad with sweet spinach and bitter leaves of frisée lettuce.*

### INGREDIENTS

*Serves 4*

225g/8oz young spinach, stems removed

1 frisée lettuce

105ml/7 tbsp groundnut (peanut) or sunflower oil

175g/6oz rindless unsmoked bacon, cut into thin strips

75g/3oz day-old bread, crusts removed and cut into short fingers

450g/1lb chicken livers

115g/4oz cherry tomatoes

salt and ground black pepper

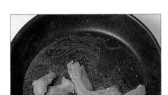

1 Place the salad leaves in a salad bowl. Heat 60ml/4 tbsp of the oil in a large frying pan. Add the bacon and cook for 3–4 minutes, or until crisp and brown. Remove the bacon with a slotted spoon and drain on a piece of kitchen paper.

2 To make the croûtons, fry the bread in the bacon-flavoured oil, tossing until crisp and golden. Drain on kitchen paper.

3 Heat the remaining 45ml/ 3 tbsp of oil in the frying pan, add the chicken livers and fry briskly for 2–3 minutes. Turn out over the salad leaves, add the bacon, croûtons and tomatoes. Season, toss and serve.

# Pan-fried Chicken Liver Salad

2 Heat 30ml/2 tbsp of the oil with the butter. When foaming, add the livers and toss over a medium-high heat for 5 minutes, until browned. Remove from the heat.

3 Remove the livers from the pan, drain them on kitchen paper, then place on top of the spinach.

*This Florentine salad uses vin santo, a sweet dessert wine from Tuscany, but this is not essential – any dessert wine will do.*

## INGREDIENTS

*Serves 4*

75g/3oz fresh baby spinach leaves

75g/3oz lollo rosso leaves

75ml/5 tbsp olive oil

15ml/1 tbsp butter

225g/8oz chicken livers, trimmed and thinly sliced

45ml/3 tbsp vin santo

50–75g/2–3oz fresh Parmesan cheese, shaved into curls

salt and ground black pepper

1 Wash and dry the spinach and lollo rosso. Tear the leaves into a large bowl, season to taste and toss gently to mix.

4 Return the pan to a medium heat, add the remaining oil and the vin santo, and stir until sizzling. Pour the hot dressing over the spinach and livers and toss to coat. Put the salad in a serving bowl and sprinkle over the Parmesan shavings. Serve immediately.

# Warm Chicken Salad with Hazelnut Dressing

*This salad combines pan-fried chicken and spinach with a light and tasty nutty dressing.*

## INGREDIENTS

*Serves 4*

45ml/3 tbsp olive oil

30ml/2 tbsp hazelnut oil

15ml/1 tbsp white wine vinegar

1 garlic clove, crushed

15ml/1 tbsp chopped fresh mixed herbs

225g/8oz baby spinach leaves

250g/9oz cherry tomatoes, halved

1 bunch spring onions
  (scallions), chopped

2 chicken breast fillets, skinned and cut
  into thin strips

salt and ground black pepper

1 First make the dressing. Place 30ml/2 tbsp of the olive oil, the hazelnut oil, vinegar, garlic and chopped herbs in a small bowl or jug (pitcher) and whisk together until thoroughly mixed. Set aside.

2 Trim any long stalks from the spinach leaves, then place in a large serving bowl with the tomatoes and spring onions, and toss together to mix.

3 Heat the remaining 15ml/1 tbsp olive oil in a frying pan, add the chicken and fry over a high heat for 7–10 minutes, or until cooked through and lightly browned.

4 Scatter the chicken pieces over the salad, give the dressing a quick whisk to blend, then drizzle it over the salad and gently toss all the ingredients together to mix. Season to taste and serve immediately.

# Warm Chicken and Mushroom Salad

*This salad needs to be served warm to make the most of the wonderful sesame and coriander flavourings. It makes a simple first course or a delicious light lunch dish.*

### INGREDIENTS

*Serves 6*

4 medium chicken breast fillets, skinned

225g/8oz mangetouts (snow peas)

2 heads decorative lettuce such as lollo rosso or oak leaf

3 carrots, peeled and cut into small matchsticks

175g/6oz/2¹/₂ cups button (white) mushrooms, sliced

6 rashers (strips) of bacon, fried and chopped

15ml/1 tbsp chopped fresh coriander (cilantro) leaves, to garnish

*For the dressing*

120ml/4fl oz/¹/₂ cup lemon juice

30ml/2 tbsp wholegrain mustard

250ml/8fl oz/1 cup olive oil

60ml/4 tbsp sesame oil

5ml/1 tsp coriander seeds, crushed

1 Mix all the dressing ingredients in a bowl. Place the chicken breasts in a shallow dish and pour on half the dressing. Chill overnight, and store the remaining dressing in the refrigerator.

2 Cook the mangetouts for 2 minutes in boiling water, then cool under running cold water to stop them cooking any further. Tear the lettuces into small pieces and mix the mangetouts, carrots, mushrooms and bacon together. Arrange all these in individual serving dishes.

3 Grill (broil) the chicken breasts until cooked through, then slice them on the diagonal into quite thin pieces. Divide among the bowls of salad, and add some dressing to each dish. Combine quickly and scatter some fresh coriander over each bowl.

# Wild Rice and Chicken Salad

*Once you have cooked the wild rice,*
*this is a very simple salad to make.*

### INGREDIENTS

Serves 4

175g/6oz/1 cup dry weight wild rice,
    boiled and cooled (see Cook's Tip)
2 celery sticks, thinly sliced
50g/2oz spring onions (scallions), chopped
115g/4oz/1$^1$/2 cups small button (white)
    mushrooms, quartered
450g/1lb/3$^3$/4 cups diced cooked
    chicken breast
120ml/4 fl oz/$^1$/2 cup vinaigrette dressing
5ml/1 tsp fresh thyme leaves
2 pears, peeled, halved and cored
25g/1oz/$^1$/4 cup walnut pieces, toasted

1 Combine the cooled cooked
wild rice with the celery, spring
onions, mushrooms and chicken
in a bowl.

2 Add the dressing and thyme;
toss well together.

3 Thinly slice the pear halves
lengthways without cutting
through the stalk end, and spread
the slices into a fan. Divide the
salad among four plates. Garnish
each with a fanned pear half and
the toasted walnuts.

COOK'S TIP

To boil wild rice, add the rice to
a large pot of salted boiling water
(about four parts water to one
part rice). Bring back to a gentle
boil and cook for 45–50 minutes,
or until the rice is tender but
still firm and has begun to
split open. Drain well.
Alternatively, put the rice in a
pan with the measured quantity
of salted water. Bring to the boil,
cover and simmer over very low
heat for 45–50 minutes, or until
tender. Cook uncovered for
the last 5 minutes to evaporate
any excess water.

# Spicy Chicken Salad

*Marinated chicken mixed with pasta and crisp vegetables makes a superb salad. Start preparations the night before if you can.*

### INGREDIENTS

*Serves 6*

5ml/1 tsp ground cumin seeds
5ml/1 tsp ground paprika
5ml/1 tsp ground turmeric
1–2 garlic cloves, crushed
30ml/2 tbsp lime juice
4 chicken breast fillets, skinned
225g/8oz rigatoni
1 red (bell) pepper, seeded and chopped
2 sticks celery, sliced thinly
1 shallot or small onion, finely chopped
25g/1oz/¼ cup stuffed green
    olives, halved
30ml/2 tbsp clear honey
15ml/1 tbsp wholegrain mustard
15–30ml/1–2 tbsp lime juice
salt and ground black pepper
mixed salad leaves, to serve

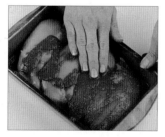

1 Mix the cumin, paprika, turmeric, garlic, seasoning and lime juice in a bowl. Rub this mixture over the chicken breast fillets. Lay the chicken in a shallow dish, cover with clear film (plastic wrap) and leave in a cool place for about 3 hours or overnight.

2 Preheat the oven to 200°C/400°F/Gas 6. Put the chicken on a grill (broiling) rack in a single layer and bake for 20 minutes. Alternatively, grill (broil) for 8–10 minutes on each side.

3 Cook the rigatoni in a large pan of salted boiling water for 8–10 minutes, or until *al dente*. Drain and rinse under cold water. Leave to drain thoroughly.

4 Put the red pepper, celery, shallot or onion and olives into a large bowl with the pasta.

5 Mix the honey, mustard and lime juice together in a bowl and pour over the pasta. Toss to coat.

6 Cut the chicken in bitesize pieces. Arrange the mixed salad leaves on a serving dish, spoon the pasta mixture in the centre and top with the spicy chicken pieces.

# Warm Stir-fried Chicken Salad

Ginger and fresh tarragon give this
salad a deliciously unusual flavour.
Arrange the salad leaves on four
individual plates, so the hot stir-fry
can be served straight from the wok,
ensuring the lettuce remains crisp
and the chicken warm.

## INGREDIENTS

Serves 4

15ml/1 tbsp fresh tarragon
2 chicken breast fillets, about 225g/8oz
   each, skinned
5cm/2in piece fresh root ginger, peeled and
   finely chopped
45ml/3 tbsp light soy sauce
15ml/1 tbsp sugar
15ml/1 tbsp sunflower oil
1 head Chinese lettuce
$^1/_2$ frisée lettuce, torn into bitesize pieces
115g/4oz/1 cup unsalted cashew nuts
2 large carrots, peeled and cut into
   fine strips
salt and ground black pepper

1 Chop the fresh tarragon. Cut
the chicken into fine strips and
place in a bowl.

2 To make the marinade,
mix together in a bowl the
tarragon, ginger, soy sauce, sugar
and seasoning.

3 Pour the marinade over the
chicken strips and leave to
marinate for 2–4 hours.

4 Strain the chicken from the
marinade, reserving the liquid.
Heat a wok or large frying pan,
then add the oil. When the oil is
hot, stir-fry the chicken for
3 minutes, add the marinade and
bubble for 2–3 minutes.

5 Slice the Chinese lettuce and
arrange on a plate with the
frisée. Toss the cashew nuts and
carrot strips together with the
chicken and sauce, pile on top
of the bed of lettuce and serve
immediately.

# Thai Chicken Salad

*This delicious salad originates from Chiang Mai, a city in the north-east of Thailand. The city is culturally very close to Laos and famous for its flavourful chicken salad.*

### INGREDIENTS

*Serves 4–6*

450g/1lb minced (ground) chicken

1 lemon grass stalk, root trimmed

3 kaffir lime leaves, finely chopped

4 fresh red chillies, seeded and chopped

60ml/4 tbsp lime juice

30ml/2 tbsp Thai fish sauce

15ml/1 tbsp roasted ground rice (see Cook's Tip)

2 spring onions (scallions), chopped

30ml/2 tbsp fresh coriander (cilantro) leaves

thinly sliced kaffir lime leaves, mixed salad leaves and fresh mint sprigs, to garnish

1 Heat a large, non-stick frying pan. Add the minced chicken and moisten with a little water. Stir constantly over a medium heat for 7–10 minutes, or until the chicken is cooked. Meanwhile, cut off the lower 5cm/2in of the lemon grass stalk and chop finely.

2 Transfer to a bowl and add the chopped lemon grass, lime leaves, chillies, lime juice, Thai fish sauce, ground rice, spring onions and coriander. Mix thoroughly.

3 Spoon the chicken into a salad bowl. Scatter sliced kaffir lime leaves over the top and garnish with salad leaves and mint.

### COOK'S TIP

Use glutinous rice for the roasted ground rice. Dry-roast the rice in a frying pan until golden brown. Remove and grind to a powder, using a mortar and pestle. When cold, store it in a glass jar in a cool and dry place.

# Chicken, Vegetable and Chilli Salad

*Crunchy fresh vegetables, chillies and gherkins give this salad plenty of flavour.*

### INGREDIENTS

*Serves 4*

225g/8oz Chinese leaves (Chinese cabbage)

2 carrots, cut in matchsticks

$^1/_2$ cucumber, cut in matchsticks

2 red chillies, seeded and cut into strips

1 small onion, sliced into fine rings

4 pickled gherkins, sliced, plus 45ml/3 tbsp of the liquid

50g/2oz/$^1/_2$ cup peanuts, lightly ground

225g/8oz cooked chicken, skinned and finely sliced

1 garlic clove, crushed

5ml/1 tsp granulated sugar

30ml/2 tbsp cider vinegar or white vinegar

salt

1 Finely slice the Chinese leaves and set aside with the carrots. Spread out the cucumber matchsticks on a board and sprinkle with salt. Set aside for 15 minutes.

2 Mix together the chilli and onions in a bowl. Add the gherkins and peanuts, and stir.

3 Tip the salted cucumber into a colander, rinse well and drain thoroughly. Using a wooden spatula, press out as much liquid from the cucumber as possible, then pat dry with kitchen paper.

4 Put the cucumber into a salad bowl and add the Chinese leaves and carrot matchsticks. Toss to mix, then add the chilli mixture and slices of cooked chicken.

5 Make a dressing by whisking the gherkin liquid with the garlic, sugar and vinegar in a small bowl or jug (pitcher). Pour over the salad, toss lightly and serve immediately.

# Hot and Sour Chicken Salad

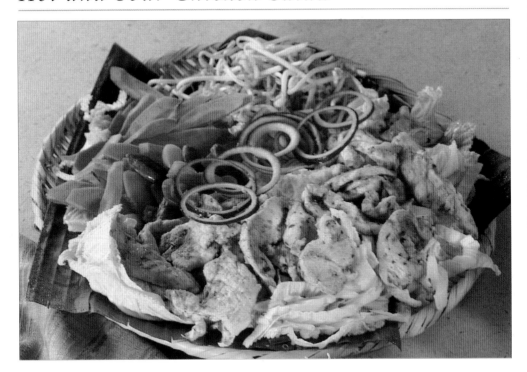

*Chicken is marinated in a delicious combination of spices, stir-fried and then served on a bed of vegetables.*

### INGREDIENTS

*Serves 4–6*

2 chicken breast fillets, skinned
1 red chilli, seeded and finely chopped
1 piece fresh root ginger, 1cm/¹/₂ in long,
    peeled and finely chopped
1 garlic clove, crushed
15ml/1 tbsp crunchy peanut butter
30ml/2 tbsp chopped coriander (cilantro)
5ml/1 tsp sugar
2.5ml/¹/₂ tsp salt
15ml/1 tbsp rice or white wine vinegar
60ml/4 tbsp vegetable oil
10ml/2 tsp Thai fish sauce (optional)
1 head Chinese leaves (Chinese cabbage)
115g/4oz/¹/₂ cup beansprouts
2 medium carrots, cut into thin sticks
1 red onion, cut into fine rings
2 large gherkins, sliced

1 Slice the chicken thinly, place in a shallow bowl and set aside. Grind the chilli, ginger and garlic in a mortar and pestle. Add the peanut butter, coriander, sugar and salt.

2 Add the vinegar, 30ml/2 tbsp of the oil and the Thai fish sauce, if using. Combine well. Cover the chicken with the spice mixture and leave to marinate for at least 2–3 hours.

3 Shred the Chinese leaves roughly and arrange with the beansprouts, carrot sticks, onion rings and sliced gherkins on a serving platter.

4 Heat the remaining 30ml/2 tbsp of oil in a wok or frying pan. Add the chicken and cook for 10–12 minutes, tossing the meat occasionally. Serve arranged on the salad.

# Curried Chicken Salad

2 Cook the pasta in a large pan of salted boiling water for 8–10 minutes, or until *al dente*. Drain and rinse thoroughly.

3 To make the sauce, mix the yogurt, curry powder, garlic, chilli and chopped coriander together in a bowl. Stir in the chicken pieces and leave to stand for 30 minutes.

*Serve this flavourful salad for lunch or supper.*

### INGREDIENTS

*Serves 4*

2 chicken breasts, cooked and skinned
175g/6oz green beans
350g/12oz multi-coloured penne
4 firm ripe tomatoes, skinned, seeded and
    cut in strips
salt and ground black pepper
coriander (cilantro) leaves, to garnish

*For the sauce*
150ml/¹/4 pint/²/3 cup low-fat yogurt
5ml/1 tsp mild curry powder
1 garlic clove, crushed
1 green chilli, seeded and finely chopped
30ml/2 tbsp chopped fresh
    coriander (cilantro)

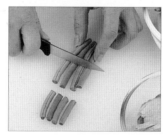

1 Cut the chicken in strips. Cut the green beans into 2.5cm/1in lengths and cook in boiling water for 5 minutes. Drain and rinse under cold water.

4 Transfer the pasta to a glass bowl and toss with the beans and tomatoes. Spoon over the chicken and sauce. Garnish with coriander leaves.

# Coronation Chicken

*A summer favourite – serve with a crisp green salad.*

*Serves 8*

$^1/_2$ lemon
1 chicken, about 2.25kg/5lb
1 onion, quartered
1 carrot, quartered
large bouquet garni
8 black peppercorns, crushed
salt
watercress sprigs or parsley,
   to garnish

*For the sauce*
1 small onion, chopped
15g/$^1/_2$ oz/1 tbsp butter
15ml/1 tbsp curry paste
15ml/1 tbsp tomato purée (paste)
120ml/4fl oz/$^1/_2$ cup red wine
bay leaf
juice of $^1/_2$ lemon, or more to taste
10–15ml/2–3 tsp apricot jam
300ml/$^1/_2$ pint/1$^1/_4$ cups mayonnaise
120ml/4fl oz/$^1/_2$ cup whipping cream
salt and ground black pepper

1 Put the lemon half in the chicken cavity, then place the chicken in a pan that fits tightly. Add the vegetables, bouquet garni, peppercorns and salt.

2 Add sufficient water to come two-thirds of the way up the chicken, bring to the boil, then cover and cook gently for 1$^1/_2$ hours, or until the juices run clear.

3 Transfer the chicken to a large bowl, pour over the cooking liquid and leave to cool. Skin, bone, then chop the chicken flesh.

4 To make the sauce, cook the onion in the butter until soft. Add the curry paste, tomato purée, wine, bay leaf and lemon juice, then cook for 10 minutes. Add the apricot jam; strain and cool.

5 Beat the sauce into the mayonnaise. Whip the cream and mayonnaise. Fold in. Add seasoning, then stir in the chicken and garnish with watercress or parsley.

# Chinese-style Chicken Salad

*Shredded chicken is served with a tasty peanut sauce.*

*Serves 4*

4 chicken breast fillets, about
    175g/6oz each

60ml/4 tbsp dark soy sauce

pinch of Chinese five-spice powder

a good squeeze of lemon juice

$^1/_2$ cucumber, peeled and cut into
    matchsticks

5ml/1 tsp salt

45ml/3 tbsp sunflower oil

30ml/2 tbsp sesame oil

15ml/1 tbsp sesame seeds

30ml/2 tbsp dry sherry

2 carrots, cut into matchsticks

8 spring onions (scallions), shredded

75g/3oz/$^3/_4$ cup beansprouts

*For the sauce*

60ml/4 tbsp crunchy peanut butter

10ml/2 tsp lemon juice

10ml/2 tsp sesame oil

1.5ml/$^1/_4$ tsp hot chilli powder

1 spring onion (scallion), finely chopped

1 Put the chicken breast fillets into a large pan and just cover with water. Add 15ml/1 tbsp of the soy sauce, the Chinese five-spice powder and lemon juice. Cover and bring to the boil, then simmer for about 20 minutes.

2 Place the cucumber match-sticks in a colander, sprinkle with the salt and cover with a weighted plate. Leave to drain for 30 minutes.

3 Heat the oils in a large frying pan or wok. Add the sesame seeds, fry for 30 seconds and then stir in the remaining soy sauce and the sherry. Add the carrots and stir-fry for 2–3 minutes. Remove and reserve.

4 Remove the chicken from the pan and leave until cool enough to handle. Discard the skins and hit the chicken lightly with a rolling pin to loosen the fibres. Slice in strips and reserve.

5 Rinse the cucumber well, pat dry with kitchen paper and place in a bowl. Add the spring onions, beansprouts, cooked carrots, pan juices and shredded chicken, and mix together. Transfer to a shallow dish. Cover and chill for about 1 hour, turning the mixture in the juices once or twice.

6 To make the sauce, cream the peanut butter with the lemon juice, sesame oil and chilli powder, adding a little hot water to form a paste, then stir in the spring onion. Arrange the chicken mixture on a serving dish and serve with the peanut butter sauce.

# Mediterranean Chicken Skewers

*Pickled onions and vegetable-wrapped chunks of chicken provide an interesting contrast of flavours in these delicious kebabs.*

## INGREDIENTS

*Serves 4*

90ml/6 tbsp olive oil

45ml/3 tbsp fresh lemon juice

1 garlic clove, finely chopped

30ml/2 tbsp chopped fresh basil

2 medium courgettes (zucchini)

1 long thin aubergine (eggplant)

300g/11oz chicken breast fillets, cut into
    5cm/2in cubes

12–16 pickled onions

1 red or yellow (bell) pepper, cut into
    5cm/2in squares

salt and ground black pepper

1 Soak four wooden skewers in water for 30 minutes. In a small bowl mix the oil with the lemon juice, garlic and basil. Season with salt and pepper.

2 Slice the courgettes and aubergine lengthways into strips 5mm/¹/₄ in thick. Cut them crossways about two-thirds of the way along their length. Discard the shorter length. Wrap half the chicken pieces with the courgette slices, and the other half with the aubergine slices.

3 Thread alternating pieces of chicken, onions and pepper on to the skewers. Lay them on a platter, and sprinkle with the flavoured oil. Leave to marinate for at least 30 minutes. Prepare a barbecue, if using.

4 Cook on the barbecue or under a hot grill (broiler) for about 10 minutes, or until the vegetables are tender and the chicken is cooked through, turning the skewers occasionally. Serve hot.

# Chicken Liver Kebabs

2 Wrap the pitted prunes around the cherry tomatoes. Prepare a barbecue, if using.

3 Thread the bacon-wrapped livers on to metal skewers with the prunes, tomatoes and mushrooms. Brush with oil. Cover the tomatoes and prunes with a strip of foil to protect them while cooking. Cook on the barbecue or under a hot grill (broiler) for 5 minutes on each side.

*These tasty kebabs may be barbecued outdoors and served with salads and baked potatoes or grilled indoors and served with rice and broccoli.*

### INGREDIENTS

*Serves 4*

115g/4oz rindless streaky (fatty) bacon rashers (strips)

350g/12oz chicken livers

12 large ready-to-eat pitted prunes

12 cherry tomatoes

8 button (white) mushrooms

30ml/2 tbsp olive oil

1 Cut each rasher of bacon into two, wrap a piece around each chicken liver and secure in position with wooden cocktail sticks (toothpicks).

4 Remove the cocktail sticks and serve the kebabs immediately.

# Sweet and Sour Chicken Kebabs

*This marinade contains sugar and will burn very easily, so cook the kebabs slowly, turning often. Serve with harlequin rice.*

INGREDIENTS

*Serves 4*

2 chicken breast fillets, skinned

8 pickling onions or 2 medium onions, peeled

4 rindless streaky (fatty) bacon rashers (strips)

3 firm bananas

1 red (bell) pepper, seeded and sliced

*For the marinade*

30ml/2 tbsp soft brown sugar

15ml/1 tbsp Worcestershire sauce

30ml/2 tbsp lemon juice

salt and ground black pepper

*For the harlequin rice*

30ml/2 tbsp olive oil

225g/8oz/2 cups cooked rice

115g/4oz/1 cup cooked peas

1 small red (bell) pepper, seeded and diced

1 Mix together the marinade ingredients. Cut each chicken breast into four pieces, add to the marinade, cover and leave for at least 4 hours or preferably overnight in the refrigerator.

2 Peel the onions, blanch them in boiling water for 5 minutes and drain. If using medium onions, quarter them after blanching. Prepare a barbecue, if using.

3 Cut each rasher of bacon in half. Peel the bananas and cut each into three pieces. Wrap a rasher of bacon around eight pieces of banana.

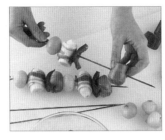

4 Thread on to four metal skewers with the chicken pieces, onions and pepper slices. Brush with the marinade.

5 Cook on a low heat on the barbecue or under a grill (broiler) for 15 minutes, turning and basting frequently with the marinade. Keep warm while you prepare the rice.

6 Heat the oil in a frying pan and add the rice, peas and diced pepper. Stir until heated through and serve with the kebabs.

# Chicken with Pineapple

*This chicken has a delicate tang and is very tender. The pineapple not only tenderizes the chicken but also gives it a slight sweetness.*

*Serves 6*

225g/8oz can pineapple chunks
5ml/1 tsp ground cumin
5ml/1 tsp ground coriander
2.5ml/$^1$/$_2$ tsp crushed garlic
5ml/1 tsp chilli powder
5ml/1 tsp salt
30ml/2 tbsp natural (plain) yogurt
15ml/1 tbsp chopped fresh coriander
   (cilantro)
orange food colouring (optional)
275g/10oz chicken, skinned and boned
$^1$/$_2$ red (bell) pepper
$^1$/$_2$ yellow or green (bell) pepper
1 large onion
6 cherry tomatoes
15ml/1 tbsp vegetable oil

1 Drain the pineapple juice into a bowl. Reserve 8 large chunks of pineapple and squeeze the juice from the remaining chunks into the bowl and set aside. You should have about 120ml/4fl oz/$^1$/$_2$ cup pineapple juice.

2 In a large mixing bowl, blend together the cumin, ground coriander, garlic, chilli powder, salt, yogurt, fresh coriander and a few drops of food colouring, if using. Pour in the reserved pineapple juice and mix together.

3 Cut the chicken into bitesize cubes, add to the mixing bowl with the yogurt and spice mixture and leave to marinate for about 1–1$^1$/$_2$ hours.

4 If using wooden skewers, soak six in water for 30 minutes. Cut the peppers and onion into bitesize chunks.

5 Prepare a barbecue, if using. Arrange the chicken pieces, peppers, onion, tomatoes and reserved pineapple chunks alternately on the skewers.

6 Baste the kebabs with the oil. Cook on the barbecue or under a hot grill (broiler) for about 15 minutes, turning and basting the chicken pieces with the marinade regularly.

7 Once the chicken pieces are cooked, remove them from the barbecue or grill and serve either with salad or plain boiled rice.

---

COOK'S TIP

~

If possible, use a mixture of chicken breast and thigh meat for this recipe.

# Citrus Kebabs

*A blend of fresh mint, cumin and citrus fruits makes these kebabs really flavoursome. Preparation time is quick, but allow at least 2 hours marinating time for the flavours to develop. Perfect served on a bed of lettuce leaves and garnished with fresh mint and orange and lemon slices.*

## INGREDIENTS

Serves 4

4 chicken breast fillets, skinned
fresh mint sprigs, to garnish
orange, lemon or lime slices, to garnish
   (optional)

*For the marinade*
finely grated rind and juice of ½ orange
finely grated rind and juice of ½ small
   lemon or lime
30ml/2 tbsp olive oil
30ml/2 tbsp clear honey
30ml/2 tbsp chopped fresh mint
1.5ml/¼ tsp ground cumin
salt and ground black pepper

1 Cut the chicken into cubes of approximately 2.5cm/1in.

2 Mix the marinade ingredients together in a glass or ceramic bowl, add the chicken cubes and leave to marinate for at least 2 hours. Prepare a barbecue, or preheat the grill (broiler), to a low heat.

3 Thread the chicken pieces on to four metal skewers and cook for 15 minutes, basting with the marinade and turning frequently, until cooked through. Serve garnished with extra mint and citrus slices if you like.

# Caribbean Chicken Kebabs

*These kebabs have a rich, Caribbean flavour and the marinade keeps them moist without the need for oil. Serve them with a colourful salad and rice.*

### INGREDIENTS

*Serves 4*

500g/1¼lb chicken breast fillets, skinned
finely grated rind of 1 lime
30ml/2 tbsp lime juice
15ml/1 tbsp rum or sherry
15ml/1 tbsp light muscovado
    (brown) sugar
5ml/1 tsp ground cinnamon
2 mangoes, peeled and cubed
rice and salad, to serve

2 Prepare a barbecue, if using. Save the marinade and thread the chicken on to the skewers, alternating with the mango cubes.

3 Cook the skewers on a barbecue or under a hot grill (broiler) for 8–10 minutes, turning occasionally and basting with the reserved marinade, until the chicken is golden brown and cooked through. Serve immediately with rice and salad.

1 If using wooden skewers, soak four in water for 30 minutes. Cut the chicken breasts into bite-size chunks and place in a bowl with the grated lime rind and juice, rum or sherry, sugar and cinnamon. Toss well, cover and leave to marinate for 1 hour.

---

COOK'S TIP

The rum or sherry adds a lovely rich flavour, but it is optional so can be omitted if you prefer to make the dish more economical.

# Turkey Sosaties with a Curried Apricot Sauce

*This is a South African way of cooking poultry in a delicious sweet-and-sour spiced sauce.*

Serves 4

15ml/1 tbsp oil
1 onion, finely chopped
1 garlic clove, crushed
2 bay leaves
juice of 1 lemon
30ml/2 tbsp curry powder
60ml/4 tbsp apricot jam
60ml/4 tbsp apple juice
salt
675g/1¹/₂ lb turkey breast fillet
60ml/4 tbsp crème fraîche

1 Heat the oil in a pan. Add the onion, garlic and bay leaves and cook over a low heat for 10 minutes, or until the onions are soft. Add the lemon juice, curry powder, apricot jam and apple juice, with salt to taste. Cook gently for 5 minutes. Leave to cool.

2 Cut the turkey into 2 cm/³/₄ in cubes and add to the marinade. Mix well, cover and leave in a cool place to marinate for at least 2 hours or chill overnight.

3 Prepare a barbecue or preheat the grill (broiler). Thread the turkey on to four metal skewers, allowing the marinade to run back into the bowl. Cook the sosaties for 6–8 minutes, turning several times, until done.

4 Meanwhile, transfer the marinade to a pan and simmer for 2 minutes. Stir in the crème fraîche and serve with the sosaties.

# Spicy Indonesian Chicken Satay

*This spicy marinade quickly gives an exotic flavour to tender chicken breasts. The satays can be cooked on a barbecue or under the grill.*

Serves 4

4 chicken breast fillets, about 175g/6oz
    each, skinned
30ml/2 tbsp deep-fried onion slices

*For the sambal kecap*
1 fresh red chilli, seeded and finely
    chopped
2 garlic cloves, crushed
60ml/4 tbsp dark soy sauce
20ml/4 tsp lemon juice or 15–25ml/
    1–1¹/₂ tbsp tamarind juice
30ml/2 tbsp hot water

1 Soak eight wooden skewers in water for 30 minutes.

2 To make the sambal kecap, mix the chilli, garlic, soy sauce, lemon or tamarind juice and hot water in a bowl. Leave to stand for 30 minutes.

3 Cut the chicken breasts into 2.5cm/1in cubes and place in a bowl with the sambal kecap. Mix thoroughly. Cover and leave in a cool place to marinate for 1 hour.

4 Tip the chicken and marinade into a sieve placed over a pan and leave to drain for a few minutes. Set the sieve aside.

5 Add 30ml/2 tbsp hot water to the marinade and bring to the boil. Lower the heat and simmer for 2 minutes, then pour into a bowl and leave to cool. When cool, add the deep-fried onions.

6 Prepare a barbecue or preheat the grill (broiler). Thread the skewers with the chicken and cook for about 10 minutes, turning regularly, until the chicken is golden brown and cooked through. Serve with the sambal kecap as a dip.

# Satay Chicken Skewers

*A spicy peanut mixture makes a perfect marinade for chicken kebabs. Allow the chicken to marinate in the mixture overnight to allow the flavours to penetrate thoroughly.*

## INGREDIENTS

*Serves 4*

4 chicken breast fillets, skinned

lemon slices, to garnish

lettuce leaves and spring onions (scallions), to serve

*For the satay marinade*

115g/4oz/¹/₂ cup crunchy peanut butter

1 small onion, chopped

1 garlic clove, crushed

30ml/2 tbsp chutney

60ml/4 tbsp olive oil

5ml/1 tsp light soy sauce

30ml/2 tbsp lemon juice

1.5ml/¹/₄ tsp chilli powder or cayenne pepper

1 Put all the satay ingredients into a food processor or blender and process until smooth. Spoon into a large dish.

2 Cut the chicken breast fillets into 2.5cm/1in cubes. Add to the satay mixture and stir to coat. Cover with clear film (plastic wrap) and chill for at least 4 hours or, better still, overnight. Soak four wooden skewers in water for 30 minutes.

3 Prepare a barbecue or preheat the grill (broiler). Thread the chicken pieces on to the skewers.

4 Cook for 10 minutes, brushing occasionally with the marinade, until done. Serve with lettuce, spring onions and lemon.

# Japanese Chicken Kebabs

*These "Yakitori" kebabs are ideal for barbecues. Make extra sauce if you like, to serve with the kebabs.*

INGREDIENTS

*Serves 4*

6 boneless chicken thighs

bunch of spring onions (scallions)

shichimi (seven-flavour spice) or paprika, to serve (optional)

*For the yakitori sauce*

150ml/$^1$/4 pint/$^2$/3 cup Japanese soy sauce

90g/3$^1$/2 oz/$^3$/4 cup sugar

25ml/1$^1$/2 tbsp sake or dry white wine

15ml/1 tbsp plain (all-purpose) flour

1 Soak 12 bamboo skewers in water for 30 minutes.

2 To make the sauce, stir the soy sauce, sugar and sake or wine into the flour in a pan. Bring to the boil, stirring. Lower the heat and simmer for 10 minutes, or until reduced by a third. Set aside.

3 Cut each chicken thigh into bitesize pieces and set aside.

4 Cut the spring onions into 3cm/ 1$^1$/4 in pieces. Prepare a barbecue or preheat the grill (broiler).

5 Thread the chicken and spring onions alternately on to the skewers. Cook on the barbecue or grill (broil) under medium heat, brushing generously several times with the sauce. Allow 5–10 minutes, or until the chicken is cooked but still moist.

6 Serve with a little extra yakitori sauce.

# Chicken Wings Teriyaki-style

*This simple, Oriental glaze can be used with any cut of chicken. Chicken wings barbecued this way are very tasty.*

INGREDIENTS

*Serves 4*

1 garlic clove, crushed

45ml/3 tbsp soy sauce

30ml/2 tbsp dry sherry

10ml/2 tsp clear honey

10ml/2 tsp grated fresh root ginger

5ml/1 tsp sesame oil

12 chicken wings

15ml/1 tbsp sesame seeds, toasted

green salad, to serve

1 Place the garlic, soy sauce, sherry, honey, ginger and sesame oil in a large bowl and beat with a fork, to mix evenly.

COOK'S TIP

Toasting the sesame seeds lightly helps to bring out their flavour. To do this, either put them in a heavy pan over a medium heat and stir until golden, or sprinkle on a baking sheet and cook under a medium grill (broiler), until golden.

2 Add the chicken wings and toss thoroughly, to coat in the marinade. Cover and leave in the refrigerator for about 30 minutes or longer if possible.

3 Cook the wings on a fairly hot barbecue for 20–25 minutes, turning occasionally and brushing with the remaining marinade.

4 Sprinkle with sesame seeds and serve with a crisp green salad.

# Blackened Cajun Chicken and Corn

*This is a classic American Deep
South method of cooking in a spiced
coating. Traditionally, the coating
should begin to char and blacken
slightly at the edges.*

## INGREDIENTS

*Serves 4*

8 chicken portions, such as drumsticks,
   thighs or wings
2 whole corn on the cob
10ml/2 tsp garlic salt
10ml/2 tsp ground black pepper
7.5ml/1$^1$/2 tsp ground cumin
7.5ml/1$^1$/2 tsp paprika
5ml/1 tsp cayenne pepper
45ml/3 tbsp butter, melted
chopped parsley, to garnish

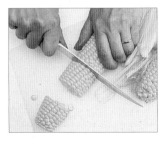

1 Cut any excess fat from the
chicken, but leave the skin on.
Slash the deepest parts with a knife,
to allow the flavours to penetrate.

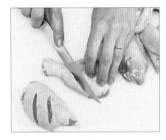

2 Pull the husks and silks off the
corn on the cob and cut them
into thick slices.

3 Prepare a barbecue. Mix
together the salt and spices.
Brush the chicken and corn with
melted butter and sprinkle the
spices over them. Toss well to
coat evenly.

4 Cook the chicken pieces over
medium-hot coals for about
25 minutes, turning occasionally,
until done. Add the corn after
15 minutes, and cook, turning
often, until golden brown. Serve
garnished with chopped parsley.

# Barbecue-cooked Jerk Chicken

*Jerk refers to the blend of herb and spice seasoning rubbed into meat before it is roasted over charcoal sprinkled with pimiento berries. In Jamaica, jerk seasoning was originally used only for pork, but jerked chicken is equally good.*

### INGREDIENTS

Serves 4

8 chicken pieces
salad leaves, to serve

*For the marinade*

5ml/1 tsp ground allspice
5ml/1 tsp ground cinnamon
5ml/1 tsp dried thyme
1.5ml/$^1$/$_4$ tsp freshly grated nutmeg
10ml/2 tsp demerara (raw) sugar
2 garlic cloves, crushed
15ml/1 tbsp finely chopped onion
15ml/1 tbsp chopped spring onion (scallion)
15ml/1 tbsp vinegar
30ml/2 tbsp oil, plus extra for brushing
15ml/1 tbsp lime juice
1 hot chilli, chopped
salt and ground black pepper

1 Combine all the marinade ingredients in a small bowl. Using a fork, mash them together well to form a thick paste.

2 Lay the chicken pieces on a plate or board and make several lengthways slits in the flesh. Rub the seasoning all over the chicken and into the slits.

3 Place the chicken in a dish, cover with clear film (plastic wrap) and leave to marinate in the refrigerator. Prepare a barbecue, if using. Shake off any excess seasoning from the chicken. Brush with oil. Place on a barbecue rack or baking sheet if grilling (broiling).

4 Cook over the barbecue coals for 30 minutes, turning often, or under a preheated grill (broiler) for 45 minutes, turning often, until done. Serve hot with salad leaves.

### COOK'S TIP

The flavour is best if you marinate the chicken overnight.

# Chicken Breasts in Spices and Coconut

*A medley of spices blended with coconut makes a fabulous marinade for barbecued chicken breasts that are perfect served with naan bread. The chicken can be prepared in advance.*

### INGREDIENTS

Serves 4

200g/7oz block creamed coconut or
   300ml/$^1$/$_2$ pint/1$^1$/$_4$ cups coconut cream
300ml/$^1$/$_2$ pint/1$^1$/$_4$ cups boiling water
3 garlic cloves, chopped
2 spring onions (scallions), chopped
1 fresh green chilli, chopped
5cm/2in piece fresh root ginger, chopped
5ml/1 tsp fennel seeds
2.5ml/$^1$/$_2$ tsp black peppercorns
seeds from 4 cardamom pods
30ml/2 tbsp ground coriander
5ml/1 tsp ground cumin
5ml/1 tsp ground star anise
5ml/1 tsp ground nutmeg
2.5ml/$^1$/$_2$ tsp ground cloves
2.5ml/$^1$/$_2$ tsp ground turmeric
4 large chicken breast fillets, skinned
onion rings and coriander (cilantro)
   sprigs, to garnish

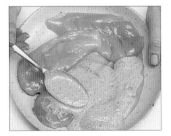

1 If using creamed coconut, break it up and put in a jug (pitcher). Pour the boiling water over and leave to dissolve. Place the garlic, spring onions, chilli, ginger and all the spices in a blender or food processor. Add the coconut mixture or the coconut cream and process to a smooth paste.

2 Make several diagonal cuts across the chicken breasts. Arrange them in one layer in a shallow dish. Spoon over half the coconut mixture and toss well to coat the chicken breasts evenly. Cover the dish and leave to marinate in the refrigerator for about 30 minutes, or overnight.

3 Prepare a barbecue. Cook the chicken over medium heat for 12–15 minutes, turning once, until well browned and thoroughly cooked. Heat the remaining coconut mixture gently, until it is boiling. Serve with the chicken, garnished with onion rings and sprigs of coriander.

# Spiced Chicken

*Almost every street-corner stall in Israel seems to sell barbecue-cooked chicken. In this recipe, the Egyptian-inspired marinade is strongly scented with cumin and cinnamon.*

### INGREDIENTS

*Serves 4*

5 garlic cloves, chopped

30ml/2 tbsp ground cumin

7.5ml/1$^1$/$_2$ tsp ground cinnamon

5ml/1 tsp paprika

juice of 1 lemon

30ml/2 tbsp olive oil

1 chicken, about 1.3kg/3lb, cut into
8 portions

salt and ground black pepper

fresh coriander (cilantro), to garnish

warmed pitta bread, salad and lemon
wedges, to serve

1 In a bowl, combine the garlic, cumin, cinnamon, paprika, lemon juice, oil, salt and pepper. Add the chicken and turn to coat thoroughly. Leave to marinate for at least 1 hour or cover and place in the refrigerator overnight.

2 Prepare a barbecue. After about 40 minutes it will be ready for cooking.

3 Cook the dark meat on the rack for 10 minutes, turning once, until done. Remove and keep warm.

4 Place the remaining chicken on the rack and cook for 7–10 minutes, turning occasionally, until golden brown and the juices run clear when pierced. Serve immediately, with pitta bread, lemon wedges and salad.

# Spiced Grilled Poussins

*The cumin and coriander coating on the poussins keeps them moist during cooking as well as giving them a delicious flavour.*

## INGREDIENTS

*Serves 4*

2 garlic cloves, roughly chopped
5ml/1 tsp ground cumin
5ml/1 tsp ground coriander
pinch of cayenne pepper
$^{1}/_{2}$ small onion, chopped
60ml/4 tbsp olive oil
2.5ml/$^{1}/_{2}$ tsp salt
2 poussins
lemon wedges, to garnish

1 Combine the garlic, cumin, coriander, cayenne pepper, onion, olive oil and salt in a blender or food processor. Process to make a paste that will spread smoothly.

2 Cut the poussins in half lengthways. Place them skin side up in a shallow dish and spread with the spice paste. Cover and leave to marinate in a cool place for 2 hours.

3 Prepare a barbecue or preheat the grill (broiler). Cook the poussins for 15–20 minutes, turning frequently, until cooked and lightly charred on the outside. Serve immediately, garnished with lemon wedges.

## VARIATION
Chicken portions and quail can also be cooked in this way.

# Poussins with Lime and Chilli

*The poussins in this recipe are flattened out – spatchcocked – so that they will cook evenly and quickly. The breast is stuffed with chilli and sun-dried tomato butter, which keeps the meat moist and tastes wonderful.*

### INGREDIENTS

Serves 4

4 poussins, about 450g/1lb each
40g/1¹/₂oz/3 tbsp butter
30ml/2 tbsp sun-dried tomato paste
finely grated rind of 1 lime
10ml/2 tsp chilli sauce
juice of ¹/₂ lime
flat leaf parsley sprigs, to garnish
lime wedges, to serve

1 Place each poussin on a board, breast side up, and press down firmly with your hand, to break the breastbone.

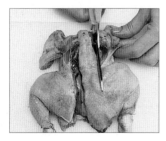

2 Turn the poussin over and, with poultry shears or strong kitchen scissors, cut down either side of the backbone and remove it.

3 Turn the poussin breast side up and flatten it neatly. Lift the breast skin carefully and gently ease your fingertips underneath, to loosen it from the flesh.

4 Mix together the butter, tomato paste, lime rind and chilli sauce. Spread about three-quarters of the mixture under the skin of each poussin, smoothing it evenly.

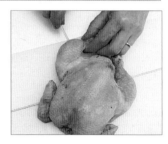

5 To hold the poussins flat during cooking, thread two skewers through each bird, crossing at the centre. Each skewer should pass through a wing and then out through a drumstick on the other side.

6 Prepare a barbecue. Mix the reserved paste with the lime juice and brush it over the skin of the poussins. Cook over medium-hot coals, turning occasionally, for 25–30 minutes, or until the juices run clear when the thickest part of the leg is pierced. Garnish with flat leaf parsley and serve with lime wedges.

---

### COOK'S TIP

If you wish to serve half a poussin per portion, you may find it easier simply to cut the birds in half lengthways. Use poultry shears or a large sharp knife to cut through the breast-bone and backbone.

# Grilled Chicken with Pica de Gallo Salsa

*This dish originates from Mexico. Its hot, fruity flavours are associated with the Tex-Mex style of cooking.*

### INGREDIENTS

*Serves 4*

4 chicken breast fillets
pinch of celery salt and cayenne
    pepper combined
30ml/2 tbsp vegetable oil
corn chips, to serve

*For the salsa*

275g/10oz watermelon
175g/6oz cantaloupe melon
1 small red onion
1–2 green chillies
30ml/2 tbsp lime juice
60ml/4 tbsp chopped fresh
    coriander (cilantro)
pinch of salt

COOK'S TIP

When handling chillies you may prefer to wear rubber gloves.

1 To make the salsa, remove the rind and as many seeds as you can from the melons. Finely dice the flesh and put it into a bowl.

2 Finely chop the onion, split the chillies (discarding the seeds which contain most of the heat) and chop. Take care when handling cut chillies. Mix with the melon.

3 Add the lime juice and coriander, and season with salt. Turn the salsa into a small bowl.

4 Prepare a barbecue or preheat a moderate grill (broiler). Slash the chicken breast fillets deeply to speed up the cooking time.

5 Season the chicken with celery salt and cayenne, brush with oil and cook for about 15 minutes, turning once until cooked through.

6 Serve the chicken on a plate, with the salsa and corn chips.

# Grilled Spatchcocked Poussins

*Spatchcocked poussins are delicious
steeped in an onion and herb sauce.*

Serves 4

4 poussins, about 450g/1lb each

olive oil

salt and ground black pepper

red (bell) pepper strips and parsley sprigs,
   to garnish

*For the sauce*

30ml/2 tbsp dry sherry

30ml/2 tbsp lemon juice

30ml/2 tbsp olive oil

50g/2oz spring onions (scallions), chopped

1 garlic clove, finely chopped

60ml/4 tbsp chopped mixed fresh herbs,
   such as tarragon, parsley, thyme,
   marjoram, lemon balm

1 Place each poussin breast down
on a chopping board and split
it along the back. Open out the bird
and turn it over, so that the breast
side is uppermost. Press the bird as
flat as possible, then thread two
metal skewers through it, across the
breast and thigh, to keep it flat.

2 Prepare a barbecue or preheat
the grill (broiler) to high.

3 Season the spatchcocked birds,
then brush them with a little
olive oil. Set them on the barbecue
15cm/6in above the coals or on the
rack in the grill (broiling) pan,
about 10cm/4in from the heat.

4 Cook for 20–25 minutes, or
until tender. Turn and brush
with more oil halfway through the
cooking time.

5 Meanwhile, to make the sauce,
whisk together the sherry,
lemon juice, olive oil, spring onions
and garlic. Season to taste.

6 When the poussins are done,
transfer them to a deep serving
platter. Whisk the herbs into the
sauce, then spoon it over the birds.
Cover tightly with another platter
or with foil and leave to rest for
15 minutes before serving,
garnished with the red pepper
strips and parsley.

# LIGHT BITES
# & LUNCHES

Tender chicken is the perfect ingredient for a light snack or lunch, and there are so
many different ways it can be enjoyed. In this chapter there are recipes from a
variety of different countries that will give you inspiration for midday eating.
They range from light bundles of vegetables and chicken, parcels made with lettuce
or lotus leaves, filled pitta and naan bread pockets to pizzas, light risottos and
stir-fries, and so much more. You will never lack ideas for a lunchtime dish,
whether you are cooking for a family or entertaining friends.

# Chicken and Pasta Omelette

*Vegetables, pasta and chicken make a tasty and substantial omelette. It is an ideal dish to make using leftovers.*

### INGREDIENTS

Serves 4–6

30ml/2 tbsp olive oil

1 large onion, chopped

2 large garlic cloves, crushed

115g/4oz rindless bacon, chopped

50g/2oz cold cooked chicken, chopped

115g/4oz leftover, lightly cooked vegetables

115g/4oz/1 cup cooked pasta or rice

4 eggs

30ml/2 tbsp chopped, mixed fresh herbs, such as parsley, chives, marjoram or tarragon, or 10ml/2 tsp dried

about 5ml/1 tsp Worcestershire sauce, to taste

15ml/1 tbsp grated mature (sharp) Cheddar cheese

salt and ground black pepper

1 Heat the oil in a large flame-proof frying pan and sauté the onion, garlic and bacon until all the fat has run out of the bacon.

2 Add the chopped chicken, vegetables and pasta or rice. Beat the eggs, herbs and Worcestershire sauce together with seasoning. Pour over the pasta or rice and vegetables, stir lightly, then leave the mixture undisturbed to cook gently for about 5 minutes.

3 When just beginning to set, sprinkle with the cheese and place under a preheated grill (broiler) until just firm and golden.

COOK'S TIP

This is surprisingly good cold, and is perfect for taking on picnics or using for packed lunches.

# Chicken and Rice Omelette

*In Japan, these rice omelettes are a favourite with children, who usually top them with a liberal helping of tomato ketchup.*

Serves 4

1 skinless, boneless chicken thigh, about
   115g/4oz, cubed

40ml/8 tsp butter

1 small onion, chopped

$^1/_2$ carrot, diced

2 shiitake mushrooms, stems removed and
   chopped

15ml/1 tbsp finely chopped fresh parsley

225g/8oz/2 cups cooked long grain
   white rice

30ml/2 tbsp tomato ketchup

6 eggs, lightly beaten

60ml/4 tbsp milk

5ml/1 tsp salt, plus extra to season

freshly ground black pepper

tomato ketchup, to serve

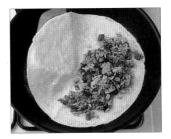

3 Beat the eggs with the milk in a bowl. Stir in the measured salt, and add pepper. Melt 5ml/1 tsp of the remaining butter in an omelette pan. Pour in a quarter of the egg mixture and stir it briefly with a fork, then allow it to set for 1 minute. Top with a quarter of the rice mixture.

4 Fold the omelette over the rice and slide it to the edge of the pan to shape it into a curve. Slide it on to a warmed plate, cover with kitchen paper and press neatly into a rectangular shape. Keep hot while cooking three more omelettes from the remaining ingredients. Serve immediately, with tomato ketchup.

1 Season the chicken. Melt 10ml/2 tsp butter in a frying pan. Fry the onion for 1 minute, then add the chicken and fry until cooked. Add the mushrooms and carrot, stir-fry over a medium heat until soft, then add the parsley. Set aside. Wipe the pan with kitchen paper.

2 Melt 10ml/2 tsp butter in the frying pan, add the rice and stir well. Mix in the fried ingredients, ketchup and black pepper. Stir well, adding salt to taste. Keep the mixture warm.

# Chicken Pancakes

*Use leftover cooked chicken and bought pancakes to make this quick and appetizing lunch.*

Serves 4

225g/8oz cooked, boned chicken
25g/1oz/2 tbsp butter
1 small onion, finely chopped
50g/2oz/scant 1 cup mushrooms,
    finely chopped
30ml/2 tbsp plain (all-purpose) flour
150ml/¼ pint/⅔ cup chicken
    stock or milk
15ml/1 tbsp chopped fresh parsley
8 small or 4 large cooked pancakes
oil, for brushing
30ml/2 tbsp grated cheese
salt and ground black pepper

3 Add the flour and then the stock or milk, stirring constantly. Boil to thicken and simmer for 2 minutes. Season with salt and black pepper.

4 Add the chicken cubes and chopped fresh parsley.

5 Divide the filling equally among the pancakes, roll them up and arrange in a greased ovenproof dish. Preheat the grill (broiler).

6 Brush the pancakes with a little oil and sprinkle with cheese. Grill (broil) until browned. Serve hot.

1 Remove the skin from the chicken and cut into cubes.

2 Heat the butter in a pan and cook the onion gently until tender. Add the mushrooms. Cook, covered, for a further 3–4 minutes.

# Chicken Pancake Parcels

*Chicken and apple might seem an unlikely combination, but make a delicious filling for these quick and easy pancakes. Crisp mangetouts and a fruity cranberry sauce make an ideal accompaniment.*

## INGREDIENTS

*Serves 4*

115g/4oz/1 cup plain (all-purpose) flour

pinch of salt

1 egg, beaten

300ml/$^1$/$_2$ pint/1$^1$/$_4$ cups milk

oil, for frying

*For the filling*

30ml/2 tbsp oil

450g/1lb/4 cups minced
  (ground) chicken

30ml/2 tbsp chopped fresh chives

2 green eating apples, cored and diced

25g/1oz/$^1$/$_4$ cup plain (all-purpose) flour

175ml/6fl oz/$^3$/$_4$ cup chicken stock

salt and ground black pepper

*For the sauce*

60ml/4 tbsp cranberry sauce

50ml/2fl oz/$^1$/$_4$ cup chicken stock

15ml/1 tbsp clear honey

15g/$^1$/$_2$ oz/2 tbsp cornflour (cornstarch)

1 To make the filling, heat the oil in a large pan and fry the chicken for 5 minutes. Add the chives and apples and then the flour. Stir in the stock and seasoning. Cook for 20 minutes.

2 To make the pancakes, sift the flour into a bowl together with a pinch of salt. Make a well in the centre and drop in the egg. Beat it in gradually with the milk to form a smooth batter. Heat the oil in a 15cm/6in omelette pan. Pour off the oil and add one-quarter of the pancake mixture. Tilt the pan to cover the base with the mixture and cook for 2–3 minutes. Turn the pancake over and cook for a further 2 minutes. Stack the pancakes on top of one another and keep warm.

3 To make the sauce, put the cranberry sauce, stock and honey into a pan. Heat gently until melted. Blend the cornflour with 20ml/4 tsp cold water, stir it in and bring to the boil. Cook, stirring, until clear.

4 Place each pancake on a warmed individual serving plate, spoon the filling into the centre and fold over around the filling. Spoon on the sauce and serve immediately.

# Chicken and Vegetable Bundles

*This popular and delicious dim sum is extremely easy to prepare and makes an ideal light lunch.*

### INGREDIENTS

*Serves 4*

4 skinless, boneless chicken thighs
5ml/1 tsp cornflour (cornstarch)
10ml/2 tsp dry sherry
30ml/2 tbsp light soy sauce
2.5ml/$^{1}/_{2}$ tsp salt
large pinch of ground white pepper
4 fresh shiitake mushrooms
1 small carrot
1 small courgette (zucchini)
50g/2oz/$^{1}/_{2}$ cup sliced, drained, canned
  bamboo shoots
1 leek, trimmed
1.5ml/$^{1}/_{4}$ tsp sesame oil

1 Remove any fat from the chicken thighs and cut each lengthways into eight strips. Place the strips in a bowl.

2 Add the cornflour, sherry and half the soy sauce to the bowl. Season, and mix well. Cover and marinate for 10 minutes.

3 Remove and discard the mushroom stalks, then cut each mushroom cap in half (or in slices if very large). Cut the carrot and courgette into eight batons, each about 5cm/2in long, then mix the mushroom halves and bamboo shoots together.

4 Bring a pan of water to the boil. Add the leek and blanch until soft. Drain thoroughly, then slit the leek down its length. Separate each layer to give eight long strips.

5 Divide the marinated chicken into eight portions. Do the same with the vegetables. Wrap a strip of leek around a portion of chicken and vegetables to make eight neat bundles. Have ready a pan with about 5cm/2in boiling water and a steamer or a heatproof plate that will fit inside it on a metal trivet.

6 Place the chicken and vegetable bundles in the steamer or on the plate. Place in the pan, cover and steam over a high heat for 12–15 minutes, or until the filling is cooked. Meanwhile, mix the remaining soy sauce with the sesame oil and use as a sauce for the bundles.

# Indonesian-style Satay Chicken

*Coconut, peanuts and chilli are the key ingredients for this popular dish. Use boneless chicken thighs to give the satays the best flavour.*

### INGREDIENTS

*Serves 4*

50g/2oz/$^1$/2 cup raw peanuts

45ml/3 tbsp vegetable oil

1 small onion, finely chopped

2.5cm/1in piece fresh root ginger, peeled and finely chopped

1 garlic clove, crushed

675g/1$^1$/2 lb chicken thighs, skinned and cut into cubes

130g/4$^1$/2 oz creamed coconut, roughly chopped, or 150ml/$^1$/4 pint/$^2$/3 cup coconut cream

15ml/1 tbsp chilli sauce

50ml/2fl oz/$^1$/4 cup crunchy peanut butter

5ml/1 tsp soft dark brown sugar

150ml/$^1$/4 pint/$^2$/3 cup milk, if using creamed coconut

1.5ml/$^1$/4 tsp salt

1 Soak four wooden skewers in water for 30 minutes. Shell and rub the skins from the peanuts, then soak them for 1 minute in a bowl with enough water to cover them. Drain the peanuts and carefully cut them into fine slivers.

2 Heat a large wok or frying pan and add 5ml/1 tsp of the oil. When the oil is hot, stir-fry the peanuts for 1 minute. Remove them with a slotted spoon and drain on kitchen paper.

3 Add the remaining oil to the pan. When the oil is hot, add the onion, ginger and garlic. Stir-fry for 2–3 minutes, or until softened but not browned. Remove and drain on kitchen paper.

4 Add the chicken and stir-fry for 3–4 minutes, or until crisp on all sides and cooked through.

5 Thread on to pre-soaked bamboo skewers and keep warm in a low oven.

6 Add the creamed coconut, if using, to the pan in small pieces and stir-fry until melted. Add the chilli sauce, peanut butter and cooked onion, ginger and garlic, and simmer for 2 minutes. Stir in the sugar, milk or coconut cream and salt and simmer for a further 3 minutes.

7 Serve the skewered chicken hot, with a dash of the hot dipping sauce sprinkled with the peanuts.

# Chicken Lettuce Parcels

*Known as* Sang Choy *in Hong Kong, this is a popular assemble-it-yourself treat. The filling – an imaginative blend of textures and flavours – is served with crisp lettuce leaves, which are used as wrappers.*

### INGREDIENTS

*Serves 6*

2 chicken breast fillets, total weight about
   350g/12oz
4 dried Chinese mushrooms, soaked for
   30 minutes in warm water to cover
30ml/2 tbsp vegetable oil
2 garlic cloves, crushed
6 drained canned water chestnuts,
   thinly sliced
30ml/2 tbsp light soy sauce
5ml/1 tsp Sichuan peppercorns, dry-fried
   and crushed
4 spring onions (scallions), finely chopped
5ml/1 tsp sesame oil
vegetable oil, for deep-frying
50g/2oz cellophane noodles
salt and ground black pepper (optional)
1 crisp lettuce, divided into leaves, and
   60ml/4 tbsp hoisin sauce, to serve

1 Remove the skin from the chicken and set aside. Chop the chicken into thin strips. Drain the mushrooms, discard the stems, and slice the caps finely. Set aside.

2 Heat the oil in a wok or large frying pan. Add the garlic, then add the chicken, and stir-fry until the pieces are cooked through and no longer pink.

3 Add the mushrooms, water chestnuts, soy sauce and peppercorns. Toss for 2–3 minutes, then season, if needed. Stir in half the spring onions, then the sesame oil. Remove from the heat. Set aside.

4 Heat the oil to 190°C/375°F. Test by dropping a cube of bread into the oil: it should brown in 60 seconds. Cut the chicken skin into strips, deep-fry until crisp and drain. Add the noodles to the oil and deep-fry until crisp. Transfer to a plate lined with kitchen paper.

5 Crush the noodles and put in a serving dish. Top with the chicken skin, chicken mixture and the remaining spring onions. Arrange the lettuce leaves on a large platter.

6 Toss the chicken and noodles to mix. Each diner can take one or two lettuce leaves, spread the inside with hoisin sauce and add a spoonful of filling, turning in the sides of the leaves and rolling them into a parcel. The parcels are eaten held in the hand.

# Sticky Chicken and Rice Parcels

*Glutinous rice gives the filling a wonderful texture in this deliciously unusual dish from China.*

### INGREDIENTS

*Serves 4*

450g/1lb/2¼ cups glutinous rice
20ml/4 tsp vegetable oil
15ml/1 tbsp dark soy sauce
1.5ml/¼ tsp five-spice powder
15ml/1 tbsp dry sherry
4 skinless and boneless chicken thighs,
  each cut into 4 pieces
8 dried Chinese mushrooms, soaked in hot
  water until soft
25g/1oz dried shrimps, soaked in hot
  water until soft
50g/2oz/½ cup sliced, drained, canned
  bamboo shoots
300ml/½ pint/1¼ cups chicken stock
10ml/2 tsp cornflour (cornstarch)
15ml/1 tbsp cold water
4 lotus leaves, soaked in warm water
  until soft
salt and ground white pepper

1 Rinse the glutinous rice until the water runs clear, then leave to soak in water for 2 hours. Drain and stir in 5ml/1 tsp of the oil and 2.5ml/½ tsp salt. Line a large steamer with a piece of clean muslin. Transfer the rice into this. Cover and steam over boiling water for 45 minutes, stirring the rice from time to time and topping up the water if needed.

2 Mix the soy sauce, five-spice powder and sherry. Put the chicken pieces in a bowl, add the marinade, stir to coat, then cover and leave to marinate for 20 minutes.

3 Drain the Chinese mushrooms, cut out and discard the stems, then chop the caps roughly. Drain the dried shrimps. Heat the remaining oil in a non-stick frying pan or wok. Stir-fry the chicken for 2 minutes, then add the mushrooms, shrimps, bamboo shoots and stock. Simmer for 10 minutes.

4 Mix the cornflour to a paste with the cold water. Add the mixture to the pan and cook, stirring, until the sauce has thickened. Add salt and white pepper to taste. Lift the cooked rice out of the steamer and let it cool slightly.

5 With lightly dampened hands, divide the rice into four equal portions. Put half of one portion in the centre of a lotus leaf. Spread it into a round and place a quarter of the chicken mixture on top. Cover with the remaining half portion of rice. Fold the leaf around the filling to make a neat rectangular parcel. Make three more parcels in the same way.

6 Prepare a steamer. Put the rice parcels, seam side down, into the steamer. Cover and steam over a high heat for about 30 minutes. Serve on individual heated plates.

---

### COOK'S TIP

The parcels can be made several days in advance and re-steamed before serving. If you do this, allow an extra 20 minutes' cooking time to ensure that the filling is hot.

# Turkey Rolls with Gazpacho Sauce

*This Spanish-style recipe uses turkey steaks wrapped around chorizo sausages and cooked on a barbecue. Served with the gazpacho sauce this makes an unusual and tasty meal.*

*Serves 4*

4 turkey breast steaks
15ml/1 tbsp red pesto or tomato
    purée (paste)
4 chorizo sausages

*For the sauce*

1 green (bell) pepper, seeded and chopped
1 red (bell) pepper, seeded and chopped
7.5cm/3in piece cucumber
1 medium-size tomato
1 garlic clove
45ml/3 tbsp olive oil
15ml/1 tbsp red wine vinegar
salt and ground black pepper

1 To make the gazpacho sauce, place the peppers, cucumber, tomato, garlic, 30ml/2 tbsp of the oil and the vinegar in a food processor and process until almost smooth. Season to taste with salt and pepper and set aside.

2 If the turkey breast steaks are quite thick, place them between two sheets of clear film (plastic wrap) and beat them with the side of a rolling pin, to flatten them.

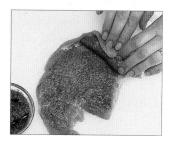

3 Spread the pesto or tomato purée over the turkey and then place a chorizo on each piece and roll up firmly.

4 Prepare a barbecue. Slice the rolls thickly and thread them on to metal skewers. Grill on a medium-hot barbecue for 10–12 minutes, turning once, until cooked through; serve with the gazpacho sauce.

# Chicken with Herb and Ricotta Stuffing

*These little chicken drumsticks are full of flavour and the stuffing and bacon helps to keep them moist and tender.*

## INGREDIENTS

*Serves 4*

60ml/4 tbsp ricotta cheese

1 garlic clove, crushed

45ml/3 tbsp mixed chopped fresh herbs, such as chives, flat leaf parsley and mint

30ml/2 tbsp fresh brown breadcrumbs

8 chicken drumsticks

8 rashers (strips) smoked streaky (fatty) bacon

5ml/1 tsp wholegrain mustard

15ml/1 tbsp sunflower oil

salt and ground black pepper

1 Mix together the ricotta cheese, garlic, herbs and breadcrumbs. Season well with salt and pepper.

2 Carefully loosen the skin from each drumstick and spoon a little of the herb stuffing under each, smoothing the skin back over firmly.

3 Wrap a bacon rasher around the wide end of each drumstick, to hold the skin in place over the stuffing.

4 Mix together the mustard and oil and brush them over the chicken. Prepare a barbecue. Cook over medium-hot coals for about 25 minutes, turning occasionally, until the juices run clear and not pink when the flesh is pierced.

# Stuffed Chicken Wings

3 Holding the large end of the bone on the third section of the wing and using a sharp knife, cut the skin and flesh away from the bone, scraping down and pulling the meat over the small end forming a pocket. Repeat this process with the remaining wing sections.

4 Fill the tiny pockets with the filling. Mix the dried bread-crumbs and the sesame seeds together. Place the breadcrumb mixture and the beaten egg in separate dishes.

5 Brush the meat with beaten egg and roll in breadcrumbs to cover. Chill and repeat to give a second layer, forming a thick coating. Chill until ready to fry.

6 Preheat the oven to 180°C/350°F/Gas 4. Heat 5cm/2in of oil in a heavy pan until hot but not smoking or the breadcrumbs will burn. Gently fry two or three wings at a time until golden brown. Remove and drain on kitchen paper. Complete the cooking in the preheated oven for 15–20 minutes, or until tender and cooked through.

*These tasty stuffed wings are excellent served for lunch or hot or cold at a buffet. They can be prepared and frozen in advance.*

INGREDIENTS

*Makes 12*

12 large chicken wings

*For the filling*

5ml/1 tsp cornflour (cornstarch)
1.5ml/$^1$/4 tsp salt
2.5ml/$^1$/2 tsp fresh thyme
pinch of ground black pepper

*For the coating*

225g/8oz/3$^1$/4 cups dried breadcrumbs
30ml/2 tbsp sesame seeds
2 eggs, beaten
oil, for deep-frying

1 Remove the wing tips and discard or use them for making stock. Skin the second joint sections, removing the two small bones, and mince (grind) the meat for the filling.

2 Mix the minced meat with the filling ingredients.

# Turkey Patties

*Turkey makes deliciously light patties, which are ideal for summer meals. You could use chicken if you prefer. Serve the patties in split and toasted buns or pieces of crusty bread, with chutney, salad leaves and chunky fries.*

### INGREDIENTS

*Serves 6*

675g/1¹/₂ lb minced (ground) turkey
1 small red onion, finely chopped
grated rind and juice of 1 lime
small handful of fresh thyme leaves
15–30ml/1–2 tbsp olive oil
salt and ground black pepper

1 Mix together the turkey, onion, lime rind and juice, thyme and seasoning. Cover and chill for up to 4 hours to allow the flavours to develop, then divide the mixture into six equal portions and shape into round patties.

2 Preheat a griddle. Brush the patties with oil, then place them on the griddle and cook for 10–12 minutes. Turn the patties over, brush with more oil and cook for 10–12 minutes on the second side, or until cooked through.

# Crispy Turkey Balls

*Turkey meat makes a good base for these spicy, Eastern-inspired balls that are great for a light lunch. Chicken can be used instead of the turkey if you prefer.*

### INGREDIENTS

*Serves 4–6*

4 thin slices of white bread, crusts removed

5ml/1 tsp olive oil

225g/8oz skinless, boneless turkey meat, roughly chopped

50g/2oz/$^1$/3 cup drained, canned water chestnuts

2 fresh red chillies, seeded and roughly chopped

1 egg white

10g/$^1$/4 oz/$^1$/4 cup fresh coriander (cilantro) leaves

5ml/1 tsp cornflour (cornstarch)

2.5ml/$^1$/2 tsp salt

1.5ml/$^1$/4 tsp ground white pepper

30ml/2 tbsp light soy sauce

5ml/1 tsp caster (superfine) sugar

30ml/2 tbsp rice vinegar

2.5ml/$^1$/2 tsp chilli oil

shredded red chillies and fresh coriander sprigs, to garnish

**1** Preheat the oven to 120°C/ 250°F/Gas $^1$/2. Brush the bread slices lightly with olive oil and cut them into 5mm/$^1$/4 in cubes. Spread over a baking sheet and bake for 15 minutes, or until dry and crisp.

**2** Meanwhile, mix together the turkey meat, water chestnuts and chillies in a food processor. Process to a coarse paste.

**3** Add the egg white, coriander leaves, cornflour, salt and pepper. Pour in half the soy sauce and process for about 30 seconds. Scrape into a bowl, cover and leave in a cool place for 20 minutes.

**4** Remove the toasted bread cubes from the oven and set them aside. Raise the oven temperature to 200°C/400°F/Gas 6. With dampened hands, divide the turkey mixture into 12 portions and form into balls.

**5** Roughly crush the toasted bread cubes, then transfer to a plate. Roll each ball in turn over the toasted crumbs until coated. Place on a baking sheet and bake for about 20 minutes, or until the coating is brown and the turkey filling has cooked through.

**6** In a small bowl, mix the remaining soy sauce with the caster sugar, rice vinegar and chilli oil. Serve this sauce with the turkey balls, garnished with shredded chillies and coriander sprigs.

# Mexican Chicken Panuchos

*These Mexican tortillas are fiddly to make, and well worth the effort. Start preparations the day before, as the onion relish needs time to allow the flavours to develop fully.*

### INGREDIENTS

Serves 6

150g/5oz/1 cup dried pinto beans, soaked
   overnight in water
1 onion, halved
5 garlic cloves, peeled
150g/5oz/1 cup masa harina
120ml/4fl oz/¹/2 cup warm water
2 chicken breast fillets, skinned
5ml/1 tsp dried oregano
25g/1oz/¹/2 cup chopped fresh
   coriander (cilantro)
2 hard-boiled eggs, sliced
oil, for shallow frying
salt and ground black pepper

*For the onion relish*
2 red Fresno chillies
5ml/1 tsp allspice berries
2.5ml/¹/2 tsp black peppercorns
5ml/1 tsp dried oregano
2 garlic cloves, peeled
2 white onions, halved and sliced thinly
100ml/3¹/2 fl oz/¹/2 cup white wine vinegar
200ml/7fl oz/ scant 1 cup cider vinegar
salt

1 To make the onion relish, dry-fry the chillies on a griddle until the skins scorch. Seal them in a plastic bag and set aside for 20 minutes. Place the allspice, black peppercorns and oregano in a food processor or blender and process until coarsely ground. Alternatively, use a pestle and mortar.

2 Dry-roast the garlic in a heavy frying pan until golden. Crush, then put in a bowl with the onions. Peel off the skins from the chillies. Slit them and scrape out the seeds. Chop the chillies.

3 Add the ground spices and chillies to the onion mixture. Mix in the vinegars and add salt to taste. Chill for at least 1 day before use.

4 Drain and rinse the pinto beans, then place in a large pan with 90ml/1¹/2 pints/3³/4 cups water. Add the onion and the whole garlic cloves. Boil and then simmer for 1¹/2 hours, or until tender.

5 To make the tortillas, mix the masa harina and a pinch of salt in a bowl. Add the warm water, a little at a time, to make a dough. Knead on a lightly floured surface for 3–4 minutes, or until smooth, then wrap the dough ball in clear film (plastic wrap) and leave to rest for 1 hour.

6 Put the chicken in a pan, add the oregano and pour in water to cover. Bring to the boil, lower the heat and simmer for 10 minutes, or until cooked. Remove from the pan, discard the water and allow the chicken cool a little. Shred the chicken into small pieces. Set aside.

> ### COOK'S TIP
> ∾
> Masa harina is a type of heavy white flour used extensively in Mexican cooking.

7 Divide the dough into 12 small pieces and roll into balls. Open a tortilla press and line both sides with plastic cut from a sandwich bag. Put a dough ball on the press and flatten it into a 6cm/2¹/2 in round. Alternatively, roll out the dough using a rolling pin. Use the remaining dough balls to make more tortillas in the same way.

8 Mash the beans and liquid to a smooth purée. Stir in the coriander and salt to taste.

9 Cook each tortilla in a hot frying pan for 15–20 seconds on each side. After a further 15 seconds on one side remove and wrap in a clean dishtowel.

10 Cut a slit in each tortilla, about 1cm/¹/2 in deep around the rim. Put a spoonful of the bean purée and a slice of hard-boiled egg in each slit.

11 Heat the oil for shallow frying in a large frying pan. Fry the tortilla pockets until they are crisp and golden brown on all sides, turning at least once during cooking. Drain them on kitchen paper and place on six individual serving plates. Top with a little of the shredded chicken and some onion relish. Season to taste and serve immediately.

# Chicken Fajitas

*Fajitas are warmed soft tortillas, filled and folded like an envelope. They are traditional Mexican fast food, delicious and easy to prepare, and a family favourite.*

## INGREDIENTS

*Serves 4*

115g/4oz/generous ¹/₂ cup white long
　grain rice
25g/1oz/3 tbsp wild rice
15ml/1 tbsp olive oil
15ml/1 tbsp sunflower oil
1 onion, cut into thin wedges
4 chicken breast fillets, skinned and cut
　into thin strips
1 red (bell) pepper, seeded and finely sliced
5ml/1 tsp ground cumin
generous pinch of cayenne pepper
2.5ml/¹/₂ tsp ground turmeric
175ml/6fl oz/³/₄ cup passata (bottled
　strained tomatoes)
120–175ml/4–6fl oz/¹/₂–³/₄ cup
　chicken stock
12 small or 8 large wheat tortillas, and
　warmed sour cream, to serve

*For the salsa*
1 shallot, roughly chopped
1 small garlic clove
¹/₂–1 fresh green chilli, seeded and
　roughly chopped
small bunch of fresh parsley
5 tomatoes
10ml/2 tsp olive oil
15ml/1 tbsp lemon juice
30ml/2 tbsp tomato juice
salt and ground black pepper

*For the guacamole*
1 large ripe avocado
2 spring onions (scallions), chopped
15–30ml/1–2 tbsp fresh lime or
　lemon juice
generous pinch of cayenne pepper
15ml/1 tbsp chopped fresh
　coriander (cilantro)

1 Cook the long grain and wild rice separately, following the instructions on the packets. Drain and set aside.

2 To make the salsa, finely chop the shallot, garlic, chilli and parsley in a blender or food processor. Spoon into a bowl. Plunge the tomatoes into boiling water for 30 seconds, then refresh in cold water. Peel away the skins, remove the seeds and chop the flesh. Stir in the chopped tomatoes, olive oil, lemon juice and tomato juice. Season to taste with salt and pepper. Cover with clear film (plastic wrap) and chill.

3 To make the guacamole, scoop the avocado flesh into a bowl. Mash it lightly with the spring onions, citrus juice, cayenne pepper, fresh coriander and seasoning, so that small pieces still remain. Cover the surface closely with clear film, and chill.

4 Heat the olive and sunflower oils in a frying pan and fry the onion wedges for 4–5 minutes, or until softened. Add the chicken strips and red pepper slices and fry until evenly browned.

5 Stir in the cumin, cayenne and turmeric. Fry, stirring, for about 1 minute, then stir in the passata and chicken stock. Bring to the boil, then lower the heat and simmer gently for 5–6 minutes, or until the chicken is cooked through. Season to taste.

6 Stir both types of rice into the chicken and cook for 1–2 minutes, or until the rice is warmed through.

7 Spoon a little of the chicken and rice mixture on to each warmed tortilla. Top with salsa, guacamole and sour cream and roll up. Alternatively, let everyone assemble their own fajitas at the table.

# Chicken Flautas

*Crisp, fried corn tortillas with a chicken and cheese filling make a delicious light meal, especially when served with a spicy tomato salsa. The secret of success is to make sure that the oil is sufficiently hot to prevent the flutes from absorbing too much of it.*

### INGREDIENTS

*Makes 12*

2 chicken breast fillets, skinned

15ml/1 tbsp vegetable oil

1 onion, finely chopped

2 garlic cloves, crushed

90g/3$^1$/$_2$ oz feta cheese, crumbled

12 corn tortillas, freshly made or a few
   days old

oil, for frying

salt and ground black pepper

*For the salsa*

3 tomatoes

juice of $^1$/$_2$ lime

small bunch of fresh coriander
   (cilantro), chopped

$^1$/$_2$ small onion, finely chopped

3 fresh Fresno chillies or similar fresh
   green chillies, seeded and chopped

1 To make the salsa, plunge the tomatoes into boiling water for 30 seconds, then refresh in cold water. Peel away the skins, remove the seeds and chop the flesh. Mix the tomatoes, lime juice, coriander, onion and chillies in a bowl. Season with salt to taste and set aside.

2 Put the chicken breasts in a large pan, add water to cover and bring to the boil. Lower the heat and simmer for 15–20 minutes, or until the chicken is cooked. Remove the chicken from the pan and let it cool a little. Using two forks, shred the chicken into small pieces. Set it aside.

3 Heat the oil in a frying pan, add the onion and garlic and fry over a low heat for about 5 minutes, or until the onion has softened but not coloured. Add the shredded chicken, with salt and pepper to taste. Mix well, remove from the heat and stir in the feta cheese.

4 Before they can be rolled, soften the tortillas by steaming three or four at a time on a plate over boiling water for a few moments until they are pliable. Alternatively, wrap them in microwave-safe film (wrap) and then heat them in a microwave oven on full power for about 30 seconds.

5 Place a spoonful of the chicken on one tortilla. Roll it tightly around the filling to make a neat cylinder. Secure with a cocktail stick (toothpick). Cover with clear film (plastic wrap) to prevent the tortilla from drying out. Repeat with the remaining tortillas.

6 Heat 2.5cm/1in oil in a frying pan until a small cube of day-old bread, added to the oil, rises to the top and bubbles at the edges. Remove the cocktail sticks. Add the rolls to the pan, a few at a time.

7 Fry the rolls for 2–3 minutes, turning frequently. Drain and serve immediately with the salsa.

---

COOK'S TIP

~

You might find it easier to keep the cocktail sticks (toothpicks) in place until after the rolls have been fried, in which case remove them before serving.

# Smoked Chicken Pizzas

*Mozzarella, yellow peppers and smoked chicken complement each other perfectly and make a really delicious topping for these individual pizzas.*

## INGREDIENTS

*Serves 4*

4 small pizza bases, about 13cm/
   5in diameter
45ml/3 tbsp olive oil
60ml/4 tbsp sun-dried tomato purée (paste)
2 yellow (bell) peppers, seeded and cut
   into thin strips
175g/6oz sliced smoked chicken
   or turkey, chopped
150g/5oz mozzarella cheese, cubed
30ml/2 tbsp chopped fresh basil
salt and ground black pepper

1 Preheat the oven to 220°C/ 425°F/Gas 7. Place the pizza bases well apart on two greased baking sheets.

2 Brush the pizza bases with 15ml/1 tbsp of the oil, then brush generously with tomato purée.

3 Stir-fry the peppers in half the remaining oil for 3–4 minutes.

4 Arrange the chicken and peppers on top of the sun-dried tomato purée.

5 Scatter over the mozzarella and basil. Season to taste with salt and black pepper.

6 Drizzle over the remaining oil and bake in the oven for 15–20 minutes, or until crisp and golden. Serve immediately.

# Chicken and Avocado Pitta Pizzas

*Pitta bread is used here to make quick bases for tasty pizzas. Use round ones if you can.*

INGREDIENTS

*Serves 4*

8 plum tomatoes, quartered

45–60ml/3–4 tbsp olive oil

1 large ripe avocado

8 round pitta breads

6–7 slices of cooked chicken, chopped

1 onion, thinly sliced

275g/10oz/2$\frac{1}{2}$ cups grated Cheddar
  cheese

30ml/2 tbsp chopped fresh
  coriander (cilantro)

salt and ground pepper

1 Preheat the oven to 230°C/
450°F/Gas 8.

4 Peel and stone (pit) the avocado.
Cut into 16 thin slices.

5 Brush the edges of the pitta
breads with oil. Arrange the
breads on two baking sheets.

6 Spread each pitta bread with
mashed tomato, covering it
almost to the edges.

7 Top each pitta bread with four
avocado slices. Sprinkle with
the chicken, then add a few onion
slices. Season to taste. Sprinkle on
the cheese.

8 Bake until the cheese begins to
melt, about 15–20 minutes.
Sprinkle with the coriander and
serve hot.

2 Place the tomatoes in a baking
dish. Drizzle over 15ml/1 tbsp
of the oil and season to taste. Bake
for 30 minutes; do not stir.

3 Remove the baking dish from
the oven and mash the
tomatoes with a fork, removing the
skins as you mash. Set aside.

# Chicken and Shiitake Mushroom Pizza

*The addition of shiitake mushrooms adds an earthy flavour to this colourful pizza, while fresh red chilli gives a hint of spiciness.*

### INGREDIENTS

Serves 3–4

45ml/3 tbsp olive oil

350g/12oz chicken breast fillets, skinned and cut into thin strips

1 bunch spring onions (scallions), sliced

1 fresh red chilli, seeded and chopped

1 red (bell) pepper, seeded and cut into thin strips

75g/3oz/generous 1 cup fresh shiitake mushrooms, wiped and sliced

45–60ml/3–4 tbsp chopped fresh coriander (cilantro)

1 pizza base, about 25–30cm/ 10–12in diameter

15ml/1 tbsp chilli oil

150g/5oz mozzarella cheese

salt and ground black pepper

1 Preheat the oven to 220°C/ 425°F/Gas 7. Heat 30ml/2 tbsp of the olive oil in a wok or large frying pan. Add the chicken, spring onions, chilli, pepper and mushrooms. Stir-fry over a high heat for 2–3 minutes, or until the chicken is firm but still slightly pink within. Season.

2 Pour off any excess oil, then set the chicken mixture aside until cool.

3 Stir the fresh coriander into the chicken mixture. Brush the pizza base with the chilli oil.

4 Spoon over the chicken mixture and drizzle over the remaining olive oil. Grate the mozzarella and sprinkle over. Bake for 15–20 minutes, or until crisp and golden. Serve immediately.

### COOK'S TIP

To make a basic pizza dough, sift 175g/6oz/1½ cups strong white bread flour and 1.5ml/¼ tsp salt into a mixing bowl. Stir in 5ml/ 1 tsp easy-blend (rapid-rise) dried yeast. Make a well in the centre of the dry ingredients and pour in 120–150ml/4–5fl oz/ ½–⅔ cup lukewarm water and 15ml/1 tbsp olive oil. Mix well. Knead the dough on a lightly floured surface for 10 minutes until smooth and elastic. Place in a greased bowl and cover with clear film (plastic wrap). Leave in a warm place to rise for about 1 hour, or until doubled in size. Knock back (punch down) the dough. Turn on to a lightly floured surface, and knead again for 2–3 minutes. Roll out as required and place on a greased baking sheet. Push up the edge of the dough to make a rim.

# Chicken Pitta Breads with Red Coleslaw

*Pitta breads are convenient for simple snacks and packed lunches, and it's easy to pack them with lots of fresh, healthy ingredients.*

## INGREDIENTS

*Serves 4*

¼ red cabbage

1 small red onion, finely sliced

2 radishes, thinly sliced

1 red apple, peeled, cored and grated

15ml/1 tbsp lemon juice

45ml/3 tbsp fromage frais or cream cheese

1 skinless chicken breast fillet, cooked,
    about 175g/6oz

4 large or 8 small pitta breads

salt and ground black pepper

chopped fresh parsley, to garnish

1 Remove the tough central spine from the cabbage leaves, then finely shred the leaves using a large sharp knife. Place the shredded cabbage in a bowl and stir in the onion, radishes, apple and lemon juice.

## COOK'S TIP
~

If the filled pitta breads need to be made more than an hour in advance, line them with crisp lettuce leaves before adding the filling.

2 Stir the fromage frais or cream cheese into the shredded cabbage mixture and season well with salt and pepper. Thinly slice the cooked chicken breast and stir into the shredded cabbage mixture until well coated.

3 Sprinkle the pitta breads with a little water, then warm them under a hot grill (broiler). Split them along one edge using a round-bladed knife. Share the filling equally among the pitta breads, then garnish with chopped fresh parsley.

# Chicken and Chorizo Tacos

*A lightly spiced filling tastes great in taco shells topped with lettuce, tomatoes and cheese. This quick dish is sure to be a success with all the family.*

### INGREDIENTS

*Serves 4*

15ml/1 tbsp vegetable oil

450g/1lb/4 cups minced (ground) chicken

5ml/1 tsp salt

5ml/1 tsp ground cumin

12 taco shells

75g/3oz chorizo sausage, minced

3 spring onions (scallions), chopped

2 tomatoes, chopped

1/2 head of lettuce, shredded

225g/8oz/2 cups grated Cheddar cheese

tomato salsa, to serve

1 Preheat the oven to 180°C/ 350°F/Gas 4.

2 Heat the oil in a non-stick frying pan. Add the chicken, salt and cumin and fry over a medium heat for 5–8 minutes, or until the chicken is cooked through. Stir frequently to prevent large lumps from forming.

3 Meanwhile, arrange the taco shells in one layer on a large baking sheet and heat in the oven for about 10 minutes, or according to the directions on the packet.

4 Add the chorizo and spring onions to the chicken and stir to mix. Cook until just warmed through, stirring occasionally.

5 To assemble each taco, place 1–2 spoonfuls of the chicken mixture in the base of a warmed taco shell. Top with a generous sprinkling of chopped tomato, shredded lettuce, and cheese.

6 Serve immediately, with tomato salsa to accompany.

# Gingered Chicken Noodles

*A blend of ginger, spices and coconut milk flavours this delicious dish, which is made in minutes. For a real Eastern touch, add a little Thai fish sauce to taste, just before serving.*

### INGREDIENTS

*Serves 4*

350g/12oz chicken breast fillet, skinned
225g/8oz courgettes (zucchini)
275g/10oz aubergine (eggplant)
about 30ml/2 tbsp oil
5cm/2in piece fresh root ginger, peeled and
   finely chopped
6 spring onions (scallions), sliced
10ml/2 tsp Thai green curry paste
400ml/14fl oz/1²/3 cups coconut milk
475ml/16 fl oz/2 cups chicken stock
115g/4oz medium egg noodles
45ml/3 tbsp chopped fresh
   coriander (cilantro)
15ml/1 tbsp lemon juice
salt and ground black pepper
chopped fresh coriander, to garnish

3 Add a little more oil, if necessary, and cook the ginger and spring onions for 3 minutes. Add the courgettes and cook for 2–3 minutes, or until beginning to turn golden. Stir in the curry paste and cook for 1 minute.

4 Add the coconut milk, stock, aubergine and chicken and simmer for 10 minutes. Add the noodles and cook for 5 minutes. Stir in the coriander and lemon juice and adjust the seasoning. Serve garnished with coriander.

1 Cut the chicken into bitesize pieces. Halve the courgettes lengthways and roughly chop them. Cut the aubergine into similarly sized pieces.

2 Heat the oil in a large pan and cook the chicken until golden. Remove with a slotted spoon and drain on kitchen paper.

# Five Ingredients Rice

*The Japanese have invented many ways to enjoy rice. Here, chicken and vegetables are cooked with short grain rice making a healthy lunch dish called Kayaku-gohan. Serve with a clear soup and tangy pickles.*

### INGREDIENTS

*Serves 4*

275g/10oz/1½ cups Japanese short
  grain rice
90g/3½ oz carrot, peeled
2.5ml/½ tsp lemon juice
90g/3½ oz gobo or canned
  bamboo shoots
225g/8oz oyster mushrooms
8 mitsuba sprigs, root part removed
7.5ml/1½ tsp dashi-no-moto (dashi stock
  granules) dissolved in 350ml/12fl oz/
  1½ cups water
150g/5oz chicken breast fillet, skinned and
  cut into 2cm/¾ in dice
30ml/2 tbsp shoyu
30ml/2 tbsp sake
25ml/1½ tbsp mirin
pinch of salt

1 Put the rice in a sieve and wash under a cold running tap until the water runs clear. Leave to drain for 30 minutes.

2 Cut the carrot into rounds, then cut the discs into flowers.

3 Fill a bowl with cold water and add the lemon juice. Peel the gobo and then slice with a knife as if you were sharpening a pencil into the bowl. Leave for 15 minutes, then drain. If using canned bamboo shoots, slice into thin matchsticks.

4 Tear the oyster mushrooms into thin strips. Chop the mitsuba sprigs into 2cm/¾ in long pieces. Put them in a sieve and pour over hot water from the kettle to wilt them. Allow to drain. Set aside.

5 Heat the water and dashi-no-moto in a pan. Add the carrots and gobo or bamboo shoots. Bring to the boil and add the chicken. Remove any scum from the surface, and add the shoyu, sake, mirin and salt.

6 Add the rice and mushrooms and cover with a lid. Bring to the boil for 5 minutes, then reduce the heat and simmer for 10 minutes. Remove from the heat without lifting the lid and leave to stand for 15 minutes. Add the mitsuba and serve.

### COOK'S TIP
Although gobo, or burdock, is a poisonous plant, the Japanese have always eaten it, but it must be cooked. It contains iron and acidic elements that are harmful if eaten raw, but after soaking in alkaline water and cooking for a short time, gobo is no longer poisonous. Mitsuba, or Japanese parsley, and gobo are available from Japanese supermarkets.

# *Adobo of Chicken and Pork*

*Four ingredients are essential in an adobo, one of the best-loved recipes from the Philippine Islands: vinegar, garlic, peppercorns and bay leaves. It is great served with plantain chips.*

### INGREDIENTS

*Serves 4*

1 chicken, about 1.3kg/3lb, or
    4 chicken quarters
350g/12oz pork leg steaks (with fat)
10ml/2 tsp sugar
60ml/4 tbsp sunflower oil
75ml/5 tbsp wine or cider vinegar
4 plump garlic cloves, crushed
2.5ml/$^1$/$_2$ tsp black peppercorns,
    crushed lightly
15ml/1 tbsp light soy sauce
4 bay leaves
2.5ml/$^1$/$_2$ tsp annatto seeds, soaked in
    30ml/2 tbsp boiling water, or
    2.5ml/$^1$/$_2$ tsp ground turmeric
salt

*For the plantain chips*
vegetable oil, for deep-frying
1–2 large plantains and/or 1 sweet potato

1 Wipe the chicken and cut into eight even-size pieces, or halve the chicken quarters, if using. Cut the pork into neat pieces. Spread out the meat on a board, sprinkle lightly with sugar and set aside.

2 Heat the oil in a wok or large pan and fry the chicken and pork pieces, in batches if necessary, until they are golden on both sides.

3 Add the vinegar, garlic, peppercorns, soy sauce and bay leaves and stir well.

4 Strain the annatto seed liquid and stir it into the pan or stir in the turmeric. Add salt to taste. Bring to the boil, cover, lower the heat and simmer for 30–35 minutes. Remove the lid and simmer for 10 minutes more.

5 Cook the plantain chips. Heat the oil. Test by dropping a cube of day-old bread into the hot oil, it should brown in 35 seconds. Peel and slice the plantains and/or sweet potato. Deep-fry them, in batches, until cooked but not brown. Drain.

6 To serve, reheat the oil and fry the plantains for a few seconds. Drain. Spoon the chicken and pork adobo into a serving dish and serve with the chips.

---

COOK'S TIP
~

Sprinkling the chicken and pork lightly with sugar turns the skin beautifully brown when fried.

---

# Fennel Stuffed with Chicken

*Fennel not only tastes delicious but it also divides into neat boat shapes, which are ideal for stuffing.*

INGREDIENTS

*Serves 4*

2 large fennel bulbs

3 eggs

30ml/2 tbsp olive oil

1 onion, chopped, or 15ml/1 tbsp
    dried onion

2 chicken breast fillets, skinned

225g/8oz/2$^1$/$_2$ cups trimmed and chopped
    oyster mushrooms

60ml/4 tbsp plain (all-purpose) flour or
    cornflour (cornstarch)

300ml/$^1$/$_2$ pint/1$^1$/$_4$ cups home-made or
    canned chicken broth, boiling

5ml/1 tsp Dijon mustard

30ml/2 tbsp sherry

salt and ground black pepper

fresh parsley sprigs, to garnish

boiled rice, to serve

1 Preheat the oven to 190°C/
375°F/Gas 5. Trim the base of
the fennel and pull each bulb apart
into four pieces. Reserve the central
part and boil the four pieces of
fennel in salted water for
3–4 minutes. Drain and leave to
cool. Boil the eggs for 10 minutes.
Allow to cool, peel and set aside.

2 Finely chop the central part of
the fennel. Sauté gently in oil
with the onion for 3–4 minutes.

3 Cut the chicken into pieces and
add to the frying pan with the
mushrooms. Cook over a medium
heat for 6 minutes, stirring. Add
the flour or cornflour and remove
from the heat.

4 Gradually add the chicken
broth, making sure the
thickener is completely absorbed.
Return to the heat and simmer
until thickened, stirring constantly.
Chop one of the eggs into the
chicken mixture, add the mustard,
sherry and seasoning to taste.

5 Arrange the fennel in a baking
dish. Spoon the filling into each
one, cover with foil and bake for
20–25 minutes. Quarter the
remaining eggs. Serve the fennel on
a bed of rice, garnished with the
eggs and parsley.

COOK'S TIP

If you find the fennel difficult to
cut, cook it before trying to cut
it. It will be much easier to deal
with once it is cooked.

# Pan-fried Chicken with Pesto

*Warm pesto accompanying pan-fried chicken makes a deliciously quick meal. Serve with pasta or rice noodles and braised vegetables.*

### INGREDIENTS

*Serves 4*

15ml/1 tbsp olive oil

4 chicken breast fillets, skinned

fresh basil leaves, to garnish

pasta or noodles and braised baby carrots
   and celery, to serve

*For the pesto*

90ml/6 tbsp olive oil

50g/2oz/$^1$/$_2$ cup pine nuts

50g/2oz/$^2$/$_3$ cup freshly grated
   Parmesan cheese

50g/2oz/1 cup fresh basil leaves

15g/$^1$/$_2$ oz/$^1$/$_4$ cup fresh parsley

2 garlic cloves, crushed

salt and ground black pepper

1 Heat the 15ml/1 tbsp oil in a frying pan. Add the chicken breasts and cook gently for 15–20 minutes, turning several times until they are tender, lightly browned and thoroughly cooked.

2 To make the pesto, place the olive oil, pine nuts, Parmesan cheese, basil leaves, parsley, garlic and salt and pepper in a blender or food processor and process until smooth and well mixed.

3 Remove the chicken from the pan, cover and keep hot. Reduce the heat slightly, then add the pesto to the pan and cook gently, stirring constantly, for a few minutes, or until the pesto has warmed through.

4 Pour the warm pesto over the chicken, then garnish with basil leaves and serve with pasta or noodles and braised baby carrots and celery.

# Mediterranean Chicken

*Chicken with a cheese filling served with fresh Mediterranean vegetables makes a perfect lunch-party dish, served simply with olive ciabatta or crusty bread.*

*Serves 4*

4 chicken breast portions, about 675g/
   1¹/₂ lb total weight
115g/4oz/1 cup soft cheese with garlic
   and herbs
450g/1lb courgettes (zucchini)
2 red (bell) peppers, seeded
450g/1lb plum tomatoes
4 celery sticks
about 30ml/2 tbsp olive oil
275g/10oz onions, roughly chopped
3 garlic cloves, crushed
8 sun-dried tomatoes, roughly chopped
5ml/1 tsp dried oregano
30ml/2 tbsp balsamic vinegar
5ml/1 tsp paprika
salt and ground black pepper
olive ciabatta or crusty bread, to serve

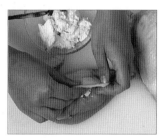

1 Preheat the oven to 190°C/
375°F/Gas 5. Loosen the skin of each chicken portion, without removing it, to make a pocket. Divide the cheese into four and push one quarter underneath the skin of each chicken portion in an even layer.

2 Cut the courgettes and peppers into similarly sized chunky pieces. Quarter the tomatoes and slice the celery sticks.

3 Heat 30ml/2 tbsp of the oil in a large, shallow flameproof casserole. Cook the onions and garlic for 4 minutes, or until soft and golden, stirring frequently.

4 Add the courgettes, peppers and celery and cook for a further 5 minutes.

5 Stir in the tomatoes, sun-dried tomatoes, oregano and balsamic vinegar. Season well.

6 Place the chicken on top, drizzle over a little more olive oil and season with salt and the paprika. Bake in the oven for 35–40 minutes, or until the chicken is golden and cooked through. Serve with plenty of olive ciabatta or crusty bread.

# Lemon Chicken with Guacamole Sauce

The avocado sauce makes an
unusual accompaniment to the
griddled chicken.

*Serves 4*

juice of 2 lemons

45ml/3 tbsp olive oil

2 garlic cloves, crushed

4 chicken breast portions, about
    200g/7oz each

2 beefsteak tomatoes, cored and cut in half

salt and ground black pepper

chopped fresh coriander (cilantro),
    for garnishing

*For the sauce*

1 ripe avocado

50ml/2 fl oz/$^1$/4 cup sour cream

45ml/3 tbsp fresh lemon juice

2.5ml/$^1$/2 tsp salt

50ml/2 fl oz/$^1$/4 cup water

1 Combine the lemon juice, oil,
garlic, 2.5ml/$^1$/2 tsp salt, and a
little pepper in a bowl. Stir to mix.

2 Arrange the chicken portions,
in one layer, in a shallow glass
or ceramic dish. Pour over the
lemon mixture and turn to coat
evenly. Cover and leave to marinate
for at least 1 hour at room temperature, or chill overnight.

3 To make the sauce, cut the
avocado in half, remove the
stone (pit), and scrape the flesh
into a food processor or blender.

4 Add the sour cream, lemon
juice, and salt and process
until smooth. Add the water and
process just to blend. If necessary,
add more water to thin the
sauce. Transfer to a bowl, taste
and adjust the seasoning, if
necessary. Set aside.

5 Preheat the grill (broiler) and
heat a ridged griddle. Remove
the chicken from the marinade and
pat dry.

6 When the griddle is hot, add
the chicken breasts and cook,
turning often, until they are cooked
through, about 10 minutes.

7 Meanwhile, arrange the tomato
halves, cut sides up, on a baking
sheet and season lightly with salt
and pepper. Grill (broil) until hot
and bubbling, about 5 minutes.

8 Place a chicken breast, tomato
half, and a dollop of avocado
sauce on each individual plate.
Sprinkle with coriander and serve.

## VARIATION

To cook on a barbecue, light the
barbecue, and when the coals are
glowing red and covered with
grey ash, spread them in a single
layer. Set an oiled grill rack about
13cm/5in above the coals and
cook the chicken breasts until
lightly charred and cooked
through, about 15–20 minutes.
Allow extra olive oil for basting.

# MIDWEEK MEALS

Weekday meals should be as exciting and adventurous as the meals we prepare at the weekends, but we don't always have a great deal of preparation time. This chapter has a collection of chicken recipes that will cater for all occasions: from tasty fast-food recipes to tried and trusted everyday classics. Thankfully, many aspects of the preparation, such as marinating, can be done in advance, which is ideal for busy people. So dip into this chapter and sample some of the enticing recipes for midweek meals.

# Grilled Chicken

*The flavour of this dish, known in Indonesia as* Ayam Bakur, *will be more intense if the chicken is marinated overnight. Celery leaves make a pretty and tasty garnish, if you have any.*

INGREDIENTS

*Serves 4*

1.3–1.6kg/3–3$^1$/$_2$ lb chicken
4 garlic cloves, crushed
2 lemon grass stems, lower 5cm/2in sliced
5ml/1 tsp ground turmeric
475ml/16fl oz/2 cups water
3–4 bay leaves
45ml/3 tbsp each dark and light soy sauce
50g/2oz/$^1$/$_4$ cup butter or margarine
salt
boiled rice, to serve

1 Cut the chicken into four or eight portions. Slash the fleshy part of each portion twice and set aside.

2 Grind the garlic, sliced lemon grass, turmeric and salt together into a paste in a food processor or with a mortar and pestle. Rub the paste into the chicken pieces and leave for at least 30 minutes or overnight. Wear rubber gloves for this, as the turmeric will stain heavily, or wash your hands immediately afterwards, if you prefer.

3 Transfer the chicken to a wok and pour in the water. Add the bay leaves and bring to the boil. Cover and cook gently for 30 minutes, adding a little more water, if necessary, and stirring from time to time.

4 Add the two soy sauces to the pan together with the butter or margarine. Cook until the chicken is well-coated and the sauce has reduced and thickened.

5 Transfer the chicken to a preheated grill (broiler) or an oven preheated to 200°C/400°F/ Gas 6. Cook for a further 10–15 minutes, turning the pieces often so they become golden brown all over. Baste with the remaining sauce during cooking. Serve with boiled rice.

# Chicken Kiev

*Cut through the crispy-coated chicken to reveal a creamy filling with just a hint of garlic.*

*Serves 4*

4 large chicken breast fillets, skinned
15ml/1 tbsp lemon juice
115g/4oz/$^1$/$_2$ cup ricotta cheese
1 garlic clove, crushed
30ml/2 tbsp chopped fresh parsley
1.5ml/$^1$/$_4$ tsp freshly grated nutmeg
30ml/2 tbsp plain (all-purpose) flour
pinch of cayenne pepper
1.5ml/$^1$/$_4$ tsp salt
115g/4oz/2 cups fresh white breadcrumbs
2 egg whites, lightly beaten
creamed potatoes, green beans and grilled
  (broiled) tomatoes, to serve

1 Place the chicken breasts between two sheets of clear film (plastic wrap) and gently beat with a rolling pin until flattened. Sprinkle with the lemon juice.

2 Mix the ricotta cheese with the garlic, 15ml/1 tbsp of the chopped parsley and the nutmeg. Shape into four 5cm/2in long rolls.

3 Put one portion of the cheese and herb mixture in the centre of each chicken breast and fold the meat over, tucking in the edges to enclose the filling completely.

4 Secure the chicken with cocktail sticks (toothpicks) pushed through the centre of each. Mix together the flour, cayenne pepper and salt, and use to dust the chicken.

5 Mix together the breadcrumbs and remaining parsley. Dip the chicken into the egg, then coat with breadcrumbs. Preheat the oven to 200°C/400°F/Gas 6. Chill for 30 minutes, then dip into the egg and breadcrumbs for a second time.

6 Put the chicken on a non-stick baking sheet. Bake in the preheated oven for 25 minutes, or until the coating is golden brown and the chicken completely cooked. Remove the cocktail sticks and serve with creamed potatoes, green beans and grilled tomatoes.

# Hunter's Chicken

*Porcini and field mushrooms give this traditional Italian chicken dish a marvellously rich flavour. Serve with creamed potatoes or polenta to soak up the lovely sauce.*

Serves 4

15g/$^1$/$_2$ oz/1 cup dried porcini mushrooms

30ml/2 tbsp olive oil

15g/$^1$/$_2$ oz/1 tbsp butter

4 chicken portions, skinned

1 large onion, thinly sliced

400g/14oz can chopped tomatoes

150ml/$^1$/$_4$ pint/$^2$/$_3$ cup red wine

1 garlic clove, crushed

leaves from 1 rosemary sprig,
    finely chopped

115g/4oz/1$^1$/$_2$ cups fresh field (portabello)
    mushrooms, thinly sliced

salt and ground black pepper

rosemary sprigs, to garnish

creamed potato or polenta, to serve
    (optional)

1 Put the porcini in a bowl, add 250ml/8fl oz/1 cup warm water and soak for 20–30 minutes. Remove the porcini from the liquid and squeeze. Strain the liquid and reserve. Finely chop the porcini.

---

V A R I A T I O N

Substitute strips of green (bell) pepper for the fresh mushrooms, if you like.

---

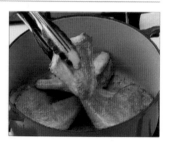

2 Heat the oil and butter in a large, flameproof casserole until foaming. Add the chicken. Sauté over a medium heat for 5 minutes, or until golden. Remove and drain on kitchen paper.

3 Add the onion and mush- rooms. Cook gently, stirring frequently, for 3 minutes, or until the onion has softened but not browned. Stir in the tomatoes, wine and reserved mushroom soaking liquid, then add the crushed garlic and chopped rosemary, with salt and pepper to taste. Bring to the boil, stirring constantly.

4 Return the chicken to the pan and coat with the sauce. Cover and simmer gently for 30 minutes.

5 Add the fresh mushrooms and mix into the sauce. Continue simmering gently for 10 minutes, or until the chicken is tender. Taste for seasoning. Serve hot, with creamed potato or polenta, if you like. Garnish with rosemary.

# Turkey with Marsala Cream Sauce

*Marsala makes a very rich and tasty sauce. The addition of lemon juice gives it a sharp edge, which helps to offset the richness.*

## INGREDIENTS

*Serves 6*

6 turkey breast steaks

45ml/3 tbsp plain (all-purpose) flour

30ml/2 tbsp olive oil

25g/1oz/2 tbsp butter

60ml/4 tbsp lemon juice

175ml/6fl oz/³/4 cup dry Marsala

175ml/6fl oz/³/4 cup double (heavy) cream

salt and ground black pepper

lemon wedges, and chopped fresh parsley, to garnish

mangetouts (snow peas) and green beans, to serve

1 Put each turkey steak between two sheets of clear film (plastic wrap) and pound with a rolling pin to flatten and stretch. Cut each in half or into quarters, cutting away and discarding any sinew.

2 Put the flour in a shallow bowl. Season well and coat the meat.

### VARIATION

Chicken breast fillets can be used instead of the turkey, and 50g/2oz/1/4 cup mascarpone cheese instead of the double cream, if you like.

3 Heat the oil and butter in a deep, heavy frying pan until sizzling. Add as many pieces of turkey as the pan will hold and sauté over a medium heat for about 3 minutes on each side until crispy and tender. Transfer to a warmed serving dish and keep hot. Repeat with the remaining turkey.

4 Lower the heat. Mix the lemon juice and Marsala together, add to the pan and raise the heat. Bring to the boil, stirring in the sediment, then add the cream. Simmer, stirring constantly, until the sauce is reduced and glossy. Taste for seasoning. Spoon over the turkey, garnish with the lemon wedges and parsley and serve immediately with the mangetouts and green beans.

# Chicken with Orange and Mustard Sauce

*The beauty of this recipe is its simplicity; the chicken continues to cook in its own juices while you prepare the sauce.*

*Serves 4*

2 large oranges

4 chicken breast fillets, skinned

5ml/1 tsp sunflower oil

salt and ground black pepper

new potatoes and sliced courgettes
(zucchini) tossed in parsley, to serve

*For the sauce*

10ml/2 tsp cornflour (cornstarch)

150ml/$^1$/4 pint/$^2$/3 cup natural
(plain) yogurt

5ml/1 tsp Dijon mustard

1 Using a sharp knife, cut a slice of peel and pith from each end of the oranges, then cut off all the peel and pith in strips, reserving the juice. Remove any remaining pith. Cut out each segment, leaving the membrane behind. Squeeze the remaining juice from the membrane.

2 Season the chicken with salt and freshly ground black pepper. Heat the oil in a non-stick frying pan and cook the chicken breasts for 5 minutes on each side. Take out of the frying pan and wrap in foil; the meat will continue to cook for a while.

3 To make the sauce, blend together the cornflour with the juice from the oranges. Add the yogurt and mustard. Put into the frying pan and slowly bring to the boil. Simmer for 1 minute.

4 Add the orange segments to the sauce and heat gently. Unwrap the chicken, check that it is cooked through and add any excess juices to the sauce. Slice on the diagonal and serve with the sauce, new potatoes and sliced courgettes tossed in parsley.

# Chicken with Yellow Pepper Sauce

*Fillets of chicken are filled with garlic cheese and accompanied by a yellow pepper sauce. Serve with tagliatelle for a tasty supper.*

Serves 4

30ml/2 tbsp olive oil

2 large yellow (bell) peppers, seeded and chopped

1 small onion, chopped

15ml/1 tbsp freshly squeezed orange juice

300ml/$^1$/2 pint/1$^1$/4 cups chicken stock

4 chicken breast fillets, skinned

75g/3oz/scant $^1$/2 cup Boursin or garlic cream cheese

12 fresh basil leaves

25g/1oz/2 tbsp butter

salt and black pepper

1 To make the yellow pepper sauce, heat half the oil in a pan and gently fry the peppers and onion until beginning to soften. Add the orange juice and stock and cook until very soft.

2 Meanwhile, lay the chicken fillets out flat and beat them out lightly.

3 Spread the chicken fillets with the Boursin or garlic cream cheese. Chop half the basil and sprinkle on top, then roll up the fillets, tucking in the ends like an envelope, and secure neatly with half a cocktail stick (toothpick).

4 Heat the remaining oil and the butter in a frying pan and fry the fillets for 7–8 minutes, turning frequently, until cooked through.

5 Meanwhile, press the pepper mixture through a sieve, or blend until smooth, then strain back into the pan. Season to taste and warm through. Serve with the fillets, garnished with the remaining basil leaves.

# *Chicken with Tarragon Cream*

*The aniseed-like flavour of tarragon has a particular affinity with chicken, especially in creamy sauces. Serve seasonal vegetables and boiled red Camargue rice with the chicken.*

### INGREDIENTS

*Serves 4*

30ml/2 tbsp light olive oil

4 chicken breast portions (about 250g/9oz
   each), skinned

3 shallots, finely chopped

2 garlic cloves, finely chopped

115g/4oz/1$^1$/$_2$ cups wild mushrooms (such
   as chanterelles or ceps) or shiitake
   mushrooms, halved

150ml/$^1$/$_4$ pint/$^2$/$_3$ cup dry white wine

300ml/$^1$/$_2$ pint/1$^1$/$_4$ cups double
   (heavy) cream

15g/$^1$/$_2$ oz/$^1$/$_4$ cup chopped mixed fresh
   tarragon and flat leaf parsley

salt and ground black pepper

sprigs of fresh tarragon and flat leaf
   parsley, to garnish

1 Heat the olive oil in a frying pan and add the chicken, skin side down. Cook for 10 minutes, turning the chicken until it is a golden brown colour on both sides.

2 Reduce the heat and cook the chicken for 10 minutes more, turning occasionally. Remove from the pan and set aside.

3 Add the shallots and garlic to the pan and cook gently, stirring, until the shallots are softened but not browned.

4 Increase the heat, add the mushrooms and stir-fry for 2 minutes. Replace the chicken, then pour in the wine. Simmer for 5–10 minutes, or until most of the wine has evaporated.

5 Add the cream and gently mix the ingredients together. Simmer for 10 minutes, or until the sauce has thickened. Stir the herbs into the sauce and season to taste. Arrange the chicken on warm plates and spoon the sauce over. Garnish with tarragon and parsley.

# Spinach-stuffed Chicken Breasts

*Large chicken breasts are filled with
a herby spinach mixture, then
topped with butter and baked until
mouthwateringly tender.*

INGREDIENTS

*Serves 6*

115g/4oz floury maincrop potatoes, diced
115g/4oz spinach leaves, finely chopped
1 egg, beaten
30ml/2 tbsp chopped fresh coriander
   (cilantro)
4 large chicken breast fillets
50g/2oz/4 tbsp butter
salt and ground black pepper
fried mushrooms, to serve

*For the sauce*

400g/14oz can chopped tomatoes
1 garlic clove, crushed
150ml/$^1$/4 pint/$^2$/3 cup hot chicken stock
30ml/2 tbsp chopped fresh coriander

1 Preheat the oven to 180°C/
350°F/Gas 4. Boil the potatoes
in a large pan of boiling water for
15 minutes, or until tender. Drain
and place them in a large bowl and
roughly mash with a fork.

2 Stir the spinach into the potato
with the egg and coriander.
Season to taste.

3 Cut almost all the way through
the chicken breasts and open
out to form a pocket in each.
Spoon the filling into the centre
and fold the chicken back over
again. Secure with wooden cocktail
sticks (toothpicks) and place in a
roasting pan.

4 Dot with butter and cover with
foil. Bake for 25 minutes.
Remove the foil and cook for a
further 10 minutes.

5 To make the sauce, heat the
tomatoes, garlic and stock in a
pan. Boil rapidly for 10 minutes.
Season and stir in the coriander.
Remove the chicken from the
oven and serve with the sauce and
fried mushrooms.

COOK'S TIP

Young spinach leaves are sweet
and are ideal for this dish.

# Chicken Spirals

*These little spirals look impressive, but they're very simple to make, and a good way to pep up plain chicken.*

Serves 4

4 chicken breast fillets, about 90g/3$^1$/2 oz
   each, skinned

20ml/4 tsp tomato purée (paste)

15g/$^1$/2 oz/$^1$/2 cup large basil leaves,
   plus extra to garnish

1 garlic clove, crushed

15ml/1 tbsp skimmed milk

30ml/2 tbsp wholemeal (whole-wheat) flour

salt and ground black pepper

passata (bottled strained tomatoes) or
   fresh tomato sauce and pasta, to serve

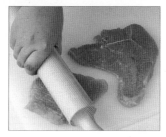

1 Place the chicken breast fillets on a board. If too thick to roll easily, flatten them slightly by beating with a rolling pin or meat mallet.

2 Spread each chicken breast with tomato purée, then top with a few basil leaves, a little crushed garlic and seasoning.

3 Roll up firmly around the filling and secure with a cocktail stick (toothpick). Brush with milk and sprinkle with flour to coat lightly.

4 Place the spirals on a foil-lined grill (broiling) pan. Cook under a medium-hot grill (broiler) for 15–20 minutes, turning them occasionally, until thoroughly cooked. Serve hot, sliced, with a spoonful or two of passata or fresh tomato sauce and accompanied with pasta sprinkled with fresh basil.

COOK'S TIP

When flattening the chicken breasts with a rolling pin, place them between two sheets of clear film (plastic wrap).

# Chicken and Beef Roulé

*A relatively simple dish to prepare, this recipe uses minced beef as a filling. It is rolled in chicken which is spread with a creamy garlic cheese that just melts in the mouth.*

### INGREDIENTS

*Serves 4*

4 boneless chicken breast fillets, about
   115g/4oz each, skinned
115g/4oz/1 cup minced (ground) beef
30ml/2 tbsp chopped fresh chives
225g/8oz/1 cup Boursin or garlic
   cream cheese
30ml/2 tbsp clear honey
salt and ground black pepper
green beans and mushrooms, to serve

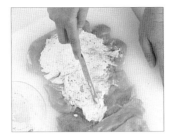

3 Place the chicken on a board and spread evenly with the cream cheese.

4 Top with the beef mixture, spreading it over evenly.

5 Roll up the chicken tightly to form a sausage shape.

6 Brush with honey and place in a roasting pan. Cook for 1 hour in the preheated oven. Remove from the pan and slice thinly. Serve with freshly cooked vegetables.

1 Preheat the oven to 190°C/ 375°F/Gas 5. Place the chicken breast fillets, side by side, between two pieces of clear film (plastic wrap). Beat with a meat mallet until 1cm/½ in thick and joined together.

2 Place the minced beef in a large pan. Fry for 3 minutes, add the fresh chives and seasoning. Cool.

# Chicken with White Wine and Garlic

*If you like a lot of garlic, use up to six cloves in this delicious recipe.*

*Serves 4*

1.6kg/3$^1$/2 lb chicken, cut into portions
1 onion, sliced
3–6 garlic cloves, crushed
5ml/1 tsp dried thyme
475ml/16fl oz/2 cups dry white wine
115g/4oz/1 cup pitted green olives (16–18)
1 bay leaf
15ml/1 tbsp lemon juice
15–25g/$^1$/2 –1oz/1–2 tbsp butter
salt and ground black pepper

1 Heat a deep frying pan. Add the chicken pieces, skin side down, and cook over medium heat for about 10 minutes, or until browned. Turn and brown the other side, 5–8 minutes more.

2 Transfer the chicken pieces to a plate and set aside.

3 Drain the excess fat from the frying pan, leaving about 15ml/1 tbsp. Add the sliced onion and 2.5ml/$^1$/2 tsp salt and cook for about 5 minutes, or until just soft. Add garlic to taste and thyme, and cook for 1 minute more.

4 Add the wine and stir, scraping up any sediment that clings to the pan. Bring to the boil and boil for 1 minute. Stir in the olives.

5 Return the chicken pieces to the pan. Add the bay leaf and season lightly with pepper. Lower the heat, cover and simmer until the chicken is cooked through, about 20–30 minutes.

6 Transfer the chicken pieces to a warmed plate. Stir the lemon juice into the sauce. Whisk in the butter to thicken the sauce slightly. Spoon over the chicken and serve.

# Chicken Meat Loaf

*Serve this herby chicken loaf either hot or cold with steamed vegetables or a crisp salad.*

*Serves 4*

15ml/1 tbsp olive oil
1 onion, chopped
1 green (bell) pepper, seeded and chopped
1 garlic clove, crushed
450g/1lb/4 cups minced (ground) chicken
50g/2oz/1 cup fresh breadcrumbs
1 egg, beaten
50g/2oz/$^1$/2 cup pine nuts
12 sun-dried tomatoes in oil, drained and
  chopped
75ml/2$^1$/2fl oz/$^1$/3 cup milk
10ml/2 tsp chopped fresh rosemary, or
  2.5ml/$^1$/2 tsp dried
5ml/1 tsp ground fennel
2.5ml/$^1$/2 tsp dried oregano
2.5ml/$^1$/2 tsp salt

1 Preheat the oven to 190°C/ 375°F/Gas 5. Heat the oil in a frying pan. Add the onion, green pepper and garlic and cook over low heat, stirring often, until just softened, about 8–10 minutes. Remove from the heat and allow to cool.

2 Place the chicken in a large bowl. Add the onion mixture and the remaining ingredients and mix thoroughly together.

3 Transfer to a 21 × 11 cm/ 8$^1$/4 × 4$^1$/2in loaf tin (pan), packing the mixture down firmly. Bake for about 1 hour, or until golden brown and cooked through. Serve hot or cold in slices.

# Chicken Pastitsio

*A traditional Greek pastitsio is a rich dish made with beef, but this lighter lower-fat version with chicken is just as tasty.*

Serves 4–6

450g/1lb/4 cups lean minced (ground) chicken

1 large onion, finely chopped

60ml/4 tbsp tomato purée (paste)

250ml/8fl oz/1 cup red wine or stock

5ml/1 tsp ground cinnamon

300g/11oz/2³/4 cups macaroni

300ml/¹/2 pint/1¹/4 cups milk

25g/1oz/2 tbsp sunflower margarine

25g/1oz/¹/4 cup plain (all-purpose) flour

5ml/1 tsp freshly grated nutmeg

2 tomatoes, sliced

60ml/4 tbsp wholemeal (whole-wheat) breadcrumbs

salt and ground black pepper

green salad, to serve

1 Preheat the oven to 220°C/425°F/Gas 7. Fry the chicken and onion in a non-stick pan without fat, stirring until lightly browned.

2 Stir in the tomato purée, red wine or stock and cinnamon. Season, then cover and simmer for 5 minutes, stirring from time to time. Remove from the heat.

3 Cook the macaroni in plenty of salted boiling water until just tender, then drain.

4 Layer the macaroni with the meat mixture in a wide ovenproof dish.

5 Place the milk, margarine and flour in a pan and whisk over a medium heat until thickened and smooth. Add the nutmeg, and season to taste.

6 Pour the sauce evenly over the pasta and meat layers. Arrange the tomato slices on top and sprinkle lines of wholemeal breadcrumbs over the surface.

7 Bake for 30–35 minutes, or until golden brown and bubbling. Serve hot with a fresh green salad.

# Minty Yogurt Chicken

*Chicken is marinated with yogurt, mint, lemon and honey and then grilled.*

INGREDIENTS

*Serves 4*

8 chicken thigh portions, skinned

15ml/1 tbsp clear honey

30ml/2 tbsp lime or lemon juice

30ml/2 tbsp natural (plain) yogurt

60ml/4 tbsp chopped fresh mint

salt and ground black pepper

new potatoes and a tomato salad, to serve

1 Slash the chicken flesh at regular intervals with a sharp knife. Place in a bowl.

2 Mix together the honey, lime or lemon juice, yogurt, seasoning and half the mint.

3 Spoon the marinade over the chicken and leave to marinate for 30 minutes. Line the grill (broiler) pan with foil and cook the chicken under a medium-hot grill until thoroughly cooked and golden brown, turning the chicken occasionally during cooking.

4 Sprinkle with the remaining mint and serve with the potatoes and tomato salad.

# *Tarragon Chicken Breasts*

*The classic French version of this dish uses a whole chicken, but bone-less breasts are quick to cook and look elegant. The combination of dried and fresh tarragon makes a wonderfully aromatic sauce.*

### INGREDIENTS

*Serves 4*

4 chicken breast fillets (about
    150–175g/5–6oz each), skinned
125ml/4fl oz/$^1$/$_2$ cup dry white wine
about 300ml/$^1$/$_2$ pint/1$^1$/$_4$ cups
    chicken stock
15ml/1 tbsp dried tarragon
1 garlic clove, finely chopped
175ml/6fl oz/$^3$/$_4$ cup whipping cream
15ml/1 tbsp chopped fresh tarragon
salt and ground black pepper
fresh tarragon sprigs, to garnish

1 Season the chicken breasts lightly with salt and pepper and put them in a pan just large enough to hold them in one layer. Pour over the wine and stock, adding more stock to cover, if necessary, then add the dried tarragon and the garlic. Bring the stock just to a simmer over a medium heat and cook gently for 8–10 minutes, or until the juices run clear when the chicken is pierced with a knife.

2 With a slotted spoon, transfer the chicken to a plate and cover to keep warm. Strain the cooking liquid into a small pan, skim off any fat and boil to reduce by two-thirds.

3 Add the cream and boil to reduce by half. Stir in the fresh tarragon and adjust the seasoning. Slice the chicken breasts, spoon over a little sauce and garnish with tarragon sprigs.

> COOK'S TIP
>
> Tarragon is traditionally paired with chicken, but you could use chopped fresh basil or parsley instead.

# *Chicken Breasts with Grapes*

*When grapes are used in a French dish, it is often called "Véronique" or sometimes "à la vigneronne" – in the style of the grape grower. Here they are cooked with chicken in a creamy sauce.*

### INGREDIENTS

*Serves 4*

4 chicken breast fillets (about 200g/7oz
    each), skinned
25g/1oz/2 tbsp butter
1 large or 2 small shallots, chopped
120ml/4fl oz/$^1$/$_2$ cup dry white wine
250ml/8fl oz/1 cup chicken stock
120ml/4fl oz/$^1$/$_2$ cup whipping cream
150g/5oz seedless green grapes (about 30)
salt and ground black pepper
fresh parsley, to garnish

1 Season the chicken breasts. Melt half the butter in a frying pan over a medium-high heat and cook the chicken breasts for 4–5 minutes on each side until golden.

2 Transfer the chicken to a plate and cover to keep warm. Add the remaining butter and sauté the shallots until just softened, stirring frequently. Add the wine, bring to the boil and boil to reduce by half, then add the stock and continue boiling to reduce by half again.

3 Add the cream to the sauce, bring back to the boil, and add any juices from the chicken. Add the grapes and cook gently for 5 minutes. Slice the chicken breasts and serve with the sauce, garnished with parsley.

# Stuffed Chicken in Bacon Coats

*Nothing could be simpler for a midweek supper than these chicken breasts stuffed with a cream cheese and chive filling. They are beautifully moist when cooked in their bacon wrapping. Serve baked potatoes and a crisp, green salad as accompaniments.*

### INGREDIENTS

*Serves 4*

4 chicken breast fillets (about 175g/6oz
    each), skinned
115g/4oz/$^1$/$_2$ cup cream cheese
15ml/1 tbsp chopped chives
8 rindless unsmoked bacon rashers (strips)
15ml/1 tbsp olive oil
ground black pepper

1 Preheat the oven to 200°C/
400°F/Gas 6. Using a sharp knife, make a horizontal slit from the side into each chicken breast.

2 Beat together the cream cheese and chives. Divide into four portions and, using a teaspoon, fill each slit with some of the cream cheese. Push the sides of the slit together to keep the filling in.

3 Wrap each breast in two rashers of bacon and place in an ovenproof dish. Drizzle the oil over the chicken and bake for 25–30 minutes, brushing occasionally with the oil, until cooked through. Season with black pepper and serve immediately.

# Southern Fried Chicken

*This is a low-fat interpretation of the original deep-fried dish popularized by Colonel Sanders in the 1950s, which is now an international fast-food favourite. Serve with potato wedges to complete the meal.*

### INGREDIENTS

*Serves 4*

15ml/1 tbsp paprika
30ml/2 tbsp plain (all-purpose) flour
4 chicken breast fillets (about 175g/6oz
    each), skinned
30ml/2 tbsp sunflower oil
150ml/¼ pint/⅔ cup sour cream
15ml/1 tbsp chopped chives
salt and ground black pepper

*For the corn cakes*
200g/7oz corn kernels
350g/12oz/4 cups mashed potato, cooled
25g/1oz/2 tbsp butter

1 Mix the paprika and flour together on a plate. Coat the chicken in the seasoned flour.

2 Heat the oil in a large frying pan and add the floured chicken breasts. Cook over a high heat until a golden brown colour on both sides. Reduce the heat and continue cooking for a further 20 minutes, turning once or twice, until the chicken is cooked right through.

3 Meanwhile, make the corn cakes. Stir the corn kernels into the cooled mashed potato and season to taste. Using lightly floured hands, shape the mixture into 12 even-size round cakes, each about 5cm/2in in diameter.

4 When the chicken is cooked, remove from the frying pan and keep hot. Melt the butter in the pan and cook the corn cakes for 3 minutes on each side, or until golden and heated through.

5 Meanwhile, mix together the sour cream with the chives in a small bowl to make a dip. Transfer the corn cakes from the frying pan to serving plates and top with the chicken breasts. Serve immediately, offering the sour cream with chives on the side.

# Chicken in Herb Crusts

*Mustard gives the chicken a piquant*
*flavour in this quick-to-prepare dish.*
*Serve with new potatoes and salad*
*for a midweek supper.*

*Serves 4*

4 chicken breast fillets, skinned
15ml/1 tbsp Dijon mustard
50g/2oz/1 cup fresh breadcrumbs
30ml/2 tbsp chopped fresh parsley
15ml/1 tbsp mixed dried herbs
25g/1oz/2 tbsp butter, melted
salt and ground black pepper

1 Preheat the oven to 180°C/
350°F/Gas 4. Place the chicken
in a greased ovenproof dish. Spread
with the mustard and season.

2 Mix the breadcrumbs and
herbs together thoroughly.

3 Press on to the chicken to coat.
Spoon over the melted butter.
Bake uncovered for 20 minutes, or
until crisp and cooked through.

COOK'S TIP

The chicken breasts can be
brushed with melted butter
instead of mustard before being
coated in the breadcrumb
mixture, if you prefer.

# Oat-crusted Chicken with Sage

*Chicken thighs and drumsticks are coated with a crisp oat and sage mixture that is simply delicious.*

Serves 4

45ml/3 tbsp skimmed milk
10ml/2 tsp English (hot) mustard
40g/1$^{1}$/$_{2}$ oz/$^{1}$/$_{2}$ cup rolled oats
45ml/3 tbsp chopped sage leaves
8 chicken thighs or drumsticks, skinned
115g/4oz/$^{1}$/$_{2}$ cup low-fat fromage frais or
    natural (plain) yogurt
5ml/1 tsp wholegrain mustard
salt and ground black pepper
fresh sage leaves, to garnish

1 Preheat the oven to 200°C/ 400°F/Gas 6. Mix together the milk and English mustard.

2 Mix the oats with 30ml/2 tbsp of the sage and the seasoning on a plate. Brush the chicken with the milk and press into the oats.

3 Place the chicken on a baking sheet and bake for about 40 minutes, or until the juices run clear, not pink, when pierced through the thickest part.

4 Mix together the low-fat fromage frais or yogurt, whole-grain mustard, remaining sage and seasoning, then serve with the chicken. Garnish the chicken with fresh sage and serve hot or cold.

# Oven "Fried" Chicken

*This healthy chicken dish is baked until crisp in the oven.*

*Serves 4*

4 large chicken pieces
50g/2oz/$^1$/$_2$ cup plain (all-purpose) flour
2.5ml/$^1$/$_2$ tsp salt
1.5ml/$^1$/$_4$ tsp pepper
1 egg
30ml/2 tbsp water
30ml/2 tbsp chopped mixed fresh herbs,
   such as parsley, basil and thyme
65g/2$^1$/$_2$ oz/1 cup dry breadcrumbs
25g/1oz/$^1$/$_3$ cup freshly grated
   Parmesan cheese
lemon wedges, for serving

1 Preheat the oven to 200°C/
400°F/Gas 6.

2 Rinse the chicken in cold water.
Pat dry with kitchen paper.

3 Combine the flour, salt and
pepper on a plate and stir with
a fork to mix. Coat the chicken
pieces on all sides with the flour
and shake off the excess.

4 Sprinkle a little water on to the
chicken pieces, and coat again
lightly with the seasoned flour.

5 Beat the egg with the water in a
shallow dish. Stir in the herbs.
Dip the chicken pieces into the egg
mixture, turning them over to coat
them thoroughly.

6 Combine the breadcrumbs and
grated Parmesan cheese on a
plate. Roll the chicken pieces in the
crumbs, patting with your fingers
to help them to adhere.

7 Place the chicken pieces in a
greased shallow dish, large
enough to hold them in one layer.
Bake until thoroughly cooked and
golden brown, 20–30 minutes. To
check that they are cooked, prick
with a fork; the juices that run out
should be clear, not pink. Serve hot,
with lemon wedges.

# Pan-fried Honey Chicken Drumsticks

*Tender chicken drumsticks are marinated in honey, lemon and soy sauce, and then quickly fried. They are sure to be popular with all the family.*

*Serves 4*

115g/4oz/scant $^1$/2 cup clear honey

juice of 1 lemon

30ml/2 tbsp soy sauce

15ml/1 tbsp sesame seeds

2.5ml/$^1$/2 tsp fresh or dried thyme leaves

12 chicken drumsticks

2.5ml/$^1$/2 tsp salt

2.5ml/$^1$/2 tsp pepper

80g/3$^1$/4 oz/$^3$/4 cup plain
  (all-purpose) flour

40g/1$^1$/2oz/3 tbsp butter or margarine

45ml/3 tbsp vegetable oil

120ml/4fl oz/$^1$/2 cup white wine

120ml/4fl oz/$^1$/2 cup chicken stock

fresh parsley sprigs, to garnish

1 In a large bowl, combine the honey, lemon juice, soy sauce, sesame seeds and thyme. Add the chicken drumsticks and mix to coat them well. Leave to marinate in a cool place for 2 hours or more, turning occasionally.

2 Mix the salt, pepper and flour in a shallow bowl. Drain the drumsticks, reserving the marinade. Roll them in the seasoned flour to coat all over.

3 Heat the butter or margarine with the oil in a large frying pan. When hot and sizzling, add the drumsticks. Brown them on all sides. Reduce the heat to medium–low and cook until the chicken is done, 12–15 minutes.

4 Test the drumsticks with a fork; the juices should be clear. Remove the drumsticks to a serving platter and keep hot.

5 Pour off most of the fat from the pan. Add the wine, stock and reserved marinade and stir well to mix in the cooking juices on the bottom of the pan. Bring to the boil and simmer until reduced by half. Check and adjust the seasoning, then spoon the sauce over the drumsticks and serve garnished with parsley.

# Blackened Chicken Breasts

*Cumin, cayenne and paprika give the coating for these chicken breasts a lovely warm piquancy. For the best flavour cook them until they begin to blacken.*

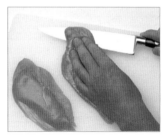

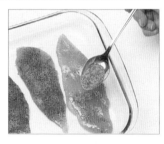

*Serves 6*

6 medium-size chicken breast
   fillets, skinned
75g/3oz/6 tbsp butter or margarine
5ml/1 tsp garlic purée (paste)
60ml/4 tbsp finely grated onion
5ml/1 tsp cayenne pepper
10ml/2 tsp sweet paprika
7.5ml/1$^1$/2 tsp salt
2.5ml/$^1$/2 tsp white pepper
5ml/1 tsp black pepper
1.5ml/$^1$/4 tsp ground cumin
5ml/1 tsp dried thyme leaves
(bell) peppers and salad leaves, to serve

1 Slice each chicken fillet in half horizontally. Flatten each slightly with the heel of the hand.

2 Melt the butter or margarine in a small pan together with the garlic purée.

3 Combine all the remaining ingredients in a shallow bowl and stir well. Brush the chicken pieces on both sides with melted butter or margarine, then sprinkle evenly with the seasoned mixture.

4 Heat a large, heavy frying pan over high heat until a drop of water sprinkled on the surface sizzles. This will take 5–8 minutes.

5 Drizzle 5ml/1 tsp of melted butter on each chicken piece. Place them in the pan in an even layer, two or three at a time. Cook until the underside begins to blacken, 2–3 minutes. Turn over and cook for 2–3 minutes more, until cooked through. Serve hot accompanied by salad.

# Chicken Breasts with Tomato-corn Salsa

*This hot tomato salsa is good with any grilled or barbecued meats.*

Serves 4

4 chicken breast fillets, about 175g/6oz
    each, skinned
30ml/2 tbsp fresh lemon juice
30ml/2 tbsp olive oil
10ml/2 tsp ground cumin
10ml/2 tsp dried oregano
15ml/1 tbsp coarse black pepper
salt

For the salsa

1 fresh hot green chilli pepper
450g/1lb tomatoes, seeded and chopped
250g/9oz/1$^1/_2$ cups corn, freshly cooked or
    thawed frozen
3 spring onions (scallions), chopped
15ml/1 tbsp chopped fresh parsley
30ml/2 tbsp chopped fresh coriander
    (cilantro)
30ml/2 tbsp fresh lemon juice
45ml/3 tbsp olive oil
5ml/1 tsp salt

1 With a meat mallet, pound the chicken breasts between two sheets of clear film (plastsic wrap) until thin.

2 In a shallow dish, combine the lemon juice, oil, cumin, oregano and pepper.

3 Add the chicken and turn to coat. Cover and leave to stand for at least 2 hours, or chill overnight in the refrigerator.

4 To make the salsa, char the chilli skin either over a gas flame or under the grill (broiler). Leave to cool for 5 minutes. Wearing rubber gloves, carefully rub off the charred skin. For a less hot flavour, discard the seeds.

5 Chop the chilli finely and place in a bowl. Add the remaining salsa ingredients and mix well.

6 Remove the chicken from the marinade. Season lightly.

7 Heat a ridged griddle. Add the chicken breasts and cook until browned, about 3 minutes. Turn and cook for 3–4 minutes more. Serve with the chilli salsa.

# Chicken, Carrot and Leek Parcels

*These intriguing parcels may sound a bit fiddly for every day, but the solution is to make them ahead of time and freeze them – ready to cook gently from frozen.*

### INGREDIENTS

*Serves 4*

4 chicken breast fillets
2 small leeks, sliced
2 carrots, grated
4 pitted black olives, chopped
1 garlic clove, crushed
15–30ml/1–2 tbsp olive oil
8 anchovy fillets
salt and ground black pepper
black olives and herb sprigs, to garnish

1 Preheat the oven to 200°C/ 400°F/Gas 6. Season the chicken well with salt and pepper.

2 Divide the leeks equally among four sheets of greased baking parchment, about 23cm/9in square. Place a piece of chicken on top of each one.

3 Mix the carrots, olives, garlic and oil together. Season lightly and place on top of the chicken portions. Top each with two of the anchovy fillets, then carefully wrap up each parcel, making sure the paper folds are underneath and the carrot mixture on top.

4 Bake for 20 minutes and serve hot, in the paper, garnished with black olives and herb sprigs.

# Chicken in a Tomato Coat

*Roasted chicken with a coating of tomato sauce and fresh tomatoes makes a tasty meal served with rice.*

### INGREDIENTS

*Serves 4–6*

1 chicken, about 1.3–2kg/3–4½lb
1 small onion
knob (pat) of butter
75ml/5 tbsp ready-made tomato sauce
30ml/2 tbsp chopped, mixed fresh herbs, such as parsley, tarragon, sage, basil and marjoram, or 10ml/2 tsp dried
150ml/¼ pint/⅔ cup dry white wine
2–3 small tomatoes, sliced
olive oil
a little cornflour (cornstarch) (optional)
salt and ground black pepper

1 Preheat the oven to 190°C/ 375°F/Gas 5. Place the chicken in a roasting pan. Put the onion, the knob of butter and some seasoning inside the chicken.

2 Spread most of the tomato sauce over the chicken and sprinkle with half the herbs and some seasoning. Pour the wine into the roasting pan.

3 Cover with foil, then roast for 1½ hours, basting occasionally. Remove the foil. Spread the chicken with the remaining sauce and the sliced tomatoes and drizzle with oil. Continue cooking for a further 20–30 minutes, or until cooked through.

4 Sprinkle the remaining herbs over the chicken, then carve. Cook the sauce with a little cornflour until thickened if you wish.

# Chicken with Lemon and Herbs

*The herbs for this recipe can be varied according to what is available; for example, parsley or thyme could be used instead of tarragon and fennel. Serve accompanied by sautéed potatoes for a quick and satisfying meal.*

### INGREDIENTS

*Serves 2*

50g/2oz/¹/4 cup butter

2 spring onions (scallions), white part only, finely chopped

15ml/1 tbsp chopped fresh tarragon

15ml/1 tbsp chopped fresh fennel

juice of 1 lemon

4 chicken thighs

salt and ground black pepper

lemon slices and herb sprigs, to garnish

1 Preheat the grill (broiler) to medium. In a small pan, melt the butter, then add the spring onions, herbs, lemon juice and salt and pepper.

2 Brush the chicken generously with the herb mixture, then grill (broil) for 10–12 minutes, basting frequently with the herb mixture.

3 Turn over, baste again, then cook for a further 10 minutes, or until the juices run clear.

4 Serve garnished with lemon and herbs.

# Chicken with Red Cabbage

*Chestnuts and red cabbage make a colourful winter dish.*

### INGREDIENTS

*Serves 4*

50g/2oz/¹/4 cup butter

4 large chicken portions, halved

1 onion, chopped

500g/1¹/4lb red cabbage, finely shredded

4 juniper berries, crushed

12 cooked peeled chestnuts

120ml/4fl oz/¹/2 cup full-bodied red wine

salt and ground black pepper

1 Heat the butter in a heavy flameproof casserole and lightly brown the chicken pieces. Transfer to a plate.

2 Add the onion and fry until soft and light golden brown. Stir in the cabbage and juniper berries, season and cook over a medium heat for 6–7 minutes, stirring once or twice.

3 Stir the chestnuts into the casserole, then tuck the chicken pieces under the cabbage so they are on the bottom of the casserole. Pour in the red wine.

4 Cover and cook gently for about 40 minutes, or until the chicken juices run clear and the cabbage is very tender. Check the seasoning and serve.

# Two-way Chicken with Vegetables

*This tender, slow-cooked chicken makes a tasty lunch or supper, with the stock and remaining vegetables providing a nourishing soup as a second meal.*

INGREDIENTS

*Serves 6*

1 chicken, about 1.3kg/3lb

2 onions, quartered

3 carrots, thickly sliced

2 celery sticks, chopped

1 parsnip or turnip, thickly sliced

50g/2oz/$^1$/2 cup button (white)
    mushrooms, roughly chopped

1–2 fresh thyme sprigs or 5ml/1 tsp
    dried thyme

4 bay leaves

large bunch of fresh parsley

115g/4oz/1 cup wholemeal (whole-wheat)
    pasta shapes

salt and ground black pepper

new potatoes or pasta, mangetouts (snow
    peas) or green beans and bread, to serve

1 Trim the chicken of any extra fat. Put it in a flameproof casserole and add the vegetables and herbs. Pour in water to cover and add salt and pepper. Bring to the boil over a medium heat, skimming off any scum. When the water boils, lower the heat and simmer for 2–3 hours.

2 Carve the chicken neatly, discarding the skin and bones, but returning any small pieces to the pan. Serve the chicken with some of the vegetables from the pan, plus new potatoes or pasta and mangetouts or green beans.

3 For the soup, remove any large pieces of parsley and thyme from the pan, let the remaining mixture cool, then chill it overnight. Next day, lift off the fat that has solidified on the surface. Reheat the soup gently.

4 When the soup comes to the boil, add the pasta shapes, with salt, if required, and cook for 10–12 minutes, or until the pasta is tender. Adjust the seasoning and garnish with parsley. Serve with wholemeal (whole-wheat) bread.

# Chicken Baked with Butter Beans and Garlic

*This simple one-pot meal combines chicken with leeks, fennel and garlic-flavoured butter beans.*

*Serves 6*

2 leeks

1 small fennel bulb

4 garlic cloves, peeled

2 x 400g/14oz cans butter (lima) beans, drained

2 large handfuls fresh parsley, chopped

300ml/$^1$/$_2$ pint/1$^1$/$_4$ cups dry white wine

300ml/$^1$/$_2$ pint/1$^1$/$_4$ cups vegetable stock

1 chicken, about 1.3kg/3lb

salt and ground black pepper

parsley sprigs, to garnish

cooked green vegetables, to serve

1 Preheat the oven to 180°C/ 350°F/Gas 4. Slit the leeks, wash out any grit, then slice them thickly. Cut the fennel into quarters, remove the core and chop the flesh roughly.

2 Mix the leeks, fennel, whole garlic cloves, butter beans and parsley in a bowl. Season to taste then spread out the mixture on the bottom of a heavy, flameproof casserole that is large enough to hold the chicken. Pour in the white wine and vegetable stock.

3 Place the chicken on top and season lightly. Bring to the boil, cover the casserole and transfer it to the oven. Bake for 1–1$^1$/$_2$ hours, or until the chicken is cooked and so tender that it falls off the bone. Garnish with parsley and serve with green vegetables.

# Chicken Börek

*This is a rich pastry parcel with a savoury filling. Serve at room temperature with a minty yogurt sauce.*

### INGREDIENTS

*Serves 4*

50g/2oz/$^1$/2 cup couscous
45ml/3 tbsp olive oil
1 onion, chopped
115g/4oz/1$^2$/3 cups mushrooms
1 garlic clove, crushed
115g/4oz/scant 1 cup diced cooked chicken
30ml/2 tbsp walnuts, chopped
30ml/2 tbsp raisins
60ml/4 tbsp chopped fresh parsley
5ml/1 tsp chopped fresh thyme
2 eggs, hard-boiled and peeled
salt and ground black pepper

*For the pastry*
400g/14oz/3$^1$/2 cups self-raising (self-rising) flour, plus extra for dusting
5ml/1 tsp salt
1 egg, plus extra for glazing
150ml/$^1$/4 pint/$^2$/3 cup natural (plain) yogurt
150ml/$^1$/4 pint/$^2$/3 cup olive oil
grated rind of $^1$/2 lemon

*For the sauce*
200ml/7fl oz/scant 1 cup natural (plain) yogurt
45ml/3 tbsp chopped fresh mint
2.5ml/$^1$/2 tsp caster (superfine) sugar
1.5ml/$^1$/4 tsp cayenne pepper
1.5ml/$^1$/4 tsp celery salt
a little milk or water, if necessary

1 Preheat the oven to 190°C/ 375°F/Gas 5. Just cover the couscous with boiling water and soak for 10 minutes, or until all the liquid is absorbed.

2 Heat the oil in a pan and soften the onion. Add the mushrooms and garlic, and cook until the juices begin to run. Increase the heat to boil off the juices.

3 Transfer the mushroom and onion mixture to a mixing bowl, add the chicken, walnuts, raisins, parsley, thyme and couscous, and stir well. Chop the eggs roughly and stir them into the mixture with seasoning to taste.

4 To make the pastry, sift the flour and salt into a bowl. Make a well in the centre, add the egg, yogurt, olive oil and lemon rind, and mix together with a round-bladed knife.

5 Turn out on to a floured surface and roll into a 30cm/12in round. Pile the filling into the centre and bring the edges over to enclose it. Turn upside down on to a baking sheet and press out flat with your hand. Glaze with beaten egg and bake for 25 minutes.

6 Meanwhile, make the sauce. Blend together all the ingredients, adding milk or water if the mixture is too thick. Spoon a little sauce over each serving.

# Chicken Breasts with Serrano Ham

*This modern Spanish dish is light
and very easy to make. It looks
fabulous, too.*

*Serves 4*

4 chicken breast fillets, skinned

4 slices Serrano ham

75g/3oz/6 tbsp butter

30ml/2 tbsp chopped capers

30ml/2 tbsp fresh thyme leaves

1 large lemon, cut lengthways into 8 slices

a few small fresh thyme sprigs

salt and ground black pepper

boiled new potatoes and steamed broccoli
    or mangetouts (snow peas), to serve

1 Preheat the oven to 200°C/
400°F/Gas 6. Wrap each
chicken breast in clear film (plastic
wrap) and beat with a rolling pin
until slightly flattened. Arrange
in a large, shallow ovenproof dish,
then top each with a slice of
Serrano ham.

2 Beat the butter with the capers,
thyme and seasoning until well
mixed. Divide the butter into
quarters and shape each into a neat
portion, then place on each ham-
topped chicken breast. Arrange
2 lemon slices on the butter and
sprinkle with small thyme sprigs.
Bake for 25 minutes, or until the
chicken is cooked through.

3 Transfer the chicken to a
warmed serving platter and
spoon the buttery juices over the
top. Serve immediately, with boiled
new potatoes and steamed broccoli
or mangetouts. Discard the lemon
slices before serving, if you prefer.

# Chicken Fillets with Olives

*This quick and tasty dish makes a good light main course.*

INGREDIENTS

*Serves 4*

90ml/6 tbsp olive oil

1 garlic clove, peeled and lightly
    crushed

1 dried chilli, lightly crushed

500g/1¼ lb chicken breast fillets, skinned,
    cut into 5mm/¼ in slices

120ml/4fl oz/½ cup dry white wine

4 tomatoes, peeled and seeded,
    cut into thin strips

about 24 black olives

6–8 fresh basil leaves, torn into pieces

salt and ground black pepper

1 Heat 60ml/4 tbsp of the olive oil in a large frying pan. Add the garlic and crushed dried chilli, and cook over low heat until the garlic is golden.

2 Raise the heat to medium and add the remaining oil. Place the chicken slices in the pan, and brown them lightly on both sides for about 2 minutes. Season with salt and pepper. Remove the chicken to a heated dish.

3 Discard the garlic and chilli. Add the wine, tomato strips and olives. Cook over medium heat for 3–4 minutes, scraping up any meat residue from the bottom of the pan.

4 Return the chicken to the pan. Sprinkle with the torn basil. Heat through for 30 seconds, and serve immediately.

# Chicken with Herbs and Lentils

*Lentils and herbs are baked with chicken to give it a lovely full flavour. Topped with garlic butter it makes a robust dish.*

## INGREDIENTS

Serves 4

115g/4oz piece of thick bacon or belly
   pork, rind removed, chopped
1 large onion, sliced
475ml/16fl oz/2 cups well-flavoured
   chicken stock
1 bay leaf
2 sprigs each parsley, marjoram
   and thyme
225g/8oz/1 cup green or brown lentils
4 chicken portions
salt and ground black pepper
25–50g/1–2oz/2–4 tbsp garlic butter
   (see Cook's Tip)

1 Fry the bacon gently in a large, heavy flameproof casserole until all the fat runs out and the bacon begins to brown. Add the onion and fry for about 2 minutes.

2 Stir in the chicken stock, bay leaf, herb stalks and some of the leafy parts (reserve some herb sprigs for garnish), lentils and seasoning. Preheat the oven to 190°C/375°F/ Gas 5.

3 Fry the chicken portions in a frying pan to brown the skin before placing on top of the lentils. Sprinkle with seasoning and some of the herbs.

4 Cover the casserole and cook in the oven for about 40 minutes, until cooked through. Serve with a dollop of garlic butter on each portion, and a few herb sprigs.

## COOK'S TIP

To make garlic butter, blend 115g/4oz/½ cup softened butter with 4 crushed garlic cloves. Form into a roll and chill. Slice into rounds. Garlic butter freezes well.

# Thai Chicken and Vegetable Stir-fry

*Lemon grass and ginger give this speedy stir-fry a delicious fragrance. You can make the dish a little hotter by adding more fresh root ginger, if you like.*

## INGREDIENTS

*Serves 4*

1 lemon grass stalk or the rind of
$^1/_2$ lemon
1cm/$^1/_2$ in piece of fresh
root ginger
1 large garlic clove
30ml/2 tbsp sunflower oil
275g/10oz lean chicken, thinly sliced
$^1/_2$ red (bell) pepper, seeded and sliced
$^1/_2$ green (bell) pepper, seeded and sliced
4 spring onions (scallions), chopped
2 medium carrots, cut into matchsticks
115g/4oz fine green beans
30ml/2 tbsp oyster sauce
pinch of sugar
salt and ground black pepper
25g/1oz/$^1/_4$ cup salted peanuts, lightly
crushed, and fresh coriander (cilantro)
leaves, to garnish
cooked rice, to serve

1 Thinly slice the lemon grass or lemon rind. Peel and chop the ginger and garlic. Heat the oil in a frying pan over a high heat. Add the lemon grass or lemon rind, ginger and garlic, and stir-fry for 30 seconds, or until brown.

2 Add the chicken and stir-fry for 2 minutes. Then add the vegetables and stir-fry for 4–5 minutes, or until the chicken is cooked and the vegetables are almost cooked.

3 Finally, stir in the oyster sauce, sugar and seasoning to taste and stir-fry for another minute to mix and blend well. Serve immediately, sprinkled with the peanuts and coriander leaves and accompanied by cooked rice.

# Chicken Stroganov

*This chicken version of the classic Russian dish – usually made with fillet of beef – is perfect served with rice mixed with chopped celery and spring onions (scallions).*

INGREDIENTS

Serves 4

4 large chicken breast fillets, skinned
45ml/3 tbsp olive oil
1 large onion, thinly sliced
225g/8oz/3 cups mushrooms, sliced
300ml/$^1$/$_2$ pint/1$^1$/$_4$ cups sour cream
salt and ground black pepper
15ml/1 tbsp chopped fresh parsley,
  to garnish

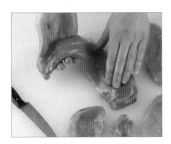

1 Divide each chicken breast into two natural fillets, place between two sheets of clear film (plastic wrap) and flatten each to a thickness of 1cm/$^1$/$_2$in with a rolling pin.

2 Cut into 2.5cm/1in strips diagonally across the fillets.

3 Heat 30ml/2 tbsp of the oil in a frying pan and cook the onion slowly until soft but not coloured.

4 Add the mushrooms and cook until golden brown. Remove and keep warm.

5 Increase the heat, add the remaining oil and fry the chicken very quickly, in small batches, for 3–4 minutes, until lightly coloured and cooked through. Remove to a dish and keep warm.

6 Return all the chicken, onions and mushrooms to the pan and season with salt and black pepper. Stir in the sour cream and bring to the boil. Sprinkle with fresh parsley and serve immediately.

# Chicken with Honey and Grapefruit

*Chicken breast portions cook very quickly and are ideal for suppers on-the-run – but be careful not to overcook them. You could substitute boneless turkey steaks or duck breast fillets for the chicken, if you prefer.*

### INGREDIENTS

*Serves 4*

4 chicken breast portions, skinned
45–60ml/3–4 tbsp clear honey
1 pink grapefruit, peeled and
    cut into 12 segments
salt and ground black pepper
noodles and salad leaves, to serve

1 Make three quite deep, diagonal slits in the chicken flesh using a large sharp knife.

2 Brush the chicken all over with some of the honey and sprinkle well with seasoning.

3 Put the chicken in a flameproof dish, uncut side uppermost, and place under a medium grill (broiler) for 2–3 minutes.

4 Turn the chicken over and place the grapefruit segments in the slits. Brush with more honey and cook for a further 5 minutes, or until tender and cooked through. If necessary, reduce the heat so that the honey glaze does not burn. Serve immediately with noodles and salad leaves.

# Crispy Chicken with Garlic Rice

*Chicken wings cooked until they are really tender have a surprising amount of meat on them, and make a very economical supper for a crowd of youngsters. Provide lots of kitchen paper, napkins and finger bowls for the sticky fingers.*

### INGREDIENTS

*Serves 4*

1 large onion, chopped
2 garlic cloves, crushed
30ml/2 tbsp sunflower oil
175g/6oz/scant 1 cup basmati rice
350ml/12fl oz/1$^1$/2 cups hot chicken stock
10ml/2 tsp finely grated lemon rind
30ml/2 tbsp chopped mixed herbs
8 or 12 chicken wings
50g/2oz/$^1$/2 cup plain (all-purpose) flour
salt and ground black pepper
fresh tomato sauce and vegetables,
    to serve

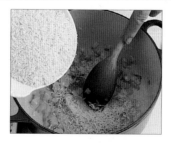

1 Preheat the oven to 200°C/ 400°F/Gas 6. Fry the onion and garlic in the oil in a large flameproof casserole, until golden. Stir in the rice and toss until all the grains are well coated in oil.

2 Stir in the stock, lemon rind and herbs and bring to the boil. Cover and cook in the middle of the oven for 40–50 minutes. Stir once or twice during cooking.

3 Meanwhile, wipe dry the chicken wings. Season the flour and use to coat the chicken portions.

4 Put the chicken wings in a small roasting pan and cook in the top of the oven for 30–40 minutes, turning once, until crispy and cooked through.

5 Serve the rice and chicken wings with a fresh tomato sauce and a selection of vegetables.

# Chicken and Bean Risotto

2 Stir in the chicken, kidney beans, corn and sultanas. Cook and stir for a further 20 minutes, or until almost all the liquid has been absorbed.

3 Meanwhile, cook the broccoli in boiling water for 5 minutes, then drain thoroughly.

4 Stir in the broccoli and chopped herbs, season to taste and serve immediately.

*Nutty-flavoured brown rice tastes good mixed with red kidney beans, corn and broccoli in this tasty risotto.*

### INGREDIENTS

*Serves 4–6*

1 onion, chopped

2 garlic cloves, crushed

1 red chilli, seeded and finely chopped

175g/6oz/2$^1$/4 cups mushrooms, sliced

2 sticks celery, chopped

225g/8oz/generous 1 cup long grain brown rice

450ml/$^3$/4 pint/scant 2 cups chicken or vegetable stock

150ml/$^1$/4 pint/$^2$/3 cup white wine

225g/8oz chicken breast fillet, skinned and diced

400g/14oz can red kidney beans, drained

200g/7oz can corn kernels

115g/4oz/$^2$/3 cup sultanas (golden raisins)

175g/6oz small broccoli florets

30–45ml/2–3 tbsp chopped fresh mixed herbs

salt and ground black pepper

1 Put the onion, garlic, chilli, mushrooms, celery, rice, stock and wine in a pan. Cover, bring to the boil and simmer for 15 minutes.

---

### COOK'S TIP

Use 5ml/1 tsp hot chilli powder in place of the fresh chilli, if you like.

---

# Stir-fried Chicken with Mangetouts

*Juicy chicken stir-fried with mangetouts, cashew nuts and water chestnuts.*

### INGREDIENTS

*Serves 4*

30ml/2 tbsp sesame oil

90ml/6 tbsp lemon juice

1 garlic clove, crushed

1cm/$^{1}/_{2}$ in piece fresh root ginger, peeled and grated

5ml/1 tsp clear honey

450g/1lb chicken breast fillets, skinned and cut into strips

115g/4oz mangetouts (snow peas), trimmed

30ml/2 tbsp groundnut (peanut) oil

50g/2oz/$^{1}/_{2}$ cup cashew nuts

6 spring onions (scallions), cut into strips

225g/8oz can water chestnuts, drained and thinly sliced

salt

saffron rice, to serve

1 Mix together the sesame oil, lemon juice, garlic, ginger and honey in a shallow non-metallic dish. Add the chicken and mix well. Cover and leave to marinate for at least 3–4 hours.

2 Blanch the mangetouts in boiling salted water for 1 minute. Drain and refresh under cold running water.

3 Drain the chicken strips and reserve the marinade. Heat the groundnut oil in a wok or large frying pan, add the cashew nuts and stir-fry for about 1–2 minutes, or until golden brown. Remove the cashew nuts from the wok or frying pan using a slotted spoon and set aside.

4 Add the chicken and stir-fry for 3–4 minutes, or until golden brown. Add the spring onions, mangetouts, water chestnuts and the reserved marinade. Cook for a few minutes, until the chicken is cooked through and the sauce is bubbling and hot. Stir in the cashew nuts and serve with saffron rice.

# Spicy Chicken Stir-fry

*The chicken is marinated in an aromatic blend of spices and then stir-fried with crisp vegetables. If you find it too spicy, serve with a spoonful of sour cream or yogurt. This dish is just as delicious hot or cold.*

### INGREDIENTS

*Serves 4*

2.5ml/$^1$/$_2$ tsp ground turmeric
2.5ml/$^1$/$_2$ tsp ground ginger
5ml/1 tsp each salt and ground
   black pepper
10ml/2 tsp ground cumin
15ml/1 tbsp ground coriander
15ml/1 tbsp caster (superfine) sugar
450g/1lb chicken breast fillet, skinned
1 bunch spring onions (scallions)
4 celery sticks
2 red (bell) peppers
1 yellow (bell) pepper
175g/6oz courgettes (zucchini)
175g/6oz mangetouts (snow peas) or
   sugar snap peas
about 45ml/3 tbsp sunflower oil
15ml/1 tbsp lime juice
15ml/1 tbsp clear honey

1 Mix together the turmeric, ginger, salt, pepper, cumin, coriander and sugar in a bowl until well combined.

2 Cut the chicken into bitesize strips. Add to the spice mixture and stir to coat the chicken pieces thoroughly. Set aside.

3 Prepare the vegetables. Cut the spring onions, celery and peppers into 5cm/2in long, thin strips. Cut the courgettes at a slight angle into thin rounds and trim the mangetouts or sugar snap peas.

4 Heat 30ml/2 tbsp of the oil in a large frying pan or wok. Stir-fry the chicken in batches until cooked through and golden brown, adding a little more oil if necessary. Remove from the pan and keep warm.

5 Add a little more oil to the pan and cook the onions, celery, peppers and courgettes over a medium heat for about 8–10 minutes, or until beginning to soften and turn golden. Add the mangetouts or sugar snap peas and cook for a further 2 minutes.

6 Return the chicken to the pan, with the lime juice and honey. Cook for 2 minutes. Adjust the seasoning and serve immediately.

# Stir-fried Turkey, Broccoli and Mushrooms

*This is a really easy, tasty dish, which*
*works well with chicken too.*

INGREDIENTS

*Serves 4*

115g/4oz broccoli florets

4 spring onions (scallions)

5ml/1 tsp cornflour (cornstarch)

45ml/3 tbsp oyster sauce

15ml/1 tbsp dark soy sauce

120ml/4fl oz/$^{1}/_{2}$ cup chicken stock

10ml/2 tsp lemon juice

45ml/3 tbsp groundnut (peanut) oil

450g/1lb turkey steaks, cut into strips
   about 5mm x5cm/$^{1}/_{4}$ x 2in

1 small onion, chopped

2 garlic cloves, crushed

10ml/2 tsp grated fresh root ginger

115g/4oz/1$^{1}/_{2}$ cups fresh shiitake
   mushrooms, sliced

75g/3oz baby corn, halved lengthways

15ml/1 tbsp sesame oil

salt and ground black pepper

egg noodles, to serve

1 Divide the broccoli florets into
smaller sprigs and cut the stalks
into thin diagonal slices.

2 Finely chop the white parts of
the spring onions and slice the
green parts into thin shreds.

3 In a bowl, blend together the
cornflour, oyster sauce, soy
sauce, stock and lemon juice.
Set aside.

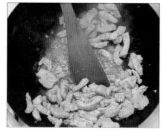

4 Heat a wok until it is hot, add
30ml/2 tbsp of the groundnut
oil and swirl it around. Add the
turkey and stir-fry for about
2 minutes, or until it is golden and
crispy at the edges, and cooked
through. Remove the turkey and
keep it warm.

5 Add the remaining groundnut
oil to the wok and stir-fry the
chopped onion, garlic and ginger
over a medium heat for about
1 minute. Increase the heat to high,
add the broccoli, mushrooms and
corn and stir-fry for 2 minutes.

6 Return the turkey to the wok,
then add the cornflour mixture
with the chopped spring onion and
seasoning. Cook, stirring, for about
1 minute, or until the sauce has
thickened. Stir in the sesame oil.
Serve immediately on a bed of egg
noodles with the finely shredded
spring onion scattered on top.

# Tequila Chicken

*In Mexico, tequila is a popular drink, and here it is combined with sherry, apples, plantains and raisins to give a most unusual sweet-and-sour flavour to chicken. Serve with rice or flour tortillas to mop up the sauce, if you like.*

### INGREDIENTS

*Serves 4*

150g/5oz/scant 1 cup raisins
120ml/4fl oz/$^1$/$_2$ cup sherry
115g/4oz/1 cup plain (all-purpose) flour
2.5ml/$^1$/$_2$ tsp salt
2.5ml/$^1$/$_2$ tsp ground black pepper
45ml/3 tbsp vegetable oil
8 skinless chicken thighs
1 onion, halved and thinly sliced
3 garlic cloves, crushed
2 tart eating apples, peeled, cored
   and diced
115g/4oz/1 cup flaked (sliced) almonds
1 ripe plantain, peeled and sliced
350ml/12fl oz/1$^1$/$_2$ cups chicken stock
250ml/8fl oz/1 cup tequila
fresh herbs, chopped, to garnish (optional)

1 Put the raisins in a bowl and pour the sherry over. Set aside to plump up. Season the flour with the salt and pepper and spread it out on a large, flat dish or soup plate. Heat 30ml/2 tbsp of the oil in a large frying pan. Dip each chicken thigh in turn in the seasoned flour, then fry in the hot oil until browned, turning occasionally. Drain on kitchen paper.

2 Heat the remaining oil. Add the onions and garlic and cook for 2–3 minutes.

3 Add the diced apples to the onion mixture with the almonds and plantain slices. Cook, stirring occasionally, for 3–4 minutes, then add the raisins with any remaining sherry. Add the chicken to the pan.

4 Pour the stock and tequila over the chicken mixture. Cover the pan with a lid and cook for 15 minutes, then take off the lid and cook for 10 minutes more or until the sauce has reduced by about half.

5 Check that the chicken thighs are cooked by lifting one out of the pan and piercing it in the thickest part with a sharp knife or skewer. Any juices that come out should be clear. If necessary, cook the chicken for a little longer before serving, sprinkled with chopped fresh herbs, if desired.

# Chicken with Mixed Vegetables

*This delectable dish is a riot of colour with a variety of contrasting textures and tastes.*

*Serves 4*

350g/12oz chicken breast fillets, skinned
20ml/4 tsp vegetable oil
300ml/$^1$/$_2$ pint/1$^1$/$_4$ cups chicken stock
75g/3oz/$^3$/$_4$ cup drained, canned
    straw mushrooms
50g/2oz/$^1$/$_2$ cup drained, canned bamboo
    shoots, sliced
50g/2oz/$^1$/$_3$ cup drained, canned water
    chestnuts, sliced
1 small carrot, sliced
50g/2oz/$^1$/$_2$ cup mangetouts (snow peas)
15ml/1 tbsp dry sherry
15ml/1 tbsp oyster sauce
5ml/1 tsp caster (superfine) sugar
5ml/1 tsp cornflour (cornstarch)
15ml/1 tbsp cold water
salt and ground white pepper

1 Put the chicken in a shallow bowl. Add 5ml/1 tsp of the oil, 1.5ml/$^1$/$_4$ tsp salt and a pinch of pepper. Cover and set aside for 10 minutes in a cool place.

2 Bring the stock to the boil in a pan. Add the chicken and cook for 12 minutes, or until tender and cooked through. Drain and slice, reserving 75ml/5 tbsp of the stock.

3 Heat the remaining oil in a non-stick frying pan or wok, add all the vegetables and stir-fry for 2 minutes. Stir in the sherry, oyster sauce, caster sugar and reserved stock. Add the chicken to the pan and cook for 2 minutes.

4 Mix the cornflour to a paste with the water. Add the mixture to the pan and cook, stirring, until the sauce thickens slightly. Season to taste with salt and pepper and serve immediately.

# Tandoori Chicken Kebabs

*This dish originates from the plains of the Punjab at the foot of the Himalayas, where food is traditionally cooked in clay ovens known as tandoors – hence the name.*

*Serves 4*

4 chicken breast fillets, about 175g/6oz
  each, skinned
15ml/1 tbsp lemon juice
45ml/3 tbsp tandoori paste
45ml/3 tbsp natural (plain) yogurt
1 garlic clove, crushed
30ml/2 tbsp chopped fresh coriander
  (cilantro)
1 small onion, cut into wedges and
  separated into layers
a little oil, for brushing
salt and ground black pepper
fresh coriander sprigs, to garnish
pilau rice and naan bread, to serve

1 Chop the chicken breasts into 2.5cm/1in cubes, place in a bowl and add the lemon juice, tandoori paste, yogurt, garlic, coriander and seasoning. Cover and leave to marinate in the refrigerator for at least 2–3 hours. Soak four wooden skewers in water for 30 minutes.

2 Preheat the grill (broiler). Thread alternate pieces of chicken and onion on to the skewers.

3 Brush the onions with a little oil, lay the kebabs on a grill rack and cook under a high heat for about 10–12 minutes, turning once, until cooked through. Garnish the kebabs with fresh coriander and serve immediately with pilau rice and naan bread.

# Chinese Chicken with Cashew Nuts

*Marinated chicken is quickly cooked with cashew nuts, spring onions and egg noodles in this tasty stir-fried dish.*

*Serves 4*

4 chicken breast fillets, about 175g/6oz
  each, skinned and sliced into strips
3 garlic cloves, crushed
60ml/4 tbsp soy sauce
30ml/2 tbsp cornflour (cornstarch)
225g/8oz dried egg noodles
45ml/3 tbsp groundnut (peanut) or
  sunflower oil
15ml/1 tbsp sesame oil
115g/4oz/1 cup roasted cashew nuts
6 spring onions (scallions), cut into
  5cm/2in pieces and halved lengthways
spring onion curls and a little chopped red
  chilli, to garnish

1 Mix the chicken, garlic, soy sauce and cornflour in a bowl. Cover and chill for 30 minutes.

2 Bring a pan of water to the boil and add the noodles. Turn off the heat and leave to stand for 5 minutes. Drain well and reserve.

3 Heat the oils in a large frying pan and add the chicken and marinade. Stir-fry for 3–4 minutes, or until golden brown and done.

4 Add the cashew nuts and spring onions to the pan and stir-fry for 2–3 minutes.

5 Add the drained noodles and stir-fry for a further 2 minutes. Serve immediately, garnished with the spring onion curls and chopped red chilli.

# Lemon Chicken Stir-fry

*This mouthwatering dish is cooked in minutes. As with all stir-fries, it is essential to prepare all the ingredients before you begin so they are ready to cook.*

INGREDIENTS

Serves 4

4 chicken breast fillets, skinned
15ml/1 tbsp light soy sauce
75ml/5 tbsp cornflour (cornstarch)
1 bunch spring onions (scallions)
1 lemon
1 garlic clove, crushed
15ml/1 tbsp caster (superfine) sugar
about 30ml/2 tbsp sherry
about 150ml/$^1$/4 pint/$^2$/3 cup chicken stock
60ml/4 tbsp olive oil
salt and ground black pepper

1 Divide the chicken breasts into two natural fillets. Place each between two sheets of clear film (plastic wrap) and flatten to 5mm/$^1$/4 in thick with a rolling pin.

2 Cut into 2.5cm/1in strips across the grain of the fillets. Put in a bowl with the soy sauce and toss to coat. Sprinkle on 60ml/4 tbsp of the cornflour, and toss.

3 Cut the spring onions diagonally into 1cm/$^1$/2 in pieces. With a swivel vegetable peeler, remove the lemon rind in thin strips and cut into fine shreds, or grate finely. Squeeze the lemon and reserve the juice. Blend the remaining cornflour into a paste with a little water.

4 Heat the oil in a wok or large frying pan and cook the chicken very quickly in small batches for 3–4 minutes, or until golden and cooked through. Remove to a dish and keep warm.

5 Add the spring onions and garlic to the pan and cook for 2 minutes.

6 Add the sugar, sherry, stock, lemon juice and cornflour mixture, with the chicken, and bring to the boil, stirring until thickened. Add more sherry or stock if necessary, and stir until the chicken is evenly covered with sauce. Season and reheat for about 2 minutes.

# Chicken with Lemon Sauce

*Succulent chicken with a refreshing lemony sauce is a sure winner.*

*Serves 4*

4 small chicken breast fillets, skinned

5ml/1 tsp sesame oil

15ml/1 tbsp dry sherry

1 egg white, lightly beaten

30ml/2 tbsp cornflour (cornstarch)

15ml/1 tbsp vegetable oil

salt and ground white pepper

chopped coriander (cilantro) leaves, spring
  onions (scallions)and lemon wedges,
  to garnish

*For the sauce*

45ml/3 tbsp fresh lemon juice

30ml/2 tbsp lime cordial

45ml/3 tbsp caster (superfine) sugar

10ml/2 tsp cornflour

90ml/6 tbsp cold water

1 Place the chicken in a shallow bowl. Mix the sesame oil with the sherry and add 2.5ml/¹/₂ tsp salt and 1.5ml/¹/₄ tsp pepper. Pour over the chicken, cover and marinate for 15 minutes.

2 Mix together the egg white and cornflour. Add the mixture to the chicken and turn to coat thoroughly. Heat the vegetable oil in a non-stick frying pan or wok and fry the chicken fillets for about 15 minutes, or until the fillets are cooked through and golden brown on both sides.

3 Meanwhile, make the sauce. Combine all the ingredients in a small pan. Add 1.5ml/¹/₄ tsp salt. Bring to the boil over a low heat, stirring constantly until the sauce is smooth and has thickened slightly.

4 Cut the chicken into pieces and arrange on a warm serving plate. Pour the sauce over the chicken, garnish with the coriander leaves, spring onions and lemon wedges and serve.

# Chilli Chicken Couscous

*Couscous makes a good base for chicken, chickpeas and vegetables, spiced up with a kick of chilli.*

INGREDIENTS

Serves 4

225g/8oz/³/4 cup couscous
1 litre/1³/4 pints/4 cups boiling water
5ml/1 tsp olive oil
400g/14oz chicken without
   skin and bone, diced
1 yellow (bell) pepper, seeded and sliced
2 large courgettes (zucchini), sliced thickly
1 small green chilli, thinly sliced,
   or 5ml/1 tsp chilli sauce
1 large tomato, diced
425g/15oz can chickpeas, drained
salt and ground black pepper
coriander (cilantro) or parsley sprigs
   to garnish

1 Place the couscous in a large bowl and pour over the boiling water. Cover and leave to stand for 30 minutes.

2 Heat the oil in a large, non-stick pan and stir-fry the chicken quickly to seal, then reduce the heat.

3 Stir in the pepper, courgettes and chilli or sauce and cook for about 10 minutes, or until the vegetables are softened.

4 Stir in the tomato and chickpeas, then add the couscous. Adjust the seasoning and stir over a medium heat until hot. Serve garnished with sprigs of fresh coriander or parsley.

# Chicken with Beans and Aubergine

*Sliced aubergine layered with beans and chicken, and then topped with yogurt, makes a hearty evening meal.*

INGREDIENTS

Serves 4

1 medium aubergine (eggplant),
   thinly sliced
15ml/1 tbsp olive oil, for brushing
450g/1lb chicken breast fillets, skinned
   and diced
1 medium onion, chopped
400g/14oz can chopped tomatoes
425g/15oz can red kidney beans, drained
15ml/1 tbsp paprika
15ml/1 tbsp chopped fresh thyme,
   or 5ml/1 tsp dried
5ml/1 tsp chilli sauce
350g/12oz/1¹/2 cups Greek (US strained
   plain) yogurt
2.5ml/¹/2 tsp freshly grated nutmeg
salt and ground black pepper

1 Arrange the aubergine in a colander and sprinkle with salt. Leave the aubergine for 30 minutes, then rinse and pat dry.

2 Preheat the oven to 190°C/375°F/Gas 5. Brush a non-stick pan with oil and fry the aubergine in batches, turning once, until golden.

3 Remove the aubergine, add the chicken and onion to the pan, and cook until lightly browned. Stir in the tomatoes, beans, paprika, thyme, chilli sauce and seasoning. In a bowl, mix together the yogurt and grated nutmeg.

4 Layer the chicken and aubergine in an ovenproof dish, finishing with aubergine. Spread the yogurt evenly over the top and bake for 50–60 minutes, or until golden.

# Chicken with Prosciutto and Cheese

*In this Italian dish, chicken is filled with prosciutto and basil and topped with a slice of Fontina cheese before it is baked. The result is absolutely wonderful.*

### INGREDIENTS

Serves 4

2 thin slices of prosciutto
4 part-boned chicken breast
    portions, skinned
4 sprigs of basil
30ml/2 tbsp olive oil
15g/$^1$/$_2$ oz/1 tbsp butter
120ml/4fl oz/$^1$/$_2$ cup dry white wine
2 thin slices of Fontina cheese
salt and ground black pepper
young salad leaves, to serve

1 Preheat the oven to 200°C/400°F/Gas 6. Lightly oil a baking dish.

2 Cut the prosciutto slices in half crossways. Open out a slit in the centre of each chicken breast, and fill each cavity with half a ham slice and a basil sprig.

> COOK'S TIP
>
> Instead of Fontina cheese you could use a Swiss mountain cheese, such as Gruyère or Emmenthal. Ask for the cheese to be sliced thinly at the delicatessen counter.

3 Heat the oil and butter in a wide, heavy frying pan until foaming. Cook the chicken breasts over a medium heat for 1–2 minutes on each side until they change colour. Transfer to the baking dish. Add the wine to the pan juices, stir until sizzling, then pour over the chicken and season to taste.

4 Top each chicken breast with a half slice of Fontina. Bake for 20 minutes, or until the chicken is cooked through. Serve hot, with young salad leaves.

# Devilled Chicken

*Chicken is marinated in lemon rind, garlic and chillies before it is quickly cooked. It can be prepared in advance, and makes a useful and quick midweek meal.*

### INGREDIENTS

Serves 4

120ml/4fl oz/$^1$/$_2$ cup olive oil
finely grated rind and juice of
    1 large lemon
2 garlic cloves, finely chopped
10ml/2 tsp finely chopped or crumbled
    dried red chillies
12 skinless, boneless chicken thighs, each
    cut into 3 or 4 pieces
salt and ground black pepper
flat leaf parsley leaves, to garnish
lemon wedges, to serve

1 Make a marinade by mixing the oil, lemon rind and juice, garlic and chillies in a large, shallow glass or china dish. Add salt and pepper to taste. Whisk well, then add the chicken pieces, turning to coat with the marinade. Cover and marinate in the refrigerator for at least 4 hours, or preferably overnight.

2 When ready to cook, prepare the barbecue or preheat the grill (broiler) and thread the chicken pieces on to eight oiled metal skewers. Cook for 6–8 minutes, turning frequently, until cooked through. Garnish with parsley leaves and serve hot, with lemon wedges for squeezing.

# *Layered Chicken and Mushroom Bake*

*A delicious and moist combination of chicken, vegetables and gravy in a simple, one-dish meal topped with crunchy slices of potato.*

INGREDIENTS

*Serves 4–6*

15ml/1 tbsp olive oil

4 large chicken breast fillets, skinned and
  cut into chunks

1 leek, finely sliced into rings

50g/2oz/$^1$/4 cup butter

25g/1oz/$^1$/4 cup plain (all-purpose) flour

475ml/16fl oz/2 cups milk

5ml/1 tsp wholegrain mustard

1 carrot, very finely diced

225g/8oz/3 cups button (white)
  mushrooms

900g/2lb maincrop potatoes, finely sliced

salt and ground black pepper

1 Preheat the oven to 180°C/
350°F/Gas 4.

2 Heat the oil in a large pan. Fry the chicken for 5 minutes, or until browned. Add the leek and fry for a further 5 minutes.

3 Add half the butter to the pan and allow it to melt. Sprinkle the flour over and stir in the milk. Cook over a low heat until thickened, then stir in the mustard.

4 Add the diced carrot with the mushrooms. Season to taste.

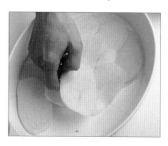

5 Line the base of a 1.75 litre/ 3 pint/7½ cup ovenproof dish with potato slices. Spoon one-third of the chicken mixture over. Cover with another layer of potatoes. Repeat layering, finishing with a layer of potatoes. Dot with the remaining butter.

6 Bake in the oven for 1½ hours, covering with foil after 30 minutes' cooking time. Serve hot.

COOK'S TIP

The liquid from the mushrooms keeps the chicken moist and the potatoes help to mop up any excess juices.

# Chicken with Potato Dumplings

*Poached chicken in a creamy sauce topped with light herb and potato dumplings makes a delicately flavoured yet hearty meal.*

INGREDIENTS

*Serves 6*

1 onion, chopped
300ml/$^1$/$_2$ pint/1$^1$/$_4$ cups vegetable stock
120ml/4fl oz/$^1$/$_2$ cup white wine
4 large chicken breast fillets, skinned
300ml/$^1$/$_2$ pint/1$^1$/$_4$ cups single
   (light) cream
15ml/1 tbsp chopped fresh tarragon
salt and ground black pepper

*For the dumplings*
225g/8oz maincrop potatoes, boiled
   and mashed
175g/6oz/1$^1$/$_4$ cups suet (US chilled,
   grated shortening)
115g/4oz/1 cup self-raising
   (self-rising) flour
50ml/2fl oz/$^1$/$_4$ cup water
30ml/2 tbsp chopped mixed fresh herbs

1 Place the onion, stock and wine in a deep pan. Add the chicken, cover and simmer for 20 minutes.

2 Remove the chicken from the stock, cut into chunks and reserve. Strain the stock and discard the onion. Reduce the stock by one-third over a high heat. Stir in the cream and tarragon and simmer until just thickened. Stir in the chicken and season with salt and ground black pepper.

3 Spoon into a 900ml/1$^1$/$_2$ pint/ 3$^3$/$_4$ cup ovenproof dish.

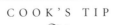

COOK'S TIP

Do not reduce the sauce too much before it is cooked in the oven as the dumplings absorb quite a lot of the liquid.

4 Preheat the oven to 190°C/ 375°F/Gas 5. Mix together the dumpling ingredients, add salt and pepper, and stir in the water to make a soft dough. Divide into six and shape into balls with floured hands. Place on top of the chicken mixture and bake uncovered for 30 minutes.

# Chicken Koftas in Tomato Sauce

*Meatballs in a tomato sauce make an ideal supper. Serve with pasta and grated cheese, if you like.*

INGREDIENTS

*Serves 4*

1 chicken, about 675g/1¹/₂lb
1 onion, grated
1 garlic clove, crushed
15ml/1 tbsp chopped fresh parsley
2.5ml/¹/₂ tsp ground cumin
2.5ml/¹/₂ tsp ground coriander
1 egg, beaten
seasoned flour, for rolling
50ml/2fl oz/¹/₄ cup olive oil
salt and ground black pepper
chopped fresh parsley, to garnish

*For the sauce*

15g/¹/₂ oz/1 tbsp butter
15g/¹/₂ oz/2 tbsp plain (all-purpose) flour
250ml/8fl oz/1 cup chicken stock
400g/14oz can chopped tomatoes, with the juice
5ml/1 tsp caster (superfine) sugar
1.5ml/¹/₄ tsp dried mixed herbs

1 Remove any skin and bone from the chicken and mince (grind) or chop finely.

2 Put into a bowl together with the onion, garlic, parsley, spices, seasoning and beaten egg.

3 Mix together thoroughly and shape into 24 × 4cm/1¹/₂in balls. Roll lightly in seasoned flour.

4 Heat the oil in a frying pan and brown the balls in small batches (this keeps the oil temperature hot and prevents the flour becoming soggy). Remove and drain on kitchen paper. There is no need to cook the balls any further at this stage as they will cook in the tomato sauce. Preheat the oven to 180°C/350°F/Gas 4.

5 To make the tomato sauce, melt the butter in a large pan. Add the flour, and then blend in the stock and tomatoes along with their juice. Add the caster sugar and mixed herbs. Bring to the boil, cover and simmer for 10–15 minutes.

6 Place the browned chicken balls into a shallow ovenproof dish and pour over the tomato sauce, cover with foil and bake in the preheated oven for 30–40 minutes. Adjust the seasoning to taste and sprinkle with parsley.

# Chicken and Tomato Hot-pot

*Here is another chicken meatball recipe, this time with a delicious tomato and rice sauce.*

### INGREDIENTS

*Serves 4*

25g/1oz white bread, crust removed
30ml/2 tbsp milk
1 garlic clove, crushed
2.5ml/$^1$/$_2$ tsp caraway seeds
225g/8oz/2 cups minced (ground) chicken
1 egg white
350ml/12fl oz/1$^1$/$_2$ cups chicken stock
400g/14oz can plum tomatoes
15ml/1 tbsp tomato purée (paste)
90g/3$^1$/$_2$ oz/$^1$/$_2$ cup easy-cook rice
salt and ground black pepper
15ml/1 tbsp chopped fresh basil,
   to garnish
carrot and courgette (zucchini) ribbons,
   to serve

4 Put the chicken stock, tomatoes and tomato purée into a large, heavy pan and bring to the boil.

5 Add the rice, stir and cook briskly for about 5 minutes. Turn the heat down to a simmer.

6 Meanwhile, shape the chicken mixture into 16 small balls. Carefully drop them into the tomato stock, and simmer for a further 8–10 minutes, or until the chicken balls and rice are cooked. Garnish with the basil, and serve with carrot and courgette ribbons.

1 Cut the bread into small cubes and put into a mixing bowl. Sprinkle over the milk and leave to soak for 5 minutes.

2 Add the garlic clove, caraway seeds, chicken, salt and freshly ground black pepper to the bread. Mix together well.

3 Whisk the egg white until stiff, then fold, half at a time, into the chicken mixture. Chill for 10 minutes in the refrigerator.

# Chicken and Chanterelle Pudding

*Chanterelle mushrooms are combined with chicken, mustard and thyme to make a flavourful filling for this traditional-style savoury pudding.*

### INGREDIENTS

*Serves 4*

1 medium onion, chopped
1 celery stick, sliced
10ml/2 tsp chopped fresh thyme
30ml/2 tbsp vegetable oil
2 chicken breast fillets, skinned
115g/4oz fresh chanterelle mushrooms,
    trimmed and sliced, or 15g/$^1$/2 oz/
    $^1$/4 cup dried, soaked in warm water
    for 20 minutes
40g/1$^1$/2oz/$^1$/3 cup plain (all-purpose) flour
300ml/$^1$/2 pint/1$^1$/4 cups chicken
    stock, boiling
5ml/1 tsp Dijon mustard
10ml/2 tsp wine vinegar
salt and ground black pepper

*For the dough*
350g/12oz/3 cups self-raising (self-
    rising) flour
2.5ml/$^1$/2 tsp salt
150g/5oz/10 tbsp chilled unsalted (sweet)
    butter, diced
75ml/5 tbsp cold water

1 Fry the onion, celery and thyme gently in oil without colouring. Cut the chicken into bitesize pieces, add to the pan with the mushrooms and cook briefly. Stir in the flour, then remove from the heat.

2 Stir in the stock. Return to the heat, simmer, stirring, to thicken, then add the mustard, vinegar and seasoning. Set aside to cool.

3 Sift the flour and salt into a bowl. Add the butter, then rub together until it resembles bread-crumbs. Add the water and mix.

4 Roll out on a floured surface into a rectangle 25 x 30cm/ 10 x 12in. Dampen a piece of muslin (cheesecloth) about twice as big as the dough. Place the dough on the muslin. Spread the chicken filling over the dough and roll up from the short end using the muslin to help. Enclose in muslin and tie each end with string.

5 Lower the pudding into a pan of boiling water, cover and simmer for 1$^1$/2 hours. Lift out, untie the string and turn on to a serving platter. Slice and serve.

# Turkey Escalopes with Capers

*Thin slices of turkey are marinated then coated in breadcrumbs and cooked very quickly. Lemon and capers add a piquancy that goes perfectly with the escalopes.*

INGREDIENTS

*Serves 2*

4 thin turkey breast escalopes
   (US scallops) (about 85g/3oz each)
1 large unwaxed lemon
2.5ml/$\frac{1}{2}$ tsp chopped fresh sage
60–75ml/4–5 tbsp extra virgin olive oil
50g/2oz/$\frac{3}{4}$ cup fine dry breadcrumbs
15ml/1 tbsp capers, rinsed and drained
salt and ground black pepper
sage leaves and lemon wedges, to garnish

1 Place the turkey escalopes between two sheets of baking parchment or clear film (plastic wrap) and pound with the flat side of a meat hammer or roll with a rolling pin to flatten to about a 5mm/$\frac{1}{4}$ in thickness.

2 With a vegetable peeler, remove four pieces of lemon rind. Cut them into thin julienne strips, cover with clear film and set aside. Grate the remainder of the lemon rind and squeeze the lemon. Put the grated rind in a large, shallow dish and add the sage, salt and pepper. Stir in 15ml/1 tbsp of the lemon juice, reserving the rest, and about 15ml/1 tbsp of the olive oil, then add the turkey, turn to coat and marinate for 30 minutes.

3 Place the breadcrumbs in another shallow dish and dip the escalopes in the crumbs, coating both sides. In a heavy frying pan heat 30ml/2 tbsp of the olive oil over a high heat, add the escalopes and cook for 2–3 minutes, turning once, until golden and cooked through. Transfer to two warmed plates and keep warm.

4 Wipe out the pan, add the remaining oil, the lemon julienne and the capers, stirring, and heat through. Spoon a little sauce over the turkey and garnish with sage leaves and lemon.

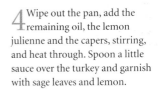

# Turkey Croquettes

3 Meanwhile, to make the sauce, heat the oil in a frying pan and fry the onion for 5 minutes, or until softened. Add the tomatoes and purée, stir and simmer for 10 minutes. Stir in the parsley, season with salt and pepper and keep the sauce warm until needed.

*A crisp patty of smoked turkey, mixed with mashed potato and spring onions, and rolled in breadcrumbs, makes a tasty midweek supper served with a tangy tomato sauce.*

### INGREDIENTS

*Serves 4*

450g/1lb maincrop potatoes, diced

3 eggs

30ml/2 tbsp milk

175g/6oz smoked turkey rashers (strips), finely chopped

2 spring onions (scallions), finely sliced

115g/4oz/2 cups fresh white breadcrumbs

vegetable oil, for deep-frying

salt and ground black pepper

*For the sauce*

15ml/1 tbsp olive oil

1 onion, finely chopped

400g/14oz can tomatoes, drained

30ml/2 tbsp tomato purée (paste)

15ml/1 tbsp chopped fresh parsley

1 Boil the potatoes for 20 minutes, or until tender. Drain and return to the pan over a low heat to make sure all the excess water evaporates.

2 Mash the potatoes with 2 eggs and the milk. Season well with salt and pepper. Stir in the turkey and spring onions. Chill for 1 hour.

4 Remove the potato mixture from the refrigerator and divide it into eight pieces. Shape each piece into a sausage shape and dip in the remaining beaten egg and then in the breadcrumbs.

5 Heat the vegetable oil in a pan or deep-fryer to 175°C/330°F. Test by dropping a cube of day-old bread into the hot oil: it should sink, rise to the surface and sizzle in 10 seconds. Deep-fry the croquettes for 5 minutes, or until golden and crisp. Serve with the sauce.

# Turkey or Chicken Schnitzel

*A schnitzel is a pounded-flat, crisp-coated, fried steak of turkey, chicken or veal. It makes an ideal quick supper as it cooks very quickly.*

### INGREDIENTS

*Serves 4*

4 turkey or chicken breast fillets (about 175g/6oz each), skinned

juice of 1 lemon

2 garlic cloves, chopped

plain (all-purpose) flour, for dusting

1–2 eggs

15ml/1 tbsp water

about 50g/2oz/¹/4 cup matzo meal

a mixture of vegetable and olive oil, for shallow frying

salt, ground black pepper and paprika

lemon wedges and a selection of vegetables, to serve

1 Place each piece of meat between two sheets of baking parchment and pound with the end of a rolling pin until it is about half its original thickness.

2 In a bowl, combine the lemon juice, garlic, salt and pepper. Coat the meat in it, then leave to marinate.

3 Meanwhile, arrange three wide plates or shallow dishes in a row. Fill one plate or dish with flour, beat the egg and water together in another and mix the matzo meal, salt, pepper and paprika together on the third.

4 Working quickly, dip each fillet into the flour, then the egg, then the matzo meal. Pat everything in well, then arrange the crumbed fillets on a plate and chill for at least 30 minutes, and up to 2 hours.

5 In a large, heavy frying pan, heat the oil to 190°C/375°F or until a cube of day-old bread dropped into the oil turns golden brown in 30–60 seconds. Carefully add the crumbed fillets (in batches if necessary) and fry until golden brown and cooked through, turning once. Remove and drain on kitchen paper. Serve immediately with lemon wedges and vegetables.

# PASTRIES
# & PIES

Versatile chicken makes a delicious filling for pastries or pies.
In this chapter is a collection of inspiring recipes from around the world
using a wide selection of flavourings in as many varied ways as possible.
For example, dainty filo pastry tartlets contain the delicate combination
of smoked chicken and peach mayonnaise, and chicken combined with
cheese and leeks is enclosed in an attractively braided jalousie.
You are sure to find the perfect pastry dish in this chapter.

# Turkey and Cranberry Bundles

*After the traditional Christmas or Thanksgiving meal, it is easy to end up with lots of turkey leftovers. These delicious filo-pastry parcels are a marvellous way of using up the small pieces of cooked turkey.*

### INGREDIENTS

*Serves 6*

450g/1lb cooked turkey, cut into chunks
115g/4oz/1 cup diced Brie
30ml/2 tbsp cranberry sauce
30ml/2 tbsp chopped fresh parsley
9 sheets filo pastry, 45 x 28cm/18 x 11in
    each, thawed if frozen
50g/2oz/¼ cup butter, melted
salt and ground black pepper
green salad, to serve

1 Preheat the oven to 200°C/400°F/Gas 6. Mix the turkey, diced Brie, cranberry sauce and chopped parsley in a large bowl. Season with salt and pepper.

2 Cut the filo sheets in half widthways to make 18 squares.

3 Layer three pieces of pastry together, brushing each with a little melted butter so that they stick together. Keep the unused pastry covered with a clean, damp dishtowel to prevent drying. Repeat with the remaining filo squares to give six pieces.

4 Divide the turkey mixture among the pastry, making neat piles on each piece. Gather up the pastry to enclose the filling in neat bundles. Place on a baking sheet, brush with melted butter and bake for 20 minutes, or until the pastry is crisp and golden. Serve hot or warm with a green salad.

---

### VARIATIONS

To make Chicken and Stilton Bundles, use cooked chicken in place of the turkey and white Stilton instead of Brie. Replace the cranberry sauce with mango chutney.

# Tunisian Chicken Parcels

*You can make these little parcels into any shape you like, but the most important thing is to encase the egg white before it starts to run out.*

*Serves 6*

45ml/3 tbsp butter, melted
1 small red onion, finely chopped
150g/5oz chicken or turkey breast fillet,
    minced (ground)
1 large garlic clove, crushed
juice of $^1/_2$ lemon
30ml/2 tbsp chopped fresh parsley
12 sheets of filo pastry, each about
    15 x 25cm/6 x 10in, thawed if frozen
6 small eggs, such as bantam, pheasant or
    guinea fowl
oil, for deep-frying
salt and ground black pepper

1 Melt half the butter in a pan and sauté the onion for about 3 minutes, or until softened. Add the meat, garlic, lemon juice, parsley and seasoning, and cook, stirring, for 2–3 minutes, or until the meat is just cooked. Set aside to cool.

2 Place one sheet of pastry lengthways on the work surface and brush with melted butter; top with a second sheet. Keep the unused pastry covered with a clean, damp dishtowel. Brush the edges with butter and place one-sixth of the mixture close to the bottom corner of the pastry. Flatten the filling, making a hollow in it.

3 Crack an egg into the hollow and be ready to fold up the pastry immediately so the egg white does not run out. Lift the right-hand corner and fold it over the filling and seal quickly, then fold the bottom left corner straight up and then fold the bottom left corner up to the right edge, forming a triangle.

4 Use the remaining pastry sheets and filling to make another five parcels, then heat the oil in a frying pan until a cube of day-old bread turns golden in about 1½ minutes. Cook the pastries, two or three at a time, until golden. Lift them out of the pan with a slotted spoon and drain on kitchen paper. Serve hot or cold.

# *Smoked Chicken with Peach Mayonnaise*

2 Place a round of pastry in each tin and brush with a little butter. Add another round of pastry, brush each again with butter, then add a third round of pastry.

3 Bake the tartlets for 5 minutes, or until the pastry is golden brown. Leave in the tins for a few moments before transferring to a wire rack to cool.

4 Place the peaches in a bowl and pour in boiling water to cover. Leave to stand for 30–60 seconds (the riper the peaches, the quicker their skins loosen). Use a slotted spoon to remove each peach from the water. Slit the skin with the point of a knife, then slip it off the fruit. Remove the stones (pits) and chop the flesh.

*These are attractive and, because smoked chicken is sold ready cooked, they require the minimum of culinary effort. The filling can be prepared a day in advance and chilled, but do not fill the pastry cases until you are ready to serve them or they will become soggy.*

INGREDIENTS

*Makes 12*

25g/1oz/2 tbsp butter, melted

3 sheets filo pastry, each 45 x 28cm / 18 x 11in, thawed if frozen

2 ripe peaches

2 smoked chicken breast fillets, skinned and finely sliced

150ml/$^1$/4 pint/$^2$/3 cup mayonnaise

grated rind of 1 lime

30ml/2 tbsp lime juice

salt and ground black pepper

fresh tarragon sprigs, lime slices and salad leaves, to garnish

1 Preheat the oven to 200°C/ 400°F/Gas 6. Brush 12 small individual tartlet tins (muffin pans) with a little of the melted butter. Using a pastry (cookie) cutter, cut each sheet of filo pastry into 12 equal rounds large enough to line the tins, allowing enough to stand up above the tops of the tins. Keep the unused pastry covered with a clean, damp dishtowel to prevent drying.

COOK'S TIP

If you are peeling a large number of peaches, blanch them in batches to avoid soaking some for too long. If left to cool for more than a few minutes, the skin is difficult to peel off easily.

5 Mix the chicken, mayonnaise, lime rind and juice, peaches and seasoning. Chill this chicken mixture for at least 30 minutes, or up to 12 hours. When ready to serve, spoon the chicken mixture into the filo tartlets and garnish with tarragon sprigs, lime slices and salad leaves.

# Old-fashioned Chicken Pie

*The chicken can be roasted and the sauce prepared a day in advance. Leave to cool completely before covering with pastry and baking. Make into four individual pies if you prefer but bake for 10 minutes less.*

## INGREDIENTS

*Serves 4*

1 chicken, about 1.6kg/3$^1$/2lb

1 onion, quartered

1 sprig fresh tarragon or rosemary

25g/1oz/2 tbsp butter

115g/4oz/1$^1$/2 cups button (white) mushrooms

30ml/2 tbsp plain (all-purpose) flour

300ml/$^1$/2 pint/1$^1$/4 cups chicken stock

115g/4oz cooked ham, diced

30ml/2 tbsp chopped fresh parsley

450g/1lb ready-made puff or flaky pastry, thawed if frozen

1 beaten egg, to glaze

salt and ground black pepper

1 Preheat the oven to 200°C/ 400°F/Gas 6. Put the chicken into a casserole together with the quartered onion and the tarragon or rosemary. Add 300ml/$^1$/2 pint/ 1$^1$/4 cups water and season. Cover and roast for about 1$^1$/4 hours, or until the chicken is cooked through.

2 Remove the chicken and strain the liquid into a measuring jug. Cool and remove any fat that settles on the surface. Make up to 300ml/$^1$/2 pint/1$^1$/4 cups with water and reserve for the sauce.

3 Remove the chicken from the bones and cut into large cubes. Melt the butter in a pan, add the mushrooms and cook for 2–3 minutes. Sprinkle in the flour and gradually blend in the stock.

4 Bring to the boil, season to taste and add the ham, chicken and parsley. Turn into a large pie dish and leave to cool.

5 Roll out the pastry on a lightly floured surface to 5cm/2in larger than the pie dish. Cut a narrow strip of pastry to place around the edge of the dish. Dampen with a little water and stick to the rim of the dish. Brush the strip with beaten egg.

6 Lay the pastry loosely over the pie, taking care not to stretch it. Press firmly on to the rim. Using a sharp knife, trim away the excess pastry and knock up the sides to encourage the pastry to rise. Crimp the edge neatly and cut a hole in the centre of the pie. This allows steam to escape during cooking. Decorate with pastry leaves, and chill until ready to bake.

7 Brush the pastry with beaten egg (taking care not to glaze over the sides of the pastry). Bake for 35–45 minutes, or until well risen and nicely browned all over.

# Chicken en Croûte

*Chicken layered with herbs and stuffing and wrapped in light puff pastry, makes an impressive dish.*

*Serves 8*

450g/1lb packet puff pastry, thawed if frozen

4 large chicken breast fillets, skinned

1 beaten egg, to glaze

*For the stuffing*

115g/4oz/1 cup thinly sliced leeks

50g/2oz/¹/3 cup chopped streaky (fatty) bacon

25g/1oz/2 tbsp butter

115g/4oz/2 cups fresh white breadcrumbs

30ml/2 tbsp chopped fresh herbs, such as parsley, thyme, marjoram and chives

grated rind of 1 large orange

orange juice or chicken stock, if necessary

1 egg, beaten

salt and ground black pepper

1 To make the stuffing, cook the sliced leeks and bacon in the butter until soft. Put the bread-crumbs into a bowl with the mixed herbs and plenty of seasoning. Add the leeks, bacon and butter with the grated orange rind, and bind together with the beaten egg. If the mixture is too dry and crumbly, you can stir in a little orange juice or chicken stock to bring it to a moist consistency.

2 Roll the pastry out to a large rectangle 30 × 40cm/12 × 16in. Trim the edges and reserve for decorating the top.

3 Place the chicken breasts between two pieces of clear film (plastic wrap) and flatten to a thickness of 5mm/¹/4in with a rolling pin. Spread a third of the leek stuffing over the centre of the pastry. Lay two chicken breasts side by side on top of the stuffing. Cover them with another third of the stuffing, then repeat with the remaining chicken breasts and the rest of the stuffing.

4 Make a cut diagonally from each corner of the pastry to the chicken. Brush the pastry with beaten egg.

5 Bring up the sides and overlap them slightly. Trim away any excess pastry before folding the ends over like a parcel. Turn over on to a greased baking tray, so that the joins are underneath. Shape neatly and trim any excess pastry.

6 With a sharp knife, lightly criss-cross the pastry into a diamond pattern. Brush with beaten egg and cut leaves from the trimmings to decorate the top. Bake at 200°C/400°F/Gas 6 for 50–60 minutes, or until well risen and golden brown on top.

# Chicken Parcels with Herb Butter

*Buttery chicken fillets are coated in herbs and wrapped in crispy filo pastry. They taste great served simply with a salad or steamed vegetables.*

*Serves 4*

4 chicken breast fillets, skinned
150g/5oz/10 tbsp butter, softened
90ml/6 tbsp chopped mixed fresh herbs,
    such as thyme, parsley, oregano and
    rosemary
5ml/1 tsp lemon juice
5 large sheets filo pastry, thawed if frozen
1 egg, beaten
30ml/2 tbsp freshly grated
    Parmesan cheese
salt and ground black pepper

1 Season the chicken fillets and fry in 25g/1oz/2 tbsp of the butter to seal and brown lightly. Allow to cool.

2 Preheat the oven to 190°C/ 375°F/Gas 5. Put the remaining butter, the herbs, lemon juice and seasoning in a food processor and process until smooth. Melt half the herb butter.

3 Take one sheet of filo pastry and brush with melted herb butter. Cover the rest of the pastry with a damp dishtowel. Fold the pastry sheet in half and brush again with butter. Place a chicken fillet about 2.5cm/1in from the top end.

4 Dot the chicken with a quarter of the remaining herb butter. Fold in the sides of the pastry, then roll up to enclose it completely. Place seam side down on a lightly greased baking sheet. Repeat with the other chicken fillets.

5 Brush the filo parcels with beaten egg. Cut the last sheet of filo into strips, then scrunch and arrange on top. Brush the parcels once again with the egg glaze, then sprinkle with Parmesan cheese. Bake for about 35–40 minutes, until golden brown. Serve hot.

# Chicken and Apricot Filo Pie

*The filling for this pie has a Middle Eastern flavour – chicken combined with apricots, bulgur wheat, nuts, herbs and spices.*

### INGREDIENTS

*Serves 6*

75g/3oz/$^1$/$_2$ cup bulgur wheat
75g/3oz/6 tbsp butter
1 onion, chopped
450g/1lb/4 cups minced (ground) chicken
50g/2oz/$^1$/$_4$ cup ready-to-eat dried
   apricots, finely chopped
25g/1oz/$^1$/$_4$ cup blanched almonds,
   chopped
5ml/1 tsp ground cinnamon
2.5ml/$^1$/$_2$ tsp ground allspice
50ml/2fl oz/$^1$/$_4$ cup Greek (US strained
   plain) yogurt
15ml/1 tbsp chopped fresh chives
30ml/2 tbsp chopped fresh parsley
6 large sheets filo pastry, thawed if frozen
salt and ground black pepper
chives, to garnish

1 Preheat the oven to 200°C/ 400°F/Gas 6.

2 Put the bulgur wheat in a bowl with 120ml/4fl oz/$^1$/$_2$ cup boiling water. Soak for 5–10 minutes, or until the water is absorbed.

3 Heat 25g/1oz/2 tbsp of the butter in a pan, and gently fry the onion and chicken until pale golden.

4 Stir in the apricots, almonds and bulgur wheat and cook for a further 2 minutes.

5 Remove from the heat and stir in the cinnamon, allspice, yogurt, chives and parsley. Season with salt and pepper.

6 Melt the remaining butter. Unroll the filo pastry and cut into 25cm/10in rounds. Keep the pastry rounds covered with a clean, damp dishtowel to prevent drying.

7 Line a 23cm/9in loose-based flan tin (quiche pan) with three of the pastry rounds, brushing each one with butter as you layer them. Spoon in the chicken mixture, cover with three more pastry rounds, brushed with melted butter as before.

8 Crumple the remaining rounds and place them on top of the pie, then brush over any remaining melted butter. Bake the pie for about 30 minutes, or until the pastry is golden brown and crisp. Serve the pie hot or cold, cut in wedges and garnished with chives.

# Chicken and Stilton Pies

*These individual chicken and
Stilton pies are wrapped in a crisp
shortcrust pastry and shaped into
pasties. They are great for lunch,
served hot or cold.*

## INGREDIENTS

*Makes 4*

350g/12oz/3 cups self-raising
  (self-rising) flour
2.5ml/$^1$/2 tsp salt
75g/3oz/6 tbsp lard or white cooking fat
75g/3oz/6 tbsp butter
60–75ml/4–5 tbsp cold water
beaten egg, to glaze

*For the filling*

450g/1lb chicken thighs, boned and skinned
25g/1oz/$^1$/4 cup chopped walnuts
25g/1oz spring onions (scallions), sliced
50g/2oz Stilton, crumbled
25g/1oz celery, finely chopped
2.5ml/$^1$/2 tsp dried thyme
salt and ground black pepper

1 Preheat the oven to 200°C/
400°F/Gas 6. Mix the flour
and salt in a bowl. Rub in the
lard and butter with your fingers
until the mixture resembles fine
breadcrumbs. Using a knife to cut
and stir, mix in the cold water to
form a stiff, pliable dough.

2 Turn out on to a work surface
and knead lightly until smooth.
Divide into four and roll out each
piece to a thickness of 5mm/$^1$/4 in.
Cut into a 20cm/8in circle.

3 Remove any fat from the
chicken thighs and cut into
small cubes. Mix with the chopped
walnuts, spring onions, Stilton,
celery, thyme and seasoning and
divide the filling equally among the
four pastry circles.

4 Brush the edge of the pastry
with beaten egg and fold over,
pinching and crimping the edges
together well. Place on a greased
baking sheet and bake in the oven
for about 45 minutes, or until
golden brown.

# Chicken, Cheese and Leek Jalousie

*A jalousie is a family-size lattice pastry roll with a mild, creamy filling. Ready-made puff pastry and cooked chicken make this a good choice for informal entertaining.*

INGREDIENTS

*Serves 6*

1 chicken, about 1.6kg/3$^1$/2 lb, roasted

2 large leeks, thinly sliced

2 garlic cloves, crushed

40g/1$^1$/2 oz/3 tbsp butter

125g/4oz/1$^2$/3 cups button (white) mushrooms, sliced

200g/7oz/scant 1 cup low-fat cream cheese

grated rind of 1 small lemon

45ml/3 tbsp chopped fresh parsley

2 x 250g/9oz blocks puff pastry, thawed if frozen

1 egg, beaten

salt and ground black pepper

fresh herbs, to garnish

1 Strip the meat from the chicken, discarding the skin and bones. Chop or shred the meat and set it aside.

2 Sauté the leeks and garlic in the butter for 10 minutes. Stir in the mushrooms and cook for 5 minutes. Leave until cold, then stir in the cream cheese, lemon rind, parsley, chicken and salt and pepper.

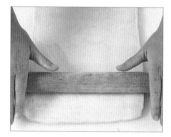

3 Stack the blocks of pastry on top of each other and roll out on a lightly floured work surface to a large rectangle, about 35 x 25cm/14 x 10in. Drape the pastry over a rolling pin and lift it on to a non-stick baking sheet.

4 Spoon the filling on to the pastry, leaving a generous margin at the top and bottom, and 10cm/4in on each side. Cut the pastry diagonally upwards at 2cm/$^3$/4 in intervals at the sides of the filling.

5 Brush the edges of the pastry with the beaten egg. Draw the pastry strips over each other in alternate crosses to "braid" the pastry. Seal the top and bottom edges.

6 Glaze the jalousie with beaten egg. Allow it to rest while you preheat the oven to 200°C/400°F/Gas 6. Bake for 15 minutes, then lower the oven temperature to 190°C/375°F/Gas 5 and bake for a further 15 minutes, or until the pastry is golden brown and crisp.

7 Allow the jalousie to stand for about 10 minutes before sliding it on to a board or platter to serve. Garnish with fresh herbs.

> ### VARIATION
> ❦
> Try a creamy blue cheese, such as Dolcelatte, for this jalousie.

# Greek Chicken Pie

This is based on a Greek chicken pie. Serve with a Greek salad of onions, feta cheese, tomatoes and cucumber.

INGREDIENTS

*Serves 4*
275g/10oz filo pastry, thawed if frozen
30ml/2 tbsp olive oil
75g/3oz/$1/2$ cup chopped toasted almonds
30ml/2 tbsp milk

*For the filling*
15ml/1 tbsp olive oil
1 medium onion, finely chopped
1 garlic clove, crushed
450g/1lb cooked chicken, boned
50g/2oz feta cheese, crumbled
2 eggs, beaten
15ml/1 tbsp chopped fresh parsley
15ml/1 tbsp chopped fresh coriander (cilantro)
15ml/1 tbsp chopped fresh mint
salt and ground black pepper

1 To make the filling, heat the oil in a large frying pan and cook the chopped onion gently until tender. Add the crushed garlic and cook for a further 2 minutes. Transfer to a bowl.

2 Remove the skin from the chicken, and mince (grind) or chop finely. Add to the onion with the rest of the filling ingredients. Mix thoroughly and season with salt and black pepper.

3 Preheat the oven to 190°C/375°F/Gas 5. Have a damp dishtowel ready to keep the filo pastry covered at all times. You will need to work fast, as the pastry dries out very quickly when exposed to air. Unravel the pastry and cut the whole batch into a 30cm/12in square.

4 Taking half the sheets (cover the remainder), brush one sheet with a little olive oil, and lay it on a well-greased 1.3 litre/$2^1/4$ pint/$5^2/3$ cup ovenproof dish.

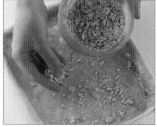

5 Sprinkle with a few almonds. Repeat with the other pastry sheets, overlapping them into the dish. Spoon in the filling and cover the pie in the same way with the rest of the overlapping pastry.

6 Fold in the edges and mark a diamond pattern on the surface with a sharp knife. Brush with milk and sprinkle on any remaining almonds. Bake for 20–30 minutes, or until golden.

# Chicken and Ham Pie

*This substantial double-crust pie is suitable for a cold buffet, picnics or any packed meals.*

INGREDIENTS

*Serves 8*

400g/14oz ready-made shortcrust pastry, thawed if frozen

800g/1³/4 lb chicken breast fillets, skinned

350g/12oz uncooked gammon (smoked or cured ham)

about 50ml/2fl oz/¹/4 cup double (heavy) cream

6 spring onions (scallions), finely chopped

15ml/1 tbsp chopped fresh tarragon

10ml/2 tsp chopped fresh thyme

grated rind and juice of ¹/2 large lemon

5ml/1 tsp freshly ground mace

beaten egg or milk, to glaze

salt and ground black pepper

1 Preheat the oven to 190°C/ 375°F/Gas 5. Roll out one-third of the pastry and use it to line a 20cm/8in pie dish 4cm/1¹/2 in deep. Place on a baking sheet.

2 Mince (grind) 115g/4oz of the chicken with the gammon, then mix with the cream, spring onions, herbs, lemon rind, 15ml/1 tbsp of the lemon juice and seasoning to make a soft mixture; add more cream if necessary.

3 Cut the remaining chicken into 1cm/¹/2 in pieces and mix with the remaining lemon juice, the mace and seasoning.

4 Make a layer of one-third of the gammon mixture in the pastry base, cover with half the chopped chicken, then add another layer of one-third of the gammon. Add all the remaining chicken followed by the remaining gammon mixture.

5 Dampen the edges of the pastry base. Roll out the remaining two-thirds of the pastry to make a lid for the pie.

6 Use the trimmings to make a lattice decoration. Make a small hole in the centre of the pie, brush the top with beaten egg or milk, then bake for about 20 minutes. Reduce the oven temperature to 160°C/325°F/Gas 3 and bake for a further 1–1¹/4 hours; cover the top with foil if the pastry becomes too brown. Transfer the pie to a wire rack and leave to cool.

# Chicken, Leek and Parsley Pie

*The flavours of chicken and leek
complement each other wonderfully.*

*Serves 4–6*

*For the pastry*

275g/10oz/2¹/₂ cups plain
    (all-purpose) flour
pinch of salt
200g/7oz/scant 1 cup butter, diced
2 egg yolks

*For the filling*

3 part-boned chicken breast portions
flavouring ingredients, such as bouquet
    garni, black peppercorns, onion
    and carrot
50g/2oz/¹/₄ cup butter
2 leeks, thinly sliced
50g/2oz/¹/₂ cup grated Cheddar cheese
25g/1oz/¹/₃ cup freshly grated
    Parmesan cheese
45ml/3 tbsp chopped fresh parsley
30ml/2 tbsp wholegrain mustard
5ml/1 tsp cornflour (cornstarch)
300ml/¹/₂ pint/1¹/₄ cups double
    (heavy) cream
beaten egg, to glaze
salt and ground black pepper
mixed green salad, to serve

1 To make the pastry, first sift the
flour and salt. Blend together
the butter and egg yolks in a food
processor or bowl until creamy.
Add the flour and process or mix
until the mixture is just coming
together. Add about 15ml/1 tbsp
cold water and process or mix for a
few seconds more. Turn out on to
a lightly floured surface and knead
lightly. Wrap in clear film (plastic
wrap) and chill for about 1 hour.

2 Meanwhile, poach the chicken
breasts in water to cover, with
the flavouring ingredients added.
Simmer until tender and cooked
through. Leave to cool in the liquid.

3 Preheat the oven to 200°C/
400°F/Gas 6. Divide the pastry
into two pieces, one slightly larger
than the other. Roll out the larger
piece on a lightly floured surface
and use to line an 18 × 28cm/
7 × 11in baking dish. Prick the base
with a fork and bake for
15 minutes. Leave to cool.

4 Lift the cooled chicken from
the poaching liquid and
discard the skins and bones. Cut
the chicken flesh into strips, then
set aside.

5 Melt the butter in a frying
pan and fry the sliced leeks over
a low heat, stirring occasionally,
until soft.

6 Stir in the Cheddar, Parmesan
and chopped parsley. Spread
half the leek mixture over the
cooked pastry base, leaving a
border all the way around.

7 Cover the leek mixture with
the chicken strips, then top
with the remaining leek mixture.
Mix together the wholegrain
mustard, cornflour and double
cream in a small bowl. Add
seasoning to taste. Pour over the
chicken and leek filling.

8 Moisten the edges of the
cooked pastry base. Roll out the
remaining pastry into a rectangle
and use to cover the pie. Brush the
lid of the pie with beaten egg, and
bake in the preheated oven for
30–40 minutes, or until the pie is
golden and crisp. Serve hot, cut
into generous square portions, with
a mixed green side salad.

# Chicken, Leek and Mixed Herb Pie

*A crisp pastry, made with fresh herbs, tops a tarragon-flavoured chicken and leek sauce to make this tempting savoury pie a popular choice.*

INGREDIENTS

*Serves 4*

175g/6oz/1¹/₂ cups plain (all-purpose) flour

pinch of salt

90g/3¹/₂oz/7 tbsp butter

15ml/1 tbsp chopped fresh mixed herbs

3 leeks, sliced

45ml/3 tbsp cornflour (cornstarch)

400ml/14fl oz/1²/₃ cups semi-skimmed (low-fat) milk

15–30ml/1–2 tbsp chopped fresh tarragon

350g/12oz chicken breast fillet, cooked, skinned and diced

200g/7oz can corn kernels, drained

salt and ground black pepper

fresh herbs and salt flakes, to garnish

1 To make the pastry, place the flour and salt in a bowl and lightly rub in 75g/3oz/6 tbsp of the butter until the mixture resembles breadcrumbs. Stir in the mixed herbs and add a little cold water to make a smooth, firm dough. Wrap the pastry in a plastic bag and chill for 30 minutes.

2 Preheat the oven to 190°C/375°F/Gas 5. Steam the leeks for about 10 minutes, or until just tender. Drain thoroughly and keep warm.

VARIATION

Use half milk and half chicken or vegetable stock, if you prefer.

3 Meanwhile, blend the cornflour with 75ml/5 tbsp of milk. Heat the remaining milk in a pan until it is just beginning to boil, then pour it on to the cornflour, stirring constantly. Return the mixture to the pan and bring to the boil, stirring constantly. Simmer for 2 minutes, stirring, until thickened.

4 Add the remaining butter to the pan with the tarragon, leeks, chicken and corn. Season to taste and mix together well.

5 Spoon the chicken into a 1.2 litre/2 pint/5 cup pie dish and place on a baking sheet. Roll out the pastry slightly larger than the pie dish. Lay it over the dish, and press to seal. Trim, decorate the top with the trimmings, if you like, and make a slit in the centre.

6 Bake for 35–40 minutes, or until the pastry is golden brown. Serve immediately, sprinkled with herbs and salt.

# Chicken and Game Pie

*Game and chicken make a rich filling for a pie, which is delicious flavoured with ginger and sherry. It makes a hearty and substantial dish for autumn meals.*

INGREDIENTS

*Serves 4*

450g/1lb boneless chicken and game meat
   (plus the carcasses and bones)
1 small onion, halved
2 bay leaves
2 carrots, halved
a few black peppercorns
15ml/1 tbsp oil
75g/3oz streaky (fatty) bacon pieces,
   rinded and chopped
15ml/1 tbsp plain (all purpose) flour
45ml/3 tbsp sweet sherry or Madeira
10ml/2 tsp ground ginger
grated rind and juice of $^1/_2$ orange
350g/12oz ready-made puff pastry,
   thawed if frozen
beaten egg or milk, to glaze
salt and ground black pepper

1 Place the carcasses and bones in a pan, with any giblets and half the onion, the bay leaves, carrots and black peppercorns. Cover with water and bring to the boil. Simmer until reduced to about 300ml/$^1/_2$ pint/1$^1/_4$ cups, then strain the stock, ready to use.

2 Cut the chicken and game meat into even-size pieces. Chop, then fry the remaining onion in the oil until softened. Then add the bacon and meat, and fry quickly to seal. Sprinkle on the flour and stir until beginning to brown. Gradually add the stock, stirring as it thickens, then add the sherry or Madeira, ginger, orange rind and juice, and seasoning. Simmer for 20 minutes.

3 Transfer to a 900ml/1$^1/_2$ pint/ 3$^3/_4$ cup pie dish and allow to cool slightly. Use a pie funnel to help hold up the pastry.

4 Preheat the oven to 220°C/ 425°F/Gas 7. Roll out the pastry to 2.5cm/1in larger than the dish. Cut off a 1cm/$^1/_2$in strip all round. Dampen the rim of the dish and press on the strip of pastry. Dampen again and then lift the pastry carefully over the pie, sealing the edges well at the rim. Trim off the excess pastry, and use to decorate the top. Brush the pie with egg or milk.

5 Bake for 15 minutes, then reduce the oven temperature to 190°C/375°F/Gas 5, for a further 25–30 minutes.

# Chicken and Mushroom Pie

*Dried and fresh mushrooms give this pie a rich flavour.*

INGREDIENTS

*Serves 6*

15g/¹/₂oz/¹/₄ cup dried porcini
   mushrooms
50g/2oz/¹/₄ cup butter
30ml/2 tbsp plain (all-purpose) flour
250ml/8fl oz/1 cup chicken stock, warmed
50ml/2fl oz/¹/₄ cup whipping cream
   or milk
1 onion, coarsely chopped
2 carrots, sliced
2 celery sticks, coarsely chopped
50g/2oz/1 cup mushrooms, quartered
450g/1lb cooked chicken meat, cubed
50g/2oz/¹/₂ cup shelled fresh or
   frozen peas
beaten egg, to glaze
salt and ground black pepper

*For the crust*

225g/8oz/2 cups plain (all-purpose) flour
1.5ml/¹/₄ tsp salt
115g/4oz/¹/₂ cup cold butter, cut in pieces
50g/2oz/¹/₄ cup lard or white cooking fat
60–120ml/4–8 tbsp iced water

1 To make the crust, sift the flour and salt into a bowl. Cut in the butter and lard until the mixture resembles breadcrumbs. Sprinkle with 90ml/6 tbsp iced water and mix until the dough holds together. Add a little more water, if necessary, 15ml/1 tbsp at a time.

2 Gather the dough into a ball and flatten into a disk. Wrap in baking parchment and chill for at least 30 minutes.

3 Place the porcini mushrooms in a small bowl. Add hot water to cover and soak until soft, about 30 minutes. Lift out of the water with a slotted spoon to leave any grit behind, and drain. Discard the soaking water.

4 Preheat the oven to 190°C/375°F/Gas 5.

5 Melt 25g/1oz/2 tbsp of the butter in a heavy pan. Whisk in the flour and cook until bubbling, whisking constantly. Add the warm stock and cook over medium heat, whisking, until the mixture boils. Cook for 2–3 minutes more. Whisk in the cream or milk. Season with salt and pepper. Put to one side.

6 Heat the remaining butter in a large, non-stick frying pan until foamy. Add the onion and carrots and cook until softened, about 5 minutes. Add the celery and fresh mushrooms and cook for 5 minutes more. Stir in the chicken, peas, and drained porcini mushrooms.

7 Add the chicken mixture to the sauce and stir. Taste for seasoning. Transfer to a 2.5 litre/4 pints/10 cup baking dish.

8 Roll out the dough to about 3mm/¹/₈in thickness. Cut out a piece about 2.5cm/1in larger all around than the dish. Lay the dough over the filling. Make a decorative crimped edge with your fingers and thumbs.

9 Cut several vents in the top crust to allow steam to escape. Brush with the egg to glaze.

10 Press together the dough trimmings, then roll out again. Cut into strips and lay them over the top crust. Glaze again. If desired, roll small balls of dough and set them in the "windows" in the lattice.

11 Bake until the top crust is browned, about 30 minutes. Serve the pie hot.

# Chicken Charter Pie

4 Roll out the pastry until about 2cm/³/₄ in larger all round than the top of the pie dish. Leave the pastry to relax while the chicken is cooling.

5 Preheat the oven to 220°C/ 425°F/Gas 7. Cut off a narrow strip around the edge of the pastry, then place the strip on the edge of the pie dish. Moisten the strip, then cover the dish with the pastry. Press the edges together.

*Rich double cream is used in the filling for this chicken pie, which originated in Cornwall, England.*

### INGREDIENTS

Serves 4

50g/2oz/¹/₄ cup butter
4 chicken legs
1 onion, finely chopped
150ml/¹/₄ pint/²/₃ cup milk
150ml/¹/₄ pint/²/₃ cup sour cream
4 spring onions (scallions), quartered
20g/³/₄ oz fresh parsley, finely chopped
225g/8oz ready-made puff pastry,
    thawed if frozen
2 eggs, beaten, plus extra to glaze
120ml/4fl oz/¹/₂ cup double (heavy) cream
salt and ground black pepper

1 Melt the butter in a heavy, shallow pan, then brown the chicken legs. Transfer them on to a plate.

2 Add the chopped onion to the pan and cook until softened. Stir the milk, sour cream, spring onions, parsley and seasoning into the pan, bring to the boil, then simmer for a couple of minutes.

3 Return the chicken to the pan with any juices, then cover tightly and cook very gently for about 30 minutes. Transfer the chicken and sauce mixture to a 1.2 litre/2 pint/5 cup pie dish and leave to cool.

6 Make a hole in the centre of the pastry and insert a small funnel of foil. Brush the pastry with egg, then bake for 15–20 minutes, until golden brown.

7 Reduce the oven temperature to 180°C/350°F/Gas 4. Mix the double cream and eggs, then pour into the pie through the funnel. Shake the pie to distribute the cream, then return to the oven for 5–10 minutes. Remove from the oven and leave in a warm place for 5–10 minutes before serving, or cool completely if serving cold.

# English Farmhouse Flan

*The lattice pastry topping makes this flan look extra special.*

*Serves 4*

225g/8oz/2 cups wholemeal
   (whole-wheat) flour
50g/2oz/$^1$/4 cup butter, cubed
50g/2oz/$^1$/4 cup lard or white cooking fat
5ml/1 tsp caraway seeds
15ml/1 tbsp oil
1 onion, chopped
1 garlic clove, crushed
225g/8oz cooked chicken, chopped
75g/3oz watercress or rocket (arugula)
   leaves, chopped
grated rind of $^1$/2 small lemon
2 eggs, lightly beaten
175ml/6fl oz/$^3$/4 cup double (heavy) cream
45ml/3 tbsp natural (plain) yogurt
a good pinch of freshly grated nutmeg
45ml/3 tbsp grated Caerphilly cheese
beaten egg, to glaze
salt and ground black pepper

3 Roll out the pastry and use to line an 18 × 28cm/7 × 11in loose-based flan tin (quiche pan). Reserve the trimmings. Prick the base and chill for 20 minutes. Place a baking sheet in the oven and preheat to 200°C/400°F/Gas 6.

4 Heat the oil in a frying pan and sauté the onions and garlic for 5–8 minutes, or until just softened. Remove from the heat and leave to cool.

5 Line the pastry case with baking parchment and fill with baking beans. Bake for 10 minutes, then remove the paper and beans and cook for 5 minutes.

6 Mix the onions, garlic, chicken, watercress or rocket and lemon rind. Spoon into the flan case. Beat the eggs, cream, yogurt, nutmeg, cheese and seasoning and pour over.

7 Roll out the pastry trimmings and cut out 1cm/$^1$/2in strips. Brush with egg, then lay in a lattice over the flan. Press the ends on to the pastry edge. Bake for 35 minutes, or until the top is golden.

1 Place the flour in a bowl with a pinch of salt. Add the butter and lard and rub into the flour with your fingertips until the mixture resembles breadcrumbs. (Alternatively, you can use a blender or food processor for this.)

2 Stir in the caraway seeds and 45ml/3 tbsp iced water and mix to a firm dough. Knead lightly on a floured surface until smooth.

# St George's Chicken Cobbler

*The St George's mushroom, so named because it emerges near to St George's Day, 23 April, combines well with chicken in this traditional English cobbler, but other wild mushrooms will also taste excellent.*

## INGREDIENTS

Serves 4

60ml/4 tbsp vegetable oil
1 medium onion, chopped
1 celery stick, sliced
1 small carrot, peeled and cut into
   julienne strips
3 chicken breast fillets, skinned
450g/1lb St George's mushrooms
75g/3oz/6 tbsp plain (all-purpose) flour
500ml/17fl oz/2¹/4 cups chicken
   stock, boiling
10ml/2 tsp Dijon mustard
30ml/2 tbsp medium sherry
10ml/2 tsp wine vinegar
salt and ground black pepper

*For the topping*
275g/10oz/2¹/2 cups self-raising (self-
   rising) flour
pinch of celery salt
pinch of cayenne pepper
115g/4oz/¹/2 cup firm unsalted (sweet)
   butter, diced
50g/2oz/¹/2 cup grated Cheddar cheese
150ml/¹/4 pint/²/3 cup cold water
beaten egg, to glaze (optional)

---

## VARIATIONS

• A mixture of bay boletus, saffron milk-caps, parasol mushroom, yellow russula, oyster or closed field (portabello) mushrooms would work well in this recipe.
• This recipe can easily be made as a pie by replacing the cobbler topping with a layer of flaky or shortcrust pastry.

---

1 Preheat the oven to 200°C/ 400°F/Gas 6. Heat the oil in a large, heavy pan, add the onion, celery and carrot and fry gently without colouring, to soften. Cut the chicken breasts into bitesize pieces, add to the vegetables and cook briefly. Add the mushrooms, fry until the juices run, then stir in the flour.

2 Remove the pan from the heat and stir in the stock gradually so that the flour is completely blended in. Return the pan to the heat, and simmer gently to thicken, stirring constantly. Add the mustard, sherry, vinegar and seasoning. Cover and keep warm.

3 To make the topping, sift the flour, celery salt and cayenne pepper into a bowl or a food processor fitted with a metal blade. Add the butter and half of the cheese, then either rub the mixture together with your fingers or process until it resembles bread-crumbs. Add the water and combine without over-mixing.

4 Turn out on to a floured board, form into a round and flatten to about a 1cm/¹/2in thickness. Cut out as many 5cm/2in shapes as you can, using a pastry (cookie) cutter.

5 Transfer the chicken mixture to a 1.2 litre/2 pint/5 cup pie dish, then overlap the cobbler shapes around the edge. Brush with beaten egg, if using, scatter over the remaining cheese and bake in the oven for 25–30 minutes, or until the topping is well risen and golden.

# Turkey and Cranberry Pie

*Fresh cranberries add a tart layer to this meaty pie, but cranberry sauce can be used if fresh are not available. The pie freezes well.*

*Serves 8*

450g/1lb pork sausage meat (bulk pork sausage)
450g/1lb/2 cups lean minced (ground) pork
15ml/1 tbsp ground coriander
15ml/1 tbsp dried mixed herbs
finely grated rind of 2 large oranges
10ml/2 tsp grated fresh root ginger or 2.5ml/$\frac{1}{2}$ tsp ground ginger
10ml/2 tsp salt
450g/1lb turkey breast fillets, skinned
115g/4oz/1 cup fresh cranberries
ground black pepper
beaten egg, to glaze
300ml/$\frac{1}{2}$ pint/1$\frac{1}{4}$ cups aspic jelly, made according to the instructions on the packet

*For the pastry*

450g/1lb/4 cups plain (all-purpose) flour
5ml/1 tsp salt
150g/5oz/10 tbsp lard or white cooking fat
150ml/$\frac{1}{4}$ pint/$\frac{2}{3}$ cup milk and water mixed

1 Preheat the oven to 180°C/ 350°F/Gas 4. Place a baking sheet in the oven to preheat. In a bowl, mix together the sausage meat, pork, coriander, herbs, orange rind, ginger and salt. Season with black pepper to taste.

2 To make the pastry, sift the flour into a large bowl with the salt. Heat the lard or white cooking fat in a small pan with the milk and water until just beginning to boil. Remove the pan from the heat and allow the mixture to cool slightly.

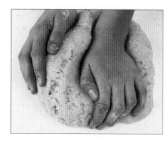

3 Quickly stir the liquid into the flour until a very stiff dough is formed. Place on a clean work surface and knead until smooth. Cut off one-third of the dough for the lid, wrap in clear film (plastic wrap) and keep in a warm place.

4 Roll out the large piece of dough on a floured surface and use to line the base and sides of a greased 20cm/8in loose-based, springform cake tin (pan). Work with the dough while it is still warm, as it will break if it becomes too cold.

5 Thinly slice the turkey breast fillets. Put them between two pieces of clear film and flatten with a rolling pin to a thickness of 3mm/$\frac{1}{8}$ in. Spoon half the pork mixture into the tin, pressing it well into the edges. Cover it with half the turkey slices and then the cranberries, followed by the remaining turkey and finally the rest of the pork mixture.

6 Roll out the remaining dough and use to cover the filling. Trim off any excess and sealing the edges with a little beaten egg. Make a steam hole in the centre of the lid and decorate the top by cutting pastry trimmings into leaf shapes. Brush with some beaten egg and bake for 2 hours. Cover the pie with foil if the top gets too brown.

7 Place the pie on a wire rack to cool. When cold, use a funnel to fill the pie with liquid aspic jelly. Leave the jelly to set for a few hours or overnight, before unmoulding the pie to serve it.

# Spiced Chicken and Egg Filo Pie

*This recipe is based on one of the most elaborate and intriguing dishes in Moroccan cuisine – bisteeya – where, traditionally, pastry is interleaved with layers of meat and spices. In this version layers of spicy meat, herby egg and almonds are enclosed in filo pastry.*

INGREDIENTS

*Serves 4*

30ml/2 tbsp sunflower oil, plus extra
    for brushing
25g/1oz/2 tbsp butter
3 chicken quarters, preferably with
    breasts attached
1¹/2 Spanish onions, very finely chopped
generous pinch of ground ginger
generous pinch of saffron threads
10ml/2 tsp ground cinnamon, plus extra
    for dusting
40g/1¹/2 oz/¹/3 cup flaked (sliced) almonds
1 large bunch fresh coriander (cilantro),
    finely chopped
1 large bunch fresh parsley, chopped
3 eggs, beaten
about 175g/6oz filo pastry, thawed if
    frozen
5–10ml/1–2 tsp icing (confectioners')
    sugar, plus extra for dusting (optional)
salt and ground black pepper

1 Heat the oil and butter in a large pan, add the chicken pieces and cook, stirring frequently, until browned. Add the onions, ginger, saffron, 2.5ml/ ¹/2 tsp of the cinnamon and 300ml/¹/2 pint/1¹/4 cups water. Season well. Bring to the boil and then cover and simmer very gently for 45–55 minutes.

2 When the chicken is cooked but still tender, transfer it to a plate. Dry-fry the almonds until golden, and set aside.

3 As soon as the cooked chicken is cool enough to handle, remove the skin and bones and cut the flesh into neat, bitesize pieces.

4 Stir the coriander and parsley into the pan and simmer the sauce until well reduced and thickened. Add the beaten eggs and cook over a very gentle heat, stirring constantly, until the eggs are lightly scrambled.

5 Preheat the oven to 180°C/ 350°F/Gas 4. Oil a shallow 25cm/10in round ovenproof dish. Place 1–2 sheets of filo pastry in an even layer over the base and sides of the dish, so that it is completely covered and the edges of the pastry sheets hang over the sides. Lightly brush the pastry with oil and make two more layers of filo, brushing with oil between the layers. Keep the unused pastry covered with a clean, damp dishtowel to prevent drying.

6 Place the chicken in the pastry case then spoon the egg and herb mixture on top. Level the surface with the back of a spoon.

7 Place a layer of filo on top of the filling (you may need to use more than one sheet of pastry) and scatter with the dry-fried almonds. Lightly sprinkle with the remaining cinnamon and the icing sugar, if using.

8 Fold the edges of the filo over the almonds and then make four further layers of filo (using one or two sheets per layer, depending on size), brushing each layer with a little oil. Tuck the filo edges down the side of the pie and brush the top layer with oil.

9 Bake the pie for 40–45 minutes, or until it is golden brown. Dust the top of the pie with icing sugar and cinnamon, creating a geometric design by using a paper template if you wish. Serve the pie immediately.

# Rich Game Raised Pie

*Terrific for stylish picnics or just as smart for a more formal special occasion, this pie looks spectacular when baked in a fluted raised pie mould.*

## INGREDIENTS

*Serves 10*

25g/1oz/2 tbsp butter
1 onion, finely chopped
2 garlic cloves, finely chopped
900g/2lb mixed boneless game meat, such
    as skinless pheasant and/or pigeon
    breast, venison and rabbit, diced
30ml/2 tbsp chopped mixed fresh herbs
1 egg, beaten
salt and ground black pepper

*For the pâté*

50g/2oz/¼ cup butter
2 garlic cloves, finely chopped
450g/1lb chicken livers, trimmed
    and chopped
60ml/4 tbsp brandy
5ml/1 tsp ground mace

*For the pastry*

675g/1½lb/6 cups strong white
    bread flour
5ml/1 tsp salt
120ml/4fl oz/½ cup milk
90ml/6 tbsp water
115g/4oz/½ cup lard or white cooking
    fat, diced
115g/4oz/½ cup butter, diced

*For the jelly*

300ml/½ pint/1¼ cups game or
    beef consommé
2.5ml/½ tsp powdered gelatine

1 Melt the butter in a small pan, then add the onion and garlic, and cook gently until softened but not coloured. Remove the pan from the heat and add the onions and garlic to the diced game meat and the chopped mixed herbs. Mix well. Season, cover and chill.

2 To make the pâté, melt the butter in a pan, add the garlic and chicken livers and cook over a medium heat, stirring frequently, until just browned. Remove the pan from the heat and stir in the brandy and ground mace. Purée the mixture in a blender or food processor until smooth, then set aside and leave to cool.

3 To make the pastry, sift the flour and salt into a bowl and make a well in the centre. Put the milk, water, lard and butter into a pan and heat gently until melted, then bring to the boil. Pour the hot liquid into the well in the flour and beat until smooth. Cover and leave until cool enough to handle.

4 Preheat the oven to 200°C/ 400°F/Gas 6. Roll out two-thirds of the pastry and use to line a 23cm/9in raised pie mould. Spoon in half the game mixture and press it down evenly. Add the pâté and then top with the remaining game.

5 Roll out the remaining pastry to form a lid. Brush the edge of the pastry case with a little water and cover with the pastry lid. Trim off the excess pastry from around the edge. Pinch the edges together to seal in the filling. Make two holes in the centre of the lid and brush the lid with beaten egg. Use the pastry trimmings to make small leaves to decorate the pie. Brush the leaves with a little beaten egg.

6 Bake the pie for 20 minutes, then cover with foil and cook for 10 minutes more. Reduce the oven temperature to 150°C/ 300°F/Gas 2. Lightly glaze the pie again with beaten egg and cook for a further 1½ hours, keeping the top covered loosely with foil.

7 Remove the pie from the oven and leave it to stand for 15 minutes to cool slightly. Increase the oven temperature to 200°C/ 400°F/Gas 6. Stand the tin on a baking sheet and remove the sides. Quickly glaze the sides of the pie with beaten egg and cover the top with foil. Cook the pie for a final 15 minutes to brown the sides. Leave the pie to cool completely, then chill overnight.

8 Next day, make the jelly. Heat the game or beef consommé in a small pan until just beginning to bubble, whisk in the gelatine until dissolved and leave to cool until just setting. Using a small funnel, carefully pour the jellied consommé into the holes in the pie. Chill until set. This pie will keep in the refrigerator for up to three days.

# Chicken Bouche

A spectacular centrepiece, this light
pastry case contains a delicious
chicken and mushroom filling with a
hint of fruit. Ideal served with freshly
cooked vegetables.

### INGREDIENTS

Serves 4

450g/1lb ready-made puff pastry, thawed
   if frozen

beaten egg, to glaze

For the filling

15ml/1 tbsp oil

450g/1lb/4 cups minced (ground) chicken

25g/1oz/$^1$/4 cup plain (all-puprose) flour

150ml/$^1$/4 pint/$^2$/3 cup milk

150ml/$^1$/4 pint/$^2$/3 cup chicken stock

4 spring onions (scallions), chopped

25g/1oz/$^1$/4 cup redcurrants

75g/3oz/scant 1 cup button (white)
   mushrooms, sliced

15ml/1 tbsp chopped fresh tarragon

salt and ground black pepper

1 Preheat the oven to 200°C/
400°F/Gas 6. Roll half the
pastry out on a lightly floured work
surface to a 25cm/10in oval. Roll
out the remainder to an oval of the
same size and draw a smaller
20cm/8in oval in the centre.

2 Brush the edge of the first
pastry shape with the beaten
egg and place the smaller oval on
top. Place on a dampened baking
sheet and bake for 30 minutes.

3 For the filling, heat the oil in a
large pan. Fry the minced
chicken for 5 minutes. Add the
flour and cook for a further
1 minute. Stir in the milk and stock
and bring to the boil.

4 Add the spring onions,
redcurrants and mushrooms.
Cook for 20 minutes.

5 Stir in the fresh tarragon and
season to taste.

6 Place the pastry bouche on a
serving plate, remove the oval
centre and spoon in the filling.
Place the oval lid on top. Serve with
freshly cooked vegetables.

## VARIATION
〜

You can also use shortcrust
pastry for this dish and cook as
a traditional chicken pie.

# Curried Chicken and Apricot Pie

*This pie is unusually sweet-sour and very moreish. Use boneless turkey instead of chicken, if you wish. Serve with steamed vegetables.*

INGREDIENTS

*Serves 6*

30ml/2 tbsp sunflower oil

1 large onion, chopped

450g/1lb chicken, boned and roughly chopped

15ml/1 tbsp curry paste or powder

30ml/2 tbsp apricot or peach chutney

115g/4oz/$^1$/2 cup ready-to-eat dried apricots, halved

115g/4oz cooked carrots, sliced

5ml/1 tsp mixed dried herbs

60ml/4 tbsp crème fraîche

350g/12oz ready-made shortcrust pastry, thawed if frozen

beaten egg or milk, to glaze

salt and ground black pepper

3 Roll out the pastry to 2.5cm/1in wider than the pie dish. Cut a strip of pastry from the edge. Dampen the rim of the dish, press on the strip, then brush with water and place the sheet of pastry on top. Press to seal.

4 Preheat the oven to 190°C/375°F/Gas 5. Trim off any excess pastry and use to make an attractive pattern on the top if you wish. Brush all over with beaten egg or milk and bake for 40 minutes, or until crisp and golden.

1 Heat the oil in a large pan and fry the onion and chicken until just colouring. Add the curry paste or powder and fry for another 2 minutes.

2 Add the chutney, apricots, carrots, herbs and crème fraîche to the pan with seasoning. Mix well and then transfer to a deep 900ml–1.2 litre/1$^1$/2 –2 pint/3$^3$/4–5 cup pie dish.

# ROASTS
# & SPECIAL
# OCCASIONS

When we are celebrating or entertaining or simply getting together with family and friends there are times when a roast is the first and only choice of dish we wish to serve. There's something very welcoming and celebratory about the delicious smell of roasting chicken as it wafts from the kitchen. In this chapter you will find many variations on the theme, using stuffings, sauces and accompaniments that are truly mouthwatering. The chapter also includes exciting recipes for special meals using chicken in different ways, so you are sure to find the right dish for any occasion.

# Traditional Roast Chicken

*Serve this favourite Sunday roast
with bacon rolls, chipolata sausages,
gravy and stuffing balls.*

Serves 4
1 chicken, about 1.8kg/4lb
4 streaky (fatty) bacon rashers (strips)
25g/1oz/2 tbsp butter
salt and ground black pepper

*For the stuffing*
25g/1oz/2 tbsp butter, melted
50g/2oz/$^1$/4 cup pitted prunes, chopped
50g/2oz/$^1$/2 cup chopped walnuts
50g/2oz/1 cup fresh breadcrumbs
1 egg, beaten
15ml/1 tbsp chopped fresh parsley
15ml/1 tbsp chopped fresh chives
30ml/2 tbsp sherry or port

*For the gravy*
30ml/2 tbsp plain (all-purpose) flour
300ml/$^1$/2 pint/1$^1$/4 cups chicken stock

1 Preheat the oven to 190°C/
375°F/Gas 5. Mix all the
stuffing ingredients together in a
bowl and season well.

2 Stuff the neck end of the
chicken quite loosely, allowing
room for the breadcrumbs to swell
during cooking. (Any remaining
stuffing can be shaped into balls
and fried to accompany the roast.)

3 Tuck the neck skin under the
bird to secure the stuffing and
hold in place with the wing tips.

4 Place in a roasting pan and
cover the breast with the
bacon rashers. Spread with the
remaining butter, cover loosely
with foil and roast for about
1$^1$/2 hours, or until the juices run
clear when the thickest part of the
leg is pierced. Baste with the juices
in the roasting pan three or four
times during cooking.

5 Remove any trussing string,
transfer to a serving plate,
cover with foil and let stand while
making the gravy. (This standing
time allows the flesh to relax and
makes carving easier.)

6 Spoon off the fat from the
juices in the pan. Blend in the
flour and cook gently until golden
brown. Add the stock and bring to
a boil, stirring until thickened.
Adjust the seasoning and strain
into a sauceboat to serve.

# Roast Chicken with Celeriac

*Celeriac has a more intense flavour than celery and makes a rich and unusual stuffing for chicken.*

INGREDIENTS

*Serves 4*

1 chicken, about 1.6kg/3$^1$/2 lb

15g/$^1$/2 oz/1 tbsp butter

*For the stuffing*

450g/1lb celeriac, chopped

25g/1oz/2 tbsp butter

3 slices bacon, chopped

1 onion, finely chopped

leaves from 1 thyme sprig, chopped

leaves from 1 small tarragon
sprig, chopped

30ml/2 tbsp chopped fresh parsley

75g/3oz/1$^1$/2 cups fresh brown
breadcrumbs

dash of Worcestershire sauce

1 egg, beaten

salt and ground black pepper

1 To make the stuffing, cook the celeriac in boiling water until tender. Drain well and chop finely.

2 Heat the butter in a pan, then gently cook the bacon and onion until the onion is soft. Stir the celeriac and herbs into the pan and cook, stirring occasionally, for 2–3 minutes. Meanwhile, preheat the oven to 200°C/400°F/Gas 6.

3 Remove the pan from the heat and stir in the fresh breadcrumbs, Worcestershire sauce, seasoning and sufficient egg to bind the mixture.

4 Place the stuffing in the neck end of the chicken. Season the skin, then rub with the remaining butter. Tuck the neck end under the bird to secure the stuffing. Roast the chicken, basting occasionally with the juices, for 1$^1$/4–1$^1$/2 hours, or until the juices run clear when the thickest part of the leg is pierced. Allow to rest for 10 minutes before carving.

# Chicken with Wild Mushrooms and Garlic

3 Pour the stock, wine and lemon juice into the roasting pan. Sprinkle over the parsley and season well. Place the chicken in the oven and cook for $1^{1}/_{2}$–$1^{3}/_{4}$ hours, or until cooked through, basting occasionally to prevent drying out.

4 Remove the chicken from the roasting pan and keep warm. Put the roasting pan on the stove and stir in the sour cream over a low heat, adding a little extra stock or water if necessary to make the juices into a thick pouring sauce.

5 Arrange the chicken on a plate, surrounded by the mushrooms. Garnish with the parsley sprigs and serve the chicken with the sauce and fresh green beans.

*Wild mushrooms surround chicken while it roasts and are then mixed with cream to make a rich accompanying sauce.*

### INGREDIENTS

*Serves 4*

45ml/3 tbsp olive or vegetable oil
1 chicken, about 1.3kg/3lb
1 large onion, finely chopped
3 celery sticks, chopped
2 garlic cloves, crushed
275g/10oz/4 cups fresh wild mushrooms,
    sliced if large
5ml/1 tsp chopped fresh thyme
250ml/8fl oz/1 cup chicken stock
250ml/8fl oz/1 cup dry white wine
juice of 1 lemon
30ml/2 tbsp chopped fresh parsley
120ml/4fl oz/$^{1}/_{2}$ cup sour cream
salt and ground black pepper
flat leaf parsley sprigs, to garnish
green beans, to serve

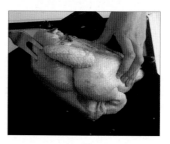

1 Preheat the oven to 190°C/ 375°F/Gas 5. Heat the oil in a roasting pan and brown the chicken all over.

2 Add the onion and fry for about 2 minutes. Add the celery, garlic, mushrooms and thyme and cook for 3 minutes.

COOK'S TIP

Always clean wild mushrooms
well to remove any grit.

# Chicken with Forty Cloves of Garlic

*This dish does not have to be exact, so do not worry if you have 35 or even 50 cloves of garlic – the important thing is that there should be lots. The smell that emanates from the oven as the chicken and garlic cook is indescribably delicious.*

## INGREDIENTS

Serves 4–5

5–6 whole heads of garlic

15g/$^1$/$_2$ oz/1 tbsp butter

45ml/3 tbsp olive oil

1 chicken, about 1.8–2kg/4–4$^1$/$_2$ lb

150g/5oz/1$^1$/$_4$ cups plain (all-purpose) flour, plus 5ml/1 tsp

75ml/5 tbsp white port, Pineau de Charentes or other white, fortified wine

2–3 fresh tarragon or rosemary sprigs

30ml/2 tbsp crème fraîche (optional)

few drops of lemon juice (optional)

salt and ground black pepper

1 Separate 3 of the heads of garlic into cloves and peel them. Remove the first layer of papery skin from the remaining heads of garlic and cut off the tops to expose the cloves. Preheat the oven to 180°C/350°F/Gas 4.

2 Heat the butter and 15ml/1 tbsp of the olive oil in a flameproof casserole. Add the chicken and cook over a medium heat, turning frequently, for 10–15 minutes, or until it is browned all over.

3 Sprinkle in 5ml/1 tsp flour and cook for 1 minute. Add the port or wine. Tuck in the whole heads of garlic and the peeled cloves with the herb sprigs. Pour over the remaining oil and season to taste.

4 Mix the main batch of flour with water to make a dough. Roll it into a sausage and press it around the rim of the casserole. Press on the lid, folding the dough up and over it to create a tight seal. Cook in the oven for 1$^1$/$_2$ hours.

5 To serve, lift off the lid to break the seal and transfer the chicken and whole garlic to a serving platter and keep warm.

6 Discard the herb sprigs, then place the casserole on the stove and whisk to combine the garlic cloves with the juices. Add the crème fraîche, if using, and lemon juice to taste. Process the sauce in a food processor or blender. Serve the garlic purée with the chicken.

# Roast Chicken with Gravy and Bread Sauce

*This is a traditional dish that makes a perfect family meal. Roast potatoes and seasonal green vegetables, such as Brussels sprouts stir-fried with chestnuts, are delicious accompaniments.*

## INGREDIENTS

*Serves 4*

50g/2oz/¹/₄ cup butter
1 onion, chopped
75g/3oz/1¹/₂ cups fresh white
   breadcrumbs
grated rind of 1 lemon
30ml/2 tbsp chopped fresh parsley
30ml/2 tbsp chopped fresh tarragon
1 egg yolk
1 chicken, about 1.5kg/3¹/₄ lb
175g/6oz rindless streaky (fatty) bacon
   rashers (strips)
salt and ground black pepper

*For the sauce*

1 onion, studded with 6 cloves
1 bay leaf
300ml/¹/₂ pint/1¹/₄ cups milk
150ml/¹/₄ pint/²/₃ cup single (light) cream
115g/4oz/2 cups fresh white breadcrumbs
10g/¹/₂oz butter

*For the gravy*

10ml/2 tsp plain (all-purpose) flour
300ml/¹/₂ pint/1¹/₄ cups well-flavoured
   chicken stock
dash of Madeira or sherry

1 Preheat the oven to 200°C/ 400°F/Gas 6. Melt half the butter in a pan and fry the onion for about 5 minutes, or until softened but not coloured.

2 Remove the pan from the heat and add the breadcrumbs, lemon rind, parsley and half the chopped tarragon. Season with salt and pepper, then mix in the egg yolk to bind the ingredients into a moist stuffing.

3 Fill the neck end of the chicken with stuffing, then truss the chicken neatly and weigh it. To calculate the cooking time, allow 20 minutes per 450g/1lb, plus 20 minutes.

4 Put the chicken in a roasting pan and season it well. Beat together the remaining butter and tarragon, then smear over the bird.

5 Arrange the bacon rashers over the top of the chicken (this helps stop the light breast meat from drying out) and roast for the calculated time. Baste the bird every 30 minutes during cooking and cover with buttered foil if the bacon begins to overbrown.

6 To make the bread sauce, put the clove-studded onion, bay leaf and milk in a small pan and bring slowly to the boil. Remove from the heat and leave the milk to stand for at least 30 minutes so that it absorbs the flavours.

7 Strain the milk into a clean pan, discard the onion and bay leaf, and add the cream and bread-crumbs. Bring to the boil, stirring constantly, then reduce the heat and simmer for 5 minutes. Keep it warm while you make the gravy and carve the chicken, then stir in the butter and season to taste.

8 Transfer the chicken to a warmed serving dish, cover tightly with foil and leave to stand for 10 minutes.

9 To make the gravy, pour off all but 15ml/1 tbsp fat from the roasting pan. Place the pan over a medium heat and stir in the flour. Cook the flour, stirring, for about 1 minute, or until golden brown, then gradually stir in the stock and Madeira or sherry. Bring to the boil, stirring constantly, then simmer, stirring, for about 3 minutes, or until thickened. Season to taste and strain into a warm sauceboat.

10 Carve the chicken and serve it immediately, with the stuffing, gravy and hot bread sauce.

## VARIATION
Cocktail sausages that have been wrapped in thin streaky bacon rashers make a delicious accompaniment to roast chicken. Roast them alongside the chicken for the final 25–30 minutes cooking time.

# Roast Chicken with Grapes and Ginger

*This dish, with its blend of spices and sweet fruit, is inspired by Moroccan cuisine. Serve with couscous, mixed with a handful of cooked chickpeas.*

### INGREDIENTS

*Serves 4*

1 chicken, about 1–1.6kg/2¼–3½ lb

115–130g/4–4½oz fresh root ginger, grated

6–8 garlic cloves, roughly chopped

juice of 1 lemon

about 30ml/2 tbsp olive oil

2–3 large pinches of ground cinnamon

500g/1¼ lb seeded red and green grapes

500g/1¼ lb seedless green grapes

5–7 shallots, chopped

about 250ml/8fl oz/1 cup chicken stock

salt and ground black pepper

1 Rub the chicken with half of the ginger, the garlic, half of the lemon juice, the olive oil, cinnamon, salt and lots of pepper. Leave to marinate.

2 Meanwhile, cut the red and green seeded grapes in half, remove the seeds and set aside. Add the whole green seedless grapes to the halved ones.

3 Preheat the oven to 180°C/ 350°F/Gas 4. Heat a heavy frying pan or flameproof casserole until hot.

4 Remove the chicken from the marinade, add to the pan and cook until browned on all sides. (There should be enough oil on the chicken to brown it but, if not, add a little extra.)

5 Put some of the shallots into the chicken cavity with the garlic and ginger from the marinade and as many of the red and green grapes as will fit inside. Roast in the oven for 40–60 minutes, or until cooked through.

---

## VARIATIONS

· This dish works with duck in place of the chicken. Marinate and roast as above, adding 15–30ml/1–2 tbsp honey to the pan sauce as it cooks.

· Use chicken breast fillets, with the skin, instead of a whole chicken. Pan-fry the chicken portions, rather than roasting them.

---

6 Remove the chicken from the pan and keep warm. Pour off any oil from the pan, reserving any sediment. Add the remaining shallots to the pan and cook for about 5 minutes, or until softened.

7 Add half the remaining red and green grapes, the remaining ginger, the stock and any juices from the roast chicken and cook over a medium-high heat until the grapes have reduced to a thick sauce. Season with salt, ground black pepper and the remaining lemon juice to taste.

8 Serve the chicken on a warmed serving dish, surrounded by the sauce and the reserved grapes.

---

## COOK'S TIP

Seeded Italia or muscat grapes have a delicious, sweet fragrance and are perfect for using in this recipe.

---

# Roast Turkey Flavoured with Mushrooms

*Explore some of the unusual wild mushrooms available to boost the flavour and succulence of roast turkey for a special occasion.*

### INGREDIENTS

*Serves 6–8*

1 turkey, about 4.5kg/10lb

butter, for basting and to finish gravy

watercress or rocket (arugula), to garnish

*For the stuffing*

50g/2oz/$^1$/4 cup unsalted (sweet) butter

1 medium onion, chopped

225g/8oz wild mushrooms, such as chanterelle, ceps, bay boletus, chicken of the woods, saffron milk-caps, Caesar's mushrooms and hedgehog fungus, trimmed and chopped

75g/3oz/1$^1$/2 cups fresh white breadcrumbs

115g/4oz pork sausages, skinned

1 small fresh truffle, sliced (optional)

5 drops truffle oil (optional)

salt and ground black pepper

*For the gravy*

75ml/5 tbsp medium sherry

400ml/14fl oz/1$^2$/3 cups chicken stock

15g/$^1$/2 oz/$^1$/4 cup dried ceps, soaked and drained

20ml/4 tsp cornflour (cornstarch)

5ml/1 tsp Dijon mustard

2.5ml/$^1$/2 tsp wine vinegar

salt and ground black pepper

---

1 Preheat the oven to 220°C/ 425°F/Gas 7. To make the stuffing, melt the butter in a pan, add the onion and fry gently without colouring. Add the mushrooms and stir until their juices begin to flow. Transfer to a bowl, add the breadcrumbs, skinned sausages and the truffle and truffle oil if using, season and stir well to combine.

2 Spoon the stuffing into the neck cavity of the turkey and enclose, fastening the skin on the underside with a skewer.

3 Rub the skin of the turkey with butter, place in a large roasting pan uncovered and roast in the oven for 50 minutes. Lower the temperature to 180°C/350°F/Gas 4 and cook for a further 2$^1$/2 hours, or until cooked through.

---

4 To make the gravy, transfer the turkey to a carving board, cover loosely with foil and keep warm. Spoon off the fat from the roasting pan and discard. Heat the remaining liquid until reduced to a sediment. Add the sherry and stir briskly with a flat wooden spoon to loosen the sediment. Stir in the ceps and chicken stock.

5 Blend the cornflour and mustard in a cup with 10ml/ 2 tsp water and the wine vinegar. Stir this mixture into the juices in the roasting pan and simmer, stirring, to thicken. Season, then stir in a knob (pat) of butter.

6 Garnish the turkey with watercress or rocket. Transfer the gravy into a warmed gravy boat and serve separately.

---

## COOK'S TIP

Other sizes of turkey can be cooked this way – allow 675g/ 1$^1$/2 lb of turkey per person and roast for 20 minutes per 450g/1lb.

# Chicken Stuffed with Forest Mushrooms

*Add the wild aroma of woodland mushrooms to a good-quality chicken to make a fantastic feast of flavour and succulence. Serve with roast potatoes and braised carrots, if you like.*

### INGREDIENTS

*Serves 4*

25g/1oz/2 tbsp unsalted (sweet) butter, plus extra for basting and to finish gravy

1 shallot, chopped

225g/8oz wild mushrooms, such as chanterelles, ceps, bay boletus, oyster, chicken of the woods, saffron milk-caps, and hedgehog fungus, trimmed and chopped

40g/1$^1$/$_2$ oz/$^3$/$_4$ cup fresh white breadcrumbs

2 egg yolks

1 chicken, about 1.8kg/4lb

$^1$/$_2$ celery stick, chopped

$^1$/$_2$ small carrot, chopped

75g/3oz potato, peeled and chopped

200ml/7fl oz/scant 1 cup chicken stock, plus extra if required

10ml/2 tsp wine vinegar

salt and ground black pepper

parsley sprigs, to garnish

1 Preheat the oven to 220°C/425°F/Gas 7. Melt the butter in a pan and gently fry the shallot without letting it colour. Add half of the chopped mushrooms and cook for 2–3 minutes, or until the moisture appears. Remove from the heat, stir in the breadcrumbs, seasoning and egg yolks, to bind.

---

### COOK'S TIP

If fresh mushrooms are not available, replace with 15g/$^1$/$_2$ oz/$^1$/$_4$ cup of the dried equivalent and soak for 20 minutes before using.

---

2 Spoon the stuffing into the neck of the chicken, enclose and fasten the skin on the underside with a skewer.

3 Rub the chicken with some extra butter and season well. Put the celery, carrot, potato and remaining mushrooms in a roasting pan. Place the chicken on top of the vegetables, add the stock and roast in the oven for 1$^1$/$_4$ hours, until cooked through.

4 Transfer the chicken to a carving board or warmed serving plate, then liquidize (blend) the vegetables and mushrooms. Pour the mixture back into the pan and heat gently, adjusting the consistency with chicken stock if necessary. Taste and adjust the seasoning, then add the vinegar and a knob (pat) of butter and stir briskly. Pour the sauce into a serving jug (pitcher) and garnish the chicken with sprigs of parsley.

# Roast Chicken with Lemon and Herbs

*A well-flavoured chicken is essential for this simple recipe – use a free-range or corn-fed bird, if possible.*

### INGREDIENTS

Serves 4

1 chicken, about 1.3kg/3lb
1 lemon, halved
small bunch thyme sprigs
1 bay leaf
15g/$^1$/$_2$ oz/1 tbsp butter, softened
60–90ml/4–6 tbsp chicken stock or water
salt and ground black pepper

1 Preheat the oven to 200°C/400°F/Gas 6. Season the chicken inside and out with salt and pepper.

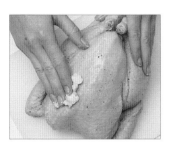

2 Squeeze the juice of one lemon half and then place the juice, the squeezed lemon half, the thyme and bay leaf in the chicken cavity. Tie the legs with string and rub the breast with butter.

3 Place the chicken on a rack in a roasting pan. Squeeze over the juice of the other lemon half. Roast the chicken for 1 hour, basting two or three times, until the juices run clear when the thickest part of the thigh is pierced.

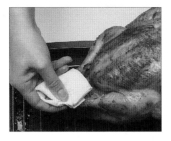

4 Pour the juices from the cavity into the roasting pan and transfer the chicken to a carving board. Cover loosely with foil and leave to stand for 10–15 minutes before carving.

5 Skim off the fat from the cooking juices. Add the stock or water and boil over a medium heat, stirring and scraping the base of the pan, until slightly reduced. Strain and serve with the chicken.

# Chicken in a Salt Crust

*Cooking food in a casing of salt gives a deliciously moist, tender result that, surprisingly, is not too salty. The technique is used in Italy and France for chicken and whole fish.*

Serves 6

1 chicken, about 1.8kg/4lb

about 2.25kg/5lb coarse sea salt

*For the garlic purée*

450g/1lb onions, quartered

2 large heads of garlic

120ml/4fl oz/$^1$/$_2$ cup olive oil

salt and ground black pepper

*For the roasted tomatoes and peppers*

450g/1lb plum tomatoes

3 red (bell) peppers, seeded and quartered

1 red chilli, seeded and finely chopped

90ml/6 tbsp olive oil

flat leaf parsley, to garnish

1 Preheat the oven to 220°C/ 425°F/Gas 7. Choose a deep ovenproof dish into which the whole chicken will fit snugly. Line the dish with a double thickness of heavy foil, allowing plenty of excess foil to overhang the top edge of the dish.

2 Truss the chicken tightly so that any salt cannot fall into the cavity. Sprinkle a thin layer of salt in the foil-lined dish, then place the chicken on top.

3 Pour the remaining salt all around and over the chicken until it is completely encased. Sprinkle the top with a little water.

4 Cover tightly with the foil and bake on the lower oven shelf for 1³/₄ hours. Meanwhile, put the onions in a small pan. Break up the heads of garlic, but leave the skins on. Add to the pan with the olive oil and seasoning.

---

### COOK'S TIP

Take the salt-crusted chicken to the table garnished with plenty of fresh mixed herbs. Once you've scraped away the salt, transfer the chicken to a clean plate to carve it.

---

5 Cover and cook over the lowest possible heat for about 1 hour or until the garlic is completely soft.

6 Plunge the tomatoes into boiling water for 30 seconds, then refresh in cold water. Peel away the skins and quarter. Put the red peppers, tomatoes and chilli in a shallow ovenproof dish and sprinkle with the oil. Bake on the shelf above the chicken for 45 minutes, or until the peppers are slightly charred.

7 Squeeze the garlic out of the skins. Process the onions, garlic and pan juices in a blender or food processor until smooth. Return the purée to the clean pan.

8 To serve the chicken, open out the foil and ease it out of the dish. Place on a large serving platter. Transfer the roasted pepper mixture to a serving dish and garnish with parsley. Reheat the garlic purée. Crack open the salt crust on the chicken, check that it is cooked through, and brush away the salt before carving and serving with the garlic purée and pepper mixture.

# Poussins Véronique

*These poussins are delicious with steamed green beans. Garnish with extra fresh tarragon, if you like.*

### INGREDIENTS

*Serves 4*

2 fresh tarragon or thyme sprigs

2 double poussins

25g/1oz/2 tbsp butter

60ml/4 tbsp white wine

grated rind and juice of $^1/_2$ lemon

15ml/1 tbsp olive oil

15ml/1 tbsp plain (all-pupose) flour

150ml/$^1/_4$ pint/$^2/_3$ cup chicken stock

115g/4oz small seedless green grapes

salt and ground black pepper

chopped fresh parsley, to garnish

1 Preheat the oven to 180°C/ 350°F/Gas 4. Put the herbs inside the cavity of each poussin and tie into a neat shape.

2 Heat the butter in a flameproof casserole, brown the poussins lightly all over and add the wine. Season, cover, and cook in the oven for 20–30 minutes, or until cooked through.

3 Remove the poussins from the casserole and cut in half with a pair of kitchen scissors, removing the backbones and small ribcage bones. Arrange in a shallow flameproof dish that will slide under the grill (broiler). Sprinkle with lemon juice and brush with oil. Grill (broil) until lightly browned. Keep warm.

4 Mix the flour into the butter and wine in the casserole, and blend in the stock. Bring to the boil, season to taste and add the lemon rind and grapes, then simmer, stirring constantly, for 2–3 minutes. Spoon the sauce over the poussins, sprinkle with chopped parsley and serve immediately.

# Spatchcock of Poussins

*Tender poussins are delicious when spatchcocked – opened out and flattened – and grilled simply with butter and herbs. Serve with boiled new potatoes and salad.*

### INGREDIENTS

*Serves 4*

4 poussins

50g/2oz/¹/4 cup butter, melted

15ml/1 tbsp lemon juice

15ml/1 tbsp chopped mixed fresh herbs,
  such as rosemary and parsley,
  plus extra to garnish

salt and ground black pepper

lemon slices, to garnish

1 Remove any trussing strings and, using kitchen scissors, cut down on each side of the backbone and remove it. Lay the poussins flat and flatten with the help of a rolling pin or mallet.

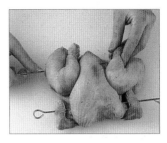

2 Thread the legs and wings on to skewers to keep the poussins flat while they are cooking.

3 Brush both sides with melted butter and season with salt and pepper to taste. Sprinkle with lemon juice and herbs.

4 Preheat the grill (broiler) to medium heat and cook skin side first for 6 minutes, or until golden brown. Turn over, brush with butter and grill (broil) for a further 6–8 minutes, or until cooked. Garnish with more chopped herbs and lemon slices.

# Pot-roast Chicken with Sausage Stuffing

*Roasting in a casserole makes these
chickens moist, tender and succulent.*

### INGREDIENTS

*Serves 6*

2 chickens, about 1.2kg/2$^{1}$/2 lb each

30ml/2 tbsp vegetable oil

350ml/12fl oz/1$^{1}$/2 cups chicken stock or
   half wine and half stock

1 bay leaf

salt and ground black pepper

*For the stuffing*

450g/1lb sausagemeat (bulk sausage)

1 small onion, chopped

1–2 garlic cloves, finely chopped

5ml/1 tsp hot paprika

2.5ml/$^{1}$/2 tsp dried chilli (optional)

2.5ml/$^{1}$/2 tsp dried thyme

1.5ml/$^{1}$/4 tsp ground allspice

40g/1$^{1}$/2 oz/$^{3}$/4 cup coarse fresh
   breadcrumbs

1 egg, beaten

1 Preheat the oven to 180°C/
350°F/Gas 4.

2 To make the stuffing, put the
sausagemeat, onion and garlic
in a frying pan and fry over a
medium heat until the
sausagemeat is lightly browned and
crumbly, stirring and turning so
that it cooks evenly. Remove from
the heat and mix in the remaining
stuffing ingredients with salt and
pepper to taste.

3 Divide the stuffing between the
chickens, packing it into the
body cavities (or, if you prefer, stuff
the neck end and bake the leftover
stuffing in a separate dish). Truss
the birds.

4 Heat the oil in a flameproof
casserole just big enough to
hold the chickens. Brown the birds
all over.

5 Add the stock, bay leaf and
seasoning. Cover and bring to
the boil, then transfer to the oven.
Pot roast for 1$^{1}$/4 hours, or until the
juices run clear when the thickest
part of the bird is pierced.

6 Untruss the chickens and spoon
the stuffing on to a serving
platter. Serve with the strained
cooking liquid.

> ### VARIATION
> ❧
> This recipe works equally well
> with guinea fowl.

# French-style Pot-roast Poussins

*An incredibly simple dish to make
that looks and tastes extra special.*

INGREDIENTS

Serves 4

15ml/1 tbsp olive oil

1 onion, sliced

1 large garlic clove, sliced

50g/2oz/scant $^1/_2$ cup diced lightly
   smoked bacon

2 poussins (just under 450g/1lb each)

30ml/2 tbsp melted butter

2 baby celery hearts, each cut into 4

8 baby carrots

2 small courgettes (zucchini), cut into chunks

8 small new potatoes

600ml/1 pint/$2^1/_2$ cups chicken stock

150ml/$^1/_4$ pint/$^2/_3$ cup dry white wine

1 bay leaf

2 fresh thyme sprigs

2 fresh rosemary sprigs

15g/$^1/_2$oz/1 tbsp butter, softened

15ml/1 tbsp plain (all-purpose) flour

salt and ground black pepper

fresh herbs, to garnish

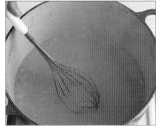

1 Preheat the oven to 190°C/
375°F/Gas 5. Heat the olive oil
in a large, flameproof casserole and
add the onion, garlic and bacon.
Sauté for 5–6 minutes, or until the
onions have softened.

2 Brush the poussins with a little
of the melted butter and season
well. Place on top of the onion
mixture.

3 Arrange the vegetables around
the poussins. Add the stock,
wine and herbs. Cover and bake for
20 minutes, then remove the lid
and brush the birds with the
remaining melted butter. Bake for a
further 25–30 minutes.

4 Transfer the poussins to a
serving plate and cut each in
half. Remove the vegetables with a
draining spoon and arrange them
around the birds. Cover with foil.

5 Discard the herbs from the pan
juices. In a bowl, mix together
the softened butter and flour to
form a paste. Bring the liquid in the
pan to the boil and then whisk in
teaspoonfuls of the paste until
thickened. Season the sauce and
serve with the poussins and
vegetables, garnished with
fresh herbs.

# Crispy Spring Chickens

*Small young chickens can be roasted in the oven fairly quickly and are delicious with a honey and sherry glaze. Serve either hot or cold.*

INGREDIENTS

*Serves 4*

2 chickens, each 900g/2lb
salt and ground black pepper

*For the glaze*
30ml/2 tbsp clear honey
30ml/2 tbsp sherry
15ml/1 tbsp vinegar

1 Preheat the oven to 180°C/ 350°F/Gas 4. Truss the birds. Place on a wire rack over the sink. Pour over boiling water to plump the flesh, and pat dry.

2 Mix the honey, sherry and vinegar together, and brush over the birds. Season well.

3 Put the rack into a roasting pan and roast the birds for 45–55 minutes, or until the juices run clear when the thickest part of the leg is pierced. Baste well during cooking with the honey glaze until crisp and golden brown.

# Chicken with Mediterranean Vegetables

*This is a delicious French alternative to a traditional roast chicken. Use a corn-fed or free-range bird, if available. This recipe also works well with guinea fowl.*

### INGREDIENTS

*Serves 4*

1 chicken, about 1.8kg/4lb
150ml/¼ pint/⅔ cup extra virgin
    olive oil
½ lemon
few sprigs of fresh thyme
450g/1lb small new potatoes
1 aubergine (eggplant), cut into
    2.5cm/1in cubes
1 red (bell) pepper, seeded and quartered
1 fennel bulb, trimmed and quartered
8 large garlic cloves, unpeeled
coarse salt and ground black pepper

1 Preheat the oven to 200°C/
400°F/Gas 6.

2 Rub the chicken all over with olive oil and season with pepper. Place the lemon half inside the bird, with a sprig or two of thyme. Put the chicken breast-side down in a large roasting pan. Roast for about 30 minutes.

3 Remove the chicken from the oven and season with salt. Turn right side up, and baste with the juices. Surround the bird with the potatoes, roll them in the pan juices, and return the roasting pan to the oven, to continue roasting.

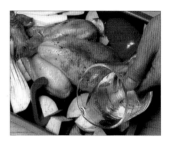

4 After 30 minutes, add the aubergine, red pepper, fennel and garlic cloves to the pan. Drizzle over the remaining oil, and season with salt and pepper. Add any remaining thyme to the vegetables. Return to the oven, and cook for 30–50 minutes more, basting and turning the vegetables occasionally.

5 To find out if the chicken is cooked, push the tip of a sharp knife between the thigh and breast. If the juices run clear, it is cooked. The vegetables should be tender and just beginning to brown. Place the vegetables in a warmed serving dish, joint the chicken and lay it on top. Skim the fat from the juices and serve in a gravy boat.

# Roast Chicken with Comté Cheese

*As it melts easily to a creamy, glossy texture with a good flavour, Comté cheese is excellent for cooking. It goes extremely well with chicken and a mushroom and vegetable sauce.*

### INGREDIENTS

*Serves 6*

75g/3oz/6 tbsp butter
30ml/2 tbsp sunflower oil
1 chicken, about 1.8kg/4lb
3 carrots, sliced in rings
2 leeks, sliced
2 celery sticks, sliced
1 litre/1³/4 pints/4 cups chicken stock
  or water
300ml/¹/2 pint/1¹/4 cups dry white wine
4 sprigs of thyme
250g/9oz/3²/3 cups button (white)
  mushrooms, halved
30ml/2 tbsp plain (all-purpose) flour
150ml/¹/4 pint/²/3 cup crème fraîche or
  double (heavy) cream
1 egg yolk
30ml/2 tbsp fresh lemon juice
freshly grated nutmeg
115g/4oz/1 cup grated Comté cheese
salt and ground black pepper

1 Heat a third of the butter with the oil in a large, flameproof casserole. Add the chicken and turn it in the fat until it is golden brown. Remove and set aside.

2 Add the vegetables to the casserole. Sauté gently for 5 minutes, then place the bird on top. Pour in the stock or water and the wine, with 1 sprig of thyme. Season well, bring to the boil, then lower the heat and cover the casserole. Simmer very gently for about 1 hour or until the chicken is cooked through.

3 Meanwhile, melt half the remaining butter in a small pan and stir-fry the mushrooms for 2–3 minutes. Do not allow them to soften or they will give up their liquid. Lift them out with a slotted spoon and set them aside. Mix the last of the butter with the flour to make a paste. Set aside too.

4 Preheat the oven to 220°C/ 425°F/Gas 7. Put the cream in a jug (pitcher) and stir in the egg yolk and lemon juice, with nutmeg to taste.

5 Transfer the cooked chicken to a shallow, heatproof dish and cover with tented foil. Remove the sprig of thyme from the casserole and discard it.

6 Return the casserole to the heat and boil rapidly until the liquid has reduced by half, then purée the stock and vegetables together in a blender or food processor. Scrape the purée back into the casserole, return to a gentle simmer and gradually whisk in the butter-and-flour paste until the sauce has thickened and is smooth. Remove from the heat again and slowly whisk in the cream mixture.

7 Surround the chicken with the mushrooms. Press half the cheese on to the chicken breast, trickle the sauce over and sprinkle over the rest of the cheese. Bake for about 15 minutes, or until the cheese is golden brown. Garnish with the remaining thyme sprigs and serve.

# Moroccan Spiced Roast Chicken with Harissa

*The spices and fruit in this stuffing give the chicken an unusual flavour. The piquant harissa sauce makes a perfect accompaniment.*

### INGREDIENTS

*Serves 4–5*

1 chicken, about 1.6kg/3½lb
30–60ml/2–4 tbsp garlic and spice
   aromatic oil
a few bay leaves
10ml/2 tsp clear honey
10ml/2 tsp tomato purée (paste)
20ml/4 tbsp lemon juice
150ml/$^1$/$_4$ pint/$^2$/$_3$ cup chicken stock
2.5–5ml/$^1$/$_2$–1 tsp harissa
salt and ground black pepper

*For the stuffing*
25g/1oz/2 tbsp butter
1 onion, chopped
1 garlic clove, crushed
7.5ml/1$^1$/$_2$ tsp ground cinnamon
2.5ml/$^1$/$_2$ tsp ground cumin
225g/8oz/1$^1$/$_3$ cups dried fruit, soaked for
   several hours (see Cook's Tip)
25g/1oz/$^1$/$_4$ cup blanched almonds,
   finely chopped

1 To make the stuffing, melt the butter in a pan. Add the onion and garlic and cook gently for 5 minutes, or until soft. Add the ground cinnamon and cumin and cook, stirring, for 2 minutes.

2 Drain the dried fruit, chop it roughly and add to the stuffing with the almonds. Season and cook for 2 minutes more. Tip into a bowl and leave to cool.

### COOK'S TIP

The stuffing can be made with mixed dried fruit or a single variety, such as apricots, instead.

3 Preheat the oven to 200°C/ 400°F/Gas 6. Stuff the neck of the chicken with the fruit stuffing, reserving any excess. Brush the garlic and spice oil over the chicken. Place the chicken in a roasting pan, tuck in the bay leaves and roast for 1–1¼ hours, basting occasionally with the juices, until cooked.

4 Remove the chicken. Pour off any excess fat from the roasting pan. Stir the honey, tomato purée, lemon juice, stock and harissa into the juices. Season. Bring to the boil, lower the heat and simmer for 2 minutes, stirring. Meanwhile, reheat any excess stuffing. Carve the chicken, and serve with the sauce and the stuffing.

# *Sherry-braised Guinea Fowl*

*Complement guinea fowl with the rich taste and aroma of sherry and wild mushrooms to make a special roast.*

## INGREDIENTS

*Serves 4*

2 young guinea fowl, tied

50g/2oz/¹/4 cup unsalted (sweet) butter

75ml/5 tbsp dry sherry

2 medium onions, sliced

1 small carrot, peeled and chopped

¹/2 celery stick, chopped

450ml/³/4 pint/scant 2 cups chicken
   stock, boiling

1 thyme sprig

1 bay leaf

225g/8oz assorted wild mushrooms, such
   as saffron milk-caps, chanterelles, oyster,
   St George's, parasol and field
   (portabello), trimmed and sliced

15ml/1 tbsp lemon juice

salt and ground black pepper

1 Preheat the oven to 190°C/
375°F/Gas 5.

2 Season the guinea fowl with salt
and pepper. Melt half of the
butter in a flameproof casserole,
add the birds and turn until
browned all over.

3 Transfer to a shallow dish,
heat the sediment in the pan,
pour in the sherry and bring to the
boil, stirring to deglaze the pan.
Pour this liquid over the birds and
set aside.

4 Wipe the casserole clean, then
melt the remaining butter. Add
the onions, carrots and celery.
Place the birds on top, cover and
cook in the oven for 40 minutes.

5 Add the stock, thyme and bay
leaf. Tie the mushrooms in a
30cm/12in square of muslin
(cheesecloth). Place in the casserole,
cover and return to the oven for a
further 40 minutes, until cooked.

6 Transfer the birds to a platter,
remove the thyme and bay leaf
and set the mushrooms in the bag
aside. Liquidize (blend) the
braising liquid and pour back into
the casserole. Add the mushrooms
from the muslin to the sauce.
Season and add lemon juice to
taste. Heat until simmering and
serve over the guinea fowl or pour
into a sauceboat.

## COOK'S TIP
~

If fresh wild mushrooms are
unavailable, replace with
15g/¹/2oz/¹/2 cup of dried saffron
milk-caps or ceps, with 75g/3oz
cultivated oyster or field
(portabello) mushrooms.

# Glazed Poussins

*Golden poussins make an impressive main course and they are also very easy to prepare. A simple mushroom risotto and refreshing side salad are suitable accompaniments.*

INGREDIENTS

Serves 4

50g/2oz/¼ cup butter

10ml/2 tsp mixed spice

30ml/2 tbsp clear honey

grated rind and juice of 2 clementines

4 poussins, about 450g/1lb each

1 onion, finely chopped

1 garlic clove, chopped

15ml/1 tbsp plain (all-purpose) flour

50ml/2fl oz/¼ cup Marsala

300ml/½ pint/1¼ cups chicken stock

small bunch of fresh coriander (cilantro),
    to garnish

1 Preheat the oven to 220°C/ 425°F/Gas 7. Heat the butter, mixed spice, honey and clementine rind and juice until the butter has melted, stirring to mix well. Remove from the heat.

2 Place the poussins in a roasting pan, brush them with the glaze, then roast for 40 minutes. Brush with any remaining glaze and baste occasionally with the pan juices during cooking. Transfer the poussins to a serving platter, cover with foil and stand for 10 minutes.

3 Skim off all but 15ml/1 tbsp of the fat from the roasting pan. Add the onion and garlic to the juices in the pan and cook on the stove until beginning to brown. Stir in the flour, then gradually pour in the Marsala, followed by the stock, whisking constantly. Bring to the boil and simmer, stirring, for 3 minutes to make a smooth, rich gravy.

4 Garnish the poussins with coriander and serve with the gravy.

# Spatchcock Poussins with Shallots and Garlic

*The word spatchcock is said to be a distortion of an 18th-century Irish expression "dispatch cock" for providing an unexpected guest with a quick and simple meal: a young chicken was prepared without frills or fuss by being split, flattened and fried or grilled.*

INGREDIENTS

Serves 2

2 poussins, about 450g/1lb each

1 shallot, finely chopped

2 garlic cloves, crushed

45ml/3 tbsp chopped mixed fresh herbs,
    such as flat leaf parsley, sage, rosemary
    and thyme

75g/3oz/6 tbsp butter, softened

salt and ground black pepper

1 To spatchcock a poussin, place it breast side down on a chopping board and split it along the back. Open out the bird and turn it over, so that the breast side is uppermost. Press the bird as flat as possible, then thread two metal skewers through it, across the breast and thigh, to keep it flat. Repeat with the second poussin and place the skewered birds on a large grill (broiling) pan.

2 Add the chopped shallot, crushed garlic and chopped mixed herbs to the butter with plenty of seasoning, and then beat well. Dot the butter over the spatchcocked poussins.

3 Preheat the grill (broiler) to high and cook the poussins for 30 minutes, turning them over halfway through. Turn again and baste with the cooking juices, then cook for a further 5–7 minutes on each side, until cooked through.

# Chicken in White Wine

*In Hungary, this chicken recipe is made with Badacsonyi wine, which has a distinctive bouquet, although any dry white wine will work.*

### INGREDIENTS

*Serves 4*

50g/2oz/$^{1}$/4 cup butter

4 spring onions (scallions), chopped

115g/4oz/$^{3}$/4 cup diced rindless
　smoked bacon

2 bay leaves

1 tarragon sprig

1 chicken, about 1.3kg/3lb

60ml/4 tbsp sweet sherry or mead

115g/4oz/1$^{2}$/3 cups button (white)
　mushrooms, sliced

300ml/$^{1}$/2 pint/1$^{1}$/4 cups Badacsonyi or
　dry white wine

salt and ground black pepper

tarragon and bay leaves, to garnish

steamed rice, to serve

1 Heat the butter in a flameproof casserole and sweat the spring onions for 1 minute. Add the bacon, bay leaves and the tarragon leaves. Cook for a further 1 minute.

---

COOK'S TIP

◆

Traditionally, this recipe was made with marc, a type of brandy.

---

2 Add the chicken to the dish and pour in the sweet sherry or mead. Cook, covered, over a very low heat for 15 minutes.

3 Add the mushrooms and wine. Cook, covered, for 1 hour. Baste the chicken with the liquid and cook, uncovered, for a further 30 minutes, or until the chicken is done and most of the liquid has evaporated.

4 Place the chicken, vegetables and bacon in a serving dish and garnish with tarragon and bay leaves. Skim the cooking liquid, season and pour into a sauceboat. Serve with rice.

# Poussins with Raisin and Walnut Stuffing

*Port-soaked raisins, walnuts and mushrooms make an unusual stuffing for poussins. Serve with tomatoes and salad leaves.*

### INGREDIENTS

*Serves 4*

4 poussins

*For the stuffing*

250ml/8fl oz/1 cup port

50g/2oz/$^1$/3 cup raisins

15ml/1 tbsp walnut oil

75g/3oz/generous 1 cup mushrooms, minced (ground)

1 large celery stick, minced (ground)

1 small onion, chopped

50g/2oz/1 cup fresh breadcrumbs

50g/2oz/$^1$/2 cup chopped walnuts

15ml/1 tbsp each chopped fresh basil and parsley, or 30ml/2 tbsp chopped parsley

2.5ml/$^1$/2 tsp dried thyme

75g/3oz/6 tbsp butter, melted

salt and ground black pepper

1 Preheat the oven to 180°C/350°F/Gas 4.

2 In a small bowl, combine the port and raisins and leave to soak for about 20 minutes.

3 Meanwhile, heat the oil in a non-stick pan. Add the mushrooms, celery, onion and 1.5ml/$^1$/4 tsp salt and cook over a low heat until softened, about 8–10 minutes. Leave to cool.

4 Drain the raisins, reserving the port. Combine the raisins, breadcrumbs, walnuts, basil, parsley and thyme in a bowl. Stir in the onion mixture and 50g/2oz/$^1$/4 cup of the butter. Add 2.5ml/$^1$/2 tsp salt and pepper to taste.

5 Fill the cavity of each poussin with the stuffing. Do not pack down. Tie the legs together, to enclose the stuffing securely.

6 Brush the poussins with the remaining butter and place in a baking dish just large enough to hold the birds comfortably. Pour over the reserved port.

7 Roast, basting occasionally, for about 1 hour. Test by piercing the thigh with a skewer; the juices should run clear. Serve immediately with some of the juices.

# Poussins with Grapes in Vermouth

*Poussins with an elegant sauce of vermouth, grapes and cream make a truly special dish, perfect for entertaining.*

Serves 4

50g/2oz/¹/₄ cup butter, softened

4 oven-ready poussins, about
    450g/1lb each

2 shallots, chopped

60ml/4 tbsp chopped fresh parsley

225g/8oz white grapes, preferably muscat,
    halved and seeded

150ml/¹/₄ pint/²/₃ cup white vermouth

5ml/1 tsp cornflour (cornstarch)

60ml/4 tbsp double (heavy) cream

30ml/2 tbsp pine nuts, toasted

salt and ground black pepper

watercress sprigs or rocket (arugula),
    to garnish

1 Preheat the oven to 200°C/ 400°F/Gas 6.

2 Spread the softened butter all over the poussins and put a hazelnut-sized piece in the cavity of each bird.

3 Mix together the shallots and parsley and place a quarter of the mixture inside each poussin. Put the poussins in a roasting pan and roast for 40–50 minutes, or until the juices run clear when the thickest part of the leg is pierced. Put the poussins on to a warm serving dish, cover and keep warm.

4 Skim off most of the fat from the roasting pan, then add the grapes and vermouth. Place the pan directly over a low flame for a few minutes to warm and slightly soften the grapes.

5 Remove the grapes with a slotted spoon, and scatter them around the poussins. Keep covered. Stir the cornflour into the cream, then add to the pan juices. Cook gently for a few minutes, stirring, until the sauce has thickened. Adjust the seasoning. Pour the sauce around the poussins. Sprinkle with the toasted pine nuts and garnish with watercress sprigs or rocket.

# Poussins Waldorf

Walnuts, apples and rice add
flavour and crunch to this roast.
Serve with salad or vegetables.

### INGREDIENTS

Serves 6

6 poussins, each about 500g/1¹/₄ lb
40–50g/1¹/₂–2oz/3–4 tbsp butter, melted
salt and ground black pepper

For the stuffing
25g/1oz/2 tbsp butter
1 onion, finely chopped
300g/11oz/2³/₄ cups cooked rice
2 celery sticks, finely chopped
2 red apples, cored and finely diced
50g/2oz/¹/₂ cup chopped walnuts
75ml/5 tbsp cream sherry or apple juice
30ml/2 tbsp lemon juice

1 Preheat the oven to 180°C/
350°F/Gas 4. To make the
stuffing, melt the butter in a small
frying pan and fry the onion,
stirring occasionally, until soft. Tip
the onion and butter into a bowl
and add the remaining stuffing
ingredients. Season with salt and
pepper and mix well.

2 Divide the stuffing among the
poussins, stuffing the body
cavities. Truss the birds and
arrange in a roasting pan. Sprinkle
with salt and pepper and drizzle
over the melted butter.

3 Roast for about 1¹/₄–1¹/₂ hours,
until the juices run clear when
the thickest part of the leg is pierced.

# Chicken Roll

*This decorative roll can be prepared and cooked the day before use and will freeze well too. Bring to room temperature about an hour before serving.*

### INGREDIENTS

*Serves 8*

1 chicken, about 2kg/4¹/₂lb

*For the stuffing*

1 medium onion, finely chopped

50g/2oz/¹/₄ cup butter, melted

350g/12oz/2 cups lean minced (ground) pork

115g/4oz streaky (fatty) bacon, chopped

15ml/1 tbsp chopped fresh parsley

10ml/2 tsp chopped fresh thyme

115g/4oz/2 cups fresh white breadcrumbs

30ml/2 tbsp sherry

1 large (US extra large) egg, beaten

25g/1oz/¹/₄ cup shelled pistachio nuts

25g/1oz/¹/₄ cup pitted black olives (about 12)

salt and ground black pepper

1 To make the stuffing, cook the chopped onion gently in 25g/1oz/2 tbsp of the butter until soft. Turn into a bowl and allow to cool. Add the remaining ingredients, mix thoroughly and season with salt and black pepper.

2 To bone the chicken, use a small, sharp knife to remove the wing tips. Turn the chicken on to its breast and cut a line down the backbone.

3 Cut the meat away from the carcass, scraping the bones clean. Carefully cut through the sinew around the leg and wing joints and scrape down the bones to free them. Remove the carcass, taking care not to cut through the skin along the breastbone.

4 To stuff the chicken, lay it flat, skin side down, and flatten as much as possible. Shape the stuffing down the centre of the chicken and fold in the sides.

5 Preheat the oven to 180°C/ 350°F/Gas 4. Sew the meat neatly together, using a needle and dark thread. Tie into a roll with fine string.

6 Put the roll, join underneath, on a rack in a roasting pan and brush with the remaining butter. Cook, uncovered, for about 1¹/₄ hours. Baste with the juices during cooking. Leave to cool. Remove the string and thread. Wrap in foil and chill until needed.

# Peanut Chicken in Pineapple Boats

*Pineapple half-shells make delightful serving containers for a creamy, spiced-chicken salad. It makes an impressive-looking dish to serve at a dinner party.*

## INGREDIENTS

*Serves 4*

2 small ripe pineapples
225g/8oz cooked chicken breast fillet, skinned and cut into bitesize pieces
2 celery sticks, diced
50g/2oz spring onions (scallions), chopped
225g/8oz seedless green grapes
40g/1$^1$/2 oz/$^1$/3 cup salted peanuts, coarsely chopped

*For the dressing*

75g/3oz/$^1$/3 cup smooth peanut butter
120ml/4fl oz/$^1$/2 cup mayonnaise
30ml/2 tbsp cream or milk
1 garlic clove, finely chopped
5ml/1 tsp mild curry powder
15ml/1 tbsp apricot jam
salt and ground black pepper

1 Cut the pineapples in half lengthways. Remove the flesh so that the shells remain intact. Cut the flesh into bitesize pieces.

2 Combine the pineapple flesh, chicken, celery, spring onions and grapes in a bowl.

3 Put all the dressing ingredients in another bowl and mix with a wooden spoon or whisk until evenly blended. Season with salt and pepper. (The dressing will be thick, until thinned by the juices from the pineapple.)

4 Add the dressing to the pineapple and chicken mix. Fold together gently but thoroughly.

5 Divide the chicken salad among the pineapple shells. Sprinkle the peanuts over the top before serving.

# Turkey with Salted Pastry

*This unusual Croatian recipe is ideal for a special occasion. The topping – pieces of crisp, salt-topped dough – are used to soak up the juices.*

INGREDIENTS

*Serves 10–12*

1 turkey, about 3kg/7lb
2 garlic cloves, halved
115g/4oz smoked bacon, finely chopped
30ml/2 tbsp chopped fresh rosemary
120ml/4fl oz/$^1$/$_2$ cup olive oil
250ml/8fl oz/1 cup dry white wine
sprigs of rosemary, to garnish
grilled (broiled) bacon, to serve

*For the salted pastry topping*
350g/12oz/3 cups plain (all-purpose)
 flour, sifted
120–150ml/4–5fl oz/$^1$/$_2$ – $^2$/$_3$ cup
 warm water
30ml/2 tbsp oil
coarse salt

1 Preheat the oven to 200°C/
400°F/Gas 6. Dry the turkey well inside and out using kitchen paper. Rub all over with the halved garlic.

2 Toss the bacon and rosemary together and use to stuff the turkey neck flap. Secure the skin underneath with a cocktail stick (toothpick). Brush with the oil.

3 Place the turkey in a roasting pan and cover loosely with foil. Cook for 45–50 minutes. Remove the foil and reduce the oven temperature to 160°C/325°F/Gas 3.

4 Baste the turkey then pour over the wine. Cook for 1 hour, basting occasionally. Reduce the temperature to 150°C/300°F/Gas 2, and cook for a further 45 minutes, basting, until cooked through.

5 To make the pastry mix the flour with a little salt, the water and oil to make a soft pliable dough. Divide equally into four.

6 Knead well, then roll out the dough on a lightly floured surface into large rounds. Sprinkle with salt. Bake for 25 minutes. Crush into pieces about 10cm/4in long. Add the pastry to the pan with the turkey for the last 6–8 minutes of cooking time. Garnish with rosemary and serve with grilled bacon.

# Parmesan Chicken Bake

*Layers of chicken, tomato sauce and Italian cheeses make an absolutely mouthwatering combination. The tomato sauce may be made the day before and left to cool. Serve with crusty bread and salad.*

## INGREDIENTS

*Serves 4*

4 chicken breast fillets, skinned
60ml/4 tbsp plain (all-purpose) flour
60ml/4 tbsp olive oil
225g/8oz mozzarella cheese, sliced
60ml/4 tbsp freshly grated Parmesan cheese
30ml/2 tbsp fresh breadcrumbs
salt and ground black pepper

*For the sauce*

15ml/1 tbsp olive oil
1 onion, finely chopped
1 celery stick, finely chopped
1 red (bell) pepper, seeded and diced
1 garlic clove, crushed
400g/14oz can chopped tomatoes with
    the juice
150ml/$^1$/4 pint/$^2$/3 cup chicken stock
15ml/1 tbsp tomato purée (paste)
10ml/2 tsp caster (superfine) sugar
15ml/1 tbsp chopped fresh basil
15ml/1 tbsp chopped fresh parsley

1 To make the tomato sauce, heat 15ml/1 tbsp olive oil in a frying pan and gently cook the onion, celery, pepper and crushed garlic in the oil until tender.

2 Add the tomatoes with their juice, the stock, purée, sugar and herbs. Season to taste and bring to the boil. Simmer for 30 minutes to make a thick sauce, stirring occasionally.

3 Divide each chicken breast into two natural fillets. Place between sheets of clear film (plastic wrap) and flatten to a thickness of 5mm/$^1$/4in with a rolling pin.

4 Season the flour. Toss the chicken breasts in the flour to coat, shaking to remove the excess.

5 Preheat the oven to 180°C/ 350°F/Gas 4. Heat the remaining oil in a large frying pan and cook the chicken quickly in batches for 3–4 minutes, or until coloured. Remove and keep warm while frying the rest of the chicken.

6 To assemble, layer the chicken pieces in a large baking dish with most of the cheeses and the thick tomato sauce, finishing with a layer of cheese and breadcrumbs on top. Bake uncovered for 20–30 minutes, or until the chicken is cooked and the top is golden.

# Chicken Tonnato

This low-fat version of the Italian dish "vitello tonnato" is made with chicken instead of veal and garnished with fine strips of red pepper instead of the traditional anchovy fillets.

**INGREDIENTS**

Serves 4

450g/1lb chicken breast fillets, skinned

1 small onion, sliced

1 bay leaf

4 black peppercorns

350ml/12fl oz/1¹/₂ cups chicken stock

200g/7oz can tuna in brine, drained

75ml/5 tbsp reduced-calorie mayonnaise

30ml/2 tbsp lemon juice

pinch of salt

2 red (bell) peppers, seeded and thinly sliced

about 25 capers, drained

mixed salad and lemon wedges, to serve

1 Put the chicken breasts in a single layer in a large, heavy pan. Add the onion, bay leaf, peppercorns and stock. Bring to the boil and reduce the heat. Cover and simmer for about 12 minutes, or until tender.

2 Turn off the heat and leave the chicken to cool in the stock, then remove with a slotted spoon. Slice the breasts thickly and arrange on a serving plate.

3 Boil the stock until reduced to about 75ml/5 tbsp. Strain through a fine sieve and cool.

4 Put the tuna, mayonnaise, lemon juice, 45ml/3 tbsp of the reduced stock and salt into a blender or food processor and purée until smooth.

5 Stir in enough of the remaining stock to make a thick, creamy sauce. Spoon the sauce over the chicken.

6 Arrange the strips of red pepper in a lattice pattern over the chicken. Put a caper in the centre of each square. Chill in the refrigerator for 1 hour and serve with fresh mixed salad and lemon wedges.

# Stuffed Chicken Breasts with Cream Sauce

*Chicken breasts filled with a leek and lime-flavoured stuffing and served in a cream sauce make an unusual and sophisticated supper.*

### INGREDIENTS

*Serves 4*

4 large chicken breast fillets, skinned

50g/2oz/$^1$/4 cup butter

3 large leeks, white and pale green
  parts only, thinly sliced

5ml/1 tsp grated lime rind

250ml/8fl oz/1 cup chicken stock or half
  stock and half dry white wine

120ml/4fl oz/$^1$/2 cup whipping or
  double (heavy) cream

15ml/1 tbsp lime juice

salt and ground black pepper

slices of lime, twisted, to garnish

1 Cut horizontally into the thickest part of each breast to make a deep, wide pocket. Take care not to cut all the way through. Set the chicken breasts aside.

2 Melt half the butter in a large, heavy frying pan over low heat. Add the leeks and lime rind and cook, stirring occasionally, for 15–20 minutes, or until the leeks are very soft but not coloured.

3 Turn the leeks into a bowl and season to taste with salt and pepper. Leave to cool. Wash and dry the frying pan.

4 Divide the leeks among the chicken breasts, and use them to fill the pockets. Secure the openings with wooden cocktail sticks (toothpicks).

5 Melt the remaining butter in the pan over medium-high heat. Add the chicken and brown lightly on both sides.

6 Add the stock and bring to the boil. Cover and simmer for 10 minutes, or until the chicken is cooked through. Turn the breasts over halfway through the cooking.

7 With a slotted spoon, remove the breasts from the pan and keep warm. Boil the cooking liquid until it is reduced by half.

8 Stir the cream into the cooking liquid and boil until reduced by about half again. Stir in the lime juice and season to taste.

9 Remove the cocktail sticks from the breasts. Cut each breast on the diagonal into 1cm/$^1$/2 in slices, pour the sauce over them and serve garnished with lime.

---

### VARIATION

For onion-stuffed chicken breasts, use 2 sweet onions, halved and thinly sliced, instead of the leeks.

# Chicken Cordon Bleu

*This is a rich dish, popular with cheese lovers. Serve simply with green beans and tiny baked potatoes, cut and filled with cream cheese.*

INGREDIENTS

*Serves 4*

4 chicken breast fillets, skinned

4 slices cooked lean ham

60ml/4 tbsp grated Gruyère or
　　Emmenthal cheese

30ml/2 tbsp olive oil

115g/4oz/1$^{3}/_{4}$ cups button (white)
　　mushrooms, sliced

60ml/4 tbsp white wine

salt and ground black pepper

watercress or rocket (arugula), to garnish

1 Place the chicken between two pieces of clear film (plastic wrap) and flatten to a thickness of 5mm/$^{1}/_{4}$ in with a rolling pin. Place the chicken on the board, outer side down, and lay a slice of ham on each. Divide the cheese between the chicken and season with a little salt and freshly ground pepper.

2 Fold the chicken breasts in half and secure with wooden cocktail sticks (toothpicks), making a large "stitch" to hold the pieces together.

3 Heat the oil in a large frying pan and brown the chicken parcels on all sides. Remove to a dish and keep warm.

4 Add the mushrooms to the pan and cook until lightly browned. Replace the chicken and pour over the wine. Cover and cook gently for 15–20 minutes, or until cooked through. Remove the cocktail sticks. Arrange the chicken and mushrooms on a serving dish, garnished with watercress or rocket.

# Crunchy Stuffed Chicken Breasts

*These tasty chicken breasts with a pine nut stuffing can be prepared in advance, kept chilled, and cooked just before serving. Serve with baby vegetables.*

## INGREDIENTS

*Serves 4*

4 chicken breast fillets, skinned
25g/1oz/2 tbsp butter
1 garlic clove, crushed
15ml/1 tbsp Dijon mustard

*For the stuffing*

15g/$^1$/$_2$ oz/1 tbsp butter
1 bunch spring onions (scallions), sliced
45ml/3 tbsp fresh breadcrumbs
25g/1oz/2 tbsp pine nuts
1 egg yolk
15ml/1 tbsp chopped fresh parsley
salt and ground black pepper
60ml/4 tbsp grated cheese

*For the topping*

2 bacon rashers (strips), finely chopped
50g/2oz/1 cup fresh breadcrumbs
15ml/1 tbsp freshly grated Parmesan cheese
15ml/1 tbsp chopped fresh parsley

1 Preheat the oven to 200°C/ 400°F/Gas 6. To make the stuffing, heat 15g/$^1$/$_2$ oz/1 tbsp of butter in a frying pan and cook the spring onions until soft. Remove from the heat and allow to cool.

2 Add the remaining ingredients and mix thoroughly.

3 To make the topping, fry the chopped bacon until crispy, drain and add to the breadcrumbs, Parmesan cheese and fresh parsley.

4 Carefully cut a deep pocket in each of the chicken breast fillets, using a sharp knife.

5 Divide the stuffing into four and use to fill the pockets. Place in a buttered ovenproof dish.

6 Melt the remaining butter, mix it with the crushed garlic and mustard, and brush liberally over the chicken. Press on the topping and bake uncovered for about 30–40 minutes, or until tender and cooked through.

# Roast Chicken with Fennel

*If you can get wild fennel, it will add character to this dish. Cultivated fennel bulb works just as well.*

### INGREDIENTS

*Serves 4–5*

1.6kg/3$^1$/2 lb roasting chicken
1 onion, quartered
120ml/4fl oz/$^1$/2 cup olive oil
2 medium fennel bulbs
1 garlic clove, peeled
pinch of freshly grated nutmeg
3–4 thin slices pancetta or bacon
120ml/4fl oz/$^1$/2 cup dry white wine
salt and ground black pepper

1 Preheat the oven to 180°C/350°F/Gas 4. Sprinkle the chicken cavity with salt and pepper. Place the onion quarters in the cavity. Rub the chicken with about 45ml/3 tbsp of the olive oil. Place in a roasting pan.

2 Cut the green fronds from the tops of the fennel bulbs. Chop the fronds together with the garlic. Place in a small bowl and mix with the nutmeg and seasoning.

3 Sprinkle the fennel mixture over the chicken, pressing it on to the oiled skin. Cover the breast with the slices of pancetta or bacon. Sprinkle with 30ml/2 tbsp of the oil. Place in the oven and roast for 30 minutes.

4 Meanwhile, boil or steam the fennel bulbs until barely tender. Remove from the heat and cut into quarters or sixths lengthways. After the chicken has been cooking for 30 minutes, remove the pan from the oven. Baste the chicken with any oils in the pan.

5 Arrange the fennel pieces around the chicken. Sprinkle the fennel with the remaining oil. Pour about half the wine over the chicken, and return to the oven.

6 After 30 minutes more, baste the chicken again. Pour on the remaining wine. Cook for 15–20 minutes, or until the juices run clear when the thickest part of the leg is pierced. Serve the chicken surrounded by the fennel.

# Chicken with Ham and Cheese

*This tasty combination comes from Italy, where it is also prepared with veal.*

### INGREDIENTS

*Serves 4*

4 small chicken breast fillets, boned
flour seasoned with salt and freshly ground black pepper, for dredging
50g/2oz/$^1$/4 cup butter
3–4 leaves fresh sage
4 thin slices prosciutto crudo, or cooked ham, cut in half
50g/2oz/$^2$/3 cup freshly grated Parmesan cheese

1 Cut each breast in half lengthways to make two flat fillets of approximately the same thickness. Dredge the chicken in the seasoned flour, and shake off the excess.

2 Preheat the grill (broiler). Heat the butter in a large, heavy frying pan and add the sage leaves. Add the chicken, in one layer, and cook over low to medium heat until cooked through and golden brown on both sides, turning as necessary. This will take about 15 minutes.

3 Remove the chicken from the heat, and arrange on a flame-proof serving dish or grill (broiling) pan. Place one piece of ham on each chicken fillet and top with the grated Parmesan. Grill for 3–4 minutes, or until the cheese has melted. Serve immediately.

# Chicken with Shallots, Garlic and Fennel

*This dish is guaranteed to be popular with garlic lovers. The fennel adds a deliciously unusual aniseed flavour.*

INGREDIENTS

Serves 4

1 chicken, about 1.6–1.8kg/3¹/₂–4lb, cut into 8 pieces, or 8 chicken joints

250g/9oz shallots, peeled

1 head garlic, separated into cloves and peeled

60ml/4 tbsp extra virgin olive oil

45ml/3 tbsp tarragon vinegar

45ml/3 tbsp white wine or vermouth (optional)

5ml/1 tsp fennel seeds, crushed

2 bulbs fennel, cut into wedges, feathery tops reserved

150ml/¹/₄ pint/²/₃ cup double (heavy) cream

5ml/1 tsp redcurrant jelly

15ml/1 tbsp tarragon mustard

caster (superfine) sugar (optional)

30ml/2 tbsp chopped fresh flat leaf parsley

salt and ground black pepper

1 Place the chicken pieces, shallots and all but one of the garlic cloves in a flameproof dish or roasting pan. Add the oil, vinegar, wine or vermouth, if using, and fennel seeds. Season with pepper, then set aside to marinate for 2–3 hours.

2 Preheat the oven to 190°C/ 375°F/Gas 5. Add the fennel to the chicken, season with salt and stir to mix.

3 Cook the chicken in the oven for 50–60 minutes, stirring once or twice. The chicken juices should run clear when the thick thigh meat is pierced.

4 Transfer the chicken and vegetables to a serving dish and keep them warm. Skim off some of the fat and bring the cooking juices to the boil, then pour in the cream. Stir, scraping up all the residue from the bottom of the pan. Whisk in the redcurrant jelly followed by the mustard. Check the seasoning, adding a little sugar if you like.

5 Chop the remaining garlic with the feathery fennel tops and mix with the parsley. Pour the sauce over the chicken and scatter the chopped garlic and herb mixture over the top. Serve immediately.

# Chicken with Spiced Figs

*The Catalans have various recipes for fruit with meat. This is quite an unusual one, but it uses one of the fruits most strongly associated with the Mediterranean – the fig.*

### INGREDIENTS

Serves 4

150g/5oz/³/₄ cup granulated sugar

120ml/4fl oz/¹/₂ cup white wine vinegar

1 lemon slice

1 cinnamon stick

450g/1lb fresh figs

120ml/4fl oz/¹/₂ cup medium sweet
   white wine

pared rind of ¹/₂ lemon

1 chicken, about 1.6kg/3¹/₂ lb, jointed into
   8 pieces

50g/2oz lardons, or thick streaky (fatty)
   bacon cut into strips

15ml/1 tbsp olive oil

50ml/2fl oz/¹/₄ cup chicken stock

salt and ground black pepper

green salad, to serve

1 Put the sugar, vinegar, lemon slice and cinnamon stick in a pan with 120ml/4fl oz/¹/₂ cup water. Bring to the boil, then simmer for 5 minutes. Add the figs, cover, and simmer for 10 minutes. Remove from the heat and leave, covered, for 3 hours.

2 Preheat the oven to 180°C/ 350°F/Gas 4. Drain the figs, and place in a bowl. Add the wine and lemon rind. Season the chicken. In a large frying pan, cook the lardons or streaky bacon strips until the fat melts. Transfer to an ovenproof dish, leaving any fat in the pan. Add the oil to the pan and brown the chicken pieces all over.

3 Drain the figs, adding the wine to the pan with the chicken. Boil until the sauce has reduced and is syrupy. Transfer the contents of the frying pan to the ovenproof dish and cook uncovered in the oven for about 20 minutes, until cooked. Add the figs and stock, cover and return to the oven for 10 minutes more. Serve with a green salad.

# Seville Chicken

*Oranges and almonds are favourite ingredients in southern Spain, especially around Seville, where the orange and almond trees are a familiar and wonderful sight.*

### INGREDIENTS

*Serves 4*

1 orange
8 chicken thighs
plain (all-purpose) flour, seasoned with
    salt and pepper
45ml/3 tbsp olive oil
1 large Spanish onion, roughly chopped
2 garlic cloves, crushed
1 red (bell) pepper, seeded and sliced
1 yellow (bell) pepper, seeded and sliced
115g/4oz chorizo sausage, sliced
50g/2oz/$^1$/2 cup flaked (sliced) almonds
225g/8oz/generous 1 cup brown
    basmati rice
about 600ml/1 pint/2$^1$/2 cups
    chicken stock
400g/14oz can chopped tomatoes
175ml/6fl oz/$^3$/4 cup white wine
generous pinch of dried thyme
salt and ground black pepper
fresh thyme sprigs, to garnish

2 Heat the oil in a large frying pan and fry the chicken pieces on both sides until nicely brown. Transfer to a plate. Add the onion and garlic to the pan and fry for 4–5 minutes, or until the onion begins to brown. Add the red and yellow peppers and fry, stirring occasionally, until slightly softened.

3 Add the chorizo, stir-fry for a few minutes, then sprinkle over the almonds and rice. Cook, stirring, for 1–2 minutes.

1 Pare a thin strip of peel from the orange and set it aside. Using a sharp knife, cut a slice of peel and pith from each end of the orange. Place cut-side down on a plate and cut off the peel and pith in strips. Cut out each segment leaving the membrane behind. Dust the chicken thighs with seasoned flour.

4 Pour in the chicken stock, tomatoes and wine and add the orange strip and thyme. Season well. Bring to simmering point, stirring, then return the chicken pieces to the pan.

5 Cover tightly and cook over a very low heat for 1–1¼ hours, or until the rice is tender and the chicken is cooked through. Just before serving, add the orange segments and allow to cook briefly to heat through. Garnish with fresh thyme and serve.

---

### COOK'S TIP

Cooking times for this dish will depend largely on the heat. If the rice seems to be drying out too quickly, add a little more stock or wine and reduce the heat. If, after 40 minutes or so, the rice is still barely cooked, increase the heat a little. Make sure the rice is kept below the liquid (the chicken can lie on the surface) and stir the rice occasionally if it seems to be cooking unevenly.

# Chicken with Sloe Gin and Juniper

*Juniper is used to make gin. The flavour of this dish is deliciously enhanced by using both sloe gin and juniper berries. Sloe gin is easy to make, but can also be bought ready-made.*

### INGREDIENTS

*Serves 8*

25g/1oz/2 tbsp butter
30ml/2 tbsp sunflower oil
8 chicken breast fillets, skinned
350g/12oz carrots, cooked
1 clove garlic, crushed
15ml/1 tbsp finely chopped parsley
50ml/2fl oz/¼ cup chicken stock
about 50ml/2fl oz/¼ cup red wine
50ml/2fl oz/¼ cup sloe gin
5ml/1 tsp crushed juniper berries
salt and ground black pepper
chopped fresh basil, to garnish

1 Melt the butter with the oil in a frying pan, and fry the chicken until browned on all sides.

2 In a food processor or blender, combine all the remaining ingredients except the basil, and blend to a smooth purée. If the mixture seems too thick, add a little more red wine or water.

3 Put the chicken breast fillets in a clean pan, pour the sauce over the top and cook over a medium heat until the chicken is cooked through – about 15 minutes. Adjust the seasoning and serve garnished with chopped fresh basil.

# Circassian Chicken

*This is a Turkish dish, which is
popular all over the Middle East.
The chicken is poached and served
cold with a flavoursome sauce.*

*Serves 6*

1 chicken, about 1.6kg/3¹/₂ lb

2 onions, quartered

1 carrot, sliced

1 celery stick, trimmed and sliced

6 peppercorns

3 slices bread, crusts removed

2 garlic cloves, roughly chopped

400g/14oz/3¹/₂ cups chopped walnuts

15ml/1 tbsp walnut oil

salt and ground black pepper

chopped walnuts and paprika, to garnish

1 Place the chicken in a large pan, with the onions, carrot, celery and peppercorns. Add water to cover, and bring to the boil. Simmer for 1 hour, uncovered, until the chicken is tender and cooked through. Leave to cool. Drain the chicken, reserving the stock.

2 Tear up the bread and soak in 90ml/6 tbsp of the chicken stock. Transfer to a blender or food processor, with the garlic and walnuts, and add 250ml/8fl oz/ 1 cup of the remaining stock. Process until smooth, then transfer to a pan.

3 Over a low heat, gradually add more chicken stock to the sauce, stirring constantly, until it is of a thick pouring consistency. Season, remove from the heat and leave to cool in the pan.

4 Skin and bone the chicken, and cut into bitesize chunks. Place in a bowl and add a little of the sauce. Stir to coat the chicken, then arrange on a serving dish. Spoon the remaining sauce over the chicken, and drizzle with the walnut oil. Sprinkle with walnuts and paprika and serve immediately.

# Chicken with Red Wine Vinegar

*This is a simple dish to prepare and tastes wonderful. It is an easy version of a modern classic in French cooking.*

### INGREDIENTS

*Serves 4*

4 chicken breast fillets, 200g/7oz each, skinned

50g/2oz/¼ cup unsalted (sweet) butter

8–12 shallots, trimmed and halved

60ml/4 tbsp red wine vinegar

2 garlic cloves, finely chopped

60ml/4 tbsp dry white wine

120ml/4fl oz/½ cup chicken stock

15ml/1 tbsp chopped fresh parsley

freshly ground black pepper

green salad, to serve

1 Cut each chicken breast in half crossways to make eight pieces.

2 Melt half the butter in a large frying pan over a medium heat. Add the chicken and cook for 3–5 minutes, or until golden brown, turning once, then season with pepper.

3 Add the shallot halves to the pan, cover and cook over a low heat for 5–7 minutes, shaking the pan and stirring occasionally.

4 Transfer the chicken to a plate. Add the vinegar to the pan and cook, stirring, for 1 minute, or until the liquid is almost evaporated. Add the garlic, wine and stock and stir to blend.

5 Return the chicken to the pan with any accumulated liquid. Cover and simmer for 2–3 minutes, or until tender and the juices run clear when pierced.

6 Transfer the chicken and shallots to a serving dish and cover to keep warm. Increase the heat and boil the cooking liquid until it has reduced by half.

7 Remove from the heat. Add the remaining butter, whisking until the sauce is thickened and glossy. Add the parsley. Pour the sauce over the chicken and shallots. Serve with a green salad.

---

### VARIATIONS
~

You could try tarragon vinegar and substitute tarragon for parsley, or raspberry vinegar and garnish with fresh raspberries.

# Grilled Poussins with Citrus Glaze

*The fresh flavour of citrus fruits complements young poultry perfectly. This recipe is suitable for many sorts of small birds, including pigeons, snipe and partridges.*

## INGREDIENTS

*Serves 4*

2 poussins, about 675g/1$^1$/$_2$ lb each

50g/2oz/$^1$/$_4$ cup butter, softened

30ml/2 tbsp olive oil

2 garlic cloves, crushed

2.5ml/$^1$/$_2$ tsp dried thyme

1.5ml/$^1$/$_4$ tsp cayenne pepper, or to taste

grated rind and juice of 1 lemon

grated rind and juice of 1 lime

30ml/2 tbsp honey

salt and ground black pepper

fresh dill, to garnish

tomato salad, to serve

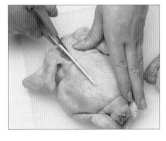

1 Using kitchen scissors or poultry shears, cut along both sides of the backbone of each bird; remove and discard. Cut the birds in half along the breastbone, then, using a rolling pin, press down to flatten.

### COOK'S TIP
If smaller poussins, about 450g/1lb each, are available, serve one per person. Increase the butter to 75g/3oz/6 tbsp, if necessary.

2 Beat the butter in a small bowl, then beat in 15ml/1 tbsp of the olive oil, the garlic, thyme, cayenne, salt and pepper, half the lemon and lime rind and 15ml/1 tbsp of the combined juice.

3 Loosen the skin of each poussin breast. With a round-bladed knife, spread the butter mixture evenly between the skin and meat.

4 Preheat the grill (broiler) and line a grill (broiling) pan with foil. In a small bowl, mix together the remaining olive oil, lemon and lime rind and juices and the honey. Place the bird halves, skin side up, on the grill pan and brush with the juice mixture.

5 Grill (broil) for 10–12 minutes, basting once or twice with the juices. Turn over and grill for 7–10 minutes, basting once, until the juices run clear when the thigh is pierced. Serve with the tomato salad, garnished with dill.

# Chicken with Apricot and Pecan Baskets

*The potato baskets make a pretty addition to the chicken and could easily have different fillings when you feel like a change.*

## INGREDIENTS

Serves 8

8 chicken breast fillets, about
    150g/5oz each
25g/1oz/2 tbsp butter
50g/2oz mushrooms, chopped
15g/$^1$/2 oz/1 tbsp chopped pecan nuts
115g/4oz/$^2$/3 cup chopped, cooked ham
50g/2oz/1 cup wholemeal
    (whole-wheat) breadcrumbs
15ml/1 tbsp chopped parsley, plus some
    whole leaves to garnish
salt and ground black pepper

*For the potato baskets*

4 large baking potatoes, about
    300g/11oz each
175g/6oz sausage meat (bulk sausage)
225g/8oz can apricots in natural juice,
    drained and quartered
1.5ml/$^1$/4 tsp cinnamon
2.5ml/$^1$/2 tsp grated orange rind
30ml/2 tbsp maple syrup
25g/1oz/2 tbsp butter
35g/1$^1$/4 oz/$^1$/4 cup chopped pecan nuts,
    plus pecan halves to garnish

*For the sauce*

15ml/1 tbsp cornflour (cornstarch)
120ml/4fl oz/$^1$/2 cup white wine
120ml/4fl oz/$^1$/2 cup chicken stock
50g/2oz/$^1$/4 cup butter
50g/2oz/scant $^1$/4 cup apricot chutney

1 Preheat the oven to 200°C/
400°F/Gas 6. Put the potatoes in the oven to bake. Cook for 1½ hours or until ready. Put the chicken between two sheets of clear film (plastic wrap) and flatten with a meat mallet. Melt the butter in a pan and sauté the mushrooms, pecan nuts and ham. Stir in the breadcrumbs, parsley and seasoning. Divide the mixture between the chicken breasts, roll up and secure each one with a cocktail stick (toothpick). Chill.

2 Mix the cornflour for the sauce with a little of the wine and stock to make a smooth paste. Put the remaining wine in a pan and add the paste. Cook, stirring, until smooth. Add the butter and chutney, and cook for 5 minutes, stirring. Turn the oven temperature down to 180°C/350°F/Gas 4.

3 Place the chicken in an oven-proof dish. Pour over the sauce. Cover with foil and bake for 20–25 minutes, until cooked through.

4 When the potatoes are cooked, cut them in half and scoop out the inside. Mash the potato in a mixing bowl.

5 Fry the sausage meat and drain off any fat. Add the remaining ingredients and cook for 1 minute. Mix together the sausage meat and potato and put in the potato shells. Sprinkle the pecans over the top, put in the oven with the chicken and bake for 20–25 minutes.

6 When the chicken is cooked, remove the cocktail sticks, slice and place on serving plates. Pour over the sauce, garnish with parsley and serve with the potato baskets.

# Chicken with Asparagus

*Canned asparagus may be used instead of fresh, but will not require any cooking – simply add at the end to warm through.*

INGREDIENTS

*Serves 4*

4 large chicken breast fillets, skinned

15ml/1 tbsp ground coriander

30ml/2 tbsp olive oil

20 slender asparagus spears, cut
    into 7.5–10cm/3–4 in lengths

300ml/$^1$/$_2$ pint/1$^1$/$_4$ cups chicken stock

15ml/1 tbsp cornflour (cornstarch)

15ml/1 tbsp lemon juice

salt and ground black pepper

15ml/1 tbsp chopped fresh parsley

1 Divide each chicken breast into two natural fillets. Place each between two sheets of clear film (plastic wrap) and flatten to a thickness of 5mm/$^1$/$_4$ in with a rolling pin. Cut into 2.5cm/1in strips diagonally. Sprinkle over the coriander, and toss to coat each piece.

2 Heat the oil in a large frying pan and fry the chicken very quickly in small batches for 3–4 minutes, until lightly coloured and cooked through. Season each batch with a little salt and freshly ground black pepper. Remove and keep warm while frying the rest of the chicken.

3 Add the asparagus and chicken stock to the pan and bring to the boil. Cook for a further 4–5 minutes, or until tender.

4 Mix the cornflour to a paste with a little cold water, stir into the sauce and cook, stirring, until thickened. Return the chicken to the pan, with the lemon juice, and reheat. Garnish with parsley and serve.

# Chicken with Morels

*Morels are among the most tasty dried mushrooms and, although expensive, a little goes a long way.*

### INGREDIENTS

*Serves 4*

40g/1¹/₂ oz/³/₄ cup dried morel
   mushrooms
250ml/8fl oz/1 cup chicken stock
50g/2oz/¹/₄ cup butter
5 or 6 shallots, thinly sliced
90g/3¹/₂ oz/1¹/₂ cups button (white)
   mushrooms, thinly sliced
1.5ml/¹/₄ tsp dried thyme
30–45ml/2–3 tbsp brandy
175ml/6fl oz/³/₄ cup double (heavy) or
   whipping cream
4 chicken breast fillets, about 200g/7oz
   each, skinned
15ml/1 tbsp vegetable oil
175ml/6fl oz/³/₄ cup champagne or dry
   sparkling wine
salt and ground black pepper

1 Put the morels in a strainer and rinse well under cold running water, shaking to remove as much grit as possible. Put them in a pan with the stock and bring to the boil over a medium-high heat. Remove the pan from the heat and leave to stand for 1 hour.

2 Remove the morels from the cooking liquid, strain the liquid through a very fine sieve or muslin-(cheesecloth-)lined strainer and reserve for the sauce. Reserve a few whole morels and slice the rest.

3 Melt half the butter in a frying pan over a medium heat. Add the shallots and cook for 2 minutes, or until softened, then add the morels and mushrooms and cook, stirring frequently, for 2–3 minutes. Season and add the thyme, brandy and 100ml/3½ fl oz/scant ½ cup of the cream. Reduce the heat and simmer gently for 10–12 minutes, or until any liquid has evaporated, stirring occasionally. Remove the morel mixture from the pan and set aside.

4 Pull off the smaller fillets from the chicken breasts (the finger-shaped piece on the underside) and reserve for another use. Make a pocket in each chicken breast by cutting a slit along the thicker edge, taking care not to cut all the way through.

5 Using a small spoon, fill each pocket with one-quarter of the mushroom mixture then, if necessary, close with a cocktail stick (toothpick).

6 Melt the remaining butter with the oil in a heavy frying pan over a medium-high heat and cook the chicken breasts on one side for 6–8 minutes, or until golden. Transfer to a plate. Add the champagne or sparkling wine to the pan and boil to reduce by half. Add the strained morel cooking liquid and boil to reduce by half again.

7 Add the remaining cream and cook over a medium heat for 2–3 minutes, or until the sauce thickens slightly and coats the back of a spoon. Adjust the seasoning. Return the chicken to the pan with any accumulated juices and the reserved whole morels, and simmer for 3–5 minutes over a medium-low heat until the chicken breasts are hot and the juices run clear when the meat is pierced.

# Chicken with Figs and Mint

*The unusual combination of figs, orange and mint makes a rich sauce to accompany tender chicken breast fillets.*

### INGREDIENTS

*Serves 4*

500g/1$^1$/4 lb/3$^1$/3 cups dried figs

$^1$/2 bottle sweet, fruity white wine

4 chicken breast fillets, about
  175–225g/6–8oz each

15ml/1 tbsp butter

30ml/2 tbsp dark orange marmalade

10 mint leaves, finely chopped, plus a few
  more to garnish

juice of $^1$/2 lemon

salt and ground black pepper

1 Place the figs in a pan with the wine and bring to the boil, then simmer very gently for about 1 hour. Leave to cool and chill overnight.

2 Fry the chicken breasts in the butter until they are cooked. Remove and keep warm. Drain any fat from the pan and pour in the juice from the figs. Boil and reduce to about 150ml/$^1$/4 pint/$^2$/3 cup.

3 Add the marmalade, chopped mint leaves and lemon juice, and simmer for a few minutes. Season to taste. When the sauce is thick and shiny, pour it over the meat. Garnish with the figs and mint leaves, and serve.

# Guinea Fowl with Whisky Cream Sauce

*Served with creamy sweet potato mash and whole baby leeks, guinea fowl is superb with a rich, creamy whisky sauce.*

INGREDIENTS

*Serves 4*

2 guinea fowl, each weighing about
   1kg/2$^1$/$_4$ lb
90ml/6 tbsp whisky
150ml/$^1$/$_4$ pint/$^2$/$_3$ cup chicken stock
150ml/$^1$/$_4$ pint/$^2$/$_3$ cup double
   (heavy) cream
20 baby leeks
salt and ground black pepper
fresh thyme sprigs, to garnish
mashed sweet potatoes, to serve

1 Preheat the oven to 200°C/ 400°F/Gas 6. Brown the guinea fowl on all sides in a roasting pan on the hob, then turn them breast uppermost and transfer the pan to the oven. Roast for about 1 hour, or until the guinea fowl are golden and cooked through. Transfer the guinea fowl to a warmed serving dish, cover with foil and keep warm.

2 Pour off the excess fat from the pan, then heat the juices on the stove and stir in the whisky. Bring to the boil and cook until reduced. Add the stock and cream and simmer again until reduced slightly. Strain and season to taste.

3 Meanwhile, trim the leeks so that they are roughly the same length as the guinea fowl breasts, then cook them whole in salted boiling water for about 3 minutes, or until tender but not too soft. Drain the leeks in a colander.

4 Carve the guinea fowl. To serve, arrange portions of mashed sweet potato on warmed serving plates, then add the carved guinea fowl and the leeks. Garnish with sprigs of fresh thyme, and season with plenty of freshly ground black pepper. Spoon a little of the sauce over each portion and serve the rest separately.

## VARIATION
*∽*

If you prefer, you can substitute brandy, Madeira or Marsala for the whisky. Or, to make a non-alcoholic version, use freshly squeezed orange juice instead.

# ONE POT
# DISHES &
# CASSEROLES

One of the best ways to blend the flavour of tender chicken with other ingredients is to cook it slowly as a one-pot dish, casserole or stew. In this chapter you will discover ingredients that you would rarely find accompanying chicken, ranging from blackberries to cocoa and prawns (shrimp), as well as a host of favourite flavourings, such as chillies, wine, mushrooms, garlic and herbs. Many of the dishes can be prepared in advance, and there are recipes suitable for everyday cooking and for special occasions.

# Chicken with Blackberries and Lemon

*This delicious dish combines some wonderful flavours, and the red wine and blackberries give it a dramatic appearance.*

### INGREDIENTS

*Serves 4*

4 part-boned chicken breast
   portions, skinned
25g/1oz/2 tbsp butter
15ml/1 tbsp sunflower oil
25g/1oz/$^1$/4 cup flour
150ml/$^1$/4 pint/$^2$/3 cup red wine
150ml/$^1$/4 pint/$^2$/3 cup chicken stock
grated rind of $^1$/2 orange plus
   15ml/1 tbsp juice
3 lemon balm sprigs, finely chopped, plus
   1 sprig to garnish
150ml/$^1$/4 pint/$^2$/3 cup double
   (heavy) cream
1 egg yolk
115g/4oz/1 cup fresh blackberries, plus
   50g/2oz/$^1$/2 cup to garnish
salt and ground black pepper

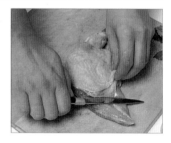

1 Preheat the oven to 180°C/ 350°F/Gas 4. Season the chicken breast portions. Heat the butter and oil in a frying pan, fry the chicken to seal it, then transfer to a flameproof casserole dish. Stir the flour into the pan, then add the wine and stock and bring to the boil. Add the orange rind and juice, and the chopped lemon balm. Pour over the chicken.

2 Cover the casserole and cook in the oven for about 40 minutes.

3 Blend the cream with the egg yolk, add some of the liquid from the casserole and stir back into the dish with the blackberries. Cover and cook for another 10–15 minutes, until the chicken is cooked. Serve garnished with blackberries and the sprig of lemon balm.

# Apricot and Chicken Casserole

*This mildly curried fruity chicken
dish served with almond rice makes
a good winter meal.*

## INGREDIENTS

*Serves 4*

15ml/1 tbsp oil
8 chicken thighs, boned and skinned
1 medium onion, finely chopped
5ml/1 tsp medium curry powder
30ml/2 tbsp plain (all-purpose) flour
450ml/³/4 pint/scant 2 cups chicken stock
juice of 1 large orange
8 dried apricots, halved
15ml/1 tbsp sultanas (golden raisins)
salt and ground black pepper

*For the rice*

225g/8oz/2 cups cooked long grain rice
15g/¹/2 oz/1 tbsp butter
50g/2oz/¹/2 cup toasted, flaked
   (sliced) almonds

1 Preheat the oven to 190°C/
375°F/Gas 5. Heat the oil in a
large frying pan. Cut the chicken
into cubes and brown quickly all
over in the oil. Add the chopped
onion and cook gently until soft
and lightly browned.

2 Transfer the chicken and onion
to a large flameproof casserole.
Sprinkle in the curry powder and
cook again for a few minutes. Add
the flour and blend in the stock
and orange juice. Bring to the
boil and season with salt and
freshly ground black pepper.

3 Add the apricots and sultanas,
cover with a lid and cook gently
for an hour, or until tender and
cooked through, in the preheated
oven. Adjust the seasoning to taste.

4 To make the almond rice,
reheat the pre-cooked rice
with the butter and season to taste.
Stir in the toasted almonds just
before serving.

# Stoved Chicken

2 Heat the butter and oil in a large, heavy frying pan, add the bacon and chicken, and brown on all sides, stirring frequently. Using a slotted spoon, transfer the chicken and bacon to the casserole. Reserve the fat in the pan.

3 Sprinkle the remaining thyme over the chicken, season with salt and pepper, then cover with the remaining onion slices, followed by a neat layer of overlapping potato slices. Season the dish well.

*This Scottish dish of slowly cooked potatoes layered with bacon and chicken has a lovely aroma of thyme and bay. It makes a perfect dish for cold autumn and winter evenings.*

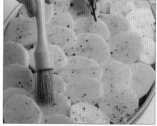

4 Pour the stock into the casserole, add the bay leaf and brush the potatoes with the reserved fat. Cover tightly and bake for about 2 hours, or until the chicken is very tender and cooked through.

5 Preheat the grill (broiler). Take the cover off the casserole and place it under the grill until the slices of potato begin to turn golden brown and crisp. Remove the bay leaf and serve hot.

### INGREDIENTS

*Serves 4*

1kg/2$^1$/4 lb baking potatoes, cut into
  5mm/$^1$/4 in slices
butter, for greasing
2 large onions, thinly sliced
15ml/1 tbsp chopped fresh thyme
25g/1oz/2 tbsp butter
15ml/1 tbsp vegetable oil
2 large bacon slices, chopped
4 large chicken pieces, halved
600ml/1 pint/2$^1$/2 cups chicken stock
1 bay leaf
salt and ground black pepper

1 Preheat the oven to 150°C/ 300°F/Gas 2. Arrange a thick layer of half the potato slices in the bottom of a lightly greased, large, heavy casserole, then cover with half the onions. Sprinkle with half of the thyme, and season with salt and pepper to taste.

# Coq au Vin

*This is a classic French country casserole, rich with the wonderful flavours of red wine and herbs.*

INGREDIENTS

Serves 6

45ml/3 tbsp light olive oil

12 shallots

225g/8oz rindless streaky (fatty) bacon
    rashers (strips), chopped

3 garlic cloves, finely chopped

225g/8oz/3 cups small mushrooms, halved

6 boneless chicken thighs

3 chicken breast fillets, halved

1 bottle red wine

salt and ground black pepper

45ml/3 tbsp chopped fresh parsley,
    to garnish

boiled potatoes, to serve

*For the bouquet garni*

3 sprigs each of fresh parsley, thyme
    and sage

1 bay leaf

4 peppercorns

*For the beurre manié*

25g/1oz/2 tbsp butter, softened

25g/1oz/$^1/_4$ cup plain (all-purpose) flour

1 Heat the oil in a large, flame-proof casserole and cook the shallots for 5 minutes, or until golden. Increase the heat, add the bacon, garlic and mushrooms and cook for a further 10 minutes, stirring frequently.

2 Use a slotted spoon to transfer the cooked ingredients to a plate, then brown the chicken portions in the oil remaining in the pan, turning them until they are golden brown all over. Return the shallots, garlic, mushrooms and bacon to the casserole and pour in the red wine.

3 Tie the bouquet garni ingredients into a small piece of muslin (cheesecloth). Add to the casserole. Bring to the boil, reduce the heat and cover the casserole, then simmer for 30–40 minutes, until the chicken is cooked through.

4 To make the beurre manié, cream the butter and flour together in a small bowl using your fingers or a spoon to make a smooth paste.

5 Add small lumps of this paste to the bubbling casserole, stirring well until each piece has melted into the liquid before adding the next. When all the paste has been added, simmer, stirring constantly, for 5 minutes.

6 Season the casserole to taste with salt and pepper and serve garnished with chopped fresh parsley and accompanied by boiled potatoes.

# Chicken and Lentil Casserole

*A casserole of wonderfully tender chicken, root vegetables and lentils, finished with crème fraîche, mustard and tarragon, makes a deliciously aromatic meal.*

### INGREDIENTS

*Serves 4*

350g/12 oz onions
350g/12 oz trimmed leeks
225g/8 oz carrots
450g/1lb swede (rutabaga)
30ml/2 tbsp oil
4 chicken pieces, about 900g/2 lb
    total weight
115g/4oz/$^1$/$_2$ cup green lentils
475ml/16 fl oz/2 cups chicken stock
300ml/$^1$/$_2$ pint/1$^1$/$_4$ cups apple juice
10ml/2 tsp cornflour (cornstarch)
45ml/3 tbsp crème fraîche
10ml/2 tsp wholegrain mustard
30ml/2 tbsp chopped fresh tarragon
salt and ground black pepper
fresh tarragon sprigs, to garnish

1 Preheat the oven to 190°C/ 375°F/Gas 5. Roughly chop the onions, leeks, carrots and swede into similarly sized pieces.

2 Heat the oil in a large, flameproof casserole. Season the chicken pieces with salt and pepper and brown them in the hot oil until golden. Drain on kitchen paper.

3 Add the onions to the pan and cook for 5 minutes, stirring, until they begin to soften and colour.

4 Stir in the leeks, carrots, swede and lentils and stir over a medium heat for 2 minutes.

5 Return the chicken to the pan. Add the stock, apple juice and seasoning. Bring to the boil and cover tightly. Cook in the oven for 50–60 minutes, or until the chicken and lentils are cooked through.

6 Place the casserole on the stove over a medium heat. Blend the cornflour with 30ml/ 2 tbsp water and add to the casserole with the crème fraîche, mustard and tarragon. Adjust the seasoning. Simmer gently for about 2 minutes, stirring, before serving garnished with tarragon sprigs.

# Country Chicken Casserole

*Succulent chicken joints in a vegetable sauce are excellent served with brown rice or pasta.*

INGREDIENTS

*Serves 4*

2 chicken breast fillets, skinned
2 chicken legs, skinned
30ml/2 tbsp plain (all-purpose) wholemeal (whole-wheat) flour
15ml/1 tbsp sunflower oil
300ml/$^1$/2 pint/1$^1$/4 cups chicken stock
300ml/$^1$/2 pint/1$^1$/4 cups white wine
30ml/2 tbsp passata (bottled strained tomatoes)
15ml/1 tbsp tomato purée (paste)
4 rashers (strips) lean smoked back bacon, chopped
1 large onion, sliced
1 garlic clove, crushed
1 green (bell) pepper, seeded and sliced
225g/8oz/3 cups button (white) mushrooms
225g/8oz carrots, sliced
1 bouquet garni
225g/8oz fresh or frozen Brussels sprouts
175g/6oz/1$^1$/2 cups fresh shelled or frozen petits pois (baby peas)
salt and ground black pepper
chopped fresh parsley, to garnish

2 Heat the oil in a large, flame-proof casserole, add the chicken and cook until browned all over. Remove the chicken using a slotted spoon, and keep warm.

5 Stir in the Brussels sprouts and petits pois, re-cover and bake for 30 minutes more, until cooked.

3 Add any remaining flour to the pan and cook for 1 minute. Gradually stir in the stock and wine, then add the passata and tomato purée.

6 Remove and discard the bouquet garni. Add seasoning to the casserole, garnish with chopped fresh parsley and serve immediately.

1 Preheat the oven to 180°C/350°F/Gas 4. Coat the chicken breast fillets and legs with the flour seasoned with salt and pepper.

4 Bring to the boil, stirring constantly, then add the chicken, bacon, onion, garlic, pepper, mushrooms, carrots and bouquet garni, and stir. Cover and bake for 1$^1$/2 hours, stirring once or twice.

VARIATION

Red wine can be used instead of white for a delicious change.

# Chicken Thighs with Lemon and Garlic

*This recipe uses classic European flavourings for chicken. Versions of it can be found in Spain and Italy. This particular recipe, however, is of French origin.*

## INGREDIENTS

*Serves 4*

600ml/1 pint/2$^1$/2 cups chicken stock
20 large garlic cloves
25g/1oz/2 tbsp butter
15ml/1 tbsp olive oil
8 chicken thighs
1 lemon, peel and pith removed and
    sliced thinly
30ml/2 tbsp plain (all-purpose) flour
150ml/$^1$/4 pint/$^2$/3 cup dry white wine
salt and ground black pepper
chopped fresh parsley or basil, to garnish
new potatoes or rice, to serve

1 Put the stock into a pan and bring to the boil. Add the garlic cloves, cover and simmer gently for 40 minutes. Heat the butter and oil in a sauté or frying pan, add the chicken thighs and cook gently on all sides until golden. Transfer to an ovenproof dish. Preheat the oven to 190°C/375°F/Gas 5.

2 Strain the stock and reserve it. Distribute the garlic and lemon slices among the chicken pieces. Add the flour to the fat in the pan in which the chicken was browned, and cook, stirring, for 1 minute. Add the wine, stirring constantly and scraping the bottom of the pan, then add the stock. Cook, stirring, until the sauce has thickened and is smooth. Season with salt and pepper.

3 Pour the sauce over the chicken, cover, and cook in the oven for 40–45 minutes, until cooked through. If a thicker sauce is required, lift out the chicken pieces, and reduce the sauce by boiling rapidly, until it is thick enough. Scatter over the chopped parsley or basil and serve with boiled new potatoes or rice.

# Chicken with Garlic

*In this recipe, garlic and onion are slowly cooked then puréed, making a fabulous sauce for the chicken. Use fresh new season's garlic if you can find it – there's no need to peel the cloves if the skin is not papery.*

### INGREDIENTS

*Serves 8*

2kg/4$^1$/$_2$ lb chicken pieces

1 large onion, halved and sliced

3 large garlic bulbs (about 200g/7oz),
    separated into cloves and peeled

150ml/$^1$/$_4$ pint/$^2$/$_3$ cup dry white wine

175ml/6fl oz/$^3$/$_4$ cup chicken stock

4–5 thyme sprigs, or 2.5ml/$^1$/$_2$ tsp
    dried thyme

1 small rosemary sprig, or a pinch of
    ground rosemary

1 bay leaf

salt and ground black pepper

1 Preheat the oven to 190°C/ 375°F/Gas 5. Pat the chicken pieces dry and season with salt and pepper.

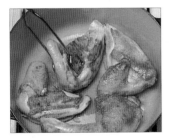

2 Put the chicken, skin side down, in a large, flameproof casserole and set over a medium-high heat. Turn frequently and transfer the chicken to a plate when browned. Cook in batches if necessary and pour off the fat after browning.

3 Add the onion and garlic to the casserole, replace the lid and cook over a medium-low heat, covered, until lightly browned, stirring frequently.

4 Add the wine to the casserole, bring to the boil and return the chicken to the casserole. Add the stock and herbs and bring back to the boil. Cover and transfer to the oven. Cook for 25 minutes, or until the chicken is tender and the juices run clear when the thickest part of the thigh is pierced.

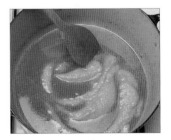

5 Remove the chicken from the pan and strain the cooking liquid. Discard the herbs, transfer the solids to a food processor and purée until smooth. Remove any fat from the cooking liquid and return to the casserole. Stir in the garlic and onion purée, add the chicken and reheat before serving.

# Chicken with Chorizo

The additions of chorizo sausage and sherry give a warm, interesting flavour to this simple Spanish casserole. Serve with rice or boiled potatoes.

### INGREDIENTS

Serves 4

1 medium chicken, jointed, or 4 chicken
   legs, halved
10ml/2 tsp ground paprika
60ml/4 tbsp olive oil
2 small onions, sliced
6 garlic cloves, thinly sliced
150g/5oz chorizo sausage
400g/14oz can chopped tomatoes
12–16 bay leaves
75ml/5 tbsp medium sherry
salt and ground black pepper
rice or potatoes, to serve

1 Preheat the oven to 190°C/ 375°F/Gas 5. Coat the chicken pieces in the paprika, making sure they are evenly covered, then season with salt. Heat the olive oil in a frying pan and fry the chicken until brown.

2 Transfer to an ovenproof dish. Add the onions to the pan and fry quickly. Add the garlic and sliced chorizo, and fry for 2 minutes.

3 Add the tomatoes, two of the bay leaves and the sherry, and bring to the boil. Pour over the chicken and cover with a lid. Bake for 45 minutes. Remove the lid and season to taste. Cook for a further 20 minutes, or until the chicken is golden and cooked through. Serve with rice or potatoes, garnished with the remaining bay leaves.

# Varna-style Chicken

*In this tasty dish from Bulgaria, the chicken is smothered in a rich tomato and mushroom sauce.*

INGREDIENTS

*Serves 8*

1 chicken, about 1.8kg/4lb, cut into
    8 pieces
2.5ml/$^1$/$_2$ tsp chopped fresh thyme
40g/1$^1$/$_2$ oz/3 tbsp butter
45ml/3 tbsp vegetable oil
3–4 garlic cloves, crushed
2 onions, finely chopped
salt and ground white pepper
basil and thyme leaves, to garnish
freshly cooked rice, to serve

*For the sauce*

120ml/4fl oz/$^1$/$_2$ cup dry sherry
45ml/3 tbsp tomato purée (paste)
a few fresh basil leaves
about 30ml/2 tbsp white wine vinegar
generous pinch of granulated sugar
5ml/1 tsp mild mustard
400g/14oz can chopped tomatoes
225g/8oz/3 cups mushrooms, sliced

3 Add the sherry, tomato purée, seasoning, basil, vinegar, sugar, mustard and tomatoes to the frying pan and bring to the boil.

---

### VARIATION
~
You could replace the cultivated mushrooms with wild if you like.

---

4 Reduce the heat and add the mushrooms. Adjust the seasoning with more sugar or vinegar to taste.

5 Pour the tomato sauce over the chicken. Bake in the oven, covered, for 45–60 minutes, or until cooked thoroughly. Serve on a bed of rice, garnished with basil and thyme.

1 Preheat the oven to 180°C/ 350°F/Gas 4. Season the chicken with salt, pepper and thyme. In a large frying pan brown the chicken in the butter and oil. Remove from the frying pan, place in an ovenproof dish and keep hot.

2 Add the garlic and onion to the frying pan and cook for about 2–3 minutes, or until just soft.

# Chicken with Chipotle Sauce

*It is important to seek out chipotle chillies for this recipe, as they impart a wonderfully rich and smoky flavour to the chicken breasts. The purée can be made ahead of time, making this a very easy recipe for entertaining.*

### INGREDIENTS

*Serves 6*

6 chipotle chillies

200ml/7fl oz/scant 1 cup water

chicken stock (see method)

3 onions

6 chicken breast fillets, skinned

45ml/3 tbsp vegetable oil

salt and ground black pepper

fresh oregano, to garnish

rice, to serve

2 Preheat the oven to 180°C/
350°F/Gas 4. Chop the flesh of the chillies roughly and put it in a food processor or blender. Add enough chicken stock to the soaking water to make it up to 400ml/14fl oz/1²/₃ cups. Pour it into the processor or blender and process until smooth.

1 Put the dried chillies in a bowl and pour over hot water to cover. Leave to stand for about 30 minutes, or until very soft. Drain, reserving the soaking water in a measuring jug (cup). Cut off the stalk from each chilli, then slit them lengthways and scrape out the seeds with a small sharp knife.

3 Peel the onions. Cut them in half, then slice them thinly. Separate the slices.

4 Trim off any fat or membrane from the chicken breasts.

5 Heat the oil in a large frying pan, add the onions and cook over a low to medium heat for about 5 minutes, or until they have softened but not coloured, stirring occasionally.

6 Using a slotted spoon, transfer the onion slices to a casserole that is large enough to hold all the chicken in a single layer. Season the onion slices.

7 Arrange the chicken on top of the onion slices. Season with salt and black pepper.

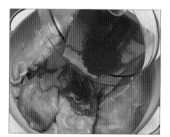

8 Pour the chipotle purée over the chicken, making sure that each piece is evenly coated.

9 Place the casserole in the preheated oven and bake for 45 minutes–1 hour, or until the chicken is cooked through, but is still moist and tender. Garnish with fresh oregano and serve with boiled white rice.

---

COOK'S TIP

Chipotle chillies are dried and smoked chillies that are often used in Mexican cooking.

# Guinea Fowl with Vegetable Stew

*Mild, sweet leeks are excellent in this light stew of guinea fowl and spring vegetables. Chicken can be used instead of the guinea fowl.*

### INGREDIENTS

Serves 4

45ml/3 tbsp olive oil

115g/4oz pancetta, cut into lardons

30ml/2 tbsp plain (all-purpose) flour

2 guinea fowl, about 1.2–1.6kg/2¹/₂–3¹/₂lb each, jointed into 4 portions each

1 onion, chopped

1 head of garlic, separated into cloves and peeled

1 bottle dry white wine

fresh thyme sprig

1 fresh bay leaf

a few parsley stalks

250g/9oz baby carrots

250g/9oz baby turnips

6 slender leeks, cut into 7.5cm/3in lengths

250g/9oz/1³/₄ cups shelled fresh peas

15ml/1 tbsp French herb mustard

15g/¹/₂oz/¹/₄ cup fresh flat leaf parsley, chopped

15ml/1 tbsp chopped fresh mint

salt and ground black pepper

1 Heat 30ml/2 tbsp of the oil in a pan and cook the pancetta over a medium heat until lightly browned, stirring occasionally. Remove from the pan and set aside.

2 Season the flour and toss the guinea fowl portions in it. Fry in the oil remaining in the pan until browned on all sides. Transfer to a flameproof casserole. Preheat the oven to 180°C/350°F/Gas 4.

3 Add the remaining oil to the pan and cook the onion gently until soft. Add the garlic and fry for 3–4 minutes, then stir in the pancetta and wine.

4 Tie the thyme, bay leaf and parsley into a bundle and add to the pan. Bring to the boil, then simmer gently for 3–4 minutes. Pour over the guinea fowl and add seasoning. Cover and cook in the oven for 40 minutes.

5 Add the baby carrots and turnips to the casserole and cook, covered, for another 30 minutes, or until the vegetables are just tender.

6 Stir in the leeks and cook for a further 15–20 minutes, or until all the vegetables and the guinea fowl are fully cooked.

7 Meanwhile, blanch the peas in boiling water for 2 minutes, then drain. Transfer the guinea fowl and vegetables to a warmed serving dish. Place the casserole over a high heat and boil the juices vigorously, stirring, until they are reduced by about half.

8 Stir in the peas and cook gently for 2–3 minutes, then stir in the mustard and adjust the seasoning. Stir in most of the parsley and the mint. Pour this sauce over the guinea fowl or return the joints and vegetables to the casserole. Scatter the remaining parsley over the top and serve immediately.

# Guinea Fowl with Cabbage

*In this French recipe guinea fowl is cooked on a bed of cabbage, leeks, onions and carrots, which give it a lovely flavour.*

### INGREDIENTS

Serves 4

1 guinea fowl, about 1.2–1.3kg/2$^1$/$_2$–3lb
15ml/1 tbsp vegetable oil
15g/$^1$/$_2$ oz/1 tbsp butter
1 large onion, halved and sliced
1 large carrot, halved and sliced
1 large leek, sliced
450g/1lb green cabbage, such as Savoy, sliced or chopped
120ml/4fl oz/$^1$/$_2$ cup dry white wine
120ml/4fl oz/$^1$/$_2$ cup chicken stock
1 or 2 garlic cloves, finely chopped
salt and ground black pepper

1 Preheat the oven to 180°C/ 350°F/Gas 4. Tie the legs of the guinea fowl with string.

2 Heat half the oil in a large, flameproof casserole over a medium-high heat and cook the guinea fowl until golden brown on all sides. Transfer to a plate.

3 Pour out the fat from the casserole and add the remaining oil with the butter. Add the onion, carrot and leek and cook over a low heat, stirring, for 5 minutes. Add the cabbage and cook for about 3–4 minutes, or until slightly wilted, stirring occasionally. Season to taste.

4 Place the guinea fowl on its side on the vegetables. Add the wine and bring to the boil, then add the stock and garlic. Cover and transfer to the oven. Cook for 25 minutes, then turn the bird on to the other side and cook for 20–25 minutes, or until it is tender and the juices run clear when the thickest part of the thigh is pierced.

5 Transfer the bird to a board and leave to stand for 5–10 minutes, then cut into four or eight pieces. With a slotted spoon, transfer the cabbage to a warmed serving dish and place the guinea fowl on top. Skim any fat from the cooking juices and serve separately.

# Italian Chicken

*Sun-dried tomatoes and pesto are a*
*winning combination in this dish.*

### INGREDIENTS

*Serves 4*

30ml/2 tbsp plain (all-purpose) flour
4 chicken portions (legs, breasts or
   quarters), skinned
30ml/2 tbsp olive oil
1 onion, chopped
2 garlic cloves, chopped
1 red (bell) pepper, seeded and chopped
400g/14oz can chopped tomatoes
30ml/2 tbsp red pesto sauce
4 sun-dried tomatoes in oil, chopped
150ml/$\frac{1}{4}$ pint/$\frac{2}{3}$ cup chicken stock
5ml/1 tsp dried oregano
8 black olives, pitted
salt and ground black pepper
chopped fresh basil and a few basil leaves,
   to garnish
tagliatelle, to serve

1 Place the flour and seasoning in a plastic bag. Add the chicken pieces and shake until coated. Heat the oil in a flameproof casserole, add the chicken and brown quickly. Remove with a spoon and set aside.

2 Lower the heat, add the onion, garlic and red pepper and cook for 5 minutes.

3 Stir in the all the ingredients, but not the olives. Bring to the boil.

4 Return the sautéed chicken portions to the casserole. Season lightly, cover and simmer for 30–35 minutes, or until the chicken is cooked.

5 Add the olives and simmer for a further 5 minutes. Transfer to a warmed serving dish, sprinkle with the chopped fresh basil and garnish with a few basil leaves. Serve with tagliatelle.

# Honey and Orange Glazed Chicken

*This way of cooking chicken breasts*
*is popular in America, Australia*
*and Great Britain. It is ideal for an*
*easy evening meal served with*
*baked potatoes and salad.*

### INGREDIENTS

*Serves 4*

4 chicken breast fillets, 175g/6oz each
15ml/1 tbsp oil
4 spring onions (scallions), chopped
1 garlic clove, crushed
45ml/3 tbsp clear honey
60ml/4 tbsp fresh orange juice
1 orange, peeled and segmented
30ml/2 tbsp soy sauce
fresh lemon balm or flat leaf parsley,
   to garnish
baked potatoes and mixed salad, to serve

1 Preheat the oven to 190°C/375°F/Gas 5. Place the chicken in a shallow roasting pan. Set aside.

2 Heat the oil in a small pan, and fry the spring onions and garlic for 2 minutes, or until softened. Add the clear honey, orange juice, orange segments and soy sauce to the pan, stirring well until the honey has melted.

3 Pour over the chicken and bake, uncovered, for about 45 minutes, basting with the honey glaze once or twice, until the chicken is cooked. Garnish with the lemon balm or parsley and serve the chicken and its sauce with baked potatoes and a salad.

# Chicken with Beans

*This substantial casserole is rich with the flavours of wine, herbs and sour cream.*

### INGREDIENTS

*Serves 4–6*

275g/10oz dried kidney or other beans, soaked overnight

8–12 chicken portions, such as thighs and drumsticks

12 bacon rashers (strips), rind removed

2 large onions, thinly sliced

250ml/8fl oz/1 cup dry white wine

2.5ml/$^1/_2$ tsp chopped fresh sage or oregano

2.5ml/$^1/_2$ tsp chopped fresh rosemary

generous pinch of freshly grated nutmeg

150ml/$^1/_4$ pint/$^2/_3$ cup sour cream

15ml/1 tbsp chilli powder or paprika

salt and ground black pepper

sprigs of rosemary and lemon wedges, to garnish

1 Preheat the oven to 180°C/ 350°F/Gas 4. Cook the beans in fast-boiling water for 20 minutes. Rinse and drain the beans well and trim the chicken portions. Season the chicken with salt and pepper.

2 Arrange the bacon around the sides and base of an ovenproof dish. Sprinkle over half of the onion and then half the beans, followed by another layer of onion and then the remaining beans.

3 In a bowl combine the wine with the sage or oregano, rosemary and nutmeg. Pour over the onion and beans. In another bowl mix together the sour cream and the chilli powder or paprika.

4 Toss the chicken in the cream mixture and place on top of the beans. Cover with foil and bake for 1$^1/_4$–1$^1/_2$ hours, until done, removing the foil for the last 15 minutes. Garnish with rosemary and lemon.

# Potted Chicken

*This is a traditional Bulgarian way of cooking chicken – in a flame-proof pot, on top of the stove – so that it cooks slowly and evenly in its own juices.*

### INGREDIENTS

*Serves 6–8*

8 chicken pieces

6–8 firm ripe tomatoes, chopped

2 garlic cloves, crushed

3 onions, chopped

60ml/4 tbsp oil or melted lard or white cooking fat

250ml/8fl oz/1 cup good chicken stock

2 bay leaves

10ml/2 tsp paprika

10 white peppercorns, bruised

handful of parsley, stalks reserved and leaves finely chopped

salt

1 Put the chicken, tomatoes and garlic in a flameproof casserole. Cover and cook gently for 10–15 minutes.

> ### VARIATION
>
> For spicy chicken, add a seeded and chopped chilli at Step 2.

2 Add the onions, oil or lard, stock, bay leaves, paprika, peppercorns and salt, and stir well.

3 Cover tightly and cook over a very low heat, stirring occasionally, for about 1$^3/_4$–2 hours, or until the chicken is cooked through. Five minutes before the end of cooking, stir in the finely chopped parsley leaves. Serve hot.

# Chicken Brunswick Stew

*This chicken stew has a spicy bite. It is warming and filling.*

### INGREDIENTS

Serves 6

1 chicken, about 1.8kg/4lb, cut
    into portions
paprika
30ml/2 tbsp olive oil
30ml/2 tbsp butter
450g/1lb chopped onions
225g/8oz chopped green or yellow
    (bell) peppers
475ml/16fl oz/2 cups chopped peeled fresh
    or canned plum tomatoes
250ml/8fl oz/1 cup white wine
475ml/16fl oz/2 cups chicken stock
    or water
15g/$^1$/2 oz/$^1$/4 cup chopped fresh parsley
2.5ml/$^1$/2 tsp hot pepper sauce
15ml/1 tbsp Worcestershire sauce
350g/12oz/2 cups corn kernels (fresh,
    frozen or canned)
185g/6$^1$/2 oz/1 cup butter (wax) beans
    (fresh or frozen)
45ml/3 tbsp plain (all-purpose) flour
salt and ground black pepper
bread rolls, rice or potatoes, to serve
    (optional)

1 Pat the chicken pieces dry, then sprinkle them lightly with salt and paprika.

2 In a large, heavy pan, heat the olive oil with the butter over medium-high heat. Heat until the mixture is sizzling and just starting to change colour.

3 Add the chicken pieces and fry until golden brown on all sides. Remove the chicken pieces with tongs and set aside.

4 Reduce the heat to low and add the chopped onions and peppers to the pan. Cook for 8–10 minutes, or until softened.

5 Raise the heat. Add the tomatoes and their juice, the wine, stock or water, parsley, and hot pepper and Worcestershire sauces. Stir and bring to the boil.

6 Return the fried chicken pieces to the pan, pushing them down in the sauce. Cover, reduce the heat, and simmer for 30 minutes, stirring occasionally.

7 Add the corn and butter beans and mix well. Partly cover and cook for 30 minutes more.

8 Tilt the pan and skim off as much of the surface fat as possible. In a small bowl, mix the flour with a little water to make a paste.

9 Gradually stir in about 175ml/ 6fl oz/$^3$/4 cup of the hot sauce from the pan. Stir the flour mixture into the stew, and mix well to distribute it evenly and thicken it. Cook for 5–8 minutes more, stirring from time to time.

10 Check the seasoning. Serve the stew in shallow soup plates or large bowls, with bread rolls, rice or potatoes, if you like.

# Chicken with Sage, Prunes and Brandy

*This stir-fry has a very rich sauce based on a good brandy – use the best you can afford.*

*Serves 4*

115g/4oz1/2 cup prunes, stoned (pitted)
1.6kg/31/2 lb chicken breast fillets, skinned
300ml/1/2 pint/11/4 cups Cognac
   or brandy
15ml/1 tbsp fresh sage, chopped
150g/5oz smoked bacon, in one piece
50g/2oz/1/4 cup butter
24 baby onions, peeled and quartered
salt and ground black pepper
fresh sage sprigs, to garnish

1 Cut the prunes into slivers. Cut the chicken breast fillets into thin pieces.

2 Mix together the prunes, chicken, Cognac or brandy and chopped sage in a non-metallic dish. Cover and leave overnight in the refrigerator to marinate.

3 Next day, strain the chicken and prunes, reserving the Cognac marinade mixture, and pat dry on kitchen towels.

4 Cut the smoked bacon into dice and set aside.

5 Heat a wok and add half the butter. When melted, add the onions and stir-fry for 4 minutes until crisp and golden. Set aside.

6 Add the bacon to the wok and stir-fry for 1 minute until it begins to release some fat. Add the remaining butter and stir-fry the chicken and prunes for 3–4 minutes, or until crisp and golden. Push the chicken mixture to one side in the wok, add the Cognac and simmer until thickened. Stir the chicken into the sauce, season well with salt and pepper, and serve garnished with sage.

# Chicken Chasseur

3 Pour off all but 15ml/1 tbsp of fat from the pan. Add the onions or shallots, mushrooms and garlic. Cook until golden, stirring frequently.

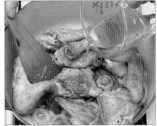

4 If using fresh tomatoes, plunge them into boiling water for 30 seconds, then refresh in cold water. Peel away the skins, remove the seeds and chop the flesh. Return the chicken to the casserole with any juices. Add the wine and bring to the boil, then stir in the stock and tomatoes.

5 Bring back to the boil, reduce the heat, cover and simmer over a low heat for about 20 minutes, or until the chicken is tender and the juices run clear when the thickest part of the meat is pierced. Tilt the pan and skim off any fat that has risen to the surface. Adjust the seasoning before serving.

*A chicken sauté is one of the classics of French cooking. Quick to prepare, it lends itself to endless variation.*

**INGREDIENTS**

Serves 4

40g/1$^{1}$/2 oz/$^{1}$/3 cup plain
   (all-purpose) flour
1.2kg/2$^{1}$/2 lb chicken pieces
15ml/1 tbsp olive oil
3 small onions or large shallots, sliced
175g/6oz/2$^{1}$/2 cups mushrooms, quartered
1 garlic clove, crushed
60ml/4 tbsp dry white wine
120ml/4fl oz/$^{1}$/2 cup chicken stock
350g/12oz tomatoes or 250ml/8fl oz/1 cup
   canned chopped tomatoes
salt and ground black pepper
fresh parsley, to garnish

1 Put the flour into a plastic bag and season. Drop each chicken piece into the bag and shake to coat with flour. Tap off the excess.

2 Heat the oil in a flameproof casserole. Fry the chicken over a medium-high heat until golden brown, turning once. Transfer to a plate and keep warm.

# Chicken with Peppers

*This colourful dish comes from the south of Italy, where sweet peppers are plentiful.*

INGREDIENTS

*Serves 4*

1 chicken, about 1.3kg/3lb cut
    into portions
3 large (bell) peppers, red, yellow or green
90ml/6 tbsp olive oil
2 medium red onions, finely sliced
2 garlic cloves, finely chopped
small piece of dried chilli, crumbled
    (optional)
120ml/4fl oz/$^1$/$_2$ cup white wine
salt and ground black pepper
2 tomatoes, fresh or canned, peeled
    and chopped
45g/3 tbsp chopped fresh parsley

1 Trim any fat and skin from the chicken. Cut the peppers in half, discard the seeds and the stem. Slice into strips.

2 Heat half the oil in a large, heavy pan or flameproof casserole. Add the onions, and cook over low heat until soft. Remove to a side dish. Add the remaining oil to the pan, raise the heat to medium, add the chicken and brown on all sides, about 6–8 minutes. Return the onions to the pan, and add the garlic and dried chilli, if using.

3 Pour in the wine, and cook until it has reduced by half. Add the peppers and stir well to coat them with the fats. Season. After 3–4 minutes, stir in the tomatoes. Lower the heat, cover the pan, and cook for 25–30 minutes, or until the peppers are soft and the chicken is cooked. Stir occasionally. Stir in the chopped parsley and serve.

# Chicken Breasts Cooked in Butter

*This simple and very delicious way of cooking chicken brings out all of its delicacy.*

INGREDIENTS

*Serves 4*

4 small chicken breast fillets, skinned
flour seasoned with salt and freshly
    ground black pepper
75g/3oz/6 tbsp butter
1 sprig fresh parsley, to garnish

1 Separate each breast into two fillets. Lightly pound the larger fillets between two sheets of clear film (plastic wrap) to flatten them. Dredge the chicken in the seasoned flour, shaking off any excess.

2 Heat the butter in a large, heavy frying pan until it bubbles. Place all the chicken fillets in the pan, in one layer if possible. Cook over moderate to high heat for 3–4 minutes, or until they are golden brown.

3 Turn the chicken over. Reduce the heat to medium-low, and continue cooking for 9–12 minutes, or until the fillets are cooked through but still springy to the touch. If the chicken begins to brown too much, cover the pan for the final minutes of cooking. Serve immediately garnished with a little parsley.

# Chicken in Creamed Horseradish

2 Wipe out the casserole, melt the butter, stir in the flour and gradually blend in the stock. Bring to the boil, stirring all the time.

3 Add the horseradish sauce and season with salt and freshly ground black pepper. Return the chicken to the casserole, cover and simmer for 30–40 minutes, or until the chicken is cooked through.

*The piquancy of horseradish gives this dish a sophisticated taste. Replace with half the quantity of fresh horseradish, if you like.*

## INGREDIENTS

*Serves 4*

30ml/2 tbsp olive oil

4 chicken portions

25g/1oz/2 tbsp butter

25g/1oz/2 tbsp plain (all-purpose) flour

450ml/$^3$/4 pint/scant 2 cups chicken stock

30ml/2 tbsp creamed horseradish
    sauce

salt and ground black pepper

15ml/1 tbsp chopped fresh parsley

mashed potatoes and green beans,
    to serve (optional)

1 Heat the oil in a large, flameproof casserole and gently brown the chicken portions on both sides over a medium heat. Remove the chicken from the casserole and keep warm.

4 Transfer to a serving dish and sprinkle with fresh parsley. Serve with mashed potatoes and green beans, if you like.

# Chicken in Green Sauce

*Slow, gentle cooking makes the chicken succulent and tender.*

*Serves 4*

25g/1oz/2 tbsp butter

15ml/1 tbsp olive oil

4 chicken portions

1 small onion, finely chopped

150ml/¹/4 pint/²/3 cup medium dry
    white wine

150ml/¹/4 pint/²/3 cup chicken stock

175g/6oz watercress or rocket (arugula)

2 thyme sprigs

2 tarragon sprigs

150ml/¹/4 pint/²/3 cup double
    (heavy) cream

salt and ground black pepper

watercress leaves or rocket (arugula),
    to garnish

1 Heat the butter and oil in a heavy, shallow pan, then brown the chicken evenly. Transfer the chicken to a plate using a slotted spoon and keep warm in the oven.

2 Add the onion to the cooking juices in the pan and cook until softened but not coloured.

3 Stir in the wine, boil for 2–3 minutes, then add the stock and bring to the boil. Return the chicken to the pan, cover tightly and cook very gently for about 30 minutes, or until the chicken juices run clear. Then transfer the chicken to a warm dish, cover the dish and keep warm.

4 Boil the cooking juices hard until reduced to about 60ml/4 tbsp. Remove the leaves from the watercress and herbs, tearing the rocket into small pieces, if using. Add the leaves to the pan with the cream and simmer over a medium heat until the sauce has thickened slightly.

5 Return the cooked chicken to the pan, season and heat through for a few minutes. Garnish with watercress leaves or rocket before serving.

# Chicken with Tomatoes and Prawns

*This tasty and unusual Piedmontese dish was created especially for Napoleon. Versions of it appear in both Italian and French recipe books.*

### INGREDIENTS

*Serves 4*

120ml/4fl oz/¹/₂ cup olive oil

8 skinless chicken thighs

1 onion, finely chopped

1 celery stick, finely chopped

1 garlic clove, crushed

350g/12oz ripe Italian plum tomatoes, peeled and roughly chopped

250ml/8fl oz/1 cup dry white wine

2.5ml/¹/₂ tsp chopped fresh rosemary

15ml/1 tbsp butter

8 small triangles thinly sliced white bread, without crusts

175g/6oz large raw prawns (shrimp), shelled

salt and ground black pepper

finely chopped flat leaf parsley, to garnish

1 Heat 30ml/2 tbsp of the oil in a frying pan. Add the chicken and sauté over a medium heat for about 5 minutes, or until it has changed colour on all sides. Transfer to a flameproof casserole.

2 Add the onion and celery to the frying pan and cook, stirring frequently, for about 3 minutes, or until softened. Add the garlic, tomatoes, wine, rosemary and seasoning. Bring to the boil, stirring.

3 Pour the tomato sauce over the chicken. Cover and cook gently for 40 minutes, or until the chicken juices run clear when pierced.

4 About 10 minutes before serving, add the remaining oil and the butter to the frying pan and heat until hot but not smoking. Add the triangles of bread and shallow fry until crisp and golden on each side. Drain.

5 Add the prawns to the casserole and heat until the prawns are cooked. Taste the sauce for seasoning. Dip one of the tips of each fried bread triangle in parsley. Serve the dish hot, garnished with the bread triangles.

# Chicken Pot au Feu

*In France, a pot au feu traditionally contains beef simmered in a rich stock, although chicken is also used. In this recipe, a lovely wine and herb-scented stock contains tender morsels of chicken and spring vegetables.*

### INGREDIENTS

*Serves 4*

1 chicken, about 2.25kg/5lb
1 parsley sprig
15ml/1 tbsp black peppercorns
1 bay leaf
300g/11oz baby carrots
175g/6oz baby leeks
25g/1oz/2 tbsp butter
15ml/1 tbsp olive oil
300g/11oz shallots, halved if large
200ml/7fl oz/scant 1 cup dry white wine
800g/1³/4 lb baby new potatoes
120ml/4fl oz/¹/2 cup double (heavy) cream
salt and ground black pepper
small bunch parsley or tarragon, chopped,
    to garnish

1 Joint the chicken into eight pieces and place the carcass in a large stockpot. Add the parsley sprig, peppercorns, bay leaf and the trimmings from the carrots and leeks. Cover with cold water and bring to the boil. Simmer for 45 minutes, then strain.

2 Meanwhile, melt the butter with the olive oil in a frying pan, then add the chicken pieces, season with salt and pepper, and brown them all over. Lift out the chicken pieces on to a plate and add the shallots to the pan. Cook over a low heat for 20 minutes, stirring occasionally, until softened, but not browned.

### COOK'S TIPS
∾
• Any leftover stock can be kept in the refrigerator and used in other recipes.
• You could use large potatoes, but they will need to be par-boiled first so that they will cook in 10–15 minutes in the pot with the other ingredients.

3 Return the chicken to the pan and add the wine. Scrape up any residue from the bottom of the pan with a wooden spoon, then add the carrots, leeks and potatoes with enough of the stock to just cover. Bring to the boil, then cover and simmer for 20 minutes, or until the chicken is cooked through. Stir in the cream and serve, garnished with the chopped parsley or tarragon.

# Chicken with Chianti

*The robust, full-bodied red wine and red pesto give this sauce a rich colour and almost spicy flavour, while the grapes add sweetness. Serve this Italian stew with grilled polenta or warm crusty bread, and accompany with a piquant salad, such as rocket or watercress, tossed with a tasty dressing.*

## INGREDIENTS

Serves 4

45ml/3 tbsp olive oil

4 part-boned chicken breast portions, skinned

1 medium red onion

30ml/2 tbsp red pesto

300ml/$^1$/2 pint/1$^1$/4 cups Chianti

300ml/$^1$/2 pint/1$^1$/4 cups water

115g/4 oz red grapes, halved lengthways and seeded if necessary

salt and ground black pepper

fresh basil leaves, to garnish

rocket (arugula) salad, to serve

1 Heat 30ml/2 tbsp of the oil in a large frying pan. Add the chicken breasts and sauté over a medium heat for about 5 minutes, or until they have changed colour on all sides. Remove with a slotted spoon and drain on kitchen paper.

2 Cut the onion in half, through the root. Trim off the root, then slice the onion halves lengthways to create thin wedges.

3 Heat the remaining oil in the pan, add the onion wedges and red pesto and cook gently, stirring constantly, for about 3 minutes, or until the onion is softened, but not browned.

4 Add the Chianti and water to the pan and bring to the boil, stirring, then return the chicken to the pan and add salt and pepper to taste.

5 Reduce the heat, then cover the pan and simmer for about 20 minutes, or until the chicken is tender and cooked through, stirring occasionally.

## COOK'S TIP

Use part-boned chicken breasts, if you can get them, in preference to boneless chicken for this dish as they have a better flavour. Chicken thighs or drumsticks could also be cooked in this way.

6 Add the grapes to the pan and cook over a low to medium heat until heated through, then taste the sauce for seasoning. Serve the chicken hot, garnished with basil and accompanied by the rocket salad.

## VARIATIONS

Use green pesto instead of red, and substitute a dry white wine such as Pinot grigio for the Chianti, then finish with seedless green grapes. A few spoonfuls of mascarpone cheese can be added at the end if you like, to enrich the sauce.

# Chicken with Mushrooms

*Strips of succulent chicken are served in a cream, mushroom and sherry sauce. Tagliatelle makes an ideal accompaniment.*

### INGREDIENTS

*Serves 4*

4 large chicken breast fillets, skinned
45ml/3 tbsp olive oil
1 onion, thinly sliced
1 garlic clove, crushed
225g/8oz/3 cups button (white)
  mushrooms, quartered
30ml/2 tbsp sherry
15ml/1 tbsp lemon juice
150ml/¹/₄ pint/²/₃ cup single (light) cream
salt and ground black pepper

1 Divide each chicken breast into two natural fillets. Place each between two sheets of clear film (plastic wrap) and flatten to a thickness of 5mm/¹/₄ in with a rolling pin. Cut into 2.5cm/1in diagonal strips.

2 Heat 30ml/2 tbsp of the oil in a large frying pan and cook the onion and crushed garlic slowly until tender.

3 Add the mushrooms and cook them for 5 minutes. Remove and keep warm.

4 Increase the heat. Add the remaining oil and fry the chicken very quickly, in small batches, for 3–4 minutes, or until lightly coloured. Season each batch with a little salt and black pepper. Remove and keep warm on a plate while frying the rest of the chicken.

5 Add the sherry and lemon juice to the pan and quickly return the chicken, onions, garlic and mushrooms, stirring to coat.

6 Stir in the cream and bring to the boil. Adjust the seasoning to taste. Serve immediately.

# Chicken Fricassée Forestier

*The term fricassée is used to describe a light stew, which is first sautéed in butter. The accompanying sauce can vary, but here wild mushrooms and bacon provide a rich flavour.*

INGREDIENTS

*Serves 4*

3 chicken breast fillets, skinned and sliced

50g/2oz/¼ cup unsalted (sweet) butter

15ml/1 tbsp vegetable oil

115g/4oz unsmoked rindless streaky (fatty) bacon, cut into pieces

75ml/5 tbsp dry sherry or white wine

1 medium onion, chopped

350g/12oz assorted wild mushrooms, trimmed and sliced

40g/1½ oz/⅓ cup plain (all-purpose) flour

500ml/17fl oz/2¼ cups chicken stock

10ml/2 tsp lemon juice

60ml/4 tbsp chopped fresh parsley

salt and ground black pepper

boiled rice, carrots and baby corn, to serve

1 Season the chicken with pepper. Heat half of the butter and the oil in a large, heavy skillet or flameproof casserole and brown the chicken and bacon pieces. Transfer to a shallow dish and pour off any excess fat.

2 Return the skillet to the heat and brown the sediment. Pour in the sherry or wine and stir with a flat wooden spoon to deglaze the pan. Pour the sherry liquid over the chicken and wipe the skillet clean.

3 Fry the onion in the remaining butter until golden brown. Add the mushrooms and cook, stirring frequently, for 6–8 minutes, or until their juices begin to run. Stir in the flour then remove from the heat. Gradually add the chicken stock and stir well until the flour is completely blended in.

4 Add the reserved chicken and bacon with the sherry juices, return to the heat and stir to thicken. Simmer for 10–15 minutes and then add the lemon juice, parsley and seasoning. Serve with plain boiled rice, carrots and baby corn.

# Tuscan Chicken

*This simple chicken casserole has all the flavours of traditional Tuscan ingredients: sweet red peppers, tomatoes and aromatic oregano.*

INGREDIENTS

*Serves 4*

8 chicken thighs, skinned

5ml/1 tsp olive oil

1 medium onion, thinly sliced

2 red (bell) peppers, seeded and sliced

1 garlic clove, crushed

300ml/$^1$/2 pint/1$^1$/4 cups passata
   (bottled strained tomatoes)

150ml/$^1$/4 pint/$^2$/3 cup dry white wine

large sprig fresh oregano, or
   5ml/1 tsp dried

400g/14oz can cannellini beans, drained

45ml/3 tbsp fresh breadcrumbs

salt and ground black pepper

1 Fry the chicken in the oil in a heavy pan until golden brown. Remove and keep hot. Add the onion and peppers to the pan and gently sauté until softened, but not brown. Stir in the crushed garlic.

2 Add the chicken, passata, wine and oregano. Season well, bring to the boil then cover the pan.

3 Lower the heat and simmer gently, stirring occasionally, for 30–35 minutes, or until the chicken is tender and the juices run clear, when pierced with the point of a knife.

4 Stir in the cannellini beans and simmer for a further 5 minutes, or until heated through. Sprinkle with the breadcrumbs and cook under a hot grill (broiler) until golden brown.

VARIATION

The wine can be replaced by chicken stock, if you prefer.

# Chicken in Creamy Orange Sauce

*This sauce is deceptively creamy – in fact it is made with low-fat fromage frais, which is virtually fat-free. The brandy adds a richer flavour, but is optional – omit it if you prefer and use orange juice alone.*

*Serves 4*

8 chicken thighs or drumsticks, skinned
45ml/3 tbsp brandy (optional)
300ml/$^{1}$/$_{2}$ pint/1$^{1}$/$_{4}$ cups orange juice
3 spring onions (scallions), chopped
10ml/2 tsp cornflour (cornstarch)
90ml/6 tbsp low-fat fromage frais or
   crème fraîche
salt and ground black pepper
rice or pasta and green salad, to serve

1 Fry the chicken pieces without fat in a non-stick or heavy pan, turning until evenly browned.

## COOK'S TIP

Cornflour helps to stabilize the fromage frais and stop it from curdling.

2 Stir in the brandy, if using, orange juice and spring onions. Bring to the boil, then cover and simmer for 15 minutes, or until the chicken is tender and the juices run clear when pierced.

3 Blend the cornflour with a little water then mix into the fromage frais or crème fraîche. Stir this into the sauce and stir over a medium heat until boiling.

4 Adjust the seasoning and serve with boiled rice or pasta and a green salad.

# Chicken Liver Stir-fry

*The final sprinkling of lemon, parsley and garlic gives this dish a delightfully fresh flavour and a wonderful aroma.*

*Serves 4*

500g/1¼lb chicken livers
75g/3oz/6 tbsp butter
175g/6oz/2½ cups field (portabello)
  mushrooms
50g/2oz/1 cup chanterelle mushrooms
3 cloves garlic, finely chopped
2 shallots, finely chopped
150ml/¼ pint/⅔ cup medium sherry
3 fresh rosemary sprigs
grated rind of 1 lemon
30ml/2 tbsp chopped fresh parsley
salt and ground black pepper
rosemary sprigs, to garnish
4 thick slices of white toast, to serve

1 Clean and trim the chicken livers to remove any gristle or muscle or discoloured parts.

2 Season the chicken livers generously with salt and ground black pepper, tossing well to coat them all thoroughly.

3 Heat a wok or frying pan and add 15g/½oz/1 tbsp of the butter. When melted, add the livers in batches (melting more butter when necessary but reserving 25g/1oz/2 tbsp for the vegetables) and flash-fry until golden brown. Drain using a slotted spoon and transfer to a plate, then place in a low oven to keep warm.

4 Cut the field mushrooms into thick slices. If large, cut the chanterelles in half.

5 Heat the wok and add the remaining butter. Stir in two-thirds of the chopped garlic and the shallots and stir-fry for 1 minute until golden brown. Stir in the mushrooms and continue to cook for a further 2 minutes.

6 Add the sherry, bring to the boil and simmer for 2–3 minutes, or until syrupy. Add the rosemary, seasoning and livers to the pan. Stir-fry for 1 minute. Garnish with the rosemary, and sprinkle with a mixture of lemon, parsley and the remaining chopped garlic. Serve with slices of toast.

# Chicken Braised in Red Wine

*Red wine is a classic partner for chicken in French cookery. It gives the dish a lovely robust sauce. For a lighter sauce, you can use white wine instead of red, as in Alsace, where the local Riesling is often cooked with chicken.*

### INGREDIENTS

*Serves 4*

1 chicken, about 1.6–1.8kg/3½–4lb, cut in pieces

25ml/1½ tbsp olive oil

225g/8oz baby onions

15g/½ oz/1 tbsp butter

225g/8oz mushrooms, quartered if large

30ml/2 tbsp plain (all-purpose) flour

750ml/1¼ pints/3 cups dry red wine

250ml/8fl oz/1 cup chicken stock, or more to cover

bouquet garni

salt and ground black pepper

3 Melt the butter in the frying pan over a medium heat and sauté the mushrooms, stirring, until golden brown.

4 Sprinkle the onions with the flour and cook for 2 minutes, stirring frequently, then add the wine and boil for 1 minute, stirring. Add the chicken, mushrooms, stock and bouquet garni. Bring to the boil, reduce the heat to very low and simmer, covered, for 45–50 minutes, or until the chicken is tender and the juices run clear when the thickest part of the meat is pierced with a knife.

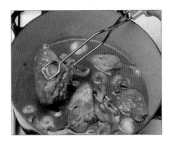

5 Transfer the chicken pieces and vegetables to a plate. Strain the cooking liquid, skim off the fat and return the liquid to the pan. Boil to reduce by one-third, then return the chicken and vegetables to the casserole and simmer for 3–4 minutes to heat through.

1 Pat the chicken pieces dry and season with salt and pepper. Put the chicken in a large, heavy frying pan, skin side down, and cook over a medium-high heat for 10–12 minutes, or until golden brown. Transfer to a plate.

2 Meanwhile, heat the oil in a large, flameproof casserole over a medium-low heat, add the onions and cook, covered, until evenly browned, stirring frequently.

# Chicken with Prawns

*This unusual combination of ingredients has its origins in a fish recipe. It is traditionally made with crayfish, although prawns or chicken can work equally well and are often easier to obtain.*

INGREDIENTS

*Serves 4*

1 chicken, about 1.3kg/3lb, cut into
    8 pieces
10ml/2 tsp vegetable oil
12 large raw prawns (shrimp) or live
    crayfish, with heads if possible
1 small onion, halved and sliced
30ml/2 tbsp plain (all-purpose) flour
175ml/6fl oz/³/4 cup dry white wine
30ml/2 tbsp brandy
300ml/¹/2 pint/1¹/4 cups chicken stock
3 medium tomatoes, cored and quartered
1 or 2 garlic cloves, finely chopped
bouquet garni
90ml/6 tbsp whipping cream
salt and ground black pepper
fresh parsley, to garnish

1 Wash the chicken pieces, then pat dry with kitchen paper and season with salt and pepper.

2 Heat the oil in a large, flame-proof casserole and cook the prawns or crayfish over a high heat until they turn a bright colour. Remove the prawns or crayfish, cool slightly and then peel away the heads and shells and reserve. Chill the peeled tails.

3 Add the chicken to the casserole, skin side down and cook over a medium-high heat for 10–12 minutes, or until golden brown all over, cooking in batches if necessary. Transfer the chicken to a plate and pour off all but 15ml/ 1 tbsp of the fat.

4 In the same casserole, cook the onion over a medium-high heat until golden, stirring frequently. Sprinkle with flour and continue cooking for 2 minutes, stirring frequently, then add the wine and brandy and bring to the boil, stirring constantly.

> ## COOK'S TIP
> 
> To prepare ahead, cook as directed up to step 6. Cool and chill the chicken and sauce. To serve, reheat over a medium-low heat for about 30 minutes. Add the prawn or crayfish tails and heat through.

5 Add the stock, prawn or crayfish heads and shells, tomatoes, garlic and bouquet garni with the chicken pieces and any juices. Bring to the boil, then reduce the heat to very low. Cover the casserole and simmer for 20–25 minutes, or until the chicken is tender and the juices run clear when the thickest part of the meat is pierced with a knife.

6 Remove the chicken from the casserole and strain the cooking liquid, pressing down on the shells and vegetables to extract as much liquid as possible. Skim off the fat and return the liquid to the pan. Add the cream and boil until it is reduced by one-third and slightly thickened.

7 Return the chicken pieces to the pan and simmer for 5 minutes. Just before serving, add the prawns or crayfish tails and heat through. Arrange on warmed plates, pour over some of the sauce and garnish with fresh parsley.

# Burgundy Chicken

*Chicken cooked in a rich wine sauce is a dinner-party classic. It is perfect accompanied by a bottle of good red wine.*

### INGREDIENTS

*Serves 4*

60ml/4 tbsp plain (all-purpose) flour

1.3kg/3lb chicken, cut into 8 portions

15ml/1 tbsp olive oil

65g/2¹/₂ oz/5 tbsp butter

20 baby onions

75g/3oz piece streaky (fatty) bacon without rind, diced

about 20 button (white) mushrooms

75cl bottle red Burgundy wine

bouquet garni

3 garlic cloves

5ml/1 tsp soft light brown sugar

salt and ground black pepper

15ml/1 tbsp chopped fresh parsley and croûtons, to garnish

1 Place 45ml/3 tbsp of the flour and the seasoning in a large plastic bag and shake each chicken joint in it until lightly coated.

2 Heat the oil and 50g/2oz/¹/₄ cup of the butter in a large flameproof casserole. Add the onions and bacon and sauté for 3–4 minutes, or until the onions have browned lightly. Add the mushrooms and fry for 2 minutes. Remove with a slotted spoon into a bowl and reserve.

3 Add the chicken pieces to the hot oil and cook until browned on all sides, about 5–6 minutes. Pour on the Burgundy wine and add the bouquet garni, garlic, soft light brown sugar and seasoning.

4 Bring to the boil, cover and simmer for 1 hour, stirring occasionally.

5 Return the reserved onions, bacon and mushrooms to the casserole, cover and cook for a further 30 minutes, until the chicken is cooked through.

6 Lift out the cooked chicken, vegetables and bacon with a slotted spoon and arrange on a warmed dish. Remove the bouquet garni and boil the liquid rapidly for 2 minutes to reduce slightly. Cream the remaining butter and flour together and whisk in teaspoonfuls of the mixture until thickened slightly. Pour over the chicken and serve garnished with parsley and croûtons.

# Chicken Stew

*This hearty Romanian stew traditionally uses a great variety of colourful seasonal vegetables and home-grown herbs, such as rosemary, marjoram and thyme.*

### INGREDIENTS

*Serves 6*

60ml/4 tbsp vegetable oil, or melted lard or white cooking fat

1 mild onion, thinly sliced

2 garlic cloves, crushed

2 red (bell) peppers, seeded and sliced

1 chicken, about 1.6kg/3¹/₂ lb

90ml/6 tbsp tomato purée (paste)

3 potatoes, diced

5ml/1 tsp chopped fresh rosemary

5ml/1 tsp chopped fresh marjoram

5ml/1 tsp chopped fresh thyme

3 carrots, cut into chunks

¹/₂ small celeriac, cut into chunks

120ml/4fl oz/¹/₂ cup dry white wine

2 courgettes (zucchini), sliced

salt and ground black pepper

chopped fresh rosemary and marjoram, to garnish

dark rye bread, to serve

1 Heat the oil or lard in a large, flameproof casserole. Add the onion and garlic and cook for 1–2 minutes, or until soft; then add the red peppers.

2 Joint the chicken into six pieces, place in the casserole and brown gently on all sides.

3 After about 15 minutes add the tomato purée, potatoes, herbs, carrots, celeriac and white wine. Season to taste with salt and pepper. Cook over a low heat, covered, for 40–50 minutes, until the chicken is cooked through.

4 Add the courgettes 5 minutes before the end of cooking. Season. Garnish with the herbs and serve with dark rye bread.

COOK'S TIP
~
You could replace the fresh herbs with 2.5ml/¹/₂ tsp dried herbs.

# Turkey Mole

*In Mexico a mole is a rich stew, traditionally served on a festive occasion. The word comes from the Aztec "molli", a chilli-flavoured sauce. There are many different types – toasted nuts, fruit and chocolate are among the classic ingredients.*

*Serves 4*

1 ancho chilli, seeded
1 guajillo chilli, seeded
115g/4oz/$^3$/4 cup sesame seeds
50g/2oz/$^1$/2 cup whole blanched almonds
50g/2oz/$^1$/2 cup shelled unsalted
    peanuts, skinned
50g/2oz/$^1$/4 cup lard or white cooking fat
    or 60ml/4 tbsp vegetable oil
1 small onion, finely chopped
2 garlic cloves, chopped
50g/2oz canned tomatoes in tomato juice
1 ripe plantain
50g/2oz/$^1$/3 cup raisins
75g/3oz/$^1$/3 cup ready-to-eat pitted prunes
5ml/1 tsp dried oregano
2.5ml/$^1$/2 tsp ground cloves
2.5ml/$^1$/2 tsp crushed allspice berries
5ml/1 tsp ground cinnamon
25g/1oz/$^1$/4 cup cocoa powder
    (unsweetened)
4 turkey breast steaks
fresh oregano, to garnish (optional)
rice and warm tortillas, to serve

1 Soak both types of dried chilli in hot water for 30 minutes, then lift them out and chop them roughly. Reserve 250ml/8fl oz/ 1 cup of the soaking liquid.

2 Spread out the sesame seeds in a heavy frying pan. Toast them over a medium heat, shaking the pan lightly so that they turn golden all over. Do not let them burn, or the sauce will taste bitter. Set aside 45ml/3 tbsp of the toasted seeds for the garnish and tip the rest into a bowl. Toast the almonds and peanuts in the same way and add them to the bowl.

3 Heat half the lard or oil in a frying pan, cook the chopped onion and garlic for 2–3 minutes, then add the chillies and tomatoes. Cook gently for 10 minutes.

4 Peel the plantain and slice it into short diagonal slices. Add it to the onion mixture with the raisins, prunes, dried oregano, spices and cocoa. Stir in the reserved water in which the chillies were soaked. Bring to the boil, stirring, then add the toasted sesame seeds, almonds and peanuts. Cook for 10 minutes, stirring, remove from the heat and allow to cool.

5 Blend the sauce in batches in a food processor or blender until smooth. The sauce should be fairly thick, but a little water may be added if necessary.

6 Heat the remaining lard or oil in a flameproof casserole. Add the turkey and brown over a medium heat.

7 Pour the sauce over the steaks and cover the casserole with foil and a tight-fitting lid. Cook over a low heat for 20–25 minutes, or until the turkey is cooked. Sprinkle with sesame seeds and chopped oregano, and serve with a rice dish and warm tortillas.

# Chicken and Egg One-pot Meal

*This Ethiopian stew is traditionally served with a pancake-like flat bread, called injera. Rice is a good substitute for the flat bread, if you prefer. The eggs are an intrinsic part of the dish so make sure everyone receives one in their portion.*

### INGREDIENTS

*Serves 4*

90ml/6 tbsp vegetable oil

6–8 onions, chopped

6 garlic cloves, chopped

10ml/2 tsp chopped fresh root ginger

250ml/8fl oz/1 cup water or chicken stock

250ml/8fl oz/1 cup passata (bottled strained tomatoes) or 400g/14oz can chopped tomatoes

1 chicken, about 1.3kg/3lb, cut into 8–12 portions

seeds from 5–8 cardamom pods

2.5ml/$^{1}$/2 tsp ground turmeric

large pinch of ground cinnamon

large pinch of ground cloves

large pinch of freshly grated nutmeg

cayenne pepper or hot paprika, to taste

4 hard-boiled eggs

salt and ground black pepper

fresh coriander (cilantro) and onion rings, to garnish

flat bread or rice, to serve

1 Heat the oil in a pan, add the onions and cook for 10 minutes. Add the garlic and ginger and cook for 1–2 minutes.

2 Add the water or chicken stock and the passata or chopped tomatoes to the pan. Bring to the boil and cook, stirring constantly, for about 10 minutes, or until the liquid has reduced and the mixture has thickened. Season with salt and pepper.

3 Add the chicken and spices to the pan and turn the chicken in the sauce. Reduce the heat, then cover and simmer, stirring occasionally, for about 1 hour, or until the chicken is cooked through. Add a little more liquid if the mixture seems too thick.

4 Remove the shells from the eggs and then prick the eggs once or twice with a fork. Add the eggs to the sauce and heat gently until warmed through. Garnish with coriander and onion rings and serve with flat bread or rice.

# Chicken with Petit Pois

This Italian dish strongly reflects the traditions of both Mediterranean and Jewish cooking. The fennel adds an aniseed flavour and the petit pois give the dish hearty substance.

Serves 4

4 chicken breast fillets, skinned
plain (all-purpose) flour, for dusting
30–45ml/2–3 tbsp olive oil
1–2 onions, chopped
$^1/_4$ fennel bulb, chopped (optional)
15ml/1 tbsp chopped fresh parsley, plus
    extra to garnish
7.5ml/1$^1/_2$ tsp fennel seeds
75ml/5 tbsp dry Marsala
120ml/4fl oz/$^1/_2$ cup chicken stock
300g/11oz/2$^3/_4$ cups petits pois
    (baby peas)
juice of 1$^1/_2$ lemons
2 egg yolks
salt and ground black pepper

1 Season the chicken with salt and pepper, then generously dust with flour. Shake off the excess flour; set aside.

2 Heat 15ml/1 tbsp oil in a pan, add the onions, fennel, if using, parsley and fennel seeds. Cook for 5 minutes.

3 Add the remaining oil and the chicken to the pan and cook for 2–3 minutes on each side, until lightly browned. Remove the chicken and onion mixture from the pan and set aside.

4 Deglaze the pan by pouring in the Marsala and cooking over a high heat until reduced to about 30ml/2 tbsp, then pour in the stock. Add the peas and return the chicken and onion mixture to the pan. Cook over a very low heat.

5 In a bowl, beat the lemon juice and egg yolks together, then slowly add 120ml/4fl oz/$^1/_2$ cup of the hot liquid from the chicken and peas, stirring well to combine.

6 Return the mixture to the pan and cook over a low heat, stirring, until the mixture thickens slightly. (Do not allow the mixture to boil or the eggs will curdle.) Serve the chicken immediately, sprinkled with a little extra parsley.

# Cubed Chicken and Vegetables

*In this popular style of Japanese cooking, vegetables are simmered with a small amount of chicken in dashi stock – a traditional stock used in Japanese recipes. It is a light meal that looks attractive when served.*

*Serves 4*

2 boneless chicken thighs, about 200g/7oz
1 large carrot, trimmed
1 konnyaku (black bean curd)
300g/11oz satoimo (taro potato) or
   small potatoes
500g/1¹/₄ lb canned bamboo
   shoots, drained
30ml/2 tbsp vegetable oil
300ml/¹/₂ pint/1¹/₄ water mixed with
   7.5ml/1¹/₂ tsp dashi-no-moto (dashi
   stock granules)
salt

*For the simmering seasonings*

75ml/5 tbsp shoyu
30ml/2 tbsp sake
30ml/2 tbsp caster (superfine) sugar
30ml/2 tbsp mirin (sweet rice wine)

1 Cut the chicken into bitesize pieces. Chop the carrot into 2cm/³/₄ in triangular chunks by cutting the carrot slightly diagonally and turning it 90° each time you cut.

2 Boil the konnyaku in rapidly boiling water for 1 minute and drain under running water. Cool, slice it crossways into 5mm/¹/₄ in thick strips. Cut a 4cm/1¹/₂ in slit down the centre of a strip without cutting the ends. Carefully push the top of the strip through the slit to make a decorative tie. Repeat with all the konnyaku.

3 Peel and halve the satoimo. Put in a colander and sprinkle with a generous amount of salt. Rub and wash under the tap. Drain. If using, peel and halve the small potatoes.

4 Halve the canned bamboo shoots, then cut into the same shape as the carrot.

5 In a pan, heat the vegetable oil and stir-fry the chicken until the surface of the meat turns white. Add the carrot, konnyaku ties, satoimo and bamboo shoots. Stir well with every new addition.

6 Add the water and dashi-no-moto and bring to the boil. Cook on a high heat for 3 minutes then reduce to medium-low. Add the simmering seasonings, cover, then simmer for 15 minutes, or until the liquid has evaporated, shaking the pan from time to time.

7 When the satoimo is soft, remove from the heat and transfer to a serving bowl. Serve immediately.

COOK'S TIP

When you cut satoimo, it produces a sticky juice. Rinsing with salt and water is the best way to wash it off.

# Hijiki Seaweed and Chicken

*The taste of hijiki is somewhere between rice and vegetable and is used in Japanese cooking. It goes well with chicken, especially when it's stir-fried with a little oil first.*

### INGREDIENTS

Serves 4

90g/3$^1$/$_2$ oz dried hijiki seaweed

150g/5oz chicken breast fillet

$^1$/$_2$ small carrot, about 5cm/2in

15ml/1 tbsp vegetable oil

100ml/3$^1$/$_2$ fl oz/scant $^1$/$_2$ cup water mixed with 1.5ml/$^1$/$_4$ tsp dashi-no-moto (dashi stock granules)

30ml/2 tbsp sake

30ml/2 tbsp caster (superfine) sugar

45ml/3 tbsp shoyu

a pinch of shichimi togarashi (seven-flavour spice) or cayenne pepper, to serve

1 Soak the hijiki in cold water for about 30 minutes. When it is crushes between the fingers it is ready to cook. Pour into a sieve and wash under running water. Drain.

2 Peel the skin from the chicken and par-boil the skin in rapidly boiling water for 1 minute, then drain. With a sharp knife, shave off all the yellow fat from the skin. Discard the clear membrane between the fat and the skin as well. Cut the skin into thin strips about 5mm/$^1$/$_4$ in wide and 2.5cm/1in long. Cut the meat into small, bitesize chunks.

3 Peel and chop the carrot into long, narrow matchsticks.

4 Heat the oil in a wok or frying pan and stir-fry the strips of chicken skin for 5 minutes, or until golden and curled up. Add the chicken meat and keep stirring until the colour changes.

5 Add the hijiki and carrot, then stir-fry for a further minute. Add the remaining ingredients. Lower the heat and cook for 5 minutes.

6 Remove the pan from the heat and leave to stand for about 10 minutes. Serve in small bowls. Sprinkle with shichimi togarashi or cayenne pepper.

# Seafood, Chicken and Vegetable Hotpot

*This Japanese dish is cooked and eaten at the table, traditionally using a clay pot. You can use a flameproof casserole or fondue pot and will need a portable table-top stove or burner.*

## INGREDIENTS

*Serves 4*

225g/8oz salmon, scaled and cut into
    5cm/2in thick steaks with bones
225g/8oz white fish (sea bream, cod, plaice,
    flounder or haddock), cleaned and
    scaled then chopped into 4 chunks
300g/11oz chicken thighs, cut into large
    bitesize chunks with bones
4 hakusai leaves (Chinese leaves), base
    part trimmed
115g/4oz spinach
1 large carrot, cut into 5mm/$^1$/4 in thick
    rounds or flower shapes
8 fresh shiitake mushrooms, stalks
    removed, or 150g/5oz oyster
    mushrooms, bases trimmed
2 thin leeks, washed and cut diagonally
    into 5cm/2in lengths
285g/10$^1$/4 oz packet tofu block, drained
    and cut into 16 cubes
salt

*For the hot-pot liquid*
12 x 6cm/4$^1$/2 x 2$^1$/2 in dashi-konbu
    (dried seaweed)
1.2 litres/2 pints/5 cups water
120ml/4fl oz/$^1$/2 cup sake

*For the condiments*
90g/3$^1$/2 oz mooli (daikon), peeled
1 dried chilli, halved and seeded
1 lemon, cut into 16 wedges
4 spring onions (scallions), chopped
2 x 5g/$^1$/8 oz packets kezuri-bushi
    (bonito flakes)
1 bottle shoyu

1 Arrange the various prepared fish and chicken on a large serving platter.

2 Boil plenty of water in a large pan and cook the hakusai for 3 minutes. Drain in a sieve and leave to cool. Add a pinch of salt to the water and boil the spinach for 1 minute, then drain in a sieve under running water.

3 Squeeze the spinach and lay it on a sushi rolling mat, then roll it up firmly. Leave to rest, then unwrap and take the cylinder out. Lay the hakusai leaves next to each other on the mat. Put the cylinder in the middle and roll again firmly. Leave for 5 minutes, then unroll and cut into 5cm/2in long cylinders.

4 Transfer the hakusai cylinders to the platter along with all the remaining vegetables and the tofu.

5 Lay the dashi-konbu on the bottom of a flameproof casserole or fondue pot. Mix the water and sake in a small bowl.

6 Insert a skewer into the cut side of the daikon three times, and insert the chilli pieces. Leave for 5 minutes, then grate finely. Drain and squeeze the liquid out. Shape the pink daikon into a mound and put in a bowl. Put all the other condiments into small bowls.

7 Fill the pot with two-thirds of the water and sake mix. Bring to the boil, then reduce the heat.

8 Transfer the casserole or fondue pot to a lighted burner at the table. Put the carrot, shiitake or oyster mushrooms, chicken and salmon into the casserole. When the colour of the meat and fish changes, add the rest of the ingredients in batches.

9 Guests pour a soy sauce into small bowls, and squeeze in a little lemon juice, then mix with a condiment. Pick up the food with chopsticks and dip into the sauce. Cook more as you go, adding water and sake as the stock reduces.

# Sichuan Chicken with Kung Po Sauce

*This recipe, which hails from the Sichuan region of Western China, has become one of the classic recipes in the Chinese repertoire.*

INGREDIENTS

*Serves 3*

2 chicken breast fillets, total weight about
    350g/12oz, skinned
1 egg white
10ml/2 tsp cornflour (cornstarch)
2.5ml/$^1$/$_2$ tsp salt
30ml/2 tbsp yellow salted beans
15ml/1 tbsp hoisin sauce
5ml/1 tsp light brown sugar
15ml/1 tbsp rice wine or
    medium-dry sherry
15ml/1 tbsp wine vinegar
4 garlic cloves, crushed
150ml/$^1$/$_4$ pint/$^2$/$_3$ cup chicken stock
45ml/3 tbsp groundnut (peanut) oil or
    sunflower oil
2–3 dried chillies, broken into small pieces
115g/4oz/1 cup roasted cashew nuts
fresh coriander (cilantro), to garnish

1 Cut the chicken into neat pieces. Lightly whisk the egg white in a dish, whisk in the cornflour and salt, then add the chicken and stir until coated.

### COOK'S TIP

Peanuts are the classic ingredient in this dish, but cashew nuts have an even better flavour.

2 In a separate bowl, mash the beans with a spoon. Stir in the hoisin sauce, brown sugar, rice wine or sherry, vinegar, garlic and stock.

3 Heat a wok, add the oil and then fry the chicken, turning constantly, for about 2 minutes, or until cooked. Drain over a bowl in order to collect the excess oil.

4 Heat the reserved oil and fry the chilli pieces for 1 minute. Return the chicken to the wok and pour in the bean sauce mixture. Bring to the boil and stir in the cashew nuts. Spoon into a heated serving dish and garnish with coriander leaves.

# GRAINS, RICE & PASTA

There are endless ways to enjoy chicken combined with pasta, grains and rice. This chapter offers recipes from around the globe, and includes traditional dishes such as fried rice, paella, jambalaya and risottos. These are hearty and filling recipes such as chicken and vegetable tagine, sophisticated pasta dishes such as pappardelle with chicken and mushrooms, as well as everyday favourites such as lasagne and cannelloni. Using combinations of herbs, spices, meats, seafood and dairy produce, the dishes in this chapter provide a wealth of choice for adventurous eating.

# Stuffed Chicken Rolls

*These delicious chicken rolls are simple to make but sophisticated enough to serve at a dinner party. Slices are arranged on a bed of tagliatelle tossed with fried wild mushrooms.*

### INGREDIENTS

Serves 4

25g/1oz/2 tbsp butter

1 garlic clove, chopped

150g/5oz/1¼ cups cooked white long grain rice

45ml/3 tbsp ricotta cheese

10ml/2 tsp chopped fresh flat leaf parsley

5ml/1 tsp chopped fresh tarragon

4 chicken breast fillets, skinned

4 slices prosciutto

15ml/1 tbsp olive oil

120ml/4fl oz/½ cup white wine

salt and ground black pepper

fresh flat leaf parsley sprigs, to garnish

cooked tagliatelle and sautéed blewit mushrooms, to serve (optional)

1 Preheat the oven to 180°C/350°F/Gas 4. Melt about 10g/¼oz/2 tsp of the butter in a small pan and fry the garlic for a few seconds without browning. Spoon into a bowl.

---

### COOK'S TIP
~

Risotto rice could be used in place of white long grain in this dish – it will make a denser stuffing for the chicken rolls.

---

2 Add the rice, ricotta, parsley and tarragon and season with salt and pepper. Stir to mix.

3 Place each chicken breast fillet in turn between two sheets of clear film (plastic wrap) and flatten by beating firmly with a rolling pin.

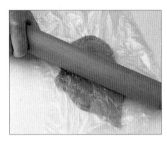

4 Divide the slices of prosciutto between the chicken, trimming the ham to fit, if necessary.

5 Place a spoonful of the rice stuffing at the wider end of each ham-topped breast. Roll up carefully and tie in place with cooking string or secure with a cocktail stick (toothpick).

6 Heat the oil and the remaining butter in a frying pan and lightly fry the chicken rolls until browned on all sides. Place side by side in a shallow baking dish and pour over the white wine.

7 Cover the dish with baking parchment and cook in the oven for 30–35 minutes, or until the chicken is tender.

8 Cut the rolls into slices and serve on a bed of tagliatelle with sautéed blewit mushrooms and a generous sprinkling of black pepper. Garnish with sprigs of flat leaf parsley.

# Joloff Chicken and Rice

*In West Africa, where this dish originated, it is usually made in large quantities, using jointed whole chickens. This version is somewhat more sophisticated, but still has the traditional flavour.*

### INGREDIENTS

*Serves 4*

2 garlic cloves, crushed
5ml/1 tsp dried thyme
4 chicken breast fillets, skinned
30ml/2 tbsp palm or vegetable oil
400g/14oz can chopped tomatoes
15ml/1 tbsp tomato purée (paste)
1 onion, chopped
450ml/$^3$/4 pint/scant 2 cups chicken stock
30ml/2 tbsp dried shrimps or
	crayfish, ground
1 fresh green chilli, seeded and
	finely chopped
350g/12oz//1$^3$/4 cups white long grain rice
750ml/1$^1$/4 pints/3 cups water
salt and ground black pepper
chopped fresh thyme, to garnish

1 Mix the garlic and thyme in a bowl. Rub the mixture into the chicken breast fillets. Heat the oil in a frying pan.

2 Add the chicken breast fillets to the pan to brown in the oil, then remove to a plate. Add the chopped tomatoes, tomato purée and onion to the pan. Cook over a medium-high heat for about 15 minutes, or until the tomatoes are well reduced, stirring occasionally at first and then more frequently as the tomatoes thicken.

3 Lower the heat, return the chicken to the pan and stir well. Cook and stir for 10 minutes, then add the stock, the shrimps or crayfish and the chilli. Bring to the boil, then simmer for 5 minutes, or until the chicken is cooked, stirring occasionally. Season to taste.

4 Meanwhile put the rice in a separate pan. Pour in the water, and top up with the sauce from the chicken. Bring to the boil, then lower the heat and cover the pan. Cook over a low heat until the liquid has been absorbed and the rice is tender.

5 Pack the rice in to four moulds and set aside. Lift out the chicken from the sauce and put on a board. If the sauce is runny, cook it over a high heat to reduce it. Unmould a rice timbale on each of four serving plates. Spoon the sauce around, then slice the chicken breasts and fan them on the sauce. Garnish with thyme sprigs and serve immediately.

# Spanish Chicken

*This colourful rice dish is ideal for entertaining. It is delicious served with a crisp green salad.*

### INGREDIENTS

*Serves 8*

30ml/2 tbsp plain (all-purpose) flour

10ml/2 tsp ground paprika

2.5ml/$^{1}/_{2}$ tsp salt

16 chicken drumsticks

50ml/2fl oz/$^{1}/_{4}$ cup olive oil

about 1.2 litres/2 pints/5 cups
    chicken stock

1 onion, finely chopped

2 garlic cloves, crushed

450g/1lb/2$^{1}/_{3}$ cups long grain rice

2 bay leaves

225g/8oz/1$^{1}/_{3}$ cups diced cooked ham

115g/4oz/1 cup pimiento-stuffed
    green olives

1 green (bell) pepper, seeded and diced

2 × 400g/14oz cans chopped tomatoes,
    with the juice

60ml/4 tbsp chopped fresh parsley

1 Preheat the oven to 180°C/350°F/Gas 4. Shake together the flour, paprika and salt in a plastic bag, add the drumsticks and toss to coat.

2 Heat the oil in a large, flameproof casserole and, working in batches, brown the chicken drumsticks slowly on all sides. Remove and keep warm.

3 Meanwhile, bring the stock to the boil and add the onion, crushed garlic, rice and bay leaves. Cook for 10 minutes. Remove from the heat and add the ham, olives, pepper, and canned tomatoes with their juice. Transfer to a shallow ovenproof dish.

4 Arrange the chicken on top, cover and bake for 30–40 minutes, or until tender. Add a little more stock if necessary to prevent the casserole from drying out. Remove the bay leaves and sprinkle over the chopped parsley to garnish before serving.

# Chicken and Chorizo

2 Add the rice, chicken stock, tomato purée and Tabasco sauce. Simmer uncovered for about 10 minutes.

3 Stir in the chicken, chorizo and peas, and simmer for a further 5 minutes. Switch off the heat, cover and leave to stand for 5 minutes more before serving.

*This spicy dish is a fast, fortifying meal for a hungry family and the perfect way to use up leftover chicken.*

*Serves 4*

45ml/3 tbsp vegetable oil
1 medium onion, chopped
1 celery stick, chopped
$^1/_2$ red (bell) pepper, chopped
400g/14oz/2 cups long grain rice
1 litre/1$^3/_4$ pints/4 cups chicken stock
15ml/1 tbsp tomato purée (paste)
3–4 dashes of Tabasco sauce
225g/8oz cold roast chicken,
   thickly sliced
115g/4oz chorizo, sliced
75g/3oz fresh or shelled frozen peas

1 Heat the oil in a heavy pan. Add the onion, celery and pepper and cook gently to soften without colouring.

VARIATION

You could use kabanos or any other cooked sausage instead of chorizo in this dish.

# Chinese Special Fried Rice

*Cooked rice fried with a selection of other ingredients is a staple Chinese dish. In this recipe a mixture of chicken, prawns and vegetables make a tasty combination.*

Serves 4

175g/6oz/scant 1 cup long grain white rice
45ml/3 tbsp groundnut (peanut) oil
1 garlic clove, crushed
4 spring onions (scallions), finely chopped
115g/4oz/scant 1 cup diced cooked chicken
115g/4oz/1 cup cooked peeled prawns
  (shrimp), rinsed if canned
50g/2oz/$^1$/2 cup fresh shelled or frozen peas
1 egg, beaten with a pinch of salt
50g/2oz/1 cup shredded lettuce
30ml/2 tbsp light soy sauce
pinch of caster (superfine) sugar
salt and ground black pepper
15ml/1 tbsp chopped roasted cashew nuts,
  to garnish

1 Rinse the long grain rice in two to three changes of warm water to wash away some of the starch. Drain well.

2 Put the rice in a pan and add 15ml/1 tbsp of the oil and 350ml/12fl oz/1$^1$/2 cups of water. Cover and bring to the boil, stir once, then cover and simmer for 12–15 minutes, or until nearly all the water has been absorbed. Turn off the heat and leave covered for 10 minutes. Fluff up with a fork and leave to cool.

3 Heat the remaining oil in a wok or frying pan, add the garlic and spring onions and stir-fry for 30 seconds.

4 Add the chicken, prawns and peas and stir-fry for 1–2 minutes, then add the cooked rice and stir-fry for a further 2 minutes. Pour in the egg and stir-fry until just set. Stir in the lettuce, soy sauce, sugar and seasoning.

5 Transfer to a warmed serving bowl, sprinkle with the chopped roasted cashew nuts and serve immediately.

# Mushroom Picker's Chicken Paella

*A good paella is based on a few well-chosen ingredients. Here, wild mushrooms combine with chicken and vegetables.*

*Serves 4*

45ml/3 tbsp olive oil

1 medium onion, chopped

1 small bulb fennel, sliced

225g/8oz assorted wild and cultivated
    mushrooms such as ceps, bay boletus,
    chanterelles, saffron milk-caps,
    hedgehog fungus, St George's, Caesar's
    and oyster mushrooms, trimmed
    and sliced

1 garlic clove, crushed

3 chicken legs, chopped through the bone

350g/12oz/1²/3 cups short-grain Spanish
    or Italian rice

900ml/1¹/2 pints/3³/4 cups chicken
    stock, boiling

1 pinch saffron threads or 1 sachet of
    saffron powder

1 thyme sprig

400g/14oz can butter (lima)
    beans, drained

75g/3oz/³/4 cup frozen peas

salt and ground black pepper

1 Heat the olive oil in a 35cm/
14in paella pan or a large frying pan. Add the onion and fennel and fry over a low heat for 3–4 minutes.

2 Add the mushrooms and garlic, and cook until the juices begin to run. Increase the heat to evaporate the juices.

3 Push the onion and mushrooms to one side. Add the chicken and fry briefly.

4 Stir in the rice, add the stock, saffron, thyme, butter beans and peas. Bring to a simmer and then cook gently for 15 minutes without stirring.

5 Season with salt and pepper. Remove from the heat and cover the surface of the paella with a circle of greased baking parchment. Cover the paper with a clean dishtowel and allow the paella to finish cooking in its own heat for about 5 minutes. Bring to the table, uncover and serve.

# Chicken Paella

*There are many variations of this basic recipe. Any seasonal vegetables can be added, together with mussels and other shellfish. Serve straight from the pan.*

### INGREDIENTS

*Serves 4*

4 chicken legs (thighs and drumsticks)
4 tomatoes
60ml/4 tbsp olive oil
1 large onion, finely chopped
1 garlic clove, crushed
5ml/1 tsp ground turmeric
115g/4oz chorizo sausage or smoked ham
225g/8oz/generous 1 cup long grain rice
600ml/1 pint/2¹/₂ cups chicken stock
1 red (bell) pepper, seeded and sliced
115g/4oz/1 cup fresh shelled or
  frozen peas
salt and ground black pepper

1 Preheat the oven to 180°C/350°F/Gas 4. Cut the chicken legs in half. Plunge the tomatoes into boiling water for 30 seconds, then refresh in cold water. Peel away the skins, remove the seeds and chop the flesh.

2 Heat the oil in a 30cm/12in paella pan or large, flameproof casserole and brown the chicken pieces on both sides. Add the onion and garlic and stir in the turmeric. Cook for 2 minutes.

3 Slice the sausage or dice the ham and add to the pan, with the rice and stock. Bring to the boil and season to taste, cover and bake for 15 minutes.

4 Remove from the oven and add the chopped tomatoes and sliced red pepper and peas. Return to the oven and cook for a further 10–15 minutes, or until the chicken is tender and the rice has absorbed the stock.

# Poussins with Dirty Rice

*This rice is called dirty not because of the bits in it (though the roux and chicken livers do "muss" it up a bit) but because jazz is called "dirty music" in New Orleans, and the rice in this recipe is certainly jazzed up.*

### INGREDIENTS

*Serves 4*

4 poussins
2 bay leaves, halved
25g/1oz/2 tbsp butter
1 lemon

*For the rice*

60ml/4 tbsp oil
25g/1oz/$^1$/4 cup plain (all-purpose) flour
50g/2oz/$^1$/4 cup butter
1 large onion, chopped
2 celery sticks, chopped
1 green (bell) pepper, seeded and diced
2 garlic cloves, crushed
200g/7oz/scant 1 cup minced (ground) pork
225g/8oz chicken livers, trimmed and sliced
Tabasco sauce
300ml/$^1$/2 pint/1$^1$/4 cups chicken stock
4 spring onions (scallions), shredded
45ml/3 tbsp chopped fresh parsley
225g/8oz/generous 1 cup American long grain rice, cooked
salt and ground black pepper

---

### COOK'S TIP

You can substitute quails for the poussins, in which case offer two per person and stuff each little bird with 10ml/2 tsp of the dirty rice before roasting for about 20 minutes.

---

1 In a small, heavy pan, make a roux by blending together 30ml/2 tbsp of the oil and the flour. When it is a chestnut-brown colour, remove the pan from the heat and place it immediately on a cold surface.

2 Heat the remaining 30ml/2 tbsp oil with the butter in a frying pan and stir-fry the onion, celery and green pepper for about 5 minutes.

3 Add the garlic and pork and stir-fry for about 5 minutes, breaking up the pork and stirring well to cook it all over.

4 Add the chicken livers and fry for 2–3 minutes, or until they have changed colour all over. Season with salt and black pepper and a dash of Tabasco sauce.

5 Stir the roux into the stir-fried mixture, then gradually add the stock. When it begins to bubble, cover and cook for 30 minutes, stirring occasionally. Uncover and cook for a further 15 minutes, stirring frequently.

6 Preheat the oven to 200°C/400°F/Gas 6. Mix the shredded spring onions and chopped parsley into the meat mixture and stir it all into the cooked rice.

7 Put $^1$/2 bay leaf and 15ml/1 tbsp rice into each poussin. Rub the outside with the butter and season with salt and pepper.

8 Put the birds on a rack in a roasting pan, squeeze the juice from the lemon over them and roast in the oven for 35–40 minutes, basting twice during cooking with the pan juices.

9 Put the remaining rice into a shallow ovenproof dish, cover it and place on a low shelf in the oven for the last 15–20 minutes of the birds' cooking time.

10 Serve the birds on a bed of dirty rice with the roasting juices (drained of fat) poured over.

# Louisiana Rice

*Chicken livers are accompanied by pork, rice, vegetables and an array of spices in this filling dish.*

Serves 4

60ml/4 tbsp vegetable oil
1 small aubergine (eggplant), diced
225g/8oz/2 cups minced (ground) pork
1 green (bell) pepper, seeded and chopped
2 celery sticks, chopped
1 onion, chopped
1 garlic clove, crushed
5ml/1 tsp cayenne pepper
5ml/1 tsp paprika
5ml/1 tsp black pepper
2.5ml/$^1$/$_2$ tsp salt
5ml/1 tsp dried thyme
2.5ml/$^1$/$_2$ tsp dried oregano
475ml/16fl oz/2 cups chicken stock
225g/8oz chicken livers, minced (ground)
150g/5oz/$^2$/$_3$ cup long grain rice
1 bay leaf
45ml/3 tbsp chopped fresh parsley
celery leaves, to garnish

1 Heat the oil in a frying pan until really hot, then add the diced aubergine and stir-fry for about 5 minutes.

2 Add the pork and cook for about 6–8 minutes, or until browned, using a wooden spoon to break up any lumps.

3 Add the chopped green pepper, celery, onion, garlic and all the spices and herbs. Cover and cook on a high heat for 5–6 minutes, stirring frequently from the bottom to scrape up and distribute the crispy brown bits.

4 Pour on the stock and stir to clean the bottom of the pan. Cover and cook for 6 minutes over a medium heat. Stir in the chicken livers, cook for 2 minutes, then stir in the rice and add the bay leaf.

5 Reduce the heat, cover and simmer for about 6–7 minutes. Turn off the heat and leave to stand for a further 10–15 minutes until the rice is tender. Remove the bay leaf and stir in the chopped parsley. Serve the rice hot, garnished with the celery leaves.

# Risotto with Chicken

*This is a classic combination of chicken and rice, cooked with prosciutto, white wine and Parmesan cheese.*

### INGREDIENTS

*Serves 4*

30ml/2 tbsp olive oil

225g/8oz chicken breast fillet, skinned and cut into 2.5cm/1in cubes

1 onion, finely chopped

1 garlic clove, finely chopped

1.5ml/$^1$/$_4$ tsp saffron threads

50g/2oz prosciutto, cut into thin strips

450g/1lb/2$^1$/$_4$ cups risotto rice, preferably arborio

120ml/4fl oz/$^1$/$_2$ cup dry white wine

1.75 litres/3 pints/7$^1$/$_2$ cups simmering chicken stock

25g/1oz/2 tbsp butter (optional)

25g/1oz/$^1$/$_3$ cup freshly grated Parmesan cheese, plus more to serve

salt and ground black pepper

3 Add the wine and bring to the boil. Simmer gently until almost all the wine is absorbed.

4 Add the simmering stock, a ladleful at a time, and cook until the rice is just tender and the risotto creamy.

5 Add the butter, if using, and Parmesan cheese and stir in well. Season with salt and pepper to taste. Serve the risotto hot, sprinkled with more Parmesan.

1 Heat the oil in a wide, heavy pan over medium-high heat. Add the chicken cubes and cook, stirring, until they start to turn white.

2 Reduce the heat to low. Add the onion, garlic, saffron and prosciutto. Cook, stirring, until the onion is soft. Stir in the risotto rice and mix well. Sauté for 1–2 minutes, stirring constantly.

# Chicken and Asparagus Risotto

*Use thick asparagus for this recipe, as fine spears overcook in this risotto. The thick ends of the asparagus are full of flavour and they become beautifully tender in the time it takes for the rice to absorb the stock.*

*Serves 4*

50g/2oz/¼ cup butter
15ml/1 tbsp olive oil
1 leek, finely chopped
115g/4oz/1½ cups oyster
 mushrooms, sliced
3 chicken breast fillets, skinned and cubed
350g/12oz asparagus
250g/9oz/1¼ cups risotto rice
900ml/1½ pints/3¾ cups simmering
 chicken stock
salt and ground black pepper
Parmesan cheese curls, to serve

1 Heat the butter with the oil in a pan until the mixture foams. Add the leek and cook gently until softened, but not coloured. Add the mushrooms and cook for 5 minutes. Remove the vegetables from the pan and set aside.

2 Increase the heat and cook the chicken until golden. Do this in batches, if necessary, and then replace them all in the pan.

3 Meanwhile, discard the woody ends from the asparagus and cut the spears in half. Set the fine tips aside. Cut the thick ends in half and add them to the pan. Replace the leek and mushroom mixture and stir in the rice.

4 Pour in a ladleful of simmering stock and cook gently, stirring occasionally, until the stock is absorbed. Continue adding the stock a ladleful at a time, simmering until the stock is absorbed, the rice is tender and the chicken is cooked.

5 Add the fine asparagus tips with the last ladleful of boiling stock for the final 5 minutes and continue cooking the risotto gently until the asparagus is tender. The whole process should take about 25–30 minutes.

6 Season the risotto to taste with salt and lots of freshly ground black pepper and spoon it into individual warm serving bowls. Top each bowl with curls of Parmesan, and serve.

COOK'S TIP
Use a cheese slicer to pare thin curls off a large piece of fresh Parmesan cheese.

# Chicken Liver Risotto

*The combination of chicken livers, bacon, parsley and thyme gives this risotto a wonderfully rich flavour.*

*Serves 2–4*

175g/6oz chicken livers
about 15ml/1 tbsp olive oil
about 25g/1oz/2 tbsp butter
about 40g/1$^1$/$_2$ oz speck or 3 rindless
 streaky (fatty) bacon rashers (strips),
 finely chopped
2 shallots, finely chopped
1 garlic clove, crushed
1 celery stick, finely sliced
275g/10oz/1$^1$/$_2$ cups risotto rice
175ml/6fl oz/$^3$/$_4$ cup dry white wine
900ml–1 litre/1$^1$/$_2$–1$^3$/$_4$ pints/3$^3$/$_4$–4 cups
 simmering chicken stock
5ml/1 tsp chopped fresh thyme
15ml/1 tbsp chopped fresh parsley
salt and ground black pepper
parsley and thyme sprigs, to garnish

1 Clean the chicken livers, removing any fat or membrane. Rinse well, pat dry and cut into small, even pieces.

2 Heat the oil and butter in a pan and fry the speck or bacon for 2–3 minutes. Add the shallots, garlic and celery and continue frying for 3–4 minutes over a low heat until the vegetables are slightly softened. Increase the heat and add the chicken livers, stir-frying for a few minutes, or until they are brown all over.

3 Add the rice. Cook, stirring, for a few minutes, then pour over the wine. Allow to boil so that the alcohol is driven off. Stir frequently, taking care not to break up the chicken livers. When all the wine has been absorbed, add the hot stock, a ladleful at a time, stirring constantly.

4 About halfway through cooking, add the thyme and seasoning. Continue to add the stock as before.

5 When the risotto is creamy and the rice is tender, stir in the parsley. Season. Remove from the heat, cover and leave to rest for a few minutes before serving, garnished with the herbs.

# *Yogurt Chicken and Rice Cake*

This Middle-Eastern speciality is traditionally flavoured with small, dried berries called zereshk, but is just as delicious when made with fresh cranberries.

### INGREDIENTS

Serves 6

40g/1$^1$/2 oz/3 tbsp butter

1 chicken, about 1.6kg/3$^1$/2 lb, cut
    into pieces

1 large onion, chopped

250ml/8fl oz/1 cup chicken stock

2 eggs, beaten

475ml/16fl oz/2 cups natural
    (plain) yogurt

2–3 saffron threads, dissolved in 15ml/
    1 tbsp warm water

5ml/1 tsp ground cinnamon

450g/1lb/2$^1$/4 cups basmati rice, soaked

1.2 litres/2 pints/5 cups boiling water

75g/3oz/$^3$/4 cup cranberries or zereshk
    (see Cook's Tip)

50g/2oz/$^1$/2 cup flaked (sliced) almonds

salt and ground black pepper

herb and radicchio salad, to serve

1 Melt two-thirds of the butter in a flameproof casserole. Fry the chicken pieces with the onion for 4–5 minutes, or until the onion is softened and the chicken has browned. Add the stock and season with salt and pepper. Bring to the boil, lower the heat and simmer for 45 minutes, or until the chicken is cooked and the stock has reduced by half.

2 Drain the chicken, reserving the stock. Cut the flesh into large pieces, discarding the skin and bones, and place in a large bowl. In a separate bowl, mix the eggs with the yogurt. Add the saffron water and cinnamon. Season lightly. Pour over the chicken and stir to coat. Cover and leave to marinate for up to 2 hours.

3 Preheat the oven to 160°C/ 325°F/Gas 3. Grease a large baking dish, about 10cm/4in deep. Drain the rice and put it in a pan. Add the boiling water and a little salt, bring back to the boil and then lower the heat and simmer gently for 10 minutes. Drain, rinse thoroughly in warm water and drain once more.

### COOK'S TIP
<br>∽<br>
If you use zereshk, wash them before use. Heat the berries then layer them with the rice.

4 Using a slotted spoon, lift the chicken pieces out of the yogurt marinade and put them on a plate. Mix half the rice into the marinade. Spread the mixture on the bottom of the baking dish. Arrange the chicken pieces in a single layer on top, then cover evenly with about half the plain rice. Sprinkle over the cranberries or zereshk, then cover with the rest of the rice.

5 Pour the reserved chicken stock over the rice. Sprinkle with flaked almonds and dot with the remaining butter. Cover tightly with foil and bake in the oven for 35–45 minutes.

6 Leave the dish to cool for a few minutes, then place it on a cold, damp dishtowel (this will help to lift the rice from the bottom of the dish). Run a knife around the inside rim of the dish. Invert a large, flat plate over the dish and turn out the rice "cake". Cut into six wedges and serve hot, with a herb and radicchio salad.

# Thai Fried Rice

*This substantial dish is based on Thai fragrant rice, which is sometimes known as jasmine rice. Chicken, red pepper and corn add colour and extra flavour.*

### INGREDIENTS

*Serves 4*

475ml/16fl oz/2 cups water

50g/2oz/1/2 cup coconut milk powder

350g/12oz/1 3/4 cups Thai fragrant
   rice, rinsed

30ml/2 tbsp groundnut (peanut) oil

2 garlic cloves, chopped

1 small onion, finely chopped

2.5cm/1in piece of fresh root ginger, grated

225g/8oz chicken breast fillets, skinned
   and cut into 1cm/1/2 in dice

1 red (bell) pepper, seeded and sliced

115g/4oz drained canned corn kernels

5ml/1 tsp chilli oil

5ml/1 tsp hot curry powder

2 eggs, beaten

salt

spring onion (scallion) shreds, to garnish

1 Pour the water into a pan and whisk in the coconut milk powder. Add the rice and bring to the boil. Lower the heat, cover and cook for 12 minutes, or until the rice is tender and the liquid has been absorbed. Spread the rice on a baking sheet and leave until cold.

2 Heat the oil in a wok, add the garlic, onion and ginger and stir-fry over a medium heat for 2 minutes.

3 Push the vegetables to the sides of the wok, add the chicken to the centre and stir-fry for 2 minutes. Add the rice and stir-fry over a high heat for about 3 minutes more until the chicken is cooked through.

4 Stir in the sliced red pepper, corn, chilli oil and curry powder, with salt to taste. Toss over the heat for 1 minute. Stir in the beaten eggs and cook for 1 minute more. Garnish with spring onion shreds and serve.

# Chicken Rice with Mint Relish

*A fresh-tasting tomato and mint relish complements this dish perfectly.*

### INGREDIENTS

*Serves 4*

250g/9oz chicken, skinned and diced

3 garlic cloves, chopped

5ml/1 tsp ground turmeric

30 45ml/2 3 tbsp olive oil

2 small–medium carrots, diced or chopped

seeds from 6–8 cardamom pods

500g/1$^1$/4 lb/2$^3$/4 cups long grain rice

250g/9oz tomatoes, chopped

750ml/1$^1$/4 pints/3 cups chicken stock

salt and ground black pepper

*For the relish*

3 tomatoes, diced

large handful of fresh mint, chopped

5–8 spring onions (scallions), thinly sliced

juice of 2 lemons

salt

1 To make the relish, put all the ingredients in a bowl and mix together. Chill until ready to serve.

2 Mix the diced chicken with half the garlic and the turmeric. Heat a little of the oil in a pan, add the chicken and fry briefly until the chicken has changed colour and is almost cooked. Remove from the pan and set aside.

3 Add the carrots to the pan with the remaining oil, then stir in the remaining garlic, cardamom seeds and the rice. Cook for 1–2 minutes.

4 Add the tomatoes and stock and bring to the boil. Cover and simmer for 10 minutes, until the rice is tender. A few minutes before the rice is cooked, add the chicken. Season to taste. Serve with relish.

# Chicken and Prawn Jambalaya

The mixture of chicken, seafood and rice suggests a close relationship to the Spanish paella, but the name is more likely to have derived from jambon (the French for ham), à la ya (Creole for rice). Jambalayas are a colourful mixture of highly flavoured ingredients, and are always made in large quantities for feasts and celebration meals.

### INGREDIENTS

Serves 10

2 chickens, about 1.6kg/3$^1$/2 lb each
450g/1lb piece raw smoked gammon
    (smoked or cured ham)
675g/1$^1$/2 lb tomatoes
50g/2oz/$^1$/4 cup lard or white cooking fat
    or bacon fat
50g/2oz/$^1$/2 cup plain (all-purpose) flour
3 medium onions, finely sliced
2 green (bell) peppers, seeded and sliced
2–3 garlic cloves, crushed
10ml/2 tsp chopped fresh thyme or 5ml/1
    tsp dried thyme
24 raw Mediterranean prawns (jumbo
    shrimp), peeled and deveined
500g/1$^1$/4 lb/2$^3$/4 cups white long grain rice
1.2 litres/2 pints/5 cups water
2–3 dashes Tabasco sauce
salt and ground black pepper
45ml/3 tbsp chopped fresh flat leaf parsley,
    plus tiny fresh parsley sprigs, to garnish

### COOK'S TIP

To devein a prawn, make a shallow cut down the centre of the curved back. Pull out the black vein with a cocktail stick (toothpick) or your fingers, then rinse the prawn thoroughly.

1 Cut each chicken into ten pieces and season well. Dice the gammon, discarding the rind and fat. Plunge the tomatoes into boiling water for 30 seconds, then refresh in cold water. Peel away the skins and chop the flesh.

2 Melt the lard or bacon fat in a large, heavy frying pan. Add the chicken pieces in batches, brown them all over, then lift them out with a slotted spoon and set them aside.

3 Reduce the heat. Sprinkle the flour into the fat in the pan and stir until the roux turns golden brown. Return the chicken pieces to the pan.

4 Add the diced gammon, onions, green peppers, tomatoes, garlic and thyme. Cook, stirring regularly, for 10 minutes, then add the prawns and mix lightly.

5 Stir the rice into the pan and pour in the water. Season with salt, pepper and Tabasco sauce. Bring to the boil, then cook gently until the rice is tender, the chicken is cooked and all the liquid has been absorbed. Add a little extra boiling water if the rice looks as though it is drying out before it is cooked.

6 Mix the parsley into the finished dish, garnish with tiny sprigs of flat leaf parsley and serve immediately.

# Lunch-box Rice with Three Toppings

*In Japan, children will often be given a rice-based lunch box such as this one. Colourful toppings and a variety of tastes hold their attention so they don't get bored.*

INGREDIENTS

*Makes 4 lunch boxes*

3 mangetouts (snow peas)

275g/10oz/scant 1¹/₂ cups Japanese short
    grain rice cooked using 375ml/
    13fl oz/scant 1²/₃ cups water, cooled

45ml/3 tbsp sesame seeds, toasted

salt

*For the egg topping*

30ml/2 tbsp caster (superfine) sugar

5ml/1 tsp salt

3 large (US extra large) eggs, beaten

*For the cod topping*

115g/4oz cod fillet, skinned and boned

20ml/4 tsp caster (superfine) sugar

5ml/1 tsp salt

5ml/1 tsp sake

2 drops of red vegetable colouring, diluted
    with a few drops of water (optional)

*For the chicken topping*

200g/7oz/1³/₄ cups minced (ground)
    raw chicken

45ml/3 tbsp sake

15ml/1 tbsp caster (superfine) sugar

15ml/1 tbsp shoyu

15ml/1 tbsp water

1 To make the egg topping, add the sugar and salt to the eggs in a pan. Cook over a medium heat, stirring as if scrambling an egg. When it is almost set, remove from the heat and stir until the egg becomes slightly dry.

2 To make the cod topping, cook the cod fillet for 2 minutes in a large pan of boiling water. Drain and dry well with kitchen paper. Skin and remove all the fish bones.

3 Put the cod and sugar into a pan, add the salt and sake, and cook over a low heat for 1 minute, stirring with a fork to flake the cod. Reduce the heat to low and add the colouring, if using. Continue to stir for 15–20 minutes, or until the cod flakes become fluffy and fibrous. Transfer to a plate.

4 To make the chicken topping, put the minced chicken, sake, sugar, shoyu and water into a small pan. Cook over a medium heat for about 3 minutes, then reduce the heat to medium-low and stir with a fork or whisk until the liquid has almost evaporated.

5 Blanch the mangetouts for about 3 minutes in lightly salted boiling water, drain and carefully slice into fine 3mm/ ¹/₈ in sticks.

6 Mix the rice with the sesame seeds in a bowl. With a wet spoon, divide the rice among four 17 x 12cm/6¹/₂ x 4¹/₂in lunch boxes. Flatten the surface using the back of a wooden spoon.

7 Spoon a quarter of the egg topping into each box to cover one-third of the rice. Cover the next third with a quarter of the cod topping, and the last section with a quarter of the chicken topping. Garnish with the mangetout sticks.

# Chicken and Split Pea Stew

*This is a Californian version of the traditional Persian Koresh, a thick, saucy stew served with rice.*

*Serves 4–6*

45–60ml/3–4 tbsp olive oil

1 large or 2 small onions, finely chopped

500g/1¼lb boneless chicken thighs

50g/2oz/¼ cup green split peas, soaked for 4 hours then drained

500ml/17fl oz/2¼ cups chicken stock

5ml/1 tsp ground turmeric

2.5ml/½ tsp ground cinnamon

1.5ml/¼ tsp freshly grated nutmeg

2 aubergines (eggplant), diced

8–10 ripe tomatoes, diced

2 garlic cloves, crushed

30ml/2 tbsp dried mint

salt and ground black pepper

fresh mint, to garnish

rice, to serve

1 Heat a little oil in a pan, add two-thirds of the onions and cook for 5 minutes. Add the chicken and cook until golden.

2 Add the split peas to the pan, then the stock, turmeric, cinnamon and nutmeg. Cook over a medium-low heat for 40 minutes, or until the split peas are tender and the chicken is cooked.

3 Heat the remaining oil in a pan, add the aubergines and remaining onions and cook until lightly browned. Add the tomatoes, garlic and mint. Season.

4 Just before serving, stir the aubergine mixture into the chicken and split pea stew. Garnish the stew with fresh mint leaves and serve with rice.

# Tagine of Chicken

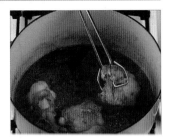

Chicken is cooked with spices and olives and served on a bed of vegetable couscous in this version of the Moroccan dish.

### INGREDIENTS

*Serves 8*

8 chicken legs (thighs and drumsticks)
30ml/2 tbsp olive oil
1 medium onion, finely chopped
2 garlic cloves, crushed
5ml/1 tsp ground turmeric
2.5ml/$^1$/$_2$ tsp ground ginger
2.5ml/$^1$/$_2$ tsp ground cinnamon
475ml/16fl oz/2 cups chicken stock
150g/5oz/1$^1$/$_4$ cups pitted green olives
1 lemon, sliced
salt and ground black pepper
fresh coriander (cilantro) sprigs, to garnish

*For the couscous*

600ml/1 pint/2$^1$/$_2$ cups chicken stock
450g/1lb couscous
4 courgettes (zucchini), thickly sliced
2 carrots, thickly sliced
2 small turnips, peeled and cubed
45ml/3 tbsp olive oil
450g/1lb can chickpeas, drained
15ml/1 tbsp chopped fresh coriander

1 Preheat the oven to 180°C/ 350°F/Gas 4. Cut the chicken legs into two through the joint.

2 Heat the oil in a large, flameproof casserole and, working in batches, brown the chicken on both sides. Drain and remove to a dish and keep warm.

3 Add the onion and crushed garlic to the flameproof casserole and cook gently until tender. Add the spices and cook for 1 minute. Pour over the stock, bring to the boil, and return the chicken. Cover and bake for 45 minutes, or until cooked. Transfer the chicken to a dish, cover and keep warm.

4 Remove any fat from the cooking liquid and boil to reduce by one-third. Meanwhile, blanch the olives and lemon slices in a pan of boiling water for 2 minutes, or until the lemon skin is tender. Drain and add to the cooking liquid, and adjust the seasoning to taste.

5 To cook the couscous, bring the stock to the boil in a large pan and sprinkle in the couscous slowly, stirring all the time. Remove from the heat, cover and leave to stand for 5 minutes.

6 Meanwhile, cook the prepared vegetables, drain and put them into a large bowl. Add the couscous and oil, and season to taste with salt and pepper. Stir the grains to fluff them up, add the chickpeas and finally the chopped coriander. Spoon on to a large serving plate, cover with the chicken, and spoon over the liquid. Garnish with the fresh coriander.

# Chicken and Vegetable Tagine

*Moroccan tagines are usually served with couscous, but in this version couscous is stirred into rice for an unusual and tasty accompaniment for the chicken and vegetables.*

INGREDIENTS

*Serves 4*

30ml/2 tbsp groundnut (peanut) oil
4 chicken breast fillets, skinned and cut
   into large pieces
1 large onion, chopped
2 garlic cloves, crushed
1 small parsnip, cut into 2.5cm/1in pieces
1 small turnip, cut into 2cm/$^3$/$_4$in pieces
3 carrots, cut into 4cm/1$^1$/$_2$in pieces
4 tomatoes, chopped
1 cinnamon stick
4 cloves
5ml/1 tsp ground ginger
1 bay leaf
1.5–2.5ml/$^1$/$_4$–$^1$/$_2$ tsp cayenne pepper
350ml/12fl oz/1$^1$/$_2$ cups chicken stock
400g/14oz can chickpeas, drained
   and skinned
1 red (bell) pepper, seeded and sliced
150g/5oz green beans, halved
1 piece of preserved lemon peel,
   thinly sliced
20–30 pitted brown or green olives
salt

*For the rice and couscous*
750ml/1$^1$/$_4$ pints/3 cups chicken stock
225g/8oz/generous 1 cup long grain rice
115g/4oz/$^2$/$_3$ cup couscous
45ml/3 tbsp chopped fresh
   coriander (cilantro)

1 Heat half of the oil in a large, flameproof casserole and fry the chicken pieces for a few minutes, or until evenly browned. Transfer to a plate.

2 Heat the remaining oil and fry the onion, garlic, parsnip, turnip and carrots together over a medium heat for 4–5 minutes, or until the vegetables are lightly flecked with brown, stirring frequently. Lower the heat, and then cover and sweat the vegetables for 5 minutes more, stirring occasionally.

3 Add the tomatoes, cook for a few minutes, then add the cinnamon stick, cloves, ginger, bay leaf and cayenne. Cook for 1–2 minutes.

4 Pour in the chicken stock, add the chickpeas and browned chicken pieces, and season with salt. Cover and simmer for 25 minutes.

5 Meanwhile, cook the rice and couscous mixture. Bring the chicken stock to the boil. Add the rice and simmer for about 5 minutes, or until almost tender. Remove the pan from the heat, stir in the couscous, cover tightly and leave for about 5 minutes.

6 When the vegetables in the tagine are almost tender, stir in the pepper slices and green beans and simmer for 10 minutes. Add the preserved lemon and olives, stir well and cook for 5 minutes more, or until the vegetables are tender and the chicken is cooked.

7 Stir the coriander into the rice and couscous mixture and pile it on to a plate. Serve the chicken tagine in the traditional dish, if you have one, or in a casserole.

# Conchiglie with Chicken Livers and Herbs

*Fresh herbs and chicken livers are a good combination, often used together on crostini in Tuscany, Italy. Here they are tossed with pasta shells to make a very tasty supper dish.*

INGREDIENTS

*Serves 4*

50g/2oz/¹/4 cup butter

115g/4oz pancetta or rindless streaky (fatty) bacon, diced

250g/9oz frozen chicken livers, thawed, drained and diced

2 garlic cloves, crushed

10ml/2 tsp chopped fresh sage

300g/11oz/2³/4 cups dried conchiglie

150ml/¼ pint/²/3 cup dry white wine

4 ripe Italian plum tomatoes, peeled and diced

15ml/1 tbsp chopped fresh flat leaf parsley

salt and ground black pepper

1 Melt half the butter in a pan, add the pancetta or bacon and fry over a medium heat for a few minutes, until it is lightly coloured.

2 Add the livers, garlic, half the sage and pepper. Increase the heat and toss the livers for about 5 minutes. Meanwhile, start cooking the pasta according to the packet instructions.

3 Pour the wine over the livers and let it sizzle, lower the heat and simmer for 5 minutes until cooked. Add the remaining butter. When it melts, mix in the tomatoes, the remaining sage and the parsley. Stir well. Add salt if needed.

4 Drain the pasta and tip it into a warmed bowl. Pour the sauce over and toss well. Serve immediately.

# Chicken and Rice Vermicelli

*This delicious dish makes a filling meal. Take care when frying vermicelli as it has a tendency to spit when added to hot oil.*

## INGREDIENTS

*Serves 4*

120ml/4fl oz/$^1$/2 cup vegetable oil
225g/8oz rice vermicelli
150g/5oz green beans, halved lengthways
1 onion, finely chopped
2 chicken breast fillets, about 175g/6oz
   each, skinned and cut into strips
5ml/1 tsp chilli powder
225g/8oz/2 cups cooked prawns (shrimp)
45ml/3 tbsp dark soy sauce
45ml/3 tbsp white wine vinegar
10ml/2 tsp caster (superfine) sugar
fresh coriander (cilantro) sprigs,
   to garnish

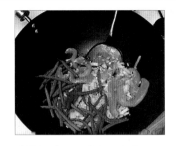

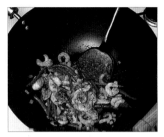

2 Heat the remaining oil, then add the green beans, chopped onion and chicken strips and stir-fry together for 3 minutes, or until the chicken strips are cooked.

3 Sprinkle in the chilli powder. Stir in the cooked prawns, soy sauce, vinegar and sugar, and stir-fry for 2 minutes.

4 Serve the chicken, prawns and vegetables on the fried vermicelli, garnished with sprigs of fresh coriander.

1 Heat a wok or frying pan, then add 60ml/4 tbsp of the oil. Break up the rice vermicelli into 7.5cm/3in lengths. When the oil is hot, fry the vermicelli in batches. Remove from the heat and keep warm.

# Farfalle with Chicken and Cherry Tomatoes

*Quick to prepare and easy to cook, this colourful dish is full of flavour. Serve it for a midweek supper, with a green salad to follow.*

*Serves 4*

350g/12oz chicken breast fillets, skinned
    and cut into bitesize pieces
60ml/4 tbsp Italian dry vermouth
10ml/2 tsp chopped fresh rosemary, plus
    4 fresh rosemary sprigs, to garnish
15ml/1 tbsp olive oil
1 onion, finely chopped
90g/3$^1$/2oz piece Italian salami, diced
275g/10oz/2$^1$/2 cups dried farfalle
15ml/1 tbsp balsamic vinegar
400g/14oz can Italian cherry tomatoes
good pinch of crushed dried red chillies
salt and ground black pepper

1 Put the chicken pieces in a large bowl, pour in the dry vermouth and sprinkle with half the chopped rosemary and salt and pepper to taste. Stir well and set aside.

2 Heat the oil in a large pan, add the onion and salami and fry over a medium heat for about 5 minutes, stirring frequently.

3 Cook the pasta for 8–10 minutes or according to the instructions on the packet.

4 Add the chicken and vermouth to the onion and salami, increase the heat to high and fry for 3 minutes, or until the chicken is white on all sides. Sprinkle the vinegar over the chicken.

5 Add the cherry tomatoes and dried chillies. Stir well and simmer for a few minutes more until the chicken is cooked. Taste the sauce for seasoning.

6 Drain the pasta and tip it into the pan. Add the remaining chopped rosemary and toss to mix the pasta and sauce together. Serve immediately in warmed bowls, garnished with the rosemary sprigs.

# Penne with Chicken, Broccoli and Cheese

*The combination of broccoli, garlic and Gorgonzola is very tasty, and goes especially well with chicken.*

## INGREDIENTS

Serves 4

115g/4oz/scant 1 cup broccoli florets, divided into tiny sprigs

50g/2oz/$^1$/4 cup butter

2 chicken breast fillets, skinned and cut into thin strips

2 garlic cloves, crushed

400g/14oz/3$^1$/2 cups dried penne

120ml/4fl oz/$^1$/2 cup dry white wine

200ml/7fl oz/scant 1 cup panna da cucina or double (heavy) cream

90g/3$^1$/2 oz Gorgonzola cheese, rind removed and diced small

salt and ground black pepper

freshly grated Parmesan cheese, to serve

1 Plunge the broccoli into a pan of salted boiling water. Bring back to the boil and boil for 2 minutes, then drain in a colander and refresh under cold running water. Shake well to remove the surplus water and set aside to drain completely.

---

## VARIATION
∾

Use leeks instead of broccoli if you prefer. Fry them with the chicken strips.

---

2 Melt the butter in a large skillet or pan, add the chicken and garlic, with salt and pepper to taste, and stir well. Fry over a medium heat for 3 minutes, or until the chicken becomes white. Meanwhile, start cooking the pasta for 8–10 minutes, or according to the instructions on the packet.

3 Pour the wine and cream over the chicken mixture in the pan, stir to mix, then simmer, stirring occasionally, for about 5 minutes, or until the sauce has reduced and thickened and the chicken is cooked through. Add the broccoli, increase the heat and toss to heat it through and mix it with the chicken. Taste for seasoning.

4 Drain the pasta and tip it in to the sauce. Add the Gorgonzola and toss well. Serve with grated Parmesan.

# Pappardelle with Chicken and Mushrooms

*Porcini mushrooms have a strong taste that goes particularly well with chicken and pasta. This is a rich and creamy dish.*

*Serves 4*

15g/$^1$/$_2$oz/$^1$/$_4$ cup dried porcini
   mushrooms
175ml/6fl oz/$^3$/$_4$ cup warm water
25g/1oz/2 tbsp butter
1 garlic clove, crushed
1 small handful fresh flat leaf parsley,
   roughly chopped
1 small leek or 4 spring onions
   (scallions), chopped
120ml/4fl oz/$^1$/$_2$ cup dry white wine
250ml/8fl oz/1 cup chicken stock
400g/14oz fresh or dried pappardelle
2 chicken breast fillets, skinned and cut
   into thin strips
105ml/7 tbsp mascarpone cheese
salt and ground black pepper
fresh basil leaves, shredded, to garnish

1 Put the dried mushrooms in a bowl. Pour in the warm water and leave to soak for 15–20 minutes. Tip into a fine sieve set over a bowl and squeeze the mushrooms with your hands to release as much liquid as possible.

2 Chop the mushrooms finely and set aside the strained soaking liquid until required.

3 Melt the butter in a pan, add the mushrooms, garlic, parsley and leek or spring onions, with seasoning. Cook over a low heat, stirring frequently, for about 5 minutes, then pour in the wine and stock and bring to the boil. Lower the heat and simmer for about 5 minutes, or until the liquid has reduced and is thickened.

4 Meanwhile, start cooking the pasta in salted boiling water for 8–10 minutes, or according to the packet instructions, adding the reserved soaking liquid from the mushrooms to the water.

5 Add the chicken and simmer for 5 minutes, or until just tender. Add the mascarpone a spoonful at a time, stirring after each addition, then add one or two spoonfuls of the water used for cooking the pasta. Season to taste.

6 Drain the pasta and tip it into a warmed large bowl. Add the chicken and sauce and toss well. Serve immediately, topped with the shredded basil leaves.

---

### VARIATION

Add 115g/4oz/1$^1$/$_2$ cups sliced button (white) or chestnut mushrooms with the chicken.

# Penne with Chicken and Ham Sauce

*A meal in itself, this colourful pasta sauce is perfect for lunch or dinner.*

### INGREDIENTS

Serves 4

350g/12oz/3 cups penne

25g/1oz/2 tbsp butter

1 onion, chopped

1 garlic clove, chopped

1 bay leaf

475ml/16 fl oz/2 cups dry white wine

150ml/$^1$/4 pint/$^2$/3 cup crème fraîche

225g/8oz cooked chicken, skinned, boned
    and diced

115g/4oz/$^2$/3 cup diced cooked lean ham

115g/4oz/1 cup grated Gouda cheese

15ml/1 tbsp chopped fresh mint

salt and ground black pepper

finely shredded fresh mint, to garnish

1 Cook the pasta in plenty of salted boiling water following the instructions on the packet.

2 Heat the butter in a large frying pan and fry the onion for 10 minutes, or until softened.

3 Add the garlic, bay leaf and wine and bring to the boil. Boil rapidly until reduced by half. Remove the bay leaf, then stir in the crème fraîche and bring back to the boil.

4 Add the chicken, ham and cheese and simmer for 5 minutes, stirring occasionally until heated through.

5 Add the mint and seasoning. Drain the pasta and turn it into a large serving bowl. Toss with the sauce immediately and garnish with shredded mint.

COOK'S TIP

Crème fraîche is a richer, full-fat French cream with a slightly acidic taste. If you can't find any, substitute sour cream.

# Tagliatelle with Chicken and Herb Sauce

*Chicken and wine is always a winning combination. Serve this dish simply with a green salad.*

### INGREDIENTS

Serves 4

30ml/2 tbsp olive oil
1 red onion, cut into wedges
350g/12oz tagliatelle
1 garlic clove, chopped
350g/12oz/2$^{1}$/$_{2}$ cups chicken, diced
300ml/$^{1}$/$_{2}$ pint/1$^{1}$/$_{4}$ cups dry vermouth
45ml/3 tbsp chopped fresh mixed herbs
150ml/$^{1}$/$_{4}$ pint/$^{2}$/$_{3}$ cup fromage frais or
    crème fraîche
salt and ground black pepper
shredded fresh mint, to garnish

1 Heat the oil in a large frying pan and fry the onion for 10 minutes until softened and the layers have separated.

2 Cook the pasta in plenty of salted boiling water following the instructions on the packet.

### COOK'S TIP
~

If you don't want to use vermouth, use dry white wine instead. Orvieto and Frascati are two Italian wines that are ideal to use in this sauce.

3 Add the garlic and chicken to the pan and fry for 10 minutes, stirring occasionally until the chicken is browned all over and cooked through.

4 Pour in the vermouth, bring to the boil, and boil rapidly until reduced by about half.

5 Stir in the herbs, fromage frais or crème fraîche and seasoning and heat through gently, but do not boil.

6 Drain the pasta thoroughly and toss it with the sauce to coat. Serve immediately, garnished with shredded fresh mint.

# Fusilli with Chicken, Tomatoes and Broccoli

*This is a really hearty meal for a hungry family. Fusilli tricolore adds to the appearance as well as tasting great.*

INGREDIENTS

*Serves 4*

675g/1$\frac{1}{2}$lb ripe but firm plum
   tomatoes, quartered
90ml/6 tbsp olive oil
5ml/1 tsp dried oregano
350g/12oz broccoli florets
1 small onion, sliced
5ml/1 tsp dried thyme
450g/1lb chicken breast fillet, skinned
   and cubed
3 garlic cloves, crushed
15ml/1 tbsp fresh lemon juice
450g/1lb/4 cups fusilli
salt and ground black pepper

1 Preheat the oven to 200°C/
400°F/Gas 6.

2 Place the tomatoes in a baking dish. Add 15ml/1 tbsp of the oil, the oregano, and 5ml/$\frac{1}{2}$ tsp salt, and stir to blend.

3 Bake until the tomatoes are just browned, about 30–40 minutes; do not stir.

4 Meanwhile, bring a large pan of salted water to the boil. Add the broccoli and cook until just tender, about 5 minutes. Drain and set aside. (Alternatively, steam the broccoli until tender.)

5 Heat 30ml/2 tbsp of the oil in a large, non-stick frying pan. Add the onion, thyme, chicken cubes and 2.5ml/$\frac{1}{2}$ tsp salt. Cook over high heat, stirring often, for 5–7 minutes. or until the meat is cooked and beginning to brown. Add the garlic and cook for 1 minute, stirring.

6 Remove from the heat. Stir in the lemon juice and season with pepper. Keep warm until the pasta is cooked.

7 Bring another large pan of salted water to the boil. Add the fusilli and cook until just tender (check the instructions on the packet for timing). Drain and place in a large bowl. Toss with the remaining oil.

8 Add the broccoli to the chicken mixture. Add to the fusilli. Add the tomatoes and stir gently to blend. Serve immediately.

# Pasta Sauce with Chicken and Tomato

*Fusilli is good with a sauce as it clings to the ridges of the pasta. This deliciously rich tomato and chicken sauce is quick to make.*

### INGREDIENTS

*Serves 4*

15ml/1 tbsp olive oil
1 onion, chopped
1 carrot, chopped
50g/2oz/1 cup sun-dried tomatoes in olive oil, drained weight
1 garlic clove, chopped
400g/14oz can chopped tomatoes, drained
15ml/1 tbsp tomato purée (paste)
150ml/½ pint/⅔ cup chicken stock
350g/12oz/3 cups fusilli
225g/8oz chicken breast fillets, skinned and diagonally sliced
salt and ground black pepper
sprigs fresh mint, to garnish

1 Heat the oil in a large frying pan and fry the chopped onion and carrot for 5 minutes, stirring from time to time.

2 Chop the sun-dried tomatoes and set aside.

3 Stir the garlic, canned tomatoes, tomato purée and stock into the onions and carrots and bring to the boil. Simmer for 10 minutes, stirring occasionally.

4 Cook the pasta in plenty of salted boiling water following the instructions on the packet.

5 Pour the sauce into a food processor or blender and process until smooth.

### COOK'S TIP

Sun-dried tomatoes are sold soaked in vegetable or olive oil. The olive oil-soaked tomatoes have a superior flavour. If using, fry the onion and carrot in 15ml/ 1 tbsp of the oil from the tomatoes.

6 Return the sauce to the pan and stir in the sun-dried tomatoes and chicken. Bring back to the boil, then simmer for 10 minutes, or until the chicken is cooked. Adjust the seasoning.

7 Drain the pasta thoroughly and toss it in the sauce. Serve immediately, garnished with sprigs of fresh mint.

# Cannelloni al Forno

*Chicken, mushroom and a hint of tarragon make a light filling for cannelloni. Serve with a salad for a substantial meal.*

### INGREDIENTS

*Serves 4–6*

450g/1lb chicken breast fillets, skinned
    and cooked
225g/8oz/3$^1$/4 cups mushrooms
2 garlic cloves, crushed
30ml/2 tbsp chopped fresh parsley
15ml/1 tbsp chopped fresh tarragon
1 egg, beaten
fresh lemon juice
12–18 cannelloni tubes
475ml/16 fl oz/2 cups ready-made
    tomato sauce
50g/2oz/$^2$/3 cup freshly grated
    Parmesan cheese
salt and ground pepper
1 fresh parsley sprig, to garnish

1 Preheat the oven to 200°C/400°F/Gas 6. Place the chicken in a blender or food processor and blend until finely minced (ground). Transfer to a bowl.

2 Place the mushrooms, garlic, parsley and tarragon in the food processor and blend until finely minced. Add to the chicken mixture.

3 Thoroughly beat the mushroom mixture into the chicken, then add the egg, salt and pepper and lemon juice to taste, and mix together well.

4 If necessary, cook the cannelloni in plenty of salted boiling water according to the instructions on the packet, then drain well on a clean dishtowel.

5 Place the filling in a piping (pastry) bag fitted with a large plain nozzle. Use this to fill each tube of cannelloni once they are cool enough to handle.

6 Lay the filled cannelloni tightly together in a single layer in a buttered shallow ovenproof dish. Spoon over the tomato sauce and sprinkle with Parmesan cheese. Bake in the oven for 30 minutes or until brown and bubbling. Serve garnished with a sprig of parsley.

# Chicken, Beef and Pork Cannelloni

*A rich mixture of chicken, beef and pork with cream and a hint of brandy makes an extremely tasty filling for cannelloni. A crisp, green salad is all that is needed to accompany it.*

### INGREDIENTS

*Serves 4*

60ml/4 tbsp olive oil

1 onion, finely chopped

1 carrot, finely chopped

2 garlic cloves, crushed

2 ripe Italian plum tomatoes, peeled and finely chopped

250g/9oz/2$^{1}$/4 cups minced (ground) chicken

130g/4$^{1}$/2 oz/$^{1}$/2 cup minced (ground) beef

130g/4$^{1}$/2 oz/$^{1}$/2 cup minced (ground) pork

30ml/2 tbsp brandy

25g/1oz/2 tbsp butter

90ml/6 tbsp *panna da cucina* or double (heavy) cream

16 dried no pre-cook cannelloni tubes

75g/3oz/1 cup freshly grated Parmesan cheese

salt and ground black pepper

green salad, to serve

*For the sauce*

50g/2oz/$^{1}$/4 cup butter

50g/2oz/$^{1}$/2 cup plain (all-purpose) flour

900ml/1$^{1}$/2 pints/3$^{3}$/4 cups milk

freshly grated nutmeg

1 Heat the oil in a pan, add the onion, carrot, garlic and tomatoes and cook over a low heat, stirring, for about 10 minutes.

2 Add all the minced meats to the pan and cook gently for about 10 minutes, stirring frequently to break up any lumps. Add the brandy, increase the heat and stir until it has reduced, then add the butter and cream and cook gently, stirring occasionally, for about 10 minutes. Allow to cool.

3 Preheat the oven to 190°C/ 375°F/Gas 5. To make the white sauce, melt the butter in a medium pan, add the flour and cook, stirring, for 1–2 minutes. Add the milk a little at a time, whisking vigorously after each addition. Bring to the boil and cook, stirring, until the sauce is smooth and thick. Grate in fresh nutmeg to taste, then season and whisk well. Remove the pan from the heat.

4 Spoon a little of the white sauce into a baking dish. Fill the cannelloni tubes with the meat mixture and place in a single layer in the dish. Pour the remaining white sauce over them, then sprinkle with the Parmesan cheese. Bake for 35–40 minutes, or until the pasta is tender when pierced with a skewer. Allow to stand for 10 minutes before serving with a green salad.

# Chicken Lasagne

*Based on the Italian beef lasagne, this is an excellent dish for entertaining guests of all ages. Serve with a green salad.*

### INGREDIENTS

*Serves 8*

30ml/2 tbsp olive oil

900g/2lb/8 cups minced (ground) raw chicken

225g/8oz/1$^{1}$/2 cups chopped rindless streaky (fatty) bacon rashers (strips)

2 garlic cloves, crushed

450g/1lb leeks, sliced

225g/8oz carrots, diced

30ml/2 tbsp tomato purée (paste)

475ml/16fl oz/2 cups chicken stock

12 sheets no pre-cook lasagne verde

salt and ground black pepper

*For the cheese sauce*

50g/2oz/$^{1}$/4 cup butter

50g/2oz/$^{1}$/2 cup plain (all-purpose) flour

600ml/1 pint/2$^{1}$/2 cups milk

115g/4oz/1 cup grated mature (sharp) Cheddar cheese

1.5ml/$^{1}$/4 tsp dry English (hot) mustard

1 Heat the oil in a large, flameproof casserole and brown the minced chicken and bacon briskly, separating the pieces with a wooden spoon. Add the crushed garlic cloves, sliced leeks and diced carrots and cook for about 5 minutes, or until softened. Add the tomato purée, stock and seasoning. Bring to the boil, cover and simmer for 30 minutes.

2 To make the sauce, melt the butter in a pan, add the flour and gradually blend in the milk, stirring until smooth. Bring to the boil, stirring all the time until thickened, and simmer for several minutes. Add half the grated cheese and the mustard, and season to taste.

3 Preheat the oven to 190°C/ 375°F/Gas 5. Layer the chicken mixture, lasagne and half the cheese sauce in a 2.5 litre/4 pint/ 10 cup ovenproof dish, starting and finishing with a layer of chicken.

4 Pour the remaining half of the cheese sauce over the top to cover and sprinkle over the remaining cheese. Bake in the preheated oven for 1 hour, or until bubbling and lightly browned on top.

# Turkey and Pasta Bake

*Slow-cooked turkey with vegetables make a well-flavoured and low-fat sauce for pasta.*

## INGREDIENTS

Serves 4

275g/10oz/2¹/₂ cups minced (ground) turkey
150g/5oz smoked turkey rashers (strips), chopped
1–2 garlic cloves, crushed
1 onion, finely chopped
2 carrots, diced
30ml/2 tbsp concentrated tomato purée (paste)
300ml/¹/₂ pint/1¹/₄ cups chicken stock
225g/8oz rigatoni
30ml/2 tbsp grated Parmesan cheese
salt and ground black pepper

3 Preheat the oven to 180°C/350°F/Gas 4. Cook the pasta in a large pan of salted boiling water for 8–10 minutes, or according to the instructions on the packet, until *al dente*. Drain thoroughly and mix with the turkey sauce.

4 Transfer to a shallow ovenproof dish and sprinkle with grated Parmesan cheese. Bake in the preheated oven for 20–30 minutes, or until lightly browned.

1 Brown the minced turkey in a non-stick pan, breaking up any large pieces with a wooden spoon, until well browned all over.

2 Add the turkey rashers, garlic, onion, carrots, purée, stock and seasoning. Bring to the boil, cover and simmer for 1 hour until tender.

# Piquant Chicken with Spaghetti

*A dash of vinegar adds piquancy to this herby chicken sauce for spaghetti. Low-fat crème fraîche makes a creamy and healthy sauce.*

### INGREDIENTS

*Serves 4*

1 onion, finely chopped

1 carrot, diced

1 garlic clove, crushed

300ml/$^1$/$_2$ pint/$1^1$/$_4$ cups vegetable stock or water

4 small chicken breast fillets, skinned

bouquet garni (bay leaf, parsley stalks and thyme)

115g/4oz/$1^1$/$_2$ cups thinly sliced button (white) mushrooms,

5ml/1 tsp wine vinegar or lemon juice

350g/12oz spaghetti

$^1$/$_2$ cucumber, peeled and cut into fingers

2 firm ripe tomatoes, skinned

30ml/2 tbsp low-fat crème fraîche

15ml/1 tbsp chopped fresh parsley

15ml/1 tbsp chopped chives

salt and ground black pepper

1 Put the onion, carrot, garlic, stock or water into a pan with the chicken and bouquet garni. Bring to the boil, cover and simmer gently for 15–20 minutes, or until tender.

2 Transfer the chicken to a plate and cover with foil. Strain the liquid, discard the vegetables and return the liquid to the pan. Add the mushrooms, wine vinegar or lemon juice and simmer for 2–3 minutes, or until tender.

3 Cook the spaghetti in a large pan of salted boiling water for 8–10 minutes, or according to the packet instructions. Drain.

4 Blanch the cucumber in boiling water for 10 seconds. Drain and rinse under cold water.

5 Cut the chicken into bitesize pieces. Boil the stock to reduce by half, then add the chicken, tomatoes, crème fraîche, cucumber and herbs. Season to taste.

6 Transfer the spaghetti to a warmed serving dish and spoon over the piquant chicken. Serve immediately.

# Spaghetti and Turkey in Cheese Sauce

*An American-Italian recipe, this dish, known as Spaghetti tetrazzini, makes an excellent family meal. It is quite filling and rich, so serve it with a tossed green salad.*

## INGREDIENTS

*Serves 4–6*

75g/3oz/6 tbsp butter

350g/12oz turkey breast fillet, cut into thin strips

2 pieces bottled roasted pepper, drained, rinsed, dried and cut into thin strips

175g/6oz dried spaghetti

50g/2oz/¹/2 cup plain (all-purpose) flour

900ml/1¹/2 pints/3³/4 cups hot milk

115g/4oz/1¹/3 cups freshly grated Parmesan cheese

1.5–2.5ml/¹/4–¹/2 tsp mustard powder

salt and ground black pepper

1 Melt 25g/1oz/2 tbsp of the butter in a pan, add the turkey and season well. Toss the turkey over a medium heat for 5 minutes, or until the meat turns white. Add the roasted pepper and toss to mix. Remove with a slotted spoon and set aside.

2 Preheat the oven to 180°C/350°F/Gas 4. Cook the pasta in salted boiling water for 8–10 minutes, or according to the instructions on the packet.

3 Meanwhile, melt the remaining butter over a low heat in the pan in which the turkey was cooked. Sprinkle in the flour and cook, stirring, for 1–2 minutes, then increase the heat to medium.

4 Add the hot milk a little at a time, whisking vigorously after each addition. Bring to the boil and cook, stirring, until the sauce is smooth and thick. Add two-thirds of the grated Parmesan, then whisk in the mustard, salt and pepper to taste. Remove the sauce from the heat.

5 Drain the pasta and return it to the pan. Mix in half the cheese sauce, then spoon the mixture around the edge of a baking dish. Stir the turkey mixture into the remaining cheese sauce and spoon into the centre of the dish. Sprinkle the remaining Parmesan evenly over the top and bake for 15–20 minutes, or until the cheese topping is just crisp. Serve hot.

# Ravioli with Pork and Turkey

*This Roman-style ravioli stuffed with minced meat and cheese is scented with fresh herbs. It makes a substantial main course.*

Serves 8

1 quantity pasta dough (see Cook's Tip)

flour, for dusting

50g/2oz/¹/4 cup butter

large bunch of fresh sage, leaves removed and roughly chopped

60ml/4 tbsp freshly grated Parmesan cheese

extra sage leaves and freshly grated Parmesan cheese, to serve

*For the filling*

25g/1oz/2 tbsp butter

150g/5oz/ minced (ground) pork

115g/4oz/1 cup minced (ground) turkey

4 fresh sage leaves, finely chopped

1 rosemary sprig, leaves removed and finely chopped

30ml/2 tbsp dry white wine

65g/2¹/2 oz/generous ¹/4 cup ricotta cheese

45ml/3 tbsp freshly grated Parmesan cheese

1 egg

freshly grated nutmeg

salt and ground black pepper

## COOK'S TIP

To make pasta dough, sift 200g/7oz/1¾ cups plain (all-purpose) flour and a pinch of salt on to a clean work surface and make a well in the centre with your fist. Pour 2 beaten eggs and 15ml/1 tbsp oil into the well. Gradually mix in the eggs with your fingers. Knead the pasta until smooth, wrap in clear film (plastic wrap) and allow to rest for at least 30 minutes before rolling out.

1 To make the filling, melt the butter in a pan, add the pork, turkey and herbs and cook gently for 5–6 minutes, stirring frequently and breaking up any lumps in the meat with a wooden spoon. Season to taste and stir well to mix thoroughly.

2 Add the wine to the pan and stir again. Simmer for 1–2 minutes, or until reduced slightly, then cover and simmer gently for about 20 minutes, stirring occasionally. With a slotted spoon, transfer the meat to a bowl and leave to cool.

3 Add the ricotta and Parmesan cheeses to the bowl with the egg and freshly grated nutmeg to taste. Stir well.

4 Using a pasta machine, roll out one-quarter of the pasta into a 90cm/36in strip. Cut the strip with a sharp knife into two 45cm/18in lengths.

5 Using a teaspoon, put 10–12 little mounds of the filling along one side of one of the pasta strips, spacing them evenly. Brush a little water on to the pasta strip around each mound, then fold the plain side of the pasta strip over the filling.

6 Starting from the folded edge, press down gently with your fingertips around each mound of filling, pushing the air out at the unfolded edge. Sprinkle lightly with flour.

7 With a fluted pasta wheel, cut along each long side, then in-between each mound to make small square shapes. Dust lightly with flour.

8 Put the ravioli in a single layer on floured dishtowels and leave to dry while repeating the process with the remaining pasta to make 80–96 ravioli altogether.

9 Drop the ravioli into a large pan of salted boiling water, bring back to the boil and boil for 4–5 minutes until the filling is cooked.

10 While the ravioli are cooking, melt the butter in a small pan, add the fresh sage leaves and stir over a medium-high heat until the sage leaves are sizzling in the butter.

11 Drain the ravioli and pour half into a warmed large bowl. Sprinkle with half the grated Parmesan, then half the sage butter. Repeat with the remaining ravioli, Parmesan and sage butter. Serve immediately, garnished with fresh sage leaves. Hand round more grated Parmesan separately.

# Turkey Lasagne

2 Blanch the broccoli in a large pan of salted boiling water for 1 minute, then drain and rinse thoroughly under cold water to prevent the broccoli from over-cooking. Drain well and set aside.

3 To make the sauce, melt the butter in a pan, stir in the flour and cook for 1 minute, still stirring. Remove from the heat and gradually stir in the milk. Return to the heat and bring the sauce to the boil, stirring constantly. Simmer for 1 minute, then add 50g/2oz/ $^2/_3$ cup of the Parmesan and plenty of salt and pepper.

*This easy pasta bake is delicious made with cooked turkey pieces and broccoli in a rich and creamy Parmesan sauce.*

### INGREDIENTS

*Serves 4*

30ml/2 tbsp olive oil
1 onion, chopped
2 garlic cloves, chopped
450g/1lb cooked turkey meat, finely diced
225g/8oz/1 cup mascarpone cheese
30ml/2 tbsp chopped fresh tarragon
300g/11oz broccoli, broken into florets
115g/4oz no pre-cook lasagne verdi
salt and ground black pepper

*For the sauce*

50g/2oz/$^1/_4$ cup butter
30ml/2 tbsp flour
600ml/1 pint/2$^1/_2$ cups milk
75g/3oz/1 cup freshly grated
   Parmesan cheese

1 Preheat the oven to 180°C/ 350°F/Gas 4. Heat the oil in a pan and cook the onion and garlic until softened. Remove from the heat, stir in the turkey, cheese and tarragon, with seasoning to taste.

---

### VARIATION
~
This dish is also good made with half ham and half turkey.

---

4 Spoon a layer of the turkey mixture into a large, shallow baking dish. Add a layer of broccoli and cover with sheets of lasagne. Coat with the cheese sauce. Repeat these layers, finishing with a layer of cheese sauce on top. Sprinkle with the remaining Parmesan and bake for 35–40 minutes.

# Bamie Goreng

*This Indonesian fried noodle dish is wonderfully versatile. You can add other vegetables, such as mushrooms, broccoli, leeks or beansprouts; just use whatever is to hand.*

## INGREDIENTS

*Serves 6–8*

450g/1lb dried egg noodles

2 eggs

25g/1oz/2 tbsp butter

90ml/6 tbsp vegetable oil

1 chicken breast fillet, skinned and sliced

115g/4oz pork fillet, sliced

115g/4oz calf's liver, finely sliced
  (optional)

2 garlic cloves, crushed

115g/4oz peeled cooked prawns (shrimp)

115g/4oz pak-choi (bok choy)

2 celery sticks, finely sliced

4 spring onions (scallions), shredded

about 60ml/4 tbsp chicken stock

dark soy sauce and light soy sauce

salt and ground black pepper

deep-fried onions and shredded spring
  onions (scallions), to garnish (optional)

3 Heat the remaining oil in a wok and fry the chicken, pork and liver (if using) with the garlic for 2–3 minutes, or until the meat has changed colour. Add the prawns, pak-choi, sliced celery and spring onions and toss to mix.

4 Add the noodles and toss over the heat until heated through and the pak-choi is lightly cooked. Add enough stock just to moisten, and season with dark and light soy sauce. Add the scrambled eggs and toss to mix. Serve immediately, garnished with onions, if you like.

1 Bring a pan of lightly salted water to the boil, add the noodles and cook them for 3–4 minutes. Drain, rinse under cold water and drain again. Set aside.

2 Put the eggs in a bowl, beat and season with salt and pepper. Heat the butter with 5ml/1 tsp oil in a small pan, add the eggs and stir over a low heat until scrambled but still quite moist. Set aside.

# Thai Fried Noodles

*Chicken is combined with prawns, pork tenderloin and Thai flavourings to make this terrific fried-noodle dish.*

*Serves 4*

225g/8oz thread egg noodles
60ml/4 tbsp vegetable oil
2 garlic cloves, finely chopped
175g/6oz pork tenderloin, sliced into
    thin strips
1 chicken breast fillet, about 175g/6oz,
    skinned and sliced into thin strips
115g/4oz/1 cup cooked peeled prawns
    (shrimp), rinsed if canned
45ml/3 tbsp lime or lemon juice
45ml/3 tbsp Thai fish sauce
30ml/2 tbsp soft light brown sugar
2 eggs, beaten
$^1/_2$ red chilli, seeded and finely chopped
50g/2oz/$^1/_4$ cup beansprouts
60ml/4 tbsp roasted peanuts, chopped
3 spring onions (scallions), cut into
    5cm/2in lengths and shredded
45ml/3 tbsp chopped fresh coriander
    (cilantro)

1 Place the noodles in a large pan of boiling water and leave to stand for about 5 minutes.

2 Meanwhile, heat 45ml/3 tbsp of the oil in a wok or large frying pan, add the garlic and cook for 30 seconds.

3 Add the pork and chicken to the pan and stir-fry on a high heat until lightly browned, then add the prawns and stir-fry for 2 minutes.

4 Add the lime or lemon juice, fish sauce and sugar and stir-fry until the sugar has dissolved.

5 Drain the noodles and add to the pan with the remaining oil. Mix well. Pour on the beaten eggs. Stir-fry until almost set, then add the chilli and beansprouts. Add half the peanuts, spring onions and coriander to the pan. Stir-fry for 2 minutes, then tip on to a serving platter. Sprinkle on the remaining ingredients, and serve at once.

# Sour Chicken Stir-fry

*There are few cookery concepts that are better suited to today's busy lifestyle than the all-in-one stir-fry. This recipe has a South-east Asian influence.*

*Serves 4*

275g/10oz Chinese egg noodles

30ml/2 tbsp vegetable oil

3 spring onions (scallions), chopped

1 garlic clove, crushed

2.5cm/1in piece fresh root ginger, peeled and grated

5ml/1 tsp hot paprika

5ml/1 tsp ground coriander

3 chicken breast fillets, skinned and sliced

115g/4oz sugar-snap peas

115g/4oz baby corn on the cob, halved

225g/8oz/1 cup fresh beansprouts

15ml/1 tbsp cornflour (cornstarch)

45ml/3 tbsp soy sauce

45ml/3 tbsp lemon juice

15ml/1 tbsp sugar

45ml/3 tbsp chopped fresh coriander (cilantro) or spring onion (scallion) tops, to garnish

1 Bring a large pan of salted water to the boil. Add the noodles and cook according to the instructions on the packet. Drain, cover and keep warm.

2 Heat the oil. Add the spring onions and cook over a gentle heat. Mix in the next five ingredients, then stir-fry for 3–4 minutes. Add the next three ingredients and steam briefly. Add the noodles.

3 Combine the cornflour, soy sauce, lemon juice and sugar in a small bowl. Add to the wok and simmer briefly to thicken. Serve garnished with chopped coriander or spring onion tops.

# CURRIES

Chicken is a popular choice to use in curried dishes and it's amazing how many different combinations of flavours there are. As well as recipes from India, there are dishes from all over Asia including Malaysia, Vietnam and Thailand. Mildly spicy curries sit alongside others that are extremely hot; and there are also many fragrantly spiced dishes and others that use fruit. There is even a selection of low-fat curries, so that you can enjoy the flavours and still eat healthily. With so many authentic and flavoursome recipes to choose from, this chapter will prove to be a curry-lover's paradise.

# Thai Red Chicken Curry

*Here chicken and potatoes are simmered in coconut milk spiced with red curry paste and Thai fish sauce, then garnished with shredded kaffir lime leaves and red chillies.*

### INGREDIENTS

*Serves 4*

1 onion
15ml/1 tbsp groundnut (peanut) oil
400ml/14fl oz/1²/₃ cups coconut milk
30ml/2 tbsp Thai red curry paste
30ml/2 tbsp Thai fish sauce
15ml/1 tbsp soft light brown sugar
225g/8oz tiny new potatoes
450g/1lb chicken breast fillets, skinned and
    cut into chunks
15ml/1 tbsp lime juice
30ml/2 tbsp chopped fresh mint
15ml/1 tbsp chopped fresh basil
2 kaffir lime leaves, shredded
1–2 fresh red chillies, seeded and
    finely shredded
salt and ground black pepper

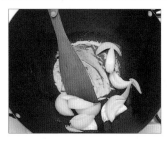

1 Cut the onion into wedges. Heat a wok until hot, then add the oil and swirl it around. Add the onion and stir-fry for 3–4 minutes.

2 Pour in the coconut milk, then bring to the boil, stirring. Stir in the curry paste, fish sauce and sugar.

3 Add the potatoes and seasoning and simmer gently, covered, for about 20 minutes.

4 Add the chicken chunks, and cook, covered, over a low heat for a further 5–10 minutes, or until the chicken is cooked and potatoes are tender.

5 Stir in the lime juice, chopped mint and basil. Serve immediately, sprinkled with the shredded kaffir lime leaves and red chillies.

### VARIATION

You can use boneless chicken thighs instead of breast fillets. Simply skin them, cut the flesh into chunks and cook in the coconut milk with the potatoes.

# Fragrant Chicken Curry

*In this dish, the mildly spiced sauce is thickened using lentils rather than the traditional onions fried in ghee.*

### INGREDIENTS

*Serves 4*

75g/3oz/scant ¹/₂ cup red lentils

30ml/2 tbsp mild curry powder

10ml/2 tsp ground coriander

5ml/1 tsp cumin seeds

475ml/16fl oz/2 cups vegetable stock

8 chicken thighs, skinned

225g/8oz fresh or frozen shredded spinach, thawed and well drained

15ml/1 tbsp chopped fresh coriander (cilantro)

salt and ground black pepper

fresh coriander (cilantro) sprigs, to garnish

white or brown basmati rice and grilled (broiled) poppadums, to serve

1 Rinse the lentils under cold running water. Put into a large pan with the curry powder, ground coriander, cumin seeds and stock.

2 Bring to the boil then lower the heat. Cover and simmer gently for 10 minutes.

3 Add the chicken and spinach. Cover and simmer gently for a further 40 minutes, or until the chicken is cooked.

4 Stir in the chopped coriander and season to taste. Serve garnished with fresh coriander and accompanied by the rice and grilled poppadums.

# Coconut Rice with Green Chicken Curry

*Use one or two fresh green chillies in this dish, according to how hot you like your curry. The mild aromatic flavour of the rice offsets the spiciness of the curry.*

### INGREDIENTS

*Serves 3–4*

4 spring onions (scallions), trimmed and
  roughly chopped
1–2 fresh green chillies, seeded and
  roughly chopped
2cm/³/4 in piece of fresh root
  ginger, peeled
2 garlic cloves
5ml/1 tsp Thai fish sauce
large bunch of fresh coriander (cilantro)
small handful of fresh parsley
30–45ml/2–3 tbsp water
30ml/2 tbsp sunflower oil
4 chicken breast fillets, skinned and cubed
1 green (bell) pepper, seeded and
  finely sliced
75g/3oz piece of creamed coconut
  dissolved in 400ml/14fl oz/1²/3 cups
  boiling water or 400ml/14fl oz can
  coconut milk
salt and ground black pepper

*For the rice*

225g/8oz/generous 1 cup Thai fragrant
  rice, rinsed
75g/3oz piece of creamed coconut
  dissolved in 400ml/14fl oz/1²/3 cups
  boiling water or 400ml/14fl oz can
  coconut milk
1 lemon grass stalk, quartered and bruised

### COOK'S TIP

Lemon grass makes the perfect partner for coconut, especially when used with chicken. In this recipe, bruise the tough, top end of the lemon grass stem in a mortar and pestle before use.

1 Put the spring onions, chillies, ginger, garlic, Thai fish sauce and fresh herbs in a food processor or blender. Pour in the water and process to a smooth paste.

2 Heat half the oil in large frying pan. Fry the chicken cubes until evenly browned. Transfer to a plate.

3 Heat the remaining oil in the pan. Stir-fry the green pepper for 3–4 minutes, then add the chilli and ginger paste. Fry, stirring, for 3–4 minutes, or until the mixture becomes fairly thick.

4 Return the chicken to the pan and add the coconut liquid. Season and bring to the boil, then lower the heat; half cover the pan and simmer for 8–10 minutes.

5 When the chicken is cooked, transfer it with the peppers to a plate. Boil the cooking liquid left in the pan for 10–12 minutes, or until it is well reduced and fairly thick.

6 Meanwhile, put the rice in a large pan. Add the coconut liquid and the bruised pieces of lemon grass. Stir in a little salt, bring to the boil, then lower the heat, cover and simmer very gently for 10 minutes, or for the time recommended on the packet. When the rice is tender, discard the pieces of lemon grass and fork the rice on to a warmed serving plate.

7 Return the chicken and peppers to the sauce, stir well and cook gently for a few minutes to heat through. Spoon the curry over the rice, and serve immediately.

# *Fragrant Thai Chicken Curry*

This flavourful and fragrant, creamy curry is quite simple to make even though it includes a variety of interesting ingredients.

### INGREDIENTS

Serves 6

400ml/14fl oz can coconut milk
6 chicken breast fillets, skinned and
    finely sliced
225g/8oz can bamboo shoots, drained
    and sliced
30ml/2 tbsp Thai fish sauce
15ml/1 tbsp soft light brown sugar
175g/6oz/scant 1 cup Thai jasmine rice
pinch of saffron threads

For the green curry paste
4 green chillies, seeded
1 lemon grass stalk, sliced
1 small onion, sliced
3 garlic cloves
1cm/$^1$/$_2$ in piece galangal or fresh root
    ginger, peeled
grated rind of $^1$/$_2$ lime
5ml/1 tsp coriander seeds
5ml/1 tsp cumin seeds
2.5ml/$^1$/$_2$ tsp shrimp or Thai fish sauce

For the garnish
1 red chilli, seeded and cut into fine strips
finely pared rind of $^1$/$_2$ lime, finely
    shredded
fresh Thai purple basil or coriander
    (cilantro), coarsely chopped

1 To make the green curry paste, put the chillies, lemon grass, onion, garlic, galangal or ginger, lime rind, coriander seeds, cumin seeds and shrimp or Thai fish sauce in a food processor or blender and process until they are reduced to a thick paste. Set aside.

2 Bring half the coconut milk to the boil in a large pan, reduce the heat and simmer for about 5 minutes, or until reduced by half. Stir in the green curry paste and simmer for a further 5 minutes.

3 Add the finely sliced chicken to the pan with the remaining coconut milk, bamboo shoots, fish sauce and sugar. Stir well to combine all the ingredients and bring the curry back to simmering point, then simmer gently for about 10 minutes, or until the chicken slices are cooked through. The mixture will look grainy or curdled during cooking, but this is quite normal.

4 Meanwhile, add the rice and saffron to a pan of salted boiling water. Reduce the heat and simmer for 10 minutes, or until tender. Drain the rice and serve it with the curry, garnished with the chilli, lime rind and Thai purple basil or coriander.

# Chicken with Spices and Soy Sauce

*This simple but delicious Chinese-influenced dish comes from Malaysia. The combination of tamarind, nutmeg, cloves and soy sauce is unusual and appetizing.*

## INGREDIENTS

*Serves 4*

1 chicken, about 1.3  1.6kg/3  3$^1$/$_2$ lb, jointed and cut into 16 pieces
3 onions, sliced
about 1 litre/1$^3$/$_4$ pints/4 cups water
3 garlic cloves, crushed
3–4 fresh red chillies, seeded and sliced, or 15ml/1 tbsp chilli powder
45ml/3 tbsp vegetable oil
2.5ml/$^1$/$_2$ tsp grated nutmeg
6 whole cloves
5ml/1 tsp tamarind pulp, soaked in 45ml/3 tbsp warm water
30–45ml/2–3 tbsp dark or light soy sauce
salt
fresh green and red chilli shreds, to garnish
plain boiled rice, to serve

1 Place the chicken pieces in a pan with one of the sliced onions. Pour over water to just cover. Bring to the boil, then reduce the heat and allow to simmer gently for about 20 minutes.

2 Grind the remaining onions with the garlic and chillies, or chilli powder, to a fine paste in a food processor or using a mortar and pestle. Heat a little of the oil in a wok or frying pan and cook the paste to bring out the flavour. Do not allow the paste to brown.

3 When the chicken has cooked for 20 minutes, lift it out of the stock and into the spicy mixture. Toss everything together over a fairly high heat so that the spices permeate the chicken. Reserve 300ml/$^1$/$_2$ pint/1$^1$/$_4$ cups of the stock to add to the pan later.

4 Stir in the nutmeg and cloves. Strain the tamarind and add the tamarind juice and the soy sauce to the chicken. Cook for a further 2–3 minutes, then add the reserved stock.

5 Taste and adjust the seasoning. Cook, uncovered, for a further 25–35 minutes, or until the chicken pieces are tender and cooked through.

6 Transfer the chicken to a bowl, topped with shredded green and red chillies, and serve with plain boiled rice.

# Red Chicken Curry with Bamboo Shoots

*Bamboo shoots have a lovely crunchy texture. It is quite acceptable to use canned whole bamboo shoots, which are crisper and of better quality than sliced shoots. Rinse before using.*

*Serves 4–6*

1 litre/1³/₄ pints/4 cups coconut milk
450g/1lb chicken breast fillets, skinned and
    cut into bitesize pieces
30ml/2 tbsp Thai fish sauce
15ml/1 tbsp sugar
225g/8oz drained canned bamboo shoots,
    rinsed and sliced
5 kaffir lime leaves, torn
salt and ground black pepper
chopped fresh red chillies and kaffir lime
    leaves, to garnish

*For the red curry paste*
5ml/1 tsp coriander seeds
2.5ml/¹/₂ tsp cumin seeds
12–15 fresh red chillies, seeded and
    roughly chopped
4 shallots, thinly sliced
2 garlic cloves, chopped
15ml/1 tbsp chopped galangal
2 lemon grass stalks, chopped
3 kaffir lime leaves, chopped
4 fresh coriander (cilantro) roots
10 black peppercorns
good pinch of ground cinnamon
5ml/1 tsp ground turmeric
2.5ml/¹/₂ tsp shrimp paste
5ml/1 tsp salt
30ml/2 tbsp vegetable oil

## VARIATION

You can use straw mushrooms instead of, or as well as, the bamboo shoots. These are available in cans from Asian stores and supermarkets. Drain well and then stir into the curry at the end of the recipe.

1 Make the curry paste. Dry-fry the coriander and cumin seeds for 1–2 minutes, then put in a mortar or food processor with the remaining ingredients except the oil and grind or process to a paste.

2 Add the oil, a little at a time, mixing or processing well after each addition. Transfer to a jar and chill until ready to use.

3 Pour half of the coconut milk into a large, heavy pan. Bring the milk to the boil, stirring constantly until it has separated.

4 Stir in 30ml/2 tbsp of the red curry paste and cook the mixture for 2–3 minutes, stirring constantly. The remaining red curry paste can be kept in the refrigerator for up to 3 months.

5 Add the chicken pieces, Thai fish sauce and sugar to the pan. Stir well, then cook for 5–6 minutes, or until the chicken changes colour and is cooked through, stirring constantly to prevent the mixture from sticking to the base of the pan.

6 Pour the remaining coconut milk into the pan, then add the sliced bamboo shoots and torn kaffir lime leaves. Bring back to the boil over a medium heat, stirring constantly to prevent the mixture sticking, then taste and add salt and pepper if necessary.

7 To serve, spoon the curry into a warmed serving dish and garnish with chopped chillies and kaffir lime leaves.

# Chicken with Thai Spices

*This is the perfect dish for a party, as the chicken and sauce can be prepared in advance and combined at the last minute.*

### INGREDIENTS

*Serves 4*

45ml/3 tbsp oil
1 onion, roughly chopped
2 garlic cloves, crushed
15ml/1 tbsp Thai red curry paste
115g/4oz creamed coconut dissolved in
    900ml/1¹/₂ pints/3³/₄ cups boiling water
2 lemon grass stalks, roughly chopped
6 kaffir lime leaves, chopped
150ml/¹/₄ pint/²/₃ cup Greek (US strained
    plain) yogurt
2 tbsp apricot jam
1 chicken, about 1.6kg/3¹/₂ lb, cooked,
    boned and skinned
30ml/2 tbsp chopped fresh
    coriander (cilantro)
salt and ground black pepper
kaffir limes leaves, shredded coconut and
    fresh coriander (cilantro), to garnish
boiled rice, to serve

1 Heat the oil in a pan. Add the onion and garlic, and fry over a low heat for 5–10 minutes, or until soft. Stir in the curry paste. Cook, stirring, for 2–3 minutes. Stir in the diluted creamed coconut, then add the lemon grass, lime leaves, yogurt and apricot jam. Stir well. Cover and simmer for 30 minutes.

2 Process the sauce in a blender or food processor, then strain it back into a clean pan, pressing as much of the puréed mixture as possible through the sieve.

3 Cut the chicken into bitesize pieces. Add to the sauce.

4 Bring the sauce back to simmering point. Stir in the fresh coriander and seasoning. Serve with rice, garnished with extra kaffir lime leaves, shredded coconut and coriander.

# Chicken with Ginger and Lemon Grass

*This Vietnamese recipe contains the unusual combination of ginger and lemon grass with mandarin orange and chillies.*

INGREDIENTS

*Serves 4–6*

3 chicken legs (thighs and drumsticks)
15ml/1 tbsp vegetable oil
2cm/$^3$/4 in piece fresh root ginger, finely chopped
1 garlic clove, crushed
1 small fresh red chilli, seeded and finely chopped
5cm/2in piece lemon grass, shredded
150ml/$^1$/4 pint/$^2$/3 cup chicken stock
15ml/1 tbsp Thai fish sauce
10ml/2 tsp sugar
2.5ml/$^1$/2 tsp salt
juice of $^1$/2 lemon
50g/2oz/$^1$/2 cup raw peanuts
2 spring onions (scallions), shredded
rind of 1 mandarin or satsuma, shredded
plain boiled rice or rice noodles, to serve

1 With the heel of a knife, chop through the narrow end of each of the chicken drumsticks. Remove the jointed parts of the chicken, then remove the skin. Rinse and pat dry with kitchen paper.

2 Heat the oil in a wok. Add the chicken, ginger, garlic, chilli and lemon grass and cook for 3–4 minutes. Add the stock, Thai fish sauce, sugar, salt and lemon juice. Cover the pan and simmer for 30–35 minutes.

3 To prepare the peanuts, the red skin must be removed. To do this grill (broil) or roast the peanuts under a medium heat until evenly brown, for 2–3 minutes. Turn the nuts out on to a clean cloth and rub briskly to loosen the skins.

4 Transfer the chicken from the pan to a warmed serving dish, and sprinkle with the roasted peanuts, shredded spring onions and the rind of the mandarin or satsuma. Serve hot with plain boiled rice or rice noodles.

# Chicken with Green Mango

*Green, unripe mango is used for cooking various dishes on the Indian subcontinent, including pickles, chutneys and some meat, chicken and vegetable dishes. This is a fairly simple chicken dish to prepare and is served with rice and dhal.*

### INGREDIENTS

*Serves 4*

1 green mango
450g/1lb/3$^1$/4 cups cubed chicken
1.5ml/$^1$/4 tsp onion seeds
5ml/1 tsp grated fresh root ginger
2.5ml/$^1$/2 tsp crushed garlic
5ml/1 tsp chilli powder
1.5ml/$^1$/4 tsp ground turmeric
5ml/1 tsp salt
5ml/1 tsp ground coriander
30ml/2 tbsp corn oil
2 onions, sliced
4 curry leaves
300ml/$^1$/2 pint/1$^1$/4 cups water
2 tomatoes, quartered
2 green chillies, chopped
30ml/2 tbsp chopped fresh
　coriander (cilantro)

1 To prepare the mango, peel, stone (pit) and slice the flesh thickly. Place the mango slices in a small bowl, cover and set aside.

2 Place the chicken cubes in a bowl and add the onion seeds, ginger, garlic, chilli powder, turmeric, salt and ground coriander. Mix the spices into the chicken and then add half the mango slices.

3 In a medium pan, heat the oil and fry the sliced onions until they turn golden brown. Add the curry leaves.

4 Gradually add the spiced chicken pieces and mango slices, stirring all the time.

5 Pour in the water, lower the heat and cook for about 12–15 minutes, stirring occasionally, until the chicken is cooked through and the water has been absorbed.

6 Add the remaining mango slices, the tomatoes, green chillies and fresh coriander. Serve hot.

# Mughlai-style Chicken

*This Mogul recipe, which comes from Andhra Pradesh, has a heady aroma of saffron and the captivating flavour of a silky almond and cream sauce.*

INGREDIENTS

*Serves 4–6*

4 chicken breast fillets, rubbed with a little
   garam masala
2 eggs, beaten with salt and pepper
90ml/6 tbsp ghee or vegetable oil
1 large onion, finely chopped
5cm/2in piece fresh root ginger,
   finely crushed
4 garlic cloves, finely crushed
4 cloves
4 green cardamom pods
5cm/2in piece cinnamon stick
2 bay leaves
15–20 saffron threads
150ml/$^1$/$_4$ pint/$^2$/$_3$ cup natural (plain)
   yogurt, beaten with 5ml/1 tsp
   cornflour (cornstarch)
75ml/2$^1$/$_2$ fl oz/$^1$/$_3$ cup double
   (heavy) cream
50g/2oz/$^1$/$_2$ cup ground almonds
salt

1 Brush the chicken fillets with the beaten eggs. In a wok or large pan, heat the ghee or vegetable oil and fry the chicken until cooked through and browned on both sides. Remove the chicken from the pan and keep warm.

2 In the same pan, fry the chopped onion, ginger, garlic, cloves, cardamom pods, cinnamon and bay leaves. When the onion turns golden, remove the pan from the heat, allow the contents to cool a little and add the saffron and yogurt mixture. Mix well to prevent the yogurt from curdling.

3 Return the chicken to the pan, along with any juices, and gently cook until the chicken is tender. Adjust the seasoning.

4 Just before serving, fold in the double cream and ground almonds. Make sure the curry is piping hot before serving.

# Goan Chicken Curry

*Coconuts grow in abundance in Goa, and so it is hardly surprising that coconut, in all of its forms, is widely used to enrich Goan cuisine.*

### INGREDIENTS

*Serves 4*

75g/3oz/1¹/₂ cups desiccated (dry unsweetened shredded) coconut

30ml/2 tbsp vegetable oil

2.5ml/¹/₂ tsp cumin seeds

4 black peppercorns

15ml/1 tbsp fennel seeds

15ml/1 tbsp coriander seeds

2 onions, finely chopped

2.5ml/¹/₂ tsp salt

8 small chicken pieces, such as thighs and drumsticks, skinned

fresh coriander (cilantro) sprigs and lemon wedges, to garnish

chutney and plain boiled rice, to serve

1 Put the desiccated coconut in a bowl with 45ml/3 tbsp water. Leave to soak for 15 minutes.

2 Heat 15ml/1 tbsp of the oil in a wok or large pan and fry the cumin seeds, peppercorns, fennel and coriander seeds over a low heat for 3–4 minutes, or until they begin to splutter.

3 Add the onions and fry for about 5 minutes, stirring occasionally, until the onion has softened and turned opaque.

4 Stir in the coconut, along with the soaking water and salt, and continue to fry for a further 5 minutes, stirring occasionally to prevent the mixture from sticking to the pan.

5 Put the coconut mixture into a food processor or blender and process to form a coarse paste. Spoon into a bowl and set aside until required.

6 Heat the remaining oil and fry the chicken for 10 minutes. Add the coconut paste and cook over a low heat for 15–20 minutes, or until golden brown and the chicken is cooked through.

7 Transfer to a warmed serving plate, and garnish with fresh coriander and lemon wedges. Serve with chutney and plain boiled rice.

### COOK'S TIP

If you prefer, make the spiced coconut mixture the day before and chill it in the refrigerator, then continue from step 6 when required.

# Balti Chicken Tikka Masala

*This recipe is based on makkhani murghi, a popular Balti dish. Serve with warm naan bread or fluffy basmati rice.*

## INGREDIENTS

*Serves 4*

4 part-boned chicken breast portions, skinned

150ml/$^1$/4 pint/$^2$/3 cup natural (plain) yogurt

2.5 cm/1 in piece fresh root ginger, grated

2 garlic cloves, crushed

5ml/1 tsp chilli powder

15ml/1 tbsp ground coriander

30ml/2 tbsp vegetable oil

30ml/2 tbsp lime juice

few drops each of yellow and red liquid food colouring, mixed to a bright orange shade

*For the masala*

450g/1lb tomatoes

75g/3oz/6 tbsp unsalted (sweet) butter

15ml/1 tbsp vegetable oil

1 onion, chopped

5ml/1 tsp salt

1 fresh green chilli, seeded and finely chopped

5ml/1 tsp garam masala

1.5ml/$^1$/4 tsp cayenne pepper

120ml/4fl oz/$^1$/2 cup double (heavy) cream

45ml/3 tbsp natural (plain) yogurt

30ml/2 tbsp roughly torn fresh coriander (cilantro) leaves

5ml/1 tsp dry-roasted cumin seeds

1 Cut each chicken portion into three or four pieces, then slash the meaty side of each piece. Put the chicken into a shallow dish. In a bowl, mix together the yogurt, ginger, garlic, chilli powder, ground coriander, oil, lime juice and colouring. Pour over the chicken and toss to coat completely, making sure that the marinade goes into the slits in the chicken. Cover and leave in the refrigerator for 6–24 hours, turning occasionally.

2 Preheat the oven to 230°C/450°F/Gas 8. Lift the chicken pieces out of the marinade, shaking off any excess, and arrange in a shallow baking tin (pan). Bake for 15–20 minutes, or until golden brown and cooked through.

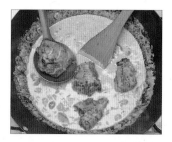

3 Meanwhile, make the masala: plunge the tomatoes into boiling water for 30 seconds, then refresh in cold water. Peel away the skins, remove the seeds and chop the flesh. Heat the butter and oil in a wok or large pan, add the onion and fry for 5 minutes, or until softened. Add the tomatoes, salt, chilli, garam masala and cayenne pepper. Cook, covered, for about 10 minutes.

4 Stir in the cream and yogurt, then simmer over a low heat for 1–2 minutes, stirring constantly. Add the chicken pieces, then stir to coat in the sauce. Serve immediately sprinkled with coriander leaves and roasted cumin seeds.

## COOK'S TIP

If you can, leave the chicken to marinate for as long as possible to allow plenty of time for it to absorb the flavourings.

# Chicken Korma

*Although kormas are traditionally rich and high in fat, this recipe uses low-fat yogurt instead of cream, which gives the sauce a delicious flavour while keeping down the fat content. To prevent the yogurt from curdling, add it very slowly to the sauce and keep stirring until it is incorporated.*

INGREDIENTS

Serves 4

675g/1¹/₂ lb chicken breast fillet, skinned

2 garlic cloves, crushed

2.5cm/1in piece fresh root ginger, roughly chopped

15ml/1 tbsp oil

3 green cardamom pods

1 onion, finely chopped

10ml/2 tsp ground cumin

1.5ml/¹/₄ tsp salt

300ml/¹/₂ pint/1¹/₄ cups natural (plain) low-fat yogurt

toasted flaked (sliced) almonds (optional) and a fresh coriander (cilantro) sprig, to garnish

plain rice, to serve

1 Remove any visible fat from the chicken fillets and cut the meat into 2.5cm/1in cubes.

2 Put the garlic and ginger into a food processor or blender with 30ml/2 tbsp water and process to a smooth, creamy paste.

3 Heat the oil in a large, heavy pan and cook the chicken cubes for 8–10 minutes, or until browned on all sides. Remove the chicken cubes with a slotted spoon and set aside.

4 Add the cardamom pods and fry for 2 minutes. Add the onion and fry for a further 5 minutes.

5 Stir in the garlic and ginger paste, cumin and salt, and cook, stirring, for a further 5 minutes.

6 Add half the yogurt, stirring in a tablespoon at a time, and cook over a low heat, until it has all been absorbed. Return the chicken to the pan.

7 Cover and simmer over a low heat for 5–6 minutes, or until the chicken is tender. Add the remaining yogurt and simmer for a further 5 minutes. Garnish with toasted flaked almonds, if using, and coriander. Serve with rice.

COOK'S TIP

Traditionally, kormas are spicy dishes with a rich, creamy texture. They are not meant to be very hot curries.

# Kashmiri Chicken Curry

*Sliced apples give this low-fat yet flavoursome dish a subtle and fruity taste.*

INGREDIENTS

Serves 4

10ml/2 tsp oil

2 medium onions, diced

1 bay leaf

2 cloves

2.5cm/1in cinnamon stick

4 black peppercorns

1 baby chicken, about 675g/1$^1$/2 lb, skinned and cut into 8 pieces

5ml/1 tsp garam masala

5ml/1 tsp grated fresh root ginger

5ml/1 tsp crushed garlic

5ml/1 tsp salt

5ml/1 tsp chilli powder

15ml/1 tbsp ground almonds

150ml/$^1$/4 pint/$^2$/3 cup natural (plain) low-fat yogurt

2 green eating apples, peeled, cored and roughly sliced

15ml/1 tbsp chopped fresh coriander (cilantro)

15g/$^1$/2 oz/$^1$/2 cup flaked (sliced) almonds, lightly toasted, and fresh coriander leaves, to garnish

1 Heat the oil in a wok or heavy frying pan and fry the onions with the bay leaf, cloves, cinnamon and peppercorns for about 3–5 minutes, or until the onions are beginning to soften but are not starting to brown.

2 Add the chicken pieces to the onions and continue to stir-fry for at least another 3 minutes.

3 Lower the heat and add the garam masala, ginger, garlic, salt, chilli powder and ground almonds and continue to stir for 2–3 minutes.

4 Pour in the yogurt and stir for 2 minutes more.

5 Add the apples and chopped coriander, cover and cook for about 10–15 minutes.

6 Check that the chicken is cooked through and serve immediately, garnished with the flaked almonds and whole coriander leaves.

# Mild Green Calcutta Curry

*Coconut milk creates a rich sauce that is sweet with dried and fresh fruit and fragrant with herbs.*

INGREDIENTS

Serves 4

4 garlic cloves, chopped

15ml/1 tbsp chopped fresh root ginger

2–3 chillies, chopped

$^1/_2$ bunch fresh coriander (cilantro) leaves, roughly chopped

1 onion, chopped

juice of 1 lemon

pinch of cayenne pepper

2.5ml/$^1/_2$ tsp curry powder

2.5ml/$^1/_2$ tsp ground cumin

2–3 pinches of ground cloves

large pinch of ground coriander

3 chicken breast fillets or thighs, skinned and cut into bitesize pieces

30ml/2 tbsp vegetable oil

2 cinnamon sticks

250ml/8fl oz/1 cup chicken stock

250ml/8fl oz/1 cup coconut milk

15–30ml/1–2 tbsp sugar

1–2 bananas

$^1/_4$ pineapple, peeled and chopped

handful of sultanas (golden raisins)

handful of raisins or currants

2–3 sprigs of fresh mint, thinly sliced

juice of $^1/_4$–$^1/_2$ lemon

salt

1 Purée the garlic, ginger, chillies, fresh coriander, onion, lemon juice, cayenne pepper, curry powder, cumin, cloves, ground coriander and salt in a food processor or blender.

2 Toss together the chicken pieces with about 15–30ml/1–2 tbsp of the spice mixture, and set aside.

3 Heat the oil in a wok or frying pan, then add the remaining spice mixture and cook over a medium heat, stirring, for 10 minutes, or until the paste is lightly browned.

4 Stir the cinnamon sticks, stock, coconut milk and sugar into the pan, bring to the boil, then reduce the heat and simmer for 10 minutes.

5 Stir the chicken into the sauce and cook for 2 minutes, or until the chicken becomes opaque.

6 Meanwhile, thickly slice the bananas. Stir all the fruit into the curry and cook for 1–2 minutes. Stir in the mint and lemon juice. Check the seasoning and add more salt, spice and lemon juice if necessary. Serve immediately with hot naan bread or steamed rice.

# Chicken Saag

*Here is a mildly spiced low-fat dish
using the popular combination of
spinach and chicken. This recipe is
best made using fresh spinach, but
if this is unavailable you can use
frozen instead.*

### INGREDIENTS

*Serves 4*

225g/8oz fresh spinach leaves, washed but
   not dried

2.5cm/1in piece root ginger, grated

2 garlic cloves, crushed

1 green chilli, roughly chopped

200ml/7fl oz/scant 1 cup water

4 tomatoes

2 bay leaves 15ml/1 tbsp oil

1.5ml/$^1$/$_4$ tsp black peppercorns

1 onion, finely chopped

10ml/2 tsp curry powder

5ml/1 tsp salt

5ml/1 tsp chilli powder

45ml/3 tbsp natural (plain) low-fat yogurt

8 chicken thighs, skinned

natural (plain) low-fat yogurt and chilli
   powder, to garnish

naan bread, to serve

1 Cook the spinach leaves,
without water, in a tightly
covered pan for 5 minutes. Put the
cooked spinach, ginger, garlic and
chilli with 50ml/2fl oz/$^1$/$_4$ cup of
the water into a food processor or
blender and process to a thick purée.
Set aside. Plunge the tomatoes into
boiling water for 30 seconds, then
refresh in cold water. Peel away the
skins and chop finely.

2 Heat the oil in a large, heavy
pan, add the bay leaves and
black peppercorns and fry for
2 minutes. Add the onion and fry
for a further 6–8 minutes, or until
the onion has browned.

3 Add the tomatoes and simmer
for about 5 minutes. Stir in the
curry powder, salt and chilli
powder and cook for 2 minutes.

4 Add the spinach purée and
150ml/$^1$/$_4$ pint/$^2$/$_3$ cup water;
simmer for 5 minutes.

5 Add the yogurt, 15ml/1 tbsp
at a time, and simmer for
5 minutes.

6 Add the chicken thighs. Cover
and cook for 25–30 minutes,
or until the chicken is cooked.
Serve on naan bread, drizzle
over some yogurt and dust with
chilli powder.

# Chicken Dhansak

*Dhansak curries originate from the Parsee community and are traditionally made with a mixture of lentils and meat.*

## INGREDIENTS

*Serves 4*

75g/3oz/scant 1/2 cup green lentils
475ml/16fl oz/2 cups chicken stock
15ml/1 tbsp oil
5ml/1 tsp cumin seeds
2 curry leaves
1 onion, finely chopped
2.5cm/1in piece fresh root ginger, chopped
1 green chilli, finely chopped
5ml/1 tsp ground cumin
5ml/1 tsp ground coriander
1.5ml/1/4 tsp salt
1.5ml/1/4 tsp chilli powder
400g/14oz can chopped tomatoes
8 chicken pieces, skinned
60ml/4 tbsp chopped fresh coriander
   (cilantro)
5ml/1 tsp garam masala
fresh coriander, to garnish
plain and yellow rice, to serve

2 Heat the oil in a large pan and fry the cumin seeds and curry leaves for 2 minutes. Add the onion, ginger and chilli and fry for about 5 minutes. Stir in the cumin, coriander, salt and chilli powder with 30ml/2 tbsp water. Add the tomatoes and the chicken. Cover and cook for 10–15 minutes.

3 Add the lentils and stock, chopped fresh coriander and garam masala and cook for a further 10 minutes, or until the chicken is cooked through. Garnish with fresh coriander and serve with spiced plain and yellow rice.

1 Rinse the lentils under cold running water. Put into a pan with the stock. Bring to the boil, cover and simmer for about 15–20 minutes. Put the lentils and stock to one side.

# Chicken Bobotie

*Perfect for a buffet party, this mild curry dish is set with savoury custard, which makes serving easy. Serve with boiled rice and chutney.*

Serves 8

2 thick slices white bread

450ml/³/₄ pint/scant 2 cups milk

30ml/2 tbsp olive oil

2 medium onions, finely chopped

45ml/3 tbsp medium curry powder

1.2kg/2¹/₂ lb/10 cups minced
  (ground) chicken

15ml/1 tbsp apricot jam, chutney or
  caster (superfine) sugar

30ml/2 tbsp wine vinegar or lemon juice

3 eggs, beaten

50g/2oz/¹/₃ cup raisins or sultanas
  (golden raisins)

butter, for greasing

12 whole almonds

salt and ground black pepper

1 Preheat the oven to 180°C/
350°F/Gas 4. Soak the bread in
150ml/¹/₄ pint/²/₃ cup of the milk.
Heat the oil in a frying pan and
gently fry the onions until tender,
then add the curry powder and
cook for a further 2 minutes.

2 Add the minced chicken, and
brown all over, separating the
grains of meat as they brown.
Remove from the heat, season with
salt and black pepper, add the
apricot jam, chutney or caster sugar
and the wine vinegar or lemon juice.

3 Mash the bread in the milk and
add to the pan with one of the
beaten eggs and the raisins.

4 Grease a 1.5 litre/2¹/₂ pint/
6¹/₄ cup shallow, ovenproof
dish with butter. Spoon in the
chicken mixture and level the top.
Cover with buttered foil and bake
in the oven for 30 minutes.

5 Meanwhile, beat the remaining
eggs and milk. Remove the dish
from the oven and lower the
temperature to 150°C/300°F/Gas 2.
Break up the meat using a fork
and pour over the egg.

6 Sprinkle the almonds over
and bake, uncovered, for
30 minutes, or until set and brown.

# Hot Chicken Curry

*This curry has a delicious thick sauce with extra colour provided by chunks of red and green pepper.*

Serves 4

30ml/2 tbsp corn oil

1.5ml/$^1$/4 tsp fenugreek seeds

1.5ml/$^1$/4 tsp onion seeds

2 onions, chopped

2.5ml/$^1$/2 tsp chopped garlic

2.5ml/$^1$/2 tsp chopped fresh root ginger

5ml/1 tsp ground coriander

5ml/1 tsp chilli powder

5ml/1 tsp salt

400g/14oz can tomatoes

30ml/2 tbsp lemon juice

350g/12oz/2$^1$/2 cups cubed chicken

30ml/2 tbsp chopped fresh
    coriander (cilantro)

3 green chillies, chopped

$^1$/2 red (bell) pepper, cut into chunks

$^1$/2 green (bell) pepper, cut into chunks

fresh coriander (cilantro) sprigs,
    to garnish

1 In a medium-size pan, heat the oil and fry the fenugreek and onion seeds until they turn a shade darker. Add the chopped onions, garlic and ginger, and fry for about 5 minutes, or until the onions turn golden brown. Reduce the heat to very low.

2 Meanwhile, in a separate bowl, mix together the ground coriander, chilli powder, salt, tomatoes and lemon juice.

3 Pour this mixture into the pan with the onions and increase the heat to medium. Stir-fry for about 3 minutes.

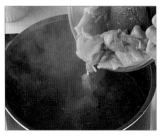

4 Add the cubed chicken and stir-fry for 5–7 minutes.

5 Add the coriander, chillies and peppers. Lower the heat, cover and simmer for 10 minutes, or until the chicken is cooked.

6 Serve hot, garnished with fresh coriander sprigs.

COOK'S TIP

For a milder version of this delicious curry, simply omit some or all of the green chillies.

# Balti Chicken Curry

*In this low-fat curry, tender pieces of
chicken are lightly cooked with fresh
vegetables and aromatic spices in the
traditional Balti style.*

## INGREDIENTS

*Serves 4*

675g/1¹/₂ lb chicken breast fillet, skinned

15ml/1 tbsp oil

2.5ml/¹/₂ tsp cumin seeds

2.5ml/¹/₂ tsp fennel seeds

1 onion, thickly sliced

2 garlic cloves, crushed

2.5cm/1in piece fresh root ginger,
  finely chopped

15ml/1 tbsp curry paste

225g/8oz broccoli, broken into florets

4 tomatoes, cut into thick wedges

5ml/1 tsp garam masala

30ml/2 tbsp chopped fresh
  coriander (cilantro)

naan bread, to serve

1 Remove any visible fat from the
chicken and cut the meat into
2.5cm/1in cubes.

2 Heat the oil in a wok or heavy
frying pan and fry the cumin
and fennel seeds for 2 minutes, or
until the seeds begin to splutter.
Add the onion, garlic and ginger
and cook for 5–7 minutes. Stir in
the curry paste and cook for a
further 2–3 minutes.

3 Add the broccoli florets and
fry for about 5 minutes. Add
the chicken cubes and fry for
5–8 minutes.

4 Add the tomato wedges to the
wok or pan with the garam
masala and the chopped fresh
coriander. Cook the curry for a
further 5–10 minutes, or until the
chicken cubes are tender. Serve
with naan bread.

# Chicken Jalfrezi

*A Jalfrezi curry is a stir-fried dish cooked with onions, ginger and garlic in a rich pepper sauce.*

Serves 4

675g/1¹/₂ lb chicken breast fillet, skinned
15ml/1 tbsp oil
5ml/1 tsp cumin seeds
1 onion, finely chopped
1 green (bell) pepper, seeded and
  finely chopped
1 red (bell) pepper, seeded and
  finely chopped
1 garlic clove, crushed
2cm/³/₄ in piece fresh root ginger,
  finely chopped
15ml/1 tbsp curry paste
1.5ml/¹/₄ tsp chilli powder
5ml/1 tsp ground coriander
5ml/1 tsp ground cumin
2.5ml/¹/₂ tsp salt
400g/14oz can chopped tomatoes
30ml/2 tbsp chopped fresh
  coriander (cilantro)
fresh coriander (cilantro) sprig, to garnish
plain rice, to serve

1 Remove any visible fat from the chicken and cut the meat into 2.5cm/1in cubes.

2 Heat the oil in a wok or heavy frying pan and fry the cumin seeds for 2 minutes, or until they splutter. Add the onion, peppers, garlic and ginger and fry for 6–8 minutes.

3 Add the curry paste and fry for about 2 minutes. Stir in the chilli powder, coriander, cumin and salt and add 15ml/1 tbsp water; fry for 2 minutes more.

4 Add the chicken cubes and fry for about 5 minutes. Add the chopped tomatoes and chopped fresh coriander. Cover the wok or frying pan with a lid and cook for about 15 minutes, or until the chicken cubes are cooked through. Garnish with a sprig of fresh coriander and serve with rice.

# Quick Chicken Curry

*Curry powder can be bought in three different strengths – mild, medium and hot. Use the type with the strength you prefer for this simple but tasty recipe.*

### INGREDIENTS

*Serves 4*

8 chicken legs (thighs and drumsticks)
30ml/2 tbsp vegetable oil
1 onion, thinly sliced
1 garlic clove, crushed
15ml/1 tbsp curry powder
15ml/1 tbsp plain (all-purpose) flour
450ml/³/4 pint/scant 2 cups chicken stock
1 beefsteak tomato
15ml/1 tbsp mango chutney
15ml/1 tbsp lemon juice
salt and ground black pepper
plain boiled rice and Indian pickles,
    to serve

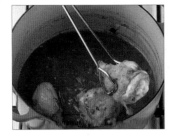

4 Bring to the boil, replace the chicken pieces, cover and simmer for 20–30 minutes, or until tender.

5 Skin the tomato by blanching in boiling water for 45 seconds, then run under cold water to loosen the skin. Peel and cut into small cubes.

6 Add to the chicken, with the mango chutney and lemon juice. Heat through gently and adjust the seasoning to taste. Serve with plenty of boiled rice and Indian pickles.

1 Cut the chicken legs in half. Heat the oil in a large, flameproof casserole and brown the chicken pieces on all sides. Remove and keep warm.

2 Add the onion and crushed garlic to the casserole and cook until soft. Add the curry powder and cook gently for 2 minutes.

3 Add the flour, and gradually blend in the chicken stock and the seasoning.

# Hot Chilli Chicken

*Not for the faint-hearted, this fiery hot, low-fat curry is made with a spicy chilli masala paste.*

Serves 4

30ml/2 tbsp tomato purée (paste)
2 garlic cloves, roughly chopped
2 fresh green chillies, roughly chopped
5 dried red chillies
2.5ml/$\frac{1}{2}$ tsp salt
1.5ml/$\frac{1}{4}$ tsp sugar
5ml/1 tsp chilli powder
2.5ml/$\frac{1}{2}$ tsp paprika
15ml/1 tbsp curry paste
15ml/1 tbsp oil
2.5ml/$\frac{1}{2}$ tsp cumin seeds
1 onion, finely chopped
2 bay leaves
5ml/1 tsp ground coriander
5ml/1 tsp ground cumin
1.5ml/$\frac{1}{4}$ tsp ground turmeric
400g/14oz can chopped tomatoes
150ml/$\frac{1}{4}$ pint/$\frac{2}{3}$ cup water
8 chicken thighs, skinned
5ml/1 tsp garam masala
sliced green chillies, to garnish
chapatis and natural (plain) low-fat
    yogurt, to serve

1 Put the tomato purée, garlic, both types of chilli, salt, sugar, chilli powder, paprika and curry paste into a processor or blender and process to a smooth paste.

2 Fry the cumin seeds in oil for 2 minutes. Add the onion and bay leaves and fry for 5 minutes.

3 Add the chilli paste and fry for 2–3 minutes. Then add the coriander, cumin and turmeric and cook for 2 minutes. Add the tomatoes and water. Bring to the boil and simmer for 5 minutes, or until the sauce thickens.

4 Add the chicken and garam masala. Cover and simmer for 25–30 minutes, or until the chicken is cooked. Garnish with sliced green chillies and serve with chapatis and yogurt.

# Chicken Biryani

*A deceptively easy curry to make, Chicken Biryani is a very popular dish with lots of flavour.*

## INGREDIENTS

Serves 4

275g/10oz/1¹/₂ cups basmati rice, rinsed

2.5ml/¹/₂ tsp salt

6 whole cardamom pods

2–3 whole cloves

1 cinnamon stick

45ml/3 tbsp vegetable oil

3 onions, sliced

675g/1¹/₂ lb chicken breast fillets, skinned and cubed

1.5ml/¹/₄ tsp ground cloves

5 cardamom pods, seeds removed and ground

1.5ml/¹/₄ tsp hot chilli powder

5ml/1 tsp ground cumin

5ml/1 tsp ground coriander

2.5ml/¹/₂ tsp black pepper

3 garlic cloves, finely chopped

5ml/1 tsp finely chopped fresh root ginger

juice of 1 lemon

4 tomatoes, sliced

30ml/2 tbsp chopped fresh coriander (cilantro)

150ml/¹/₄ pint/²/₃ cup natural (plain) yogurt

2.5ml/¹/₂ tsp saffron strands soaked in 10ml/2 tsp hot milk

45ml/3 tbsp toasted flaked (sliced) almonds and fresh coriander sprigs, to garnish

natural (plain) yogurt, to serve

1 Preheat the oven to 190°C/375°F/Gas 5. Bring a pan of water to the boil and add the rice, salt, cardamom pods, cloves and cinnamon stick. Boil for 2 minutes and then drain, leaving the whole spices in the rice.

2 Heat the oil in a pan and fry the onions for 8 minutes, or until browned. Add the cubed chicken followed by all the ground spices, the garlic, ginger and lemon juice. Stir-fry for 5 minutes.

3 Transfer the chicken mixture to a casserole and lay the sliced tomatoes on top. Sprinkle over the fresh coriander, spoon over the natural yogurt and top with the drained rice.

4 Drizzle the saffron and milk over the rice and pour over 150ml/¹/₄ pint/²/₃ cup of water.

5 Cover tightly and bake in the oven for 1 hour. Transfer to a warmed serving platter and remove the whole spices from the rice. Garnish with toasted almonds and fresh coriander and serve with extra natural yogurt.

# Balti Chicken Madras

*This is a fairly hot low-fat chicken curry which is excellent served with either plain boiled rice, pilau rice or naan bread.*

## INGREDIENTS

*Serves 4*

275g/10oz chicken breast fillet, skinned
45ml/3 tbsp tomato purée (paste)
large pinch of ground fenugreek
1.5ml/¼ tsp ground fennel seeds
5ml/1 tsp grated fresh root ginger
7.5ml/1½ tsp ground coriander
5ml/1 tsp crushed garlic
5ml/1 tsp chilli powder
1.5ml/¼ tsp ground turmeric
30ml/2 tbsp lemon juice
5ml/1 tsp salt
300ml/½ pint/1¼ cups water
15ml/1 tbsp oil
2 medium onions, diced
2–4 curry leaves
2 green chillies, seeded and chopped
15ml/1 tbsp fresh coriander
  (cilantro) leaves

1 Remove any visible fat from the chicken breast fillet and cut the meat into bitesize cubes.

### COOK'S TIP

Always take care not to be over-generous when you are using ground fenugreek as it can be quite bitter.

2 Mix the tomato purée in a bowl with the fenugreek, fennel seeds, ginger, coriander, garlic, chilli powder, turmeric, lemon juice, salt and water.

3 Heat the oil in a wok or heavy frying pan and fry the onions together with the curry leaves until the onions are golden brown.

4 Add the chicken pieces to the onions and stir for about 1 minute to seal the meat.

5 Pour in the prepared spice mixture and continue to stir the chicken for about 2 minutes.

6 Lower the heat and cook for 8–10 minutes until the chicken is thoroughly cooked. Add the chillies and fresh coriander and serve immediately.

# *Karahi Chicken with Mint*

2 Heat the oil in a frying pan or large pan and stir-fry the spring onions for about 2 minutes until soft.

3 Add the boiled chicken strips to the pan and stir-fry them for about 3 minutes over a medium heat.

4 Gradually add the ginger, dried chilli, lemon juice, fresh coriander, fresh mint, tomatoes and salt, and gently stir to blend all the flavours together.

5 Transfer to a serving dish and garnish with the fresh mint and coriander sprigs.

*For this tasty dish, the chicken is first boiled before being quickly stir-fried in a little oil.*

### INGREDIENTS

*Serves 4*

275g/10oz chicken breast fillet, skinned
   and cut into strips
300ml/$^1/_2$ pint/1$^1/_4$ cups water
30ml/2 tbsp soya oil
2 bunches spring onions (scallions),
   roughly chopped
5ml/1 tsp grated fresh root ginger
5ml/1 tsp crushed dried red chilli
30ml/2 tbsp lemon juice
15ml/1 tbsp chopped fresh
   coriander (cilantro)
15ml/1 tbsp chopped fresh mint
3 tomatoes, seeded and roughly chopped
5ml/1 tsp salt
mint and coriander sprigs, to garnish

1 Put the chicken and water into a pan, bring to the boil and lower the heat to medium. Cook for about 10 minutes, or until the water has evaporated and the chicken is cooked. Remove from the heat and set aside.

# Tandoori Chicken

*A famous Indian chicken dish,
Tandoori Chicken is cooked in a clay
oven called a tandoor. This dish is
extremely popular in the West and
appears on many Indian restaurant
menus. Although the authentic
tandoori flavour is very difficult to
achieve in conventional ovens, this
version is delicious nevertheless.*

### INGREDIENTS

Serves 4

4 chicken quarters
175ml/6fl oz/³/4 cup natural (plain)
   low-fat yogurt
5ml/1 tsp garam masala
5ml/1 tsp chopped fresh root ginger
5ml/1 tsp chopped garlic
7.5ml/1¹/2 tsp chilli powder
1.5ml/¹/4 tsp ground turmeric
5ml/1 tsp ground coriander
15ml/1 tbsp lemon juice
5ml/1 tsp salt
a few drops red food colouring
30ml/2 tbsp corn oil

*For the garnish*
mixed salad leaves
lime wedges
1 tomato, quartered

1 Skin, rinse and pat dry the
chicken quarters. Make two slits
into the flesh of each piece, place in
a dish and set aside.

2 Mix together the yogurt, garam
masala, ginger, garlic, chilli
powder, turmeric, ground
coriander, lemon juice, salt, red
food colouring and oil, and beat
until well mixed together.

3 Cover the chicken with the
yogurt and spice mixture and
leave to marinate for 3 hours.

4 Preheat the oven to 240°C/
475°F/Gas 9. Transfer the
chicken to an ovenproof dish.

5 Bake in the oven for 20–25
minutes, or until the chicken
is cooked right through and
browned on top.

6 Remove from the oven, transfer
to a dish and garnish with the
salad leaves, lime and tomato.

# Simple Curried Chicken

*A tasty curry that needs very little time for preparation.*

*Serves 4*

450g/1lb tomatoes or canned
   chopped tomatoes
30ml/2 tbsp vegetable oil
1 onion, chopped
1 green or red (bell) pepper, seeded
   and diced
1 garlic clove, finely chopped
25ml/1$^1$/2 tbsp curry powder
2.5ml/$^1$/2 tsp dried thyme
30ml/2 tbsp lemon juice
120ml/4fl oz/$^1$/2 cup water
50g/2oz currants or raisins
salt and ground black pepper
1.6kg/3$^1$/2 lb chicken, skinned and cut
   into 8 pieces
cooked rice, to serve

1 Preheat the oven to 180°C/350°F/Gas 4. If using fresh tomatoes plunge them into boiling water for 30 seconds, then refresh in cold water. Peel away the skins, remove the seeds and chop the flesh. Set aside.

2 Heat the oil in a flameproof casserole or a deep frying pan that has a lid and an ovenproof handle. Add the onion, diced green or red pepper and garlic. Cook, stirring occasionally, until the vegetables are soft but not too brown.

3 Stir in the curry powder and thyme, then add the tomatoes, lemon juice and water. Bring to the boil, stirring frequently. Stir in the currants or raisins. Season to taste.

4 Put the chicken pieces in the frying pan or casserole, arranging them in one layer. Turn to coat them with the sauce. Cover the pan and transfer to the oven. Cook for about 40 minutes, or until the chicken is tender. Turn the pieces halfway through cooking.

5 Remove the chicken and sauce to a warmed serving platter. Serve with freshly boiled rice.

### VARIATION

For Curried Chicken Casserole, omit the diced pepper and cook 25ml/1$^1$/2 tbsp finely chopped fresh ginger and 1 green chilli, seeded and finely chopped, with the onion and garlic. In step 3, stir in the curry powder with 450ml/$^3$/4 pint/scant 2 cups natural (plain) yogurt; omit the tomatoes, lemon juice and water. Add the chicken pieces, cover and cook in the oven at a lower temperature of 160°C/325°F/Gas 3 for 1–1$^1$/4 hours.

# Spicy Masala Chicken

*These chicken pieces are marinated and then grilled and have a sweet-and-sour taste. They can be served hot or cold with a salad and rice.*

Serves 6

12 chicken thighs
90ml/6 tbsp lemon juice
5ml/1 tsp chopped fresh root ginger
5ml/1 tsp chopped garlic
5ml/1 tsp crushed dried red chillies
5ml/1 tsp salt
5ml/1 tsp soft brown sugar
30ml/2 tbsp clear honey
30ml/2 tbsp chopped fresh
   coriander (cilantro)
1 green chilli, finely chopped
30ml/2 tbsp vegetable oil
fresh coriander (cilantro) sprigs, to garnish

1 Prick the chicken thighs with a fork, rinse, pat dry and set aside in a bowl.

2 In a large mixing bowl, make the marinade by mixing together the lemon juice, ginger, garlic, crushed dried red chillies, salt, sugar and honey.

3 Transfer the chicken thighs to the spice mixture and coat well. Set aside for about 45 minutes.

4 Preheat the grill (broiler) to medium. Add the fresh coriander and chopped green chilli to the chicken thighs and place them in a flameproof dish.

5 Pour any remaining marinade over the chicken and baste with the oil.

6 Grill (broil) the chicken thighs under the preheated grill for 15–20 minutes, turning and basting occasionally, until they are cooked.

7 Transfer the chicken to a serving dish and garnish with a few sprigs of fresh coriander.

# Karahi Chicken with Fresh Fenugreek

2 In a mixing bowl, combine the garlic, chilli powder and salt with the tomato purée.

3 Heat the oil in a large pan. Lower the heat and add the tomato purée and spice mixture.

*Fresh fenugreek is a flavour that not many people are familiar with. This recipe is a good introduction to this delicious herb.*

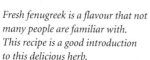

### INGREDIENTS

*Serves 4*

115g/4oz chicken thigh meat, skinned and
   cut into strips
115g/4oz chicken breast fillet, skinned and
   cut into strips
2.5ml/$^1$/$_2$ tsp chopped garlic
5ml/1 tsp chilli powder
2.5ml/$^1$/$_2$ tsp salt
10ml/2 tsp tomato purée (paste)
30ml/2 tbsp soya oil
1 bunch fenugreek leaves
15ml/1 tbsp chopped fresh
   coriander (cilantro)
300ml/$^1$/$_2$ pint/1$^1$/$_4$ cups water
rice or chapatis, to serve

1 Bring a pan of water to the boil, add the chicken and cook for 5–7 minutes. Drain.

4 Add the chicken pieces and stir-fry for 5–7 minutes. Lower the heat again.

5 Add the fenugreek leaves and fresh coriander. Continue to stir-fry for 5–7 minutes.

6 Pour in the water. Cover and cook for about 5 minutes and serve hot with rice or chapatis.

### COOK'S TIP
∽
When preparing fresh fenugreek, use only the leaves and discard the stems, which are very bitter.

# Chicken in Cashew Nut Sauce

*This chicken dish has a deliciously thick and nutty sauce, and it is best served with plain boiled rice.*

*Serves 4*

2 onions
30ml/2 tbsp tomato purée (paste)
50g/2oz/$^1$/$_2$ cup cashew nuts
7.5ml/1$^1$/$_2$ tsp garam masala
5ml/1 tsp crushed garlic
5ml/1 tsp chilli powder
15ml/1 tbsp lemon juice
1.5ml/$^1$/$_4$ tsp ground turmeric
5ml/1 tsp salt
15ml/1 tbsp natural (plain) low-fat yogurt
30ml/2 tbsp corn oil
15ml/1 tbsp chopped fresh
    coriander (cilantro)
15ml/1 tbsp sultanas (golden raisins)
450g/1lb/3$^1$/$_4$ cups cubed chicken
175g/6oz/2$^1$/$_4$ cups button (white)
    mushrooms, halved
300ml/$^1$/$_2$ pint/1$^1$/$_4$ cups water
chopped fresh coriander (cilantro),
    to garnish

1 Cut the onions into quarters then place them in a food processor or blender and process for about 1 minute.

2 Add the tomato purée, cashew nuts, garam masala, garlic, chilli powder, lemon juice, turmeric, salt and yogurt. Process for a further 1–1$^1$/$_2$ minutes.

3 In a pan, heat the oil, lower the heat to medium and pour in the spice mixture from the food processor. Fry for about 2 minutes, turning down the heat if necessary.

4 Add the fresh coriander, sultanas and cubed chicken and continue to stir-fry for a further 1 minute.

5 Add the mushrooms, pour in the water and bring to a simmer. Cover and cook over a low heat for about 10 minutes, or until the chicken is cooked through and the sauce is thick. Cook for a little longer if necessary.

6 Serve garnished with chopped fresh coriander.

# Balti Chicken Vindaloo

*This is rather a hot low-fat curry and is probably one of the best-known Indian dishes, especially in the West.*

INGREDIENTS

Serves 4

1 large potato
150ml/¼ pint/⅔ cup malt vinegar
7.5ml/1½ tsp crushed coriander seeds
5ml/1 tsp crushed cumin seeds
7.5ml/1½ tsp chilli powder
1.5ml/¼ tsp ground turmeric
5ml/1 tsp crushed garlic
5ml/1 tsp grated fresh root ginger
5ml/1 tsp salt
7.5ml/1½ tsp paprika
15ml/1 tbsp tomato purée (paste)
large pinch of ground fenugreek
300ml/½ pint/1¼ cups water
225g/8oz chicken breast fillet, skinned
    and cubed
15ml/1 tbsp oil
2 medium onions, sliced
4 curry leaves
2 green chillies, chopped

1 Peel the potato, cut it into large, irregular shapes, place in a bowl of water and set aside.

COOK'S TIP

The best thing to drink with a hot curry is either iced water or a yogurt-based lassi.

2 In a bowl, mix together the vinegar, coriander, cumin, chilli powder, turmeric, garlic, ginger, salt, paprika, tomato purée, fenugreek and water.

3 Pour this spice mixture over the chicken and set aside.

4 Heat the oil in a wok or heavy frying pan and quickly fry the onions with the curry leaves for 3–4 minutes without burning.

5 Lower the heat and add the chicken mixture to the pan with the spices. Continue to stir-fry for a further 2 minutes. Drain the potato pieces and add to the pan. Cover with a lid and cook over a medium-low heat for 5–7 minutes, or until the sauce has thickened slightly and the chicken and potatoes are cooked through.

6 Add the chopped green chillies before serving.

# Chicken in a Spicy Lentil Sauce

Traditionally, this dish is made with lamb, but it is equally delicious, and low in fat, if chicken is substituted. The lentils are flavoured with a tarka, which is poured over the dish just before serving.

INGREDIENTS

Serves 4

30ml/2 tbsp chana dhal
50g/2oz/$^1$/4 cup masoor dhal
15ml/1 tbsp oil
2 medium onions, chopped
5ml/1 tsp crushed garlic
5ml/1 tsp grated fresh root ginger
2.5ml/$^1$/2 tsp ground turmeric
7.5ml/1$^1$/2 tsp chilli powder
5ml/1 tsp garam masala
2.5ml/$^1$/2 tsp ground coriander
7.5ml/1$^1$/2 tsp salt
175g/6oz chicken breast fillet, skinned
   and cubed
45ml/3 tbsp fresh coriander
   (cilantro) leaves
1–2 green chillies, seeded and chopped
30–45ml/2–3 tbsp lemon juice
300ml/$^1$/2 pint/1$^1$/4 cups water
2 tomatoes, peeled and halved

For the tarka

5ml/1 tsp oil
2.5ml/$^1$/2 tsp cumin seeds
2 garlic cloves
2 dried red chillies
4 curry leaves

1 Boil the chana dhal and masoor dhal together in a pan of water until soft and mushy. Set aside.

2 Heat the oil in a wok or heavy frying pan and fry the onions until soft and golden brown. Stir in the garlic, ginger, turmeric, chilli powder, garam masala, ground coriander and salt.

3 Next, add the chicken pieces and stir-fry for 5–7 minutes to seal in the juices and lightly brown the meat.

4 Add half the fresh coriander, the green chillies, lemon juice and water and cook for a further 3–5 minutes until the chicken is cooked, before pouring in the chana dhal and masoor dhal, followed by the tomatoes.

5 Add the remaining coriander. Remove the pan from the heat and set aside.

6 To make the tarka, heat the oil and add the cumin seeds, whole garlic cloves, dried chillies and curry leaves. Heat for about 30 seconds and, while it is still hot, pour it over the top of the dhal. Serve immediately.

COOK'S TIP
~
Chana dhal is made from split, small chickpeas; masoor dhal is made from split lentils.

# Balti Chicken in Orange and Pepper Sauce

*Orange, ginger, coriander, garlic and black pepper make a delicious sauce for chicken in this low-fat curry.*

### INGREDIENTS

*Serves 4*

225g/8oz low-fat fromage frais or
   ricotta cheese
50ml/2fl oz/¹/₄ cup natural (plain)
   low-fat yogurt
120ml/4fl oz/¹/₂ cup orange juice
7.5ml/1¹/₂ tsp grated fresh root ginger
5ml/1 tsp crushed garlic
5ml/1 tsp freshly ground black pepper
5ml/1 tsp salt
5ml/1 tsp ground coriander
1 chicken, about 675g/1¹/₂lb, skinned and
   cut into 8 pieces
15ml/1 tbsp oil
1 bay leaf
1 large onion, chopped
15ml/1 tbsp fresh mint leaves
1 green chilli, seeded and chopped

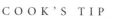

1 In a small bowl whisk together the fromage frais or ricotta cheese, yogurt, orange juice, ginger, garlic, pepper, salt and coriander.

### COOK'S TIP

If you prefer the taste of curry leaves, you can use them instead of the bay leaf, but you need to double the quantity.

2 Pour this over the chicken and set aside for 3–4 hours.

3 Heat the oil with the bay leaf in a wok or heavy frying pan and fry the onion until soft.

4 Pour in the chicken mixture and stir-fry for 3–5 minutes over a medium heat. Lower the heat, cover and cook for 7–10 minutes, until the chicken is cooked through, adding a little water if the sauce is too thick. Add the fresh mint and chilli, and serve.

# Balti Chicken in Hara Masala Sauce

*This fruity low-fat chicken dish has a creamy sauce with a kick of chilli. It looks attractive too.*

*Serves 4*

1 crisp green eating apple, peeled, cored
    and cut into small cubes
60ml/4 tbsp fresh coriander
    (cilantro) leaves
30ml/2 tbsp fresh mint leaves
120ml/4fl oz/$^{1}/_{2}$ cup natural (plain)
    low-fat yogurt
45ml/3 tbsp low fat fromage frais or
    ricotta cheese
2 medium green chillies, seeded
    and chopped
1 bunch spring onions
    (scallions), chopped
5ml/1 tsp salt
5ml/1 tsp sugar
5ml/1 tsp crushed garlic
5ml/1 tsp grated fresh root ginger
15ml/1 tbsp oil
225g/8oz chicken breast fillet, skinned
    and cubed
25g/1oz/2 tbsp sultanas (golden raisins)

1 Place the apple, 45ml/3 tbsp of the coriander, the mint, yogurt, fromage frais or ricotta cheese, chillies, spring onions, salt, sugar, garlic and ginger in a food processor and process for about 1 minute, using the pulsing action.

2 Heat the oil in a frying pan, pour in the yogurt mixture and cook over a low heat for 2 minutes.

3 Next, add the chicken cubes and blend everything together. Cook over a medium-low heat for 12–15 minutes, or until the chicken is fully cooked through.

4 Finally, add the sultanas and remaining 15ml/1 tbsp fresh coriander leaves before serving.

# HOT & SPICY

Countries such as Mexico, Malaysia, Thailand, Indonesia, the Caribbean and
Morocco are renowned for their use of spices and hot flavourings in everyday
dishes.  In this chapter, chillies, turmeric, cumin and garam masala come into their
own. These are just a few of the aromatic flavourings that are used to add colour,
texture and heat to a whole range of rice dishes, casseroles, taco and tortilla
fillings, roasts, pan-cooked dishes, fried dishes and kebabs.

# Chicken Piri-piri

*This is a classic Portuguese African dish, based on a hot sauce made from Angolan chillies. Chicken and vegetables are layered over rice and casseroled with the spicy piri-piri sauce.*

*Serves 4*

4 chicken breast fillets
30–45ml/2–3 tbsp olive oil
1 large onion, finely sliced
2 carrots, cut into thin strips
1 large parsnip or 2 small parsnips, cut into thin strips
1 red (bell) pepper, seeded and sliced
1 yellow (bell) pepper, seeded and sliced
1 litre/1³/4 pints/4 cups chicken stock
3 tomatoes, peeled, seeded and chopped
generous dash of piri-piri sauce
15ml/1 tbsp tomato purée (paste)
¹/2 cinnamon stick
1 fresh thyme sprig, plus extra fresh thyme, to garnish
1 bay leaf
275g/10oz/1¹/2 cups white long grain rice
15ml/1 tbsp lime or lemon juice
salt and ground black pepper

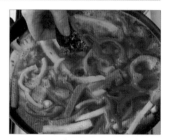

1 Preheat the oven to 180°C/ 350°F/Gas 4. Rub the chicken skin with a little salt and pepper. Heat 30ml/2 tbsp of the oil in a large frying pan and brown the chicken fillets on all sides. Transfer to a plate.

2 Add some more oil if necessary and fry the onion for 2–3 minutes, or until slightly softened. Add the carrots, parsnip and peppers, stir-fry for a few minutes and then cover and sweat for 4–5 minutes, or until quite soft.

3 Pour in the chicken stock, then add the tomatoes, piri-piri sauce, tomato purée and cinnamon stick. Stir in the thyme and bay leaf. Season to taste and bring to the boil. Using a ladle, spoon off 300ml/¹/2 pint/1¹/4 cups of the liquid and set aside in a small pan.

4 Put the rice in the bottom of a casserole. Using a slotted spoon, scoop the vegetables out of the pan and spread them over the rice. Arrange the chicken on top. Pour over the spicy chicken stock from the pan, cover the casserole tightly and cook in the oven for about 45 minutes, or until both the rice and chicken are tender.

5 Meanwhile, heat the reserved chicken stock, adding a few more drops of piri-piri sauce and the lime or lemon juice.

6 To serve, spoon the piri-piri chicken and rice on to warmed serving plates. Serve the remaining sauce separately or poured over the chicken.

# Chicken and Tomatillo Chimichangas

*These rolled chicken pancakes are a common sight on street stalls along the Mexican border with Texas. They use tomatillos – rather like a small, meaty tomato – and chipotle chilli, a spicy, dry, smoked chilli.*

## INGREDIENTS

*Serves 4*

2 chicken breast fillets, skinned
1 chipotle chilli, seeded
15ml/1 tbsp vegetable oil
2 onions, finely chopped
4 garlic cloves, crushed
2.5ml/$^1$/$_2$ tsp ground cumin
2.5ml/$^1$/$_2$ tsp ground coriander
2.5ml/$^1$/$_2$ tsp ground cinnamon
2.5ml/$^1$/$_2$ tsp ground cloves
300g/11oz/scant 2 cups drained canned tomatillos (Mexican green tomatoes)
400g/14oz/2$^2$/$_3$ cups cooked pinto beans
8 x 20–25cm/8–10in fresh wheat flour tortillas
oil, for frying
salt and ground black pepper

1 Put the chicken breast fillets in a large pan, pour over water to cover and add the chilli. Bring to the boil, lower the heat and simmer for 10 minutes, or until the chicken is cooked through and the chilli has softened. Remove the chilli and chop it finely. Lift the chicken breasts out of the pan and put them on a plate. Leave to cool slightly, then shred with two forks.

2 Heat the oil in a frying pan. Fry the onions until translucent, then add the garlic and ground spices and cook for 3 minutes more. Add the tomatillos and pinto beans. Cook over a medium heat for 5 minutes, stirring constantly to break up the tomatillos and some of the beans. Simmer gently for 5 minutes more. Add the chicken and seasoning.

3 Wrap the tortillas in foil and place them on a plate. Stand the plate over boiling water for about 5 minutes, or until they become pliable. Alternatively, wrap them in microwave-safe film and heat them in a microwave on full power for 1 minute.

4 Spoon one-eighth of the bean filling into the centre of a tortilla, fold in both sides, then fold the bottom of the tortilla up and the top down to form a neat parcel. Secure with a wooden cocktail stick (toothpick).

5 Heat the oil in a large frying pan and fry the chimichangas in batches until crisp, turning once. Remove them from the oil with a slotted spoon and drain on kitchen paper. Serve hot.

# Chicken Pilau

*This spicy dish is a complete meal on its own, but also makes a good accompaniment to curries.*

INGREDIENTS

*Serves 4*

400g/14oz/2 cups basmati rice

75g/3oz/6 tbsp butter

1 onion, sliced

1.5ml/$^1$/4 tsp mixed onion and
    mustard seeds

3 curry leaves

5ml/1 tsp grated fresh root ginger

5ml/1 tsp crushed garlic

5ml/1 tsp ground coriander

5ml/1 tsp chilli powder

7.5ml/1$^1$/2 tsp salt

2 tomatoes, sliced

1 potato, cubed

50g/2oz/$^1$/2 cup fresh shelled or
    frozen peas

175g/6oz/1$^1$/4 cups cubed chicken

60ml/4 tbsp chopped fresh coriander
    (cilantro)

2 green chillies, chopped

750ml/1$^1$/4 pints/3 cups water

1 Wash, then soak the rice in cold water for 30 minutes. Set aside in a sieve.

2 In a medium pan, melt the butter and fry the sliced onion until golden.

3 Add the onion and mustard seeds, the curry leaves, ginger, garlic, ground coriander, chilli powder and salt. Stir-fry for about 2 minutes.

4 Add the tomatoes, potato, peas and chicken, and mix well.

5 Add the drained rice and stir gently to combine.

6 Add the coriander and chopped green chillies. Mix and stir-fry for a further 1 minute. Pour in the water. Bring to the boil and lower the heat. Cover and cook for about 20 minutes.

## VARIATION

You can substitute low-fat spread for the butter, if you prefer.

# Chicken in Green Almond Sauce

*This casserole with its spicy sauce originates from Mexico.*

### INGREDIENTS

*Serves 6*

1 chicken, about 1.6kg/3¹/₂ lb, cut into
    serving pieces
475ml/16fl oz/2 cups chicken stock
1 onion, chopped
1 garlic clove, chopped
115g/4oz/2 cups coarsely chopped fresh
    coriander (cilantro)
1 green (bell) pepper, seeded and chopped
1 jalapeño chilli, seeded and chopped
275g/10oz can tomatillos (Mexican
    green tomatoes)
115g/4oz/1 cup ground almonds
30ml/2 tbsp corn oil
salt
fresh coriander sprig, to garnish
rice, to serve

1 Put the chicken pieces into a flameproof casserole or shallow pan. Pour in the stock, bring to a simmer, cover and cook for about 45 minutes, or until tender. Drain the stock into a measuring jug (pitcher) and set aside.

2 Put the onion, garlic, coriander, green pepper, chilli, tomatillos with their juice and the almonds in a food processor. Purée fairly coarsely.

3 Heat the oil in a frying pan, add the almond mixture and cook over a low heat, stirring with a wooden spoon, for 3–4 minutes. Scrape into the casserole or pan with the chicken.

4 Make the stock up to 475ml/ 16fl oz/2 cups with water, if necessary. Stir it into the casserole or pan. Mix gently and simmer just long enough to blend the flavours and heat the chicken pieces through. Add salt to taste. Serve at once, garnished with coriander and accompanied by rice.

### COOK'S TIP

If the colour of the sauce seems a little pale, add 2–3 outer leaves of dark green cos lettuce. Cut out the central veins, chop the leaves and add at step 2.

# Roast Spicy Chicken

*An American favourite: crisp,
roasted, spicy chicken with garlic.*

## INGREDIENTS

*Serves 4*

1 chicken, about 1.6kg/3$^1$/$_2$ lb
juice of 1 lemon
4 garlic cloves, crushed
15ml/1 tbsp cayenne pepper
15ml/1 tbsp paprika
15ml/1 tbsp dried oregano
2.5ml/$^1$/$_2$ tsp coarse black pepper
10ml/2 tsp olive oil
5ml/1 tsp salt

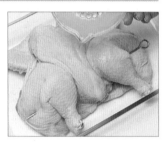

1 With a sharp knife or poultry shears, remove the backbone from the chicken. Turn it breast side up. With the heel of your hand, press down to break the breastbone, and open the chicken flat like a book. Insert a skewer through the chicken, at the thighs, to keep it flat during cooking.

2 Place the chicken in a shallow dish and pour over the lemon juice to coat.

3 In a small bowl, combine the garlic, cayenne, paprika, oregano, pepper and oil. Mix well. Rub evenly over the surface of the chicken.

4 Cover and leave to marinate for 2–3 hours at room temperature, or chill overnight (return to room temperature before roasting).

5 Season the chicken with salt on both sides. Transfer to a shallow roasting pan.

6 Put the pan in a cold oven and set the temperature to 200°C/ 400°F/Gas 6. Roast for about 1 hour, or until the chicken is cooked, turning occasionally and basting with the pan juices. To test, prick with a skewer: the juices that run out should be clear.

COOK'S TIP

Roasting chicken in an oven that has not been preheated produces a particularly crispy skin.

# Sweet-spiced Chicken

*Make sure you allow plenty of time
for the chicken wings to marinate
so the spicy flavours develop well,
then use a wok or a large frying pan
for stir-frying.*

*Serves 4*

1 red chilli, finely chopped

5ml/1 tsp chilli powder

5ml/1 tsp ground ginger

rind of 1 lime, finely grated

12 chicken wings

50ml/2fl oz/$^1$/4 cup sunflower oil

15ml/1 tbsp fresh coriander (cilantro),
    chopped

30ml/2 tbsp soy sauce

50ml/2fl oz/$^1$/4 cup clear honey

lime rind and fresh coriander sprigs,
    to garnish

1 Mix the fresh chilli, chilli
powder, ground ginger and
lime rind together. Rub the mixture
into the chicken skins and leave for
at least 2 hours to allow the
flavours to penetrate.

2 Heat a wok or large frying pan
and add half of the oil. When
the oil is hot, add half the wings
and stir-fry for 10 minutes, turning
regularly until crisp and golden.
Drain on kitchen paper. Repeat
with the remaining wings.

3 Add the coriander to the hot
wok and stir-fry for 30 seconds,
then return the wings to the wok
and stir-fry for 1 minute.

4 Stir in the soy sauce and honey,
and stir-fry for 1 minute. Serve
the chicken wings hot with the
sauce drizzled over them, garnished
with lime rind and coriander.

# Chicken with Sauce Piquante

*Sauce Piquante goes with everything that runs, flies or swims in Louisiana – you will even find Alligator Sauce Piquante on menus. It is based on the brown Cajun roux and chilli peppers give it heat: vary the heat by the number you use.*

### INGREDIENTS

Serves 4

4 chicken legs or 2 legs and 2 breast
   portions
75ml/2$^1$/2 fl oz/$^1$/3 cup cooking oil
50g/2oz/$^1$/2 cup plain (all purpose) **flour**
1 medium onion, chopped
2 celery sticks, sliced
1 green (bell) pepper, seeded and diced
2 garlic cloves, crushed
1 bay leaf
2.5ml/$^1$/2 tsp dried thyme
2.5ml/$^1$/2 tsp dried oregano
1–2 red chillies, seeded and
   finely chopped
400g/14oz can tomatoes, chopped, with
   the juice
300ml/$^1$/2 pint/1$^1$/4 cups chicken stock
salt and ground black pepper
watercress or rocket (arugula), to garnish
boiled potatoes, to serve

1 Halve the chicken legs through the joint, or the breasts across the middle, to give eight pieces.

2 In a heavy pan, fry the chicken in the oil until brown on all sides. Set aside as they are cooked.

3 Strain the oil from the pan into a flameproof casserole. Heat it and stir in the flour. Stir constantly over a low heat until the roux is the colour of peanut butter.

4 Tip in the onion, celery and pepper and stir over the heat for 2–3 minutes.

5 Add the garlic, bay leaf, thyme, oregano and chillies. Stir for 1 minute, then turn down the heat and stir in the tomatoes with their juice.

6 Return the casserole to the heat and gradually stir in the stock. Add the chicken pieces, cover and leave to simmer for 45 minutes, or until the chicken is cooked through.

7 If there is too much sauce or if it looks too runny, remove the lid for the last 10–15 minutes of the cooking time and turn up the heat a little to reduce and thicken the sauce.

8 Check the seasoning and serve garnished with watercress or rocket and accompanied by boiled potatoes.

### COOK'S TIP

If you prefer to err on the side of caution with chilli heat, use just 1 chilli and pep up the seasoning at the end with a dash or two of Tabasco sauce.
The oil in chillies clings to your skin and could hurt if you then rub your eyes. Scrape out the seeds under running cold water and wash your hands after handling chillies.

# Cajun Chicken

*Ham, chorizo and prawns
accompany chicken for this
wonderful spicy Cajun rice dish.*

### INGREDIENTS

*Serves 4*

1 chicken, about 1.2kg/2¹/₂ lb

1¹/₂ onions

1 bay leaf

4 black peppercorns

1 parsley sprig

30ml/2 tbsp vegetable oil

2 garlic cloves, chopped

1 green (bell) pepper, seeded and chopped

1 celery stick, chopped

225g/8oz/generous 1 cup long grain rice

115g/4oz chorizo sausage, sliced

115g/4oz/²/₃ cup chopped, cooked ham

400g/14oz can chopped tomatoes
    with herbs

2.5ml/¹/₂ tsp hot chilli powder

2.5ml/¹/₂ tsp cumin seeds

2.5ml/¹/₂ tsp ground cumin

5ml/1 tsp dried thyme

115g/4oz/1 cup cooked, peeled prawns
    (shrimp)

dash of Tabasco sauce

salt and ground black pepper

chopped parsley, to garnish

1 Place the chicken in a large, flameproof casserole and pour over 600ml/1 pint/2¹/₂ cups water. Add the half onion, the bay leaf, peppercorns and parsley, and bring to the boil. Cover and simmer gently for about 1¹/₂ hours.

2 When the chicken is cooked, lift it out of the stock, remove the skin and carcass and chop the meat. Strain the stock, leave to cool and reserve.

3 Chop the remaining onion and heat the oil in a large frying pan. Add the onion, garlic, green pepper and celery. Fry for about 5 minutes, then stir in the rice, coating the grains with the oil. Add the sausage, ham and reserved chicken and fry for a further 2–3 minutes, stirring frequently.

4 Pour in the tomatoes and 300ml/¹/₂ pint/1¹/₄ cups of the reserved stock, and add the chilli, cumin and thyme. Bring to the boil, then cover and simmer gently for 20 minutes, or until the rice is tender and the liquid absorbed.

5 Stir in the prawns and Tabasco. Cook for a further 5 minutes, then season well and serve hot, garnished with chopped parsley.

# Chicken with Cajun Sauce

*Sizzling fried chicken served in a hot and tasty tomato sauce.*

*Serves 4*

1 chicken, 1.6kg/3¹/₂ lb, cut into 8 pieces
90g/3¹/₂ oz/³/₄ cup plain (all-purpose) flour
250ml/8fl oz/1 cup buttermilk or milk
vegetable oil, for frying
salt and ground black pepper
chopped spring onions (scallions), and fresh coriander sprigs, to garnish

*For the sauce*
115g/4oz/¹/₂ cup lard or vegetable oil
65g/2¹/₂ oz/9 tbsp plain (all-purpose) flour
2 onions, chopped
2–3 celery sticks, chopped
1 large green (bell) pepper, seeded and chopped
2 garlic cloves, finely chopped
225g/8oz tomatoes
250ml/8fl oz/1 cup passata (bottled strained tomatoes)
450ml/³/₄ pint/scant 2 cups red wine or chicken stock
2 bay leaves
15ml/1 tbsp soft brown sugar
5ml/1 tsp grated orange rind
2.5ml/¹/₂ tsp cayenne pepper

1 Heat the lard or oil in a large pan and stir in the flour. Cook over a medium heat, stirring for 15–20 minutes.

2 Add the onions, celery, green pepper and garlic and cook, stirring, until softened.

3 Plunge the tomatoes into boiling water for 30 seconds, then refresh in cold water. Peel away the skins and chop the flesh. Stir in the tomatoes and remaining sauce ingredients with seasoning. Bring to the boil and simmer for 1 hour, until rich and thick.

4 Meanwhile, prepare the chicken. Put the flour in a plastic bag and season with salt and pepper. Dip each piece of chicken in buttermilk or milk, then dredge in the flour to coat lightly all over. Shake off the excess flour. Set the chicken aside for 20 minutes to let the coating set before frying.

5 Heat the vegetable oil 2.5cm/1in deep in a large pan until it is very hot and starting to sizzle. Fry the chicken pieces, turning them once, for about 30 minutes, or until deep golden brown all over and cooked through.

6 Drain the chicken on kitchen paper. Add them to the sauce and sprinkle with spring onions.

# Moroccan Spiced Roast Poussin

*Half-poussins taste great served with a spicy apricot and rice stuffing.*

Serves 4

75g/3oz/³/4 cup cooked long grain rice
1 small onion, finely chopped
finely grated rind and juice of 1 lemon
30ml/2 tbsp chopped mint
45ml/3 tbsp chopped dried apricots
30ml/2 tbsp natural (plain) yogurt
10ml/2 tsp ground turmeric
10ml/2 tsp ground cumin
2 × 450g/1lb poussins
salt and ground black pepper
lemon slices and mint sprigs, to garnish

1 Preheat the oven to 200°C/ 400°F/Gas 6. Mix together the rice, onion, lemon rind, mint and apricots. Stir in half each of the lemon juice, yogurt, turmeric, cumin, and add salt and pepper.

2 Stuff the poussins with the rice mixture at the neck end only. Any stuffing left over can be served separately. Place the poussins on a rack in a roasting pan.

3 Mix together the remaining lemon juice, yogurt, turmeric and cumin, then brush over the poussins. Cover loosely with foil and cook the birds in the oven for 30 minutes.

4 Remove the foil and roast for a further 15 minutes, or until golden brown and the juices run clear, not pink, when pierced.

5 Cut the poussins in half with a sharp knife or poultry shears, and serve with any leftover rice stuffing. Garnish with lemon slices and fresh mint sprigs.

# Sticky Ginger Chicken

*This sweet, gingery glaze for chicken drumsticks turns dark and sticky under the grill and tastes marvellous.*

Serves 4

30ml/2 tbsp lemon juice
30ml/2 tbsp muscovado (molasses) sugar
5ml/1 tsp grated fresh root ginger
10ml/2 tsp soy sauce
8 chicken drumsticks, skinned
ground black pepper
lettuce and crusty bread, to serve

1 Mix together the lemon juice, muscovado sugar, grated ginger, soy sauce and pepper to make a glaze for the chicken.

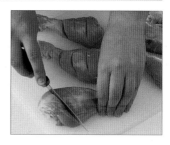

2 With a sharp knife, slash the chicken drumsticks about three times through the thickest part, then toss the chicken in the glaze.

3 Cook the chicken drumsticks under a hot grill (broiler) or on a barbecue, turning occasionally and brushing with the glaze, until the chicken is dark gold and the juices run clear, not pink, when pierced with a skewer. Serve on a bed of lettuce with crusty bread, if you like.

# Moroccan Chicken Couscous

*A subtly spiced and fragrant dish with a fruity sauce.*

### INGREDIENTS

*Serves 4*

15ml/1 tbsp butter
15ml/1 tbsp sunflower oil
4 chicken portions, about 175g/6oz each
2 onions, finely chopped
2 garlic cloves, crushed
2.5ml/$^1/_2$ tsp ground cinnamon
1.5ml/$^1/_4$ tsp ground ginger
1.5ml/$^1/_4$ tsp ground turmeric
30ml/2 tbsp orange juice
10ml/2 tsp clear honey
salt
fresh mint sprigs, to garnish

*For the couscous*

350g/12oz/2 cups couscous
5ml/1 tsp salt
10ml/2 tsp caster (superfine) sugar
30ml/2 tbsp sunflower oil
2.5ml/$^1/_2$ tsp ground cinnamon
pinch of freshly grated nutmeg
15ml/1 tbsp orange flower water
30ml/2 tbsp sultanas (golden raisins)
50g/2oz/$^1/_2$ cup chopped blanched
   almonds
45ml/3 tbsp chopped pistachio nuts

1 Heat the butter and oil in a large pan and add the chicken portions, skin side down. Fry for 3–4 minutes, or until the skin is golden, then turn over.

2 Add the onions, garlic, spices and a pinch of salt and pour over the orange juice and 300ml/$^1/_2$ pint/1$^1/_4$ cups water. Cover and bring to the boil, then reduce the heat and simmer for about 30 minutes.

3 Meanwhile, place the couscous and salt in a bowl and cover with 350ml/12fl oz/1$^1/_2$ cups water. Stir once and leave to stand for 5 minutes. Add the caster sugar, 15ml/1 tbsp of the oil, the cinnamon, nutmeg, orange flower water and sultanas, and mix well.

4 Heat the remaining 15ml/ 1 tbsp of the oil in a pan and lightly fry the almonds until golden. Stir into the couscous with the pistachio nuts.

5 Line a steamer with baking parchment and spoon in the couscous. Sit the steamer over the chicken (or over a pan of boiling water) and steam for 10 minutes.

6 Remove the steamer and keep covered. Stir the honey into the chicken liquid and boil rapidly for 3–4 minutes. Spoon the couscous on to a warmed serving platter and top with the chicken, with a little of the sauce spooned over. Garnish with fresh mint and serve with the remaining sauce.

# *Nasi Goreng*

*This dish is originally from Thailand.
The bland flavour of crispy prawn
crackers make an ideal accompaniment spicy flavour of the dish.*

*Serves 4*

1 green chilli
225g/8oz/generous 1 cup long grain rice
2 eggs
30ml/2 tbsp vegetable oil
2 spring onions (scallions), roughly chopped
2 cloves garlic, crushed
225g/8oz cooked chicken, cut into strips
225g/8oz/2 cups cooked prawns
45ml/3 tbsp dark soy sauce
prawn crackers, to serve

1 Remove and discard the seeds
from the chilli. Chop the flesh
finely and set aside.

2 Rinse the rice and then cook for
10–12 minutes in 475ml/
16fl oz/2 cups water in a pan with a
tight-fitting lid. When cooked,
refresh under cold water.

3 Lightly beat the eggs. Heat
15ml/1 tbsp of oil in a small
frying pan and swirl in the beaten
egg. When cooked on one side, flip
over and cook on the other side.
Remove from the pan and leave to
cool. Cut the omelette into strips.

4 Place the spring onions, chilli
and garlic in a blender or food
processor and blend to a paste.

5 Heat a wok, and then add the
remaining oil. When the oil is
hot, add the chilli paste and stir-fry
for 1 minute. Stir the chicken and
prawns into the chilli paste, and
cook until heated through.

6 Add the rice and stir-fry for
3–4 minutes. Stir in the soy
sauce. Serve with prawn crackers,
and the strips of omelette.

# Chicken Satay

*Here is one of the classic spicy foods
of the East. The chicken pieces should
be large, otherwise they will not
absorb the marinade satisfactorily.*

*Serves 4*

4 chicken breast fillets, skinned
10ml/2 tsp light brown sugar

*For the marinade*
5ml/1 tsp cumin seeds
5ml/1 tsp fennel seeds
7.5ml/1$^{1}$/2 tsp coriander seeds
6 shallots or small onions, chopped
1 garlic clove, crushed
1 lemon grass stalk, root trimmed
3 macadamia nuts or 6 cashew nuts
2.5ml/$^{1}$/2 tsp ground turmeric

*For the sauce*
4 shallots or small onions, sliced
2 garlic cloves, crushed
1cm/$^{1}$/2 in cube shrimp paste
6 cashew nuts or almonds
2 lemon grass stalks, trimmed, lower
    5cm/2in sliced
45ml/3 tbsp sunflower oil
5–10ml/1–2 tsp chilli powder
400ml/14fl oz can coconut milk
60–75ml/4–5 tbsp tamarind water or
    30ml/2 tbsp tamarind concentrate
    mixed with 45ml/3 tbsp water
15ml/1 tbsp soft brown sugar
175g/6oz/$^{1}$/2 cup crunchy peanut butter

1 Cut the chicken into thin strips,
sprinkle with the sugar and
set aside.

2 Make the marinade. Dry-fry
the spices, then grind them to a
powder. Put the shallots or onions
in a mortar or a food processor and
add the garlic. Roughly chop the
lower 5cm/2in of the lemon grass
and add it to the onions with the
nuts, ground spices and turmeric.
Grind or process to a paste.

3 Add the chicken pieces and stir
well until coated. Cover loosely
with clear film (plastic wrap) and
leave to marinate for at least
4 hours.

4 Prepare the sauce. Pound or
process the shallots or onions
with the garlic and shrimp paste.
Add the nuts and the lower parts of
the lemon grass stalks. Process to a
fine purée. Heat the oil in a wok
and fry the purée for 2–3 minutes.
Add the chilli powder and cook for
2 minutes more.

5 Stir in the coconut milk and
bring slowly to the boil. Reduce
the heat and stir in the tamarind
water and brown sugar. Add the
peanut butter and cook over a low
heat, stirring gently, until fairly
thick. Keep warm. Soak 16 bamboo
skewers in water for 30 minutes.
Prepare the barbecue, if using.

6 Thread the chicken on to the
bamboo skewers. Barbecue or
grill (broil) for about 5 minutes, or
until golden and tender, brushing
with oil occasionally. Serve with the
hot peanut sauce.

# Chicken Rendang

*This spicy Malaysian dish is marvellous as part of a buffet. Serve it with prawn crackers or with boiled rice and deep-fried anchovies.*

### INGREDIENTS

Serves 4

1 chicken, about 1.3kg/3lb
5ml/1 tsp sugar
75g/3oz/1 cup desiccated (dry
    unsweetened shredded) coconut
4 small red or white onions,
    roughly chopped
2 garlic cloves, chopped
2.5cm/1in piece fresh root ginger, peeled
    and sliced
1–2 lemon grass stalks, root trimmed
2.5cm/1in piece fresh galangal, peeled
    and sliced
75ml/5 tbsp groundnut (peanut) oil or
    vegetable oil
10–15ml/2–3 tsp chilli powder or to taste
400ml/14fl oz can coconut milk
10ml/2 tsp salt
fresh chives and deep-fried anchovies,
    to garnish

1 Joint the chicken into 8 pieces and remove the skin, sprinkle with the sugar and leave to stand for 1 hour.

2 Dry-fry the coconut in a wok or large frying pan over a medium heat, turning constantly until it is crisp and golden. Transfer the fried coconut to a food processor and process to an oily paste. Transfer to a bowl and reserve.

3 Add the onions, garlic and ginger to the processor. Cut off the lower 5cm/2in of the lemon grass, chop and add to the processor with the galangal. Process to a fine paste.

4 Heat the oil in a wok or large pan and fry the onion mixture for a few minutes. Reduce the heat, stir in the chilli powder and cook for 2–3 minutes, stirring constantly. Spoon in 120ml/ 4fl oz/¹/₂ cup of the coconut milk and add salt to taste.

5 As soon as the mixture bubbles, add the chicken pieces, turning them until they are well coated with the spices. Pour in the coconut milk, stirring constantly to prevent curdling. Bruise the top of the lemon grass stalks and add to the wok or pan. Cover and cook gently for 40–45 minutes, or until the chicken is tender and cooked through.

6 Just before serving, stir in the coconut paste. Bring to just below boiling point, then simmer for 5 minutes. Transfer to a serving bowl and garnish with fresh chives and deep-fried anchovies.

# Chicken and Mushroom Donburi

*"Donburi" means a one-dish meal that is eaten from a bowl, and takes its name from the eponymous Japanese porcelain food bowl. The rice here is completely plain but is nevertheless an integral part of the dish and offsets the spicy ingredients.*

### INGREDIENTS

*Serves 4*

275g/10oz/1¹/₂ cups Japanese rice or Thai fragrant rice, rinsed
10ml/2 tsp groundnut (peanut) oil
50g/2oz/¹/₄ cup butter
2 garlic cloves, crushed
2.5cm/1in piece of fresh root ginger, grated
5 spring onions (scallions), diagonally sliced
1 green fresh chilli, seeded and finely sliced
3 chicken breast fillets, skinned and cut into thin strips
150g/5oz tofu, cut into small cubes
115g/4oz/1³/₄ cups shiitake mushrooms, stalks discarded and cups sliced
15ml/1 tbsp Japanese rice wine
30ml/2 tbsp light soy sauce
10ml/2 tsp granulated sugar
400ml/14fl oz/1²/₃ cups chicken stock

1 Put the rice in a pan, and add 600ml/1 pint/2¹/₂ cups water. Bring to the boil, then lower the heat, cover and simmer for 8–10 minutes or according to the instructions on the packet. Remove the pan from the heat and leave to stand, covered, for 5 minutes.

2 While the rice is cooking, heat the oil and half the butter in a large frying pan. Stir-fry the garlic, ginger, spring onions and chilli for 1–2 minutes, or until slightly softened. Add the strips of chicken and fry, in batches, until all the pieces are evenly browned.

3 Transfer the chicken mixture to a plate and add the tofu to the pan. Stir-fry for a few minutes, then add the mushrooms. Stir-fry for 2–3 minutes over a medium heat until the mushrooms are tender.

4 Stir in the rice wine, soy sauce and sugar and cook briskly for 1–2 minutes, stirring constantly. Return the chicken to the pan, toss over the heat for about 2 minutes, then pour in the stock. Stir well and cook over a low heat for 5–6 minutes, or until bubbling.

5 Spoon the rice into individual serving bowls and pile the chicken mixture on top, making sure that each portion gets a generous amount of chicken sauce.

# Stir-fried Chicken with Basil and Chilli

This quick and easy chicken dish is an excellent introduction to Thai cuisine. Thai basil, which is sometimes known as holy basil, has a unique, pungent flavour that is both spicy and sharp. Deep-frying the leaves adds another dimension to this dish.

## INGREDIENTS

Serves 4–6

45ml/3 tbsp vegetable oil

4 garlic cloves, thinly sliced

2–4 fresh red chillies, seeded and finely chopped

450g/1lb chicken breast fillet, skinned and cut into bitesize pieces

45ml/3 tbsp Thai fish sauce

10ml/2 tsp dark soy sauce

5ml/1 tsp sugar

10–12 Thai basil leaves

2 fresh red chillies, seeded and finely chopped and about 20 deep-fried Thai basil leaves, to garnish

1 Heat the oil in a wok or large frying pan. Add the garlic and chillies and stir-fry over a medium heat for 1–2 minutes, or until the garlic is golden.

## COOK'S TIP

To deep-fry Thai basil leaves, first make sure that the leaves are completely dry or they will splutter when added to the oil.

2 Add the pieces of chicken to the wok or pan and stir-fry until the chicken changes colour.

3 Stir in the Thai fish sauce, soy sauce and sugar. Continue to stir-fry the mixture for 3–4 minutes, or until the chicken is fully cooked with the sauce.

4 Stir in the fresh Thai basil leaves. Spoon the entire mixture on to a warm serving platter, or individual serving dishes and garnish with the sliced chillies and deep-fried Thai basil.

# Chicken and Basil Coconut Rice

*For this dish, the rice is simmered with coconut so it absorbs the flavour of the chillies, basil and spices.*

### INGREDIENTS

Serves 4

350g/12oz/1³/4 cups Thai fragrant
   rice, rinsed
30–45ml/2–3 tbsp groundnut (peanut) oil
1 large onion, finely sliced into rings
1 garlic clove, crushed
1 fresh red chilli, seeded and finely sliced
1 fresh green chilli, seeded and finely sliced
generous handful of basil leaves
3 chicken breast fillets, about 350g/12oz,
   skinned and finely sliced
5mm/¹/4 in piece of lemon grass, pounded
   or finely chopped
50g/2oz piece of creamed coconut
   dissolved in 600ml/1 pint/2¹/2 cups
   boiling water or 300ml/¹/2 pint/
   1¹/4 cups coconut milk mixed with
   300ml/¹/2 pint/1¹/4 cups water
salt and ground black pepper

1 Bring a pan of lightly salted water to the boil. Add the rice to the pan and boil for about 6 minutes, or until partially cooked. Drain.

2 Heat the oil in a frying pan and fry the onion rings for 5–10 minutes, or until golden and crisp. Lift out, drain on kitchen paper and set aside.

3 Fry the garlic and chillies in the oil remaining in the pan for 2–3 minutes, then add the basil leaves and fry briefly until they begin to wilt. Remove a few leaves and set them aside for the garnish, then add the chicken slices with the lemon grass and fry for 2–3 minutes, or until golden.

4 Add the rice. Stir-fry for a few minutes to coat the grains, then pour in the coconut liquid. Cook for 4–5 minutes, or until the rice is tender, adding a little more water if necessary. Adjust the seasoning. Pile the rice into a warmed serving dish, scatter with the fried onion rings and basil leaves, and serve at once.

# Indonesian Pineapple Rice

*This way of presenting rice not only looks spectacular, but it also tastes so good that it can easily be served solo.*

### INGREDIENTS

Serves 4

75g/3oz/³/4 cup raw peanuts
1 large pineapple
45ml/3 tbsp groundnut or sunflower oil
1 onion, chopped
1 garlic clove, crushed
2 chicken breast fillets (about 225g/8oz)
225g/8oz/generous 1 cup Thai fragrant
   rice, rinsed
600ml/1 pint/2¹/2 cups chicken stock
1 lemon grass stalk, bruised
2 thick slices of ham
1 fresh red chilli, seeded and very
   finely sliced
salt

1 Dry-fry the peanuts in a non-stick frying pan until golden. When cool, grind one-sixth of them in a coffee or herb mill and chop the remainder.

2 Cut a lengthways section of pineapple, slicing through the leaves, then cut out the flesh to leave a neat shell. Chop 115g/4oz of the pineapple into cubes, saving the remainder for another dish.

3 Heat the oil in a pan and fry the onion and garlic for 3–4 minutes, or until soft. Cut the chicken into thin strips, add to the pan and stir-fry over a medium heat for a few minutes, or until evenly brown.

4 Add the rice to the pan. Toss with the chicken mixture for a few minutes, then pour in the stock, with the lemon grass and a little salt. Bring to just below boiling point, then lower the heat, cover the pan and simmer gently for 10–12 minutes, or until the rice and the chicken pieces are tender.

5 Cut the ham into julienne strips. Stir the chopped peanuts, the pineapple cubes and the ham into the rice, then spoon the mixture into the pineapple shell. Sprinkle the ground peanuts and the sliced chilli over the top and serve.

# Bang Bang Chicken

*Use toasted sesame seed paste to give an authentic flavour to the sauce for this Sichuan dish. Bang Bang Chicken is perfect for parties.*

INGREDIENTS

*Serves 4*

3 chicken breast fillets (about 450g/1lb)
1 garlic clove, crushed
2.5ml/$^1$/$_2$ tsp black peppercorns
1 small onion, halved
1 large cucumber, peeled, seeded and cut
  into thin strips
salt and ground black pepper

*For the sauce*

45ml/3 tbsp toasted sesame paste
15ml/1 tbsp light soy sauce
15ml/1 tbsp wine vinegar
2 spring onions (scallions), finely chopped
2 garlic cloves, crushed
5 x 1cm/2 x $^1$/$_2$ in piece fresh root ginger,
  peeled and cut into matchsticks
15ml/1 tbsp Sichuan peppercorns, dry-
  fried and crushed
5ml/1 tsp light brown sugar

*For the chilli oil*

60ml/4 tbsp groundnut (peanut) oil
5ml/1 tsp chilli powder

1 Place the chicken in a pan. Just cover with water, add the garlic, peppercorns and onion and bring to the boil. Skim the surface, stir in salt and pepper to taste, then cover the pan. Cook for 25 minutes, or until the chicken is cooked through. Drain, reserving the stock.

2 Make the sauce by mixing the toasted sesame paste with 45ml/3 tbsp of the chicken stock, saving the rest for soup. Add the soy sauce, vinegar, spring onions, garlic, ginger and crushed pepper-corns to the sesame mixture. Stir in sugar to taste.

3 Make the chilli oil by gently heating the oil and chilli powder together until foaming. Simmer for 2 minutes, cool, then strain off the red-coloured oil and discard the sediment.

4 Spread out the cucumber strips on a platter. Cut the chicken breasts into pieces of about the same size as the cucumber strips and arrange them on top. Pour over the sauce, drizzle on the chilli oil and serve.

# Caribbean Chicken with Pigeon Pea Rice

*Golden, spicy caramelized chicken tops a richly flavoured vegetable rice in this hearty and delicious supper dish. Pigeon peas are a common ingredient in Caribbean cooking.*

### INGREDIENTS

Serves 4

5ml/1 tsp allspice

2.5ml/$^1$/2 tsp ground cinnamon

5ml/1 tsp dried thyme

pinch of ground cloves

1.5ml/$^1$/4 tsp freshly grated nutmeg

4 chicken breast fillets, skinned

45ml/3 tbsp groundnut or sunflower oil

15g/$^1$/2 oz/1 tbsp butter

1 onion, chopped

2 garlic cloves, crushed

1 carrot, diced

1 celery stick, chopped

3 spring onions (scallions), chopped

1 fresh red chilli, seeded and thinly sliced

400g/14oz can pigeon peas

225g/8oz/generous 1 cup long grain rice

120ml/4fl oz/$^1$/2 cup coconut milk

550ml/18fl oz/2$^1$/2 cups chicken stock

30ml/2 tbsp demerara (raw) sugar

salt and cayenne pepper

1 Mix together the allspice, cinnamon, thyme, cloves and nutmeg. Rub the mixture all over the pieces of chicken. Set aside for 30 minutes.

2 Heat 15ml/1 tbsp of the oil with the butter in a pan. Fry the onion and garlic over a medium heat until soft and beginning to brown. Add the carrot, celery, spring onions and chilli. Sauté for a few minutes, then stir in the pigeon peas, rice, coconut milk and chicken stock. Season with salt and cayenne pepper. Bring to the boil, then cover, cook and simmer over a low heat for about 25 minutes.

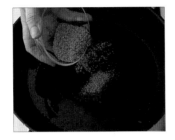

3 About 10 minutes before the rice mixture is cooked, heat the remaining oil in a frying pan, add the sugar and cook, but do not stir, until it begins to caramelize.

4 Carefully add the chicken to the pan. Cook for 8–10 minutes, or until the chicken has a browned, glazed appearance and is cooked through. Transfer the chicken to a board and slice it thickly. Serve the pigeon pea rice in individual bowls, with the chicken on top.

# Caribbean Peanut Chicken

*Peanut butter is used a lot in Caribbean dishes. It adds richness, as well as a delicious depth of flavour.*

### INGREDIENTS

*Serves 4*

4 chicken breast fillets, skinned and cut into thin strips

225g/8oz/generous 1 cup white long grain rice

30ml/2 tbsp groundnut (peanut) oil

15g/¹/₂ oz/1 tbsp butter, plus extra for greasing

1 onion, finely chopped

2 tomatoes, peeled, seeded and chopped

1 fresh green chilli, seeded and sliced

60ml/4 tbsp smooth peanut butter

450ml/³/₄ pint/scant 2 cups chicken stock

lemon juice, to taste

salt and ground black pepper

lime wedges and sprigs of fresh flat leaf parsley, to garnish

*For the marinade*

15ml/1 tbsp sunflower oil

1–2 garlic cloves, crushed

5ml/1 tsp chopped fresh thyme

25ml/1¹/₂ tbsp medium curry powder

juice of half a lemon

1 Mix all the marinade ingredients in a bowl and stir in the chicken. Cover with clear film (plastic wrap) and set aside in a cool place for 2–3 hours.

2 Cook the rice in lightly salted boiling water. Drain and transfer to a buttered casserole.

3 Preheat the oven to 180°C/350°F/Gas 4. Heat 15ml/1 tbsp of the oil with the butter in a flameproof casserole and fry the chicken pieces for 4–5 minutes, or until evenly brown.

4 Transfer the chicken to a plate. Add the remaining oil to the casserole and fry the onion for 5–6 minutes. Stir in the tomatoes and chilli. Cook over a low heat for 3–4 minutes, stirring occasionally. Remove the pan from the heat.

5 Mix the peanut butter with the chicken stock. Stir into the tomato and onion mixture, then add the chicken. Stir in the lemon juice, season to taste, then spoon the mixture over the rice.

6 Cover the casserole. Cook in the oven for 15–20 minutes, or until piping hot and cooked through. Use a large spoon to toss the rice with the chicken mixture. Serve immediately, garnished with the lime wedges and parsley sprigs.

# *Chicken with Spiced Rice*

*This hot dish for entertaining. It
can be prepared in advance and
reheated in the oven. Serve with
traditional curry accompaniments.*

INGREDIENTS

*Serves 8*

900g/2lb boneless chicken thighs

60ml/4 tbsp olive oil

2 large onions, thinly sliced

1–2 green chillies, seeded and finely chopped

5ml/1 tsp grated fresh root ginger

1 garlic clove, crushed

15ml/1 tbsp hot curry powder

150ml/$^1$/4 pint/$^2$/3 cup chicken stock

150ml/$^1$/4 pint/$^2$/3 cup natural
(plain) yogurt

30ml/2 tbsp chopped fresh coriander
(cilantro)

salt and ground black pepper

*For the rice*

450g/1lb/2$^1$/4 cups basmati rice

2.5ml/$^1$/2 tsp garam masala

900ml/1$^1$/2 pints/3$^3$/4 cups chicken stock
or water

50g/2oz/scant $^1$/2 cup raisins or sultanas
(golden raisins)

25g/1oz/$^1$/4 cup toasted chopped almonds

1 Put the basmati rice into a sieve and wash under cold running water to remove any starchy powder coating the grains. Then put into a bowl and cover with cold water and leave to soak for 30 minutes. The grains will absorb some water so that they will not stick together in a solid mass while cooking.

2 Preheat the oven to 160°C/ 325°F/Gas 3. Cut the chicken into cubes of approximately 2.5cm/1in. Heat 30ml/2 tbsp of the oil in a large, flameproof casserole. Add one onion and cook until softened. Add the finely chopped chillies, ginger, garlic and curry powder and continue cooking for a further 2 minutes, stirring from time to time.

3 Add the stock and seasoning, and bring slowly to the boil. Add the chicken. Cover and cook in the oven for 20 minutes, or until cooked.

4 Remove from the oven and stir in the yogurt.

5 Meanwhile, heat the remaining oil in a flameproof casserole and cook the remaining onion gently until tender and lightly browned. Add the drained rice, garam masala and stock or water. Bring to the boil, cover and cook in the oven with the chicken for 20–35 minutes, or until tender and all the stock has been absorbed.

6 To serve, stir the raisins or sultanas and toasted almonds into the rice. Spoon half the rice into a large, deep serving dish, cover with the chicken and then the remaining rice. Sprinkle with chopped coriander to garnish.

# Balti Chicken with Green and Red Chillies

*Minced chicken is seldom cooked in Indian or Pakistani homes. However, it works very well in this recipe.*

### INGREDIENTS

*Serves 4*

275g/10oz chicken breast fillet, skinned and cubed
2 thick red chillies
3 thick green chillies
30ml/2 tbsp oil
6 curry leaves
3 medium onions, sliced
7.5ml/1¹/₂ tsp crushed garlic
5ml/1 tsp chilli powder
7.5ml/1¹/₂ tsp ground coriander
7.5ml/1¹/₂ tsp grated fresh root ginger
5ml/1 tsp salt
15ml/1 tbsp lemon juice
30ml/2 tbsp chopped fresh coriander (cilantro)
chapatis and lemon wedges, to serve

1 Boil the cubed chicken in water for about 10 minutes, or until soft and cooked through. Remove with a slotted spoon.

## COOK'S TIP

Taste this dish during cooking as it is quite mild, especially if you seed the chillies, and you may find that it needs some additional spices to suit your palate.

2 Place the chicken in a food processor to mince (grind).

3 Cut the chillies in half lengthways and remove the seeds, if desired. Cut the flesh into strips and set aside.

4 Heat the oil in a wok or frying pan and fry the curry leaves and onions until the onions are a soft golden brown. Lower the heat and add the garlic, chilli powder, ground coriander, ginger and salt.

5 Add the minced chicken and stir-fry for 3–5 minutes.

6 Add the lemon juice, the prepared chilli strips and most of the fresh coriander. Stir-fry for a further 3–5 minutes, then serve, garnished with the remaining fresh coriander and accompanied by warm chapatis and lemon wedges.

# Chicken with Panir and Peas

*This is rather an unusual combination, but it really works well. Serve with plain boiled rice.*

### INGREDIENTS

Serves 4

1 chicken, about 675g/1$^1$/$_2$lb
30ml/2 tbsp tomato purée (paste)
45ml/3 tbsp natural (plain) low-fat yogurt
7.5ml/1$^1$/$_2$ tsp garam masala
5ml/1 tsp crushed garlic
5ml/1 tsp grated fresh root ginger
pinch of ground cardamom
15ml/1 tbsp chilli powder
1.5ml/$^1$/$_4$ tsp ground turmeric
5ml/1 tsp salt
5ml/1 tsp sugar
10ml/2 tsp oil
2.5cm/1in cinnamon stick
2 black peppercorns
300ml/$^1$/$_2$ pint/1$^1$/$_4$ cups water
115g/4oz/1 cup cubed panir
30ml/2 tbsp fresh coriander (cilantro) leaves
2 green chillies, seeded and chopped
50g/2oz/$^1$/$_4$ cup low-fat fromage frais or ricotta cheese
75g/3oz/$^3$/$_4$ cup fresh shelled or thawed frozen peas

1 Skin the chicken and cut it into 6–8 equal pieces.

---

#### COOK'S TIP
～

Panir is an Indian cheese made from whole milk.

---

2 Mix the tomato purée, yogurt, garam masala, garlic, ginger, cardamom, chilli powder, turmeric, salt and sugar in a bowl.

3 Heat the oil with the whole spices in a wok or heavy frying pan, then pour the sauce mixture into the oil. Lower the heat and cook gently for about 3 minutes, then pour in the water and bring to a simmer.

4 Add the chicken pieces and stir-fry for about 2 minutes, then cover the pan and cook over a medium heat for about 15 minutes.

5 Add the panir cubes to the pan, followed by half the coriander and half the green chillies. Mix well and cook for a further 5–7 minutes.

6 Stir in the fromage frais or ricotta cheese and peas, heat through and serve garnished with the reserved coriander and chillies.

# Chicken and Coriander Potatoes

*The potatoes are cooked separately in the oven before being added to spicy chicken. Make sure you start the preparation in good time, as the chicken takes 2 hours to marinate.*

*Serves 4*

150ml/$^1$/4 pint/$^2$/3 cup natural (plain) low-fat yogurt
25g/1oz/$^1$/4 cup ground almonds
7.5ml/1$^1$/2 tsp ground coriander
2.5ml/$^1$/2 tsp chilli powder
5ml/1 tsp garam masala
15ml/1 tbsp coconut milk
5ml/1 tsp crushed garlic
5ml/1 tsp grated fresh root ginger
30ml/2 tbsp chopped fresh coriander (cilantro)
1 red chilli, seeded and chopped
225g/8oz chicken breast fillet, skinned and cubed
15ml/1 tbsp oil
2 medium onions, sliced
3 green cardamom pods
2.5cm/1in cinnamon stick
2 cloves
salt and ground black pepper

*For the potatoes*

15ml/1 tbsp oil
8 baby potatoes, thickly sliced
1.5ml/$^1$/4 tsp cumin seeds
15ml/1 tbsp finely chopped fresh coriander (cilantro)

---

## VARIATION

Any variety of fresh mint may also be added to the potatoes, if you like.

---

1 In a bowl, mix together the yogurt, ground almonds, ground coriander, chilli powder, garam masala, coconut milk, garlic, ginger, half the fresh coriander and half the red chilli.

2 Place the chicken pieces in the mixture, mix well and leave to marinate for about 2 hours.

3 Meanwhile, start to prepare the potatoes. Heat the oil in a wok or heavy frying pan. Add the sliced potatoes, cumin seeds and fresh coriander and quickly stir-fry for 2–3 minutes. Season with salt and pepper to taste.

4 Transfer the potatoes to a heatproof dish, cover and cook in a preheated oven at 180°C/350°F/Gas 4 for 30 minutes, or until the potatoes are cooked through. Test with a skewer.

5 About halfway through the potatoes' cooking time, heat the oil with the onions, cardamom pods, cinnamon and cloves for about 1$^1$/2 minutes.

6 Add the chicken mixture to the onions and stir-fry for 5–7 minutes. Lower the heat, cover and cook for 5–7 minutes. Season to taste. Top with the potatoes and garnish with coriander and chilli.

# Indian Spiced Chicken

These tender marinated chicken pieces can be served hot or cold.

### INGREDIENTS

*Serves 4*
1 chicken, about 1.8kg/4lb
mixed salad leaves and lemon wedges,
    to serve

*For the marinade*
150ml/$^1$/4 pint/$^2$/3 cup natural (plain) low-
    fat yogurt
5ml/1 tsp ground paprika
10ml/2 tsp grated fresh root ginger
1 garlic clove, crushed
10ml/2 tsp garam masala
2.5ml/$^1$/2 tsp salt
red food colouring (optional)
juice of 1 lemon

1 Joint the chicken and divide it into eight pieces, using a sharp knife.

2 Mix all the marinade ingredients in a large dish, add the chicken pieces and mix to coat with the marinade. Chill for 4 hours or overnight to allow the flavours to penetrate the flesh.

3 Preheat the oven to 200°C/ 400°F/Gas 6. Remove the chicken pieces from the marinade and arrange them in a single layer in a large, ovenproof dish. Bake for 30–40 minutes, or until cooked through. Reserve the marinade.

4 Baste with a little of the marinade while cooking. Arrange on a bed of salad leaves and serve hot or cold, with wedges of lemon.

# Red-hot Chicken

*A good party dish. The chicken is marinated the night before so all you have to do on the day is to cook it in a very hot oven and serve with wedges of lemon and a green salad.*

INGREDIENTS

Serves 4

1 chicken, 1.8kg/4lb, cut into 8 pieces
juice of 1 large lemon
150ml/¹/4 pint/²/3 cup natural (plain)
    low-fat yogurt
3 garlic cloves, crushed
30ml/2 tbsp olive oil
5ml/1 tsp ground turmeric
10ml/2 tsp paprika
5ml/1 tsp grated fresh root ginger or
    2.5ml/¹/2 tsp ground ginger
10ml/2 tsp garam masala
5ml/1 tsp salt
a few drops red food colouring (optional)

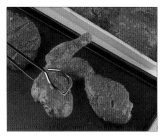

3 Mix together the remaining ingredients and pour the sauce over the chicken pieces, turning them to coat thoroughly. Cover with clear film (plastic wrap) and chill overnight.

4 Preheat the oven to 220°C/ 425°F/Gas 7. Remove the chicken from the marinade and arrange in a single layer on a shallow baking sheet. Bake for 15 minutes, turn over, and cook for a further 15 minutes, or until cooked.

1 Skin the chicken pieces and cut two slits in each piece.

2 Arrange in a single layer in a glass or ceramic dish and pour over the lemon juice.

# Chilli Chicken

*Serve as a simple supper dish with boiled potatoes and broccoli, or as a party dish with rice.*

INGREDIENTS

*Serves 4*

12 chicken thighs
15ml/1 tbsp olive oil
1 onion, thinly sliced
1 garlic clove, crushed
5ml/1 tsp chilli powder or 1 red chilli, chopped
400g/14oz can chopped tomatoes
5ml/1 tsp caster (superfine) sugar
425g/15oz can red kidney beans, drained
salt and ground black pepper

1 Cut the chicken into large cubes, removing all skin and bones. Heat the oil in a large flame-proof casserole and brown the chicken on all sides. Remove with a slotted spoon and keep warm.

2 Add the onion and garlic to the casserole and cook gently until soft. Stir in the chilli powder or chopped red chilli and cook for 2 minutes. Add the tomatoes with their juice, seasoning and sugar. Bring to the boil.

3 Replace the chicken, cover the casserole and simmer for about 30 minutes, or until cooked through.

4 Add the red kidney beans and gently cook for a further 5 minutes to heat them through before serving.

# Ginger Chicken Wings

*Here is a really quick dish that is full of flavour. Chicken wings coated in a spicy yogurt sauce are quickly cooked and then sprinkled with ginger.*

*Serves 4*

10–12 chicken wings, skinned
175ml/6fl oz/³/₄ cup natural (plain)
   low-fat yogurt
7.5ml/1¹/₂ tsp grated fresh root ginger
5ml/1 tsp salt
5ml/1 tsp Tabasco sauce
15ml/1 tbsp tomato ketchup
5ml/1 tsp crushed garlic
15ml/1 tbsp lemon juice
15ml/1 tbsp fresh coriander (cilantro)
   leaves
15ml/1 tbsp oil
2 medium onions, sliced
15ml/1 tbsp shredded fresh root ginger

1 Place the chicken wings in a glass or china bowl. Pour the yogurt into a separate bowl with the ginger, salt, Tabasco sauce, tomato ketchup, garlic, lemon juice and half the fresh coriander leaves. Whisk everything together, then pour the mixture over the chicken wings and stir gently to coat.

2 Heat the oil in a wok or heavy frying pan and fry the onions until soft.

3 Add the chicken and cook over a medium heat, stirring occasionally, for 10–15 minutes, or until cooked through.

4 Add the remaining coriander and the shredded ginger, and serve hot.

VARIATION

You can substitute other cuts of chicken for the wings, but increase the cooking time.

# Jeera Chicken

3 Add the chillies, garlic and ginger and fry for about 2 minutes.

4 Add the ground coriander, ground cumin and salt and cook for a further 2–3 minutes.

*This aromatic dish has a delicious, distinctive taste of cumin. Serve simply with cooling cucumber raita.*

### INGREDIENTS

*Serves 4*

45ml/3 tbsp cumin seeds
15ml/1 tbsp oil
2.5ml/$^{1}/_{2}$ tsp black peppercorns
4 green cardamom pods
2 green chillies, finely chopped
2 garlic cloves, crushed
2.5cm/1in piece fresh root ginger, grated
5ml/1 tsp ground coriander
10ml/2 tsp ground cumin
2.5ml/$^{1}/_{2}$ tsp salt
8 chicken pieces, such as thighs and
    drumsticks, skinned
5ml/1 tsp garam masala
fresh coriander (cilantro) and chilli
    powder, to garnish
cucumber raita, to serve

1 Dry-roast 15ml/1 tbsp of the cumin seeds in a small, heavy frying pan for 5 minutes, or until they turn a few shades darker and give off a roasted aroma. Set aside.

2 Heat the oil in a large, heavy pan and fry the remaining cumin seeds, black peppercorns and cardamom pods for about 2–3 minutes.

5 Add the chicken. Cover and simmer for 20–25 minutes.

6 Add the garam masala and reserved toasted cumin seeds and cook for a further 5 minutes. Garnish with fresh coriander and chilli powder and serve with cucumber raita.

# Chicken Dopiazza

*Dopiazza translates literally as "two onions" and describes this chicken dish in which two types of onion – large and small – are used at different stages during the cooking process.*

INGREDIENTS

Serves 4

30ml/2 tbsp oil

8 small onions, halved

4 tomatoes

2 bay leaves

8 green cardamom pods

4 cloves

3 dried red chillies

8 black peppercorns

2 onions, finely chopped

2 garlic cloves, crushed

2.5cm/1in piece fresh root ginger, finely chopped

5ml/1 tsp ground coriander

5ml/1 tsp ground cumin

2.5ml/$^1$/$_2$ tsp ground turmeric

5ml/1 tsp chilli powder

2.5ml/$^1$/$_2$ tsp salt

120ml/4fl oz/$^1$/$_2$ cup water

8 chicken pieces, such as thighs and drumsticks, skinned

plain rice, to serve

1 Heat half the oil in a large, heavy pan and fry the small onions for 10 minutes, or until golden brown. Remove and set aside. Plunge the tomatoes into boiling water for 30 seconds, then refresh in cold water. Peel away the skins and finely chop the flesh.

2 In the remaining oil fry the bay leaves, cardamom pods, cloves, chillies and peppercorns for 2 minutes. Add the onions, garlic and ginger and fry for 5 minutes. Stir in the spices and salt.

3 Add the tomatoes and water and simmer for 5 minutes, or until the sauce thickens. Add the chicken and cook for 15 minutes.

4 Add the reserved onions, then cover and cook for 10 minutes, or until the chicken is cooked through. Serve with boiled rice.

COOK'S TIP

To make the onions easy to peel, quickly soak them in boiling water.

# *Index*

# Acknowledgements

The publishers would like to thank the following contributors:

*Recipe creators:* Catherine Atkinson, Michelle Berriedale-Johnson, Angela Boggiano, Ruby le Bois, Carla Capalbo, Lesley Chamberlain, Jacqueline Clark, Maxine Clark, Carole Clements, Andy Clevely, Elizabeth Wolf-Cohen, Trish Davies, Roz Denny, Sarah Edmonds, Joanna Farrow, Christine France, Yasuko Fukuoka, Sarah Gates, Shirley Gill, Brian Glover, Rosamund Grant, Caroline Handslip, Deh-Ta Hsiung, Shehzad Husain, Christine Ingram, Peter Jordan, Manisha Kanani, Emi Kazuko, Lucy Knox, Elisabeth Lambert Ortiz, Lesley Mackley, Norma MacMillan, Sue Maggs, Kathy Man, Sally Mansfield, Elizabeth Martin, Jane Milton, Sallie Morris, Katherine Richmond, Keith Richmond, Anne Sheasby, Marlena Spieler, Jenny Stacey, Liz Trigg, Laura Washburn, Steven Wheeler, Kate Whiteman and Jeni Wright.

*Photographers:* Karl Adamson, Edward Allwright, David Armstrong, Steve Baxter, Nicki Dowey, James Duncan, Rafi Fernandez, John Freeman, Ian Garlick, Michelle Garrett, John Heseltine, Amanda Heywood, Janine Hosegood, Dave Jordan, Dave King, Don Last, Clare Lewis, Sara Lewis, William Lingwood, Patrick McLeavy, Thomas Odulate, Peter Reilly, Craig Robertson, Simon Smith, Sam Stowell and Sunil Vikayaki.